FIVE PLAYS

by

GERHART HAUPTMANN

TRANSLATED BY
THEODORE H. LUSTIG

WITH A GENERAL INTRODUCTION
AND PREFACES TO THE PLAYS BY
JOHN GASSNER

BANTAM BOOKS / NEW YORK

FIVE PLAYS BY GERHART HAUPTMANN

Published as a Bantam Classic / May 1961

CONTENTS

INTRODUCTION

BY JOHN GASSNER

Gerhart Hauptmann: A Pioneer of Modern Drama

In retrospect it seems to be one of life's little ironies and art's large paradoxes that Hauptmann should have become a major figure in the modern theatre. It was not at all the art of the drama that first beckoned to him; he came to the theatre only after vacillations that might have led him into several different professions. He stands out as an arch-realist or "naturalist" although his own highest ambitions led him to abandon naturalistic drama early in his career and aim for eminence as a dramatic poet. An aura of social and literary radicalism adheres to his reputation even though his convictions faltered rapidly and he lapsed into mysticism and neo-romanticism, earning the sarcasm of the British critic Ashley Dukes, who noted that Hauptmann had "the steadiness of a weather-vane." For all that, however, Hauptmann became the grand old man of German literature and represented its liberal and realistic aspirations to the world until his reputation was overshadowed by Thomas Mann's after World War I. Hauptmann, who was intrinsically neither a great man nor a great artist, was thrust into greatness in the 1890's when the period and the person were joined in wedlock.

1

Born on November 15, 1862 to a prosperous Silesian inn-keeper, Gerhart Hauptmann was expected to pursue a business career; his practical parents did not easily relinquish their son to the arts. They sent him to an institute of technology in the commercial city of Breslau where he was to specialize in science. (An awareness of scientific thought did indeed infuse the early part of his playwriting career with objectivity and scientism in stern reaction against romantic subjectivity and emotionalism.) Practicality being the order of the day in the rapidly growing Prussian economy, Hauptmann was next sent to an uncle's estate, where he was expected to master the profitable science of agronomy. But there was another side to the formative background of his life and it inclined him to the pursuit of art, poetry, and even fantasy. He was exposed in childhood to the mystical pietism of the Moravian sect which had taken root in Silesia and had won the adherence of both his mother and grandfather. A delicate child, moreover, he gave himself up to observation and reflection. He became the poet of the Silesian countryside. Its landscape, dialect, and folk life proved one of the main sources of his art, as did, later on, the country around Berlin, the lake-side village of Erkner, where he spent the early years of his marriage.

Having failed in preparatory studies for admission to the university and showing little aptitude for scientific pursuits, young Hauptmann came closer to his vocation when he enrolled in an art school at Breslau and then turned to the study of sculpture in Rome. Unsuccessful in art, but cushioned against adversity by the wealth of the rich girl he married at the age of twenty-three (she had supported him during the four years of his engagement to her), he wrote poetry and fiction, including the affectingly clinical story of a widower victimized by sex, *Bahnwärter Thiel* (*Signal-Man Thiel*), published in 1887. He became a member of the advanced literary circles of Germany which combined creative interests with social and political idealism, and he joined the Berlin literary club *Durch* ("Through" or "Forward") made up of highly articulate young socialists, scientists, journalists, and progressive men of letters.

The young Hauptmann could not but share their social sympathies and their cult of science—that is, the Darwinism and determinism that led them to propound a bleak view of human behavior and destiny. Whether he looked about him at home or looked abroad, he could not fail to encounter representations of social reality, on the one hand, and avowals of scientific philosophy on the other. He could not have escaped the latter even in his own family, for his elder brother Carl (1858–1921), later a novelist and a playwright too, started out as a serious student of science. It was Carl who brought him to the University of Jena to attend the lectures of the celebrated biologist Ernst Haeckel, the popularizer of Darwinism and mechanistic philosophy. Sociological influences on the impressionable young man also emanated from German and Russian writers, who made the working class and the peasantry their special province, and from the founders of the modern socialist movement, Karl Marx, Friedrich Engels, and Ferdinand Lassalle. As for literary influences, the example of Ibsen was particularly potent. The first play produced by the Berlin avant-garde theatre with which Hauptmann was associated was *Ghosts*, Ibsen's attack on convention which included in its armament the biological concept of heredity and the forbidden subject of venereal disease.

Especially rousing too was the example of the French writers, from Flaubert to Zola, who developed a program for new or intensified representations of reality. Zola had called upon writers to make their work a scrap or fragment of life —this in his polemical work, *The Experimental Novel*, in 1880. About ten years later, his disciple Jean Jullien, one of the stanchest supporters of the *Théâtre Libre* of Paris, coined the better known term of "slice-of-life." Tabooed and distasteful subjects became the staples of the literary marketplace, and a display of life's raw material, compounded of the commonplace and the scabrous, became doubly serviceable to the literary rebels of Hauptmann's generation: they used it to express their revolt against bourgeois convention and at the same time to draw attention to themselves, if not indeed to purvey profitable sensationalism to the very public they despised in the time-honored tradition of literary bohemians. Thus there arose in Germany no less than in France, though somewhat later, a style of writing that went considerably beyond the surface realism discreetly parcelled out by mid-Victorian writers. Instead of the palliatives of genteel or journalistic reformers, the young radicals favored the surgery of laying the facts bare and bleeding on the author's operating table. No subject was considered too indelicate for a writer dedicated to "truth," no reality too raw, no convention too unassailable. It is no wonder that the cries of outraged clerics and citizens rang throughout Europe and America and that censorship battles were fought both officially and unofficially—and are still being fought. The famed objectivity of this ultra-realistic or "naturalistic" style of literature did not accomplish much pacification. It is true that consistent naturalists refrained from commentary and that they allowed the facts to speak for themselves. But it was they who selected and publicized the facts that spoke only too well for themselves.

The major naturalists, moreover, did considerably more than display reality. They also tried to document it, and they subjected it to analysis in terms of the prevailing mechanistic philosophy, discarding all "unreal" explanations and consolations whether romantic or religious, fanciful or devout. Two facets of human reality concerned them especially and seemed to pre-empt everything on their horizon whenever they dealt with character or behavior—namely, the *instinctual* and the *environmental*. According to the quasi-scientific and quasi-sociological zealots of naturalism, who had little belief in free will or rationality as a decisive factor, moral judgments had scant relevance, if any. The individual was utterly *conditioned*. Behavior was determined by forces over which reason could exercise little control—except, one supposes, insofar as reason could introduce new scientific and sociological factors such as the practice of eugenics. Men were to be observed as products of their conditioning by nature and nurture, by their instincts and by their environment; and against some factors—primarily, the sexual instinct and heredity—it was virtually impossible for the individual to struggle. Drama (as well as fiction) was deemed to be closest to reality when it was amoral and "natural"—natural in the ideal sense of observing the forces of nature scrupulously, contriving nothing, but simply recording whatever is observable and verifiable.

With Naturalism arose a virtually new view of tragedy—as entrapment and destruction by ordinary rather than extraordinary, commonplace rather than heroic, forces. The tragedy of the common man became possible at last, provided, one is permitted to assume, his plight was uncommonly interesting. Above all, it became necessary to revise the entire concept of "tragedy of Fate," which is the kind of tragedy the Greeks allegedly excelled at writing. Fate, far from being regarded as the whim of the gods or as a mystical force, was destiny shaped by genetic, instinctual, and environmental factors. It was to these doctrines that Hauptmann succumbed in the stimulating company of fellow-intellectuals and artists congregated in Berlin during the last two decades of the nineteenth century. Hauptmann gave himself up to the new doctrine with all the ardor of youth and of an impressionable character. If he did not adhere to doctrinaire "Zolaism" for long or succeed with any marked consistency, he nevertheless became the leading exponent of Naturalism in the Central European theatre. From the new movement, Hauptmann reaped great benefit, deriving from it a vigorous dramatic technique and a style notable for authentic colloquialism and vivid dialect.

Invigorated by doctrine and supported by comrades-at-arms who were already distinguishing themselves in literature, science, and journalism, Hauptmann also found a theatrical enterprise ready to receive his nascent talent. First a member of the avant-garde literary club *Durch,* then the center of a literary colony in the suburbs of Berlin, Hauptmann soon became the special playwright of the *Freie Bühne* or "Free Stage" established in the capital in 1889 by the critic turned producer and stage director Otto Brahm. The latter succeeded so quickly in revolutionizing the German stage that he was made the director of Berlin's largest theatre, the *Deutsches Theater.* Brahm developed an effective style of realistic stage production, giving scrupulous attention to details of environment and stage appearance, and training an efficient ensemble in the arts of natural speech and movement. Brahm is said to have once asked one of his actors whether a particular bit of stage business by this performer would produce a "grand effect." The latter proudly replied that it would, whereupon Brahm ordered him to discard it at once.

Having already revealed a flair for verse and fiction, Hauptmann turned to playwriting at the urging of the eccentric bellwether of German literature, Arnold Holz, a lover of Walt Whitman's poetry and the co-author of naturalistic works of fiction and drama, who offered to collaborate with him. Holz is said to have even supplied the title and inspired the merciless, fatalistic conclusion of Hauptmann's first play, *Vor Sonnenaufgang.* Acclaimed for its exemplification of the aims of the naturalist movement, *Before Sunrise* was quickly accepted for production by the *Freie Bühne,* and the play became a sensation in Berlin even after the prudent deletion of a scene in which a woman was to be shown in labor. The Silesian dialect of the natives was scrupulously reproduced in the play and neatly contrasted with the Berlin dialect of one speaker and the High German speech of the educated characters. Authenticity of dialogue was paralleled in this work by scrupulous attention to the environment of the Silesian peasantry demoralized by drink and by the sudden wealth being drawn from recently discovered coal fields. The action provided an early specimen of naturalism in Germany: a drunken father lusts after his daughter while his second wife is betraying him with his future son-in-law. Moreover, Hauptmann's intellectual hero, Dr. Loth, proves himself a devotee of eugenics. This principled (and rather prissy) young sociologist declines to marry the one decent person in the village on discovering that alcoholism is hereditary in her family; and the abandoned girl, feeling herself trapped in her environment, kills herself while her drunken father sings a bawdy song in the background!

A doctrinaire adherence to eugenics combined with a description of the effects of industrialization on a peasantry suddenly enriched by the discovery of coal underground, *Before Sunrise* was impressive as a social document at the same time that it was gruesomely powerful as a play—a combination familiar to contemporary playgoers through some of the plays of Tennessee Williams. Despite stiff characterization, dramaturgic awkwardness and the evident strain of trying to hew close to formula in treating the themes of heredity and environment, the young playwright towered over his contemporaries in Germany. His faults seemed less important to his admirers than his forthrightness and vitality.

Hauptmann followed this *Tobacco Road* kind of drama, in which hereditary alcoholism fills the role of tragic Fate, with another lurid work in 1890, *Das Friedensfest,* or *The Feast of Reconciliation.* It was another depressing family drama, although located on a higher social level. The ailing and long-absent father of the family meets his estranged son at Christmas at the home they had both left, but the effort to effect a reconciliation ends in a bitter quarrel over facts dredged up from the past, and the father, thinking that the son is about to strike him as he had done on an earlier occasion, suffers a fatal stroke. Here Hauptmann produced a "family catastrophe" (the subtitle of the play) with a superabundance of morbid detail.

It was with still another family drama, *Lonely Lives* (*Einsame Menschen*) that followed in 1891, that Hauptmann first won a wide public and became internationally known. A study of a "problematical character," a weak scholarly idealist dominated by devoted parents and married to a self-effacing, unintellectual woman, *Lonely Lives* dramatized the stalemate of lives lived in quiet desperation. When he has to renounce an emancipated and spirited woman who has entered his life, the unhappy scholar destroys himself in an unwonted access of rebellion. Except for the drastic conclusion, *Lonely Lives* was an inexorably naturalistic drama of attrition of the will and entrapment. The scholarly Vockerat is trapped by meddling ministrations of kind parents, pious and conservative, who keep him within the strict bounds of matrimony when he yearns for a more stimulating companion than his wife. And, raging with despair, he is even more profoundly hobbled by the pathos of his wife, the devoted Käthe, who knows how inadequate she is for her crippled Faust and pitifully cries out her knowledge to him when she sobs *"Ich genüge dir nicht."* A life of frustration was here closely observed and personally felt by Hauptmann, who had become dissatisfied with his own marriage, which he was to terminate before long. Atmospheric and psychological interest enriched the texture of a play for which no particular excitement but a good deal of human reality could be claimed in its time, and perhaps in our own as well.

It was not family but social drama, however, that brought Hauptmann to the peak of his reputation and importance. *The Weavers (Die Weber)*, the next play in 1892, was a veritable summation of attempts to give realistic art a comprehensive significance. With *The Weavers*, Hauptmann took playwriting out of the boudoirs of bourgeois drama into areas of conflict that came to be designated in our century as "proletarian drama." The play dealt with workers and their employers, and embroiled the former with the state itself when they started smashing the newly-introduced machinery they blamed for their economic distress. Economics entered the theatre as a direct *motif* virtually for the first time with Hauptmann's picture of the depressed condition of the Silesian weavers when the Industrial Revolution came to Eastern Germany in the 1840's. By comparison with Hauptmann's account of their desperate condition, his earlier pictures of unhappiness in middle-class homes seemed almost inconsequential.

Although Hauptmann endeavored to be a consistent naturalist—he tried to remain detached from the play in order to create an objective "document"—it is plain that he became an "engaged" writer. He was moved by the sufferings of the weavers and understood, if he could not approve, their going berserk. His play was also inevitably swept into a larger contemporary significance, and this is exactly what the authorities had feared in opposing stage productions of the work. The *Freie Bühne* had to be revived in order to present this pioneering play on the stage at all, and when it was finally presented in 1894 to the general public at the *Deutsches Theater*, the production ignited a demonstration in the audience. Hissed from the orchestra and acclaimed from the balcony, *The Weavers* became the most controversial play since Ibsen's *Ghosts*, and by comparison with Hauptmann, the Scandinavian master seemed for a time the outdated hero of a revolution that had passed into the limbo of history and been supplanted by a more imperative issue. Although written with accuracy of detail and seeming detachment, the play was not a mere "slice of life."

Without melodramatic villainy or exceptional nobility on any character's part, this drama with a collective hero in lowly circumstances moved Hauptmann's contemporaries profoundly. Its emotional power was as compelling as it was elementary, and the American critic James Huneker was altogether accurate in describing the work as "a symphony in five movements with one grim, leading motive—hunger." Infused with life by their sympathetic author, Hauptmann's weavers simply refused to remain figures on the checkerboard of economic reality and historical process. Hauptmann also brought the play to a shattering climax in propelling his weavers *en masse* from a state of numb despair to an explosion of rage and violence, and he introduced both revolutionary implications and mordant irony into the concluding scene: soldiers have been sent to the region to quell the uprising of the machine-wrecking rioters, but the enraged weavers hurl themselves on the military with whatever weapons are at hand. The only person killed on stage, by a stray bullet fired by the soldiers, is the passive old weaver Hilse whose pietist beliefs require resignation to suffering in this world for the sake of happiness in the other.

It would be more accurate, of course, to call this work an epic rather than a "symphony," and it was toward epic action that Hauptmann moved again when he wrote *Florian Geyer* (1896), producing a group drama of the sixteenth century in which the German people constituted a collective character as well as a chorus while the action kept a single tragic figure in the foreground. This central character is the "black knight" Florian Geyer who, turning upon his own class, led the peasants against their feudal masters during the Protestant Reformation. The crushing of the rebellion and the death of its lonely leader constituted poignant political drama. Despite diffuseness and discursiveness, *Florian Geyer* was a noteworthy achievement in dramatic realism, and a victory for the principle that history is an affair of the multitude rather than of isolated heroic figures. Hauptmann's towering ambition in this work did him great credit as a dramatist who was willing to thrust the drama far beyond the narrow confines of the problem play while at the same time keeping his argument within the bounds of social reality. His work also stood in plain contrast to the long-standing romantic tradition that took its warrant in Germany from the historical plays of Friedrich Schiller. As might have been expected at the time of its composition, the play was a failure on the stage. But it was acclaimed as a work of major significance when revived shortly after the collapse of the German Empire at the close of World War I. *Florian Geyer* did not indeed exhaust its author's epic vein; he returned to it much later in writing *The White Redeemer,* a poetic drama dealing with the conquest of Mexico.

2

In the 1890's, Hauptmann's talent became so fertile and his search for fields to cultivate was so persistent that he was not satisfied with experiments in the naturalistic handling of family drama and epic action. He supplemented his efforts with attempts to write naturalistic comedy and tragedy. His first (and relatively inconsequential) work, *Colleague Crampton,* written in the same year as *The Weavers,* was a comic character-study of failure. The comedy revolved around a down-at-heels, dissipated painter who loses his professorship and sponges on his daughter and her lover —to whom he loftily imparts instruction in art. But *Colleague Crampton* was only an exercise in comedy, an excellent Falstaffian character sketch, rather than a fully realized play. It was with its successor, *The Beaver Coat* (*Der Biberpeltz*), that Hauptmann proved himself adept in comedy while relinquishing no particle of his naturalistic handling of character and environment. Written in 1893 from long observation of the country around Berlin, and steeped in scorn for police bureaucracy (with which the author had tangled over local productions of *The Weavers*), the new play

came to be regarded as an outstanding "peasant comedy."
It could be called with equal accuracy a "naturalistic comedy," for which there was precedent in the composition of
many a so-called *comédie rosse*, or gross and amoral comedy,
by the Parisian writers who wrote for Antoine's *Théâtre
Libre* after 1887. Whether or not we regard the play as
completely successful and fresh, it commands and probably
will long continue to command interest on the strength of
its vivid characters. One of these is the washerwoman,
Mrs. Wolff, a devoted wife and mother who lets no scruples
stand in her way in promoting the welfare of her family with
petty peculations, vast pretence, and extravagant prevarica-
tions. Mrs. Wolff is one of those characters of the comic
stage whose very impudence enhances their vitality, as has
been noted in the case of Falstaff. Almost as successful a
character-creation was the figure of the bureaucratic police
official or local magistrate, von Wehrhahn, whom Mrs. Wolff
hoodwinks so masterfully.

Hauptmann's political satire is transparent, and in Germany, a country ridden with officialdom, von Wehrhahn and
his Dogberry associates could long continue to be objects of
gratifying lampooning. But the cream of the jest lies in the
conception of the heroine and her depredations as a trav-
esty on the ruling economic and social philosophy of the
nineteenth century middle class, which Hauptmann's socialist associates could not have failed to call to his attention. A
saturnine point-of-view shapes the portrait of Hauptmann's
Rabelaisian heroine. It defines itself for us as we observe Mrs.
Wolff using all her brash resourcefulness to further the for-
tunes of her family. Unswervingly loyal to her own interests,
she represents the ultimate in *laissez-faire* "social Darwinism," reduced to comic or farcical terms. For this de-
signing woman, whom nothing puts out of countenance, the
"struggle for existence" is the sole reality, and the sacrosanct
Victorian "survival of the fittest" the only moral principle.
This picaresque piece, with its considerable underpinning of
satire, could recall for later generations the trenchant amor-
alism of Bertolt Brecht's *The Threepenny Opera* and *Mother
Courage*.

With *The Beaver Coat* Hauptmann brought to a climax
German folk farce and the genre of naturalistic comedy which
is (or pretends to be) so "objective" as to be outrageously
amoral. With the sequel, *The Conflagration* (*Der rote Han*),
in 1901, he brought his thieving heroine to a final peak of

rosserie or crassness before allowing her to die (and die, undetected) when she burns her house down in order to collect the insurance and a commission for her architect son-in-law to replace the building with a new one.

In 1898 Hauptmann, already successful in locating the common man at the center of social drama and comedy with such plays as *The Weavers* and *The Beaver Coat,* attempted the even bolder experiment of creating tragedy using a simple, inarticulate character in *Fuhrmann Henschel (Drayman Henschel).* The experiment was partially successful because Henschel's simple soul has qualities of grandeur. He is a monolithic figure who somehow possesses stature as a lumbering yet noble sufferer. Henschel has a deep sensibility even if his intelligence and expressiveness are limited. Ever since the eighteenth century, progressive thinkers such as the French *philosophe* Diderot and the German critic-playwright Lessing had advanced claims for considering of the common man a proper subject for tragedy. In *Drayman Henschel,* Hauptmann was one of the few playwrights to confirm these claims with effective tragic portraiture in humble surroundings and common circumstances. It is no doubt significant that even as late as 1949 an American playwright, Arthur Miller, writing in one of the bastions of democracy, found it necessary to justify his choice of a little man, Willy Loman, for tragic treatment in *Death of a Salesman.* In *Drayman Henschel,* a vital man, strong in body and spirit, is broken when, violating his oath to his dying wife not to succumb to their lusty housemaid, he marries the latter and is driven to suicide by her heartlessness and infidelity. Written with simple power and compassion, *Drayman Henschel* remains one of the most compelling dramas of the naturalistic stage. Unvarnished in dialogue and "unintellectual" in argument, unfashionable in an age of superficial theatricality and trivial emotion, this is one of those monolithic works which it is difficult to assess cleverly and easy to deprecate brightly. But it is, with *The Weavers,* perhaps the most perdurable of Hauptmann's achievements.

3

At about the same time that he wrote this powerful play, Hauptmann also resumed his concern with German middle-class life and its frustrations. He produced two of his most impressive works in this genre when he wrote

Michael Kramer in 1900 and *Gabriel Schilling's Flight* in 1906. In the former, a teacher of painting who has missed the greatness he had hoped to attain, seeks fulfillment through his son's talent. Hauptmann evokes pathos from the hypersensitive son's inability to live up to his father's expectations and his infatuation with a common girl which exposes him to ridicule and drives him to suicide. The play, moreover, approached tragic tension in the father's effort to live through the son and in his ultimate realization of failure. In *Gabriel Schilling's Flight*, an artist is ground to death between the upper and nether millstones of a mistress and a wife. Both as a drama of sexual conflict and a study in artistic temperament, the play was noteworthy for its tensions, if tiresome with pathos. A later play about the life of an artist, a subject of which Hauptmann did not seem to tire, was his late tragicomedy *Peter Brauer* (1921) revolving around a lazy and alcoholic bungler.

It was nevertheless with environments and characters of the lower social strata that Hauptmann continued to be most impressive. This was evident when he produced *Rose Bernd* in 1903 and *Die Ratten,* or *The Rats,* in 1911. *Rose Bernd* belongs to the genre of "naturalistic tragedy," although the term tragedy should be reserved perhaps for characters possessed of richer sensibility than Hauptmann's robust peasant heroine, who is first seduced by the local squire and then forced to yield to a blackmailing foreman while carrying the squire's child. The discovery of her condition after a quarrel, in the course of which her fiancé loses an eye, and her final desperation follow with harrowing inevitability in a work that is both unrelenting and compassionate. Successfully skirting the banality of the once popular theme of the poor working girl seduced by a well-to-do villain, Hauptmann won another victory for Naturalism. *Rose Bernd* made a strong impression in its time and remains an effective example of the naturalists' concern with environment and instinct. Hauptmann continued his naturalistic interest in sexuality in his later years when he published *Dorothea Angermann* (1921), in which a preacher's daughter is demoralized by a cook.

The Rats, a work of theatrical sophistication, also contains a strong naturalistic strain. Here the central drama is caused by a childless woman of the Berlin slums who buys an illegitimate child, pretends to her husband that she has given birth to it, and has its mother murdered to secure possession of the child. This portion of the play is used to invalidate the romantic view of art which is advanced by an old-fashioned showman who comically gets involved in this grim drama without realizing it. The blending of the two themes proved provocative in a manner later associated with the theatrical ingenuities of Pirandello. But the chief value of *The Rats* lay in its premise that tragedy can transpire under lowly and sordid circumstances—a naturalistic premise, of course—which Hauptmann elaborated with lifelike and lively detail.

Hauptmann's inclination to blend raw reality with theatrical and imaginative elements started as early as 1893 when he produced the widely known play *Hannele's Himmelfahrt,* or *The Ascension of Hannele,* often called simply *Hannele.* The blending signified in the eclectic author's case a division of loyalties, for he was drawn to opposite poles—realism and romantic fantasy. In *Hannele* he managed to strike a balance even more successfully than in *The Rats,* but the workhouse details of the play were sufficiently pungent to offend some members of the audience—such as the German prince who disposed of it in his diary as "a horrible play" and found it necessary "to revive our spirits with champagne and caviar."

Essentially a very simple play, *Hannele* starts out as a sordid picture of life in a workhouse and brings into this miserable environment the poor, mistreated Hannele who tries to drown herself. As the little girl lies on her death-bed she has visions that transport her from her dismal past into a fairy-tale future in which the village schoolmaster is transformed into Christ. Alternating literary German with dialect, and mingling dream and reality, Hauptmann pleased both the realistically and poetically inclined factions of the German public, and *Hannele* won singular success. It still commands interest as a *tour de force* of playwriting, even though its sentiment becomes cloying and its technique has lost whatever originality it once possessed.

Partly a "dream play," *Hannele* marked a satisfactory transition for Hauptmann from realism to poetry. The first product of Hauptmann's complete conversion—or, we should say rather, his reconversion—to poetry came in 1896 with *Die versunkene Glocke,* or *The Sunken Bell,* which played in many countries and was altogether successful in theatres already inclining toward neo-romanticism and symbolism. A new Symbolist movement had taken hold in Europe under the influence of Maeterlinck's mysterious and mystical style of drama. It infiltrated German literary circles, and in Austria found a spokesman endowed with poetic genius in Hugo von Hofmannsthal, who is best known as the librettist of Richard Strauss' operas. Hauptmann, who had won one reputation by 1893 as the German theatre's greatest realist, gained a second reputation within three years as Germany's leading poet-playwright. It would be unfair, however, to attribute the writing of this and other more or less poetic pieces to opportunism on Hauptmann's part. There was a personal basis for his concern in *The Sunken Bell* with the problem of an artist who is torn between human compassion and aspirations to freedom, between the call of common humanity and the seductions of a creative imagination.

Hauptmann had long felt himself in this situation as an artist just as his loyalties as a man were severely tried when he found himself alienated from his wife whose fortune had sheltered his literary career, and in love with another woman. To a considerable degree it was his own division that he dramatized in inventing the symbolic fairy tale of *The Sunken Bell*, and it was himself he saw in the central figure of the master-worker Heinrich, the bell-founder who abandons his wife and climbs to the mountaintop where he falls in love with the pagan mountain sprite Rautendelein. Heinrich, however, cannot enjoy his happiness as a free spirit for long. He is pulled down to earth, back to common reality, by the tolling of a bell in the valley when his abandoned wife, having drowned herself, tolls a sunken bell with her dead hand. Unable to survive in the valley after having lived awhile on the heights, Heinrich dies. As he has been warned above,

> He who has flown so high
> Into the very Light, as you have flown,
> Must perish if he once fall back to Earth.

Hauptmann in 1896 must have applied this warning to himself, but actually the reverse proved to be true in his case. When he returned to "earth" in such plays as *Drayman Henschel, Rose Bernd,* and *The Rats,* he was *not* destroyed; he remained a considerable playwright and amply deserved the Nobel Prize awarded to him in 1912, along with honorary degrees from Oxford, Columbia, and other universities.

There can be no doubt that the dramatically weakest of his

works, even when some literary distinction could be claimed for them, were the plays he pitched on the altitudes of poetic drama. The rarefied literary air, to which Hauptmann was not altogether unaccustomed (he had published verse in his youth including an epic called *Das Promethidenlos*), could not sustain as much dramatic life in his plays as did the mire of his social dramas and naturalistic comedies and tragedies. His "ironical masque" *Schluck and Jau*, in 1899, inspired by the Induction of *The Taming of the Shrew*, was an experiment in changes of personality in which a coarse peasant is led to believe for a while that he is a prince. This work is reminiscent of Calderon's *Life Is a Dream* and an anticipation of Pirandellian drama. It is saved from aridity only by the earthy vitality of the two tramps who are the objects of the experiment in personality transformation. In the largely static *Poor Henry* (*Der arme Heinrich*) of the year 1902, Hauptmann retold a famous medieval legend with occasional literary power but also with great verbosity. In the tiresome *Griselda*, published in 1909, he retold another medieval legend, that of the patient Griselda to whom both Boccacio and Chaucer had paid their respects; but it cannot be said that Hauptmann's effort came to much. *Pippa Dances* (*Und Pippa Tanzt*), a "fairy-play" published in 1906, deteriorated after a vivid first-act tavern scene into snarled symbolism; the girl Pippa was the symbol of Beauty destroyed by brutish materialism and visible after her death only to visionaries.

Numerous quasi-romantic literary plays by the master-naturalist failed to sustain his early reputation. Among these were plays built on interesting notions but otherwise undistinguished, such as *Der Bogen der Odysseus* (*Ulysses' Bow*, 1914), in which Odysseus fears disillusionment if he should return home; and *Hamlet in Wittenberg* (1935), in which Shakespeare's prince is seen in his student days immediately prior to receiving the news of his father's death. A third play, *Der weisse Heiland* (*The White Redeemer, 1920*), dramatized the conquest of Mexico with sympathy for the natives and their trusting ruler Montezuma who submits to the white-skinned Spaniards in the belief that Cortez is the "white savior" of Aztec solar mythology. But even this work proved too discursive and static for the stage. Only *Die goldene Harfe* (*The Golden Harp*), in 1933, made sufficiently active drama with its story of the rivalry of two brothers for a girl who chooses the physically weaker and, in the end, spiritually stronger young man.

The romanticism that sent the latter-day Hauptmann to remote periods and places in these and other plays (including a Prospero romance, *Indipohdi,* in 1920), amounted to an anticlimax for one of the most distinguished careers in the modern theatre, which at its peak before World War I led critics to rank Hauptmann with Ibsen and Strindberg. In the opinion of some students of German literature, Hauptmann's declining powers as a playwright were compensated for by his work in fiction. He made an impression with four novels: *The Fool in Christ, Emanuel Quint* (1910), a Tolstoyan novel about a Christ-like Silesian carpenter; a symbolical novel *Atlantis* (1912); a rhapsodic love story *The Heretic of Soana* (1918); and *The Island of the Great Mother* (1924), a romance about the founding of a Utopian matriarchy on a South Sea island. But, even at its best, Hauptmann's fiction remains secondary to his work as a dramatist, and his reputation now rests mainly on *The Weavers, Hannele, The Beaver Coat, Drayman Henschel,* and *Rose Bernd*—the five plays given in this Bantam volume in welcome new translations.

It is no easy task to put Hauptmann's dialogue, especially the Silesian dialect, into equivalent English for the stage; the equivalents for German dialects in early translations tended to be repellent and rapidly became outmoded. Hauptmann also followed the naturalistic practice of supplying lengthy stage directions to convey the reality of the environment and to present action unaccompanied by extensive dialogue.

Hauptmann died on June 6, 1946, after having weathered the Nazi period of reaction—unlike Thomas Mann and other self-exiled men of letters—as a resident of Germany. The Hitler regime was pleased to have this literary lion on exhibition and honored him in 1942, on his eightieth birthday, with the publication of his collected works in 17 volumes. It was during this time (1941–42) that, returning to the classics, he also wrote two full-length Iphigenia plays and one-act dramas on Agamemnon and Electra, as a dramatic cycle. Feeling too old and too attached to Germany, he could not bring himself to leave the country and he tried to lose himself in his writing. He refrained from denouncing the barbarities of Hitlerism, and his passiveness naturally disappointed his old admirers. He did indeed leave on his death a hidden protest against Nazi policies and practices. But for a man once so closely identified with humanitarian ideals, the last decade and a half of his life was a moral as well as a literary anti-climax. One could recall to Hauptmann's disadvantage the German emperor's words, spoken many years before—"I know that Hauptmann is the most eminent German writer, but I still cannot forgive him his *Weavers*." The man the world respects and is likely to remember longest is the playwright whose significant work was completed before the outbreak of World War I.

FIVE PLAYS
by
GERHART HAUPTMANN

PREFACE TO *The Weavers*

Otto Brahm's *Freie Bühne* proved so successful with his pioneering productions of Hauptmann's first play *Before Sunrise* and other naturalistic works such as Strindberg's *Miss Julie* and Tolstoy's *The Power of Darkness* that he suspended operations after the second season. There appeared to be no need for such an operation once the cause of progressive theatre had been won in Berlin. Nevertheless, he soon found it necessary to revive the *Freie Bühne* when Adolf L'Arronge, the manager of the *Deutsches Theater*, who had taken over *Lonely Lives* for Brahm, rejected Hauptmann's next work. The play was the historical social drama *The Weavers*, and Brahm could have no better justification for reassembling his avant-garde associates for another of his series of special Sunday noon performances.

It is not difficult to understand why even a progressive commercial management would be wary of *The Weavers*. The play was not only grimily and grimly naturalistic, it was inflammatory; the hungry weavers were transformed by their anger from creatures who evoked pity to creatures who inspired fear with the fury which led them to pillage their employer's home and to destroy the newly-installed machines of the Industrial Revolution in Eastern Germany. Such an uprising had occurred in the 1840's, but was already a remote historical occurrence in the 1890's and should have been viewed perhaps with reassuring "esthetic distance." But this blind revolt of the "masses" was anything but remote when regarded as an early, inchoate example of "class war" and a symbol of the continuing struggle of a class-conscious working class against capitalism under the leadership of the growing Social Democratic party in Germany. Any fears L'Arronge may have felt concerning the revolutionary implications of the work were fully substantiated when Brahm staged the play later on at the *Deutsches*

21

Theater. First the German emperor, Kaiser Wilhelm I, had the imperial coat-of-arms removed from the theatre after the government's failure to dissuade the management from presenting the play. Then on the opening night, with the liberal side of the Berlin public rallying to the work already known from its *Freie Bühne* première on February 26, 1893, the Socialist leader August Bebel led a demonstration in the balcony with his supporters picking up the song of the weavers' protest, *Bloody Justice*.

It appeared that *The Weavers* was not only a play, but a cause, though not an exclusively political one. Both the *Freie Bühne* and its offshoot in Berlin, the *Freie Volksbühne* or Free People's Stage, doubled their subscription membership as a result of this work. Under the French title of *Les Tisserands* the play also became a noteworthy production of the *Freie Bühne's* parent organization in Paris, André Antoine's *Théâtre Libre,* on May 29, 1893. It was the second production of a foreign play by this famous institution (the first was Strindberg's *Miss Julie*), and appropriately so, since the young Hauptmann was so patently indebted to Zola's and Antoine's ventures in Naturalism. Antoine was especially attracted to the play because he liked to infuse life into crowd scenes, and he took pride in this production, for which he had been obliged to borrow money from a friend. He called the work "the masterpiece of a social drama still in its infancy," and recalled that "from act to act, the public, deeply stirred, did not stop applauding." As for his staging of the work or "spectacle" (as he called it), he felt as if he had attained the pinnacle of his career as a stage director and feared that everything coming after this production would be an anticlimax. He declared that "the end of my effort is on the horizon," for he had poured into the work "all the power, resources, and energy" that was in him. He noted that "the second act with the Song of the Weavers, which serves as a *leitmotiv* and rumbles continually behind the scene, had a prodigious effect." In Act Four "in the overrunning of the manufacturer's house, the illusion of terror was so intense that the whole orchestra stood up." The last scene culminating in the death of the God-trusting old weaver Hilse in the fusillade "was carried out amid applause."

The historical nature of *The Weavers* may require some comment: The play was based on the 1844 revolt of the Silesian Weavers, previously celebrated in Heinrich Heine's

ballad *Die Schlesichen Weber,* "The Silesian Weavers." It
was actually a small incident, part of a long struggle in a
land where for centuries weavers had worked hand-looms at
home for employers who supplied the yarn and marketed the
finished product. Matters reached a crisis by 1844 owing to a
crop failure (the weavers tilled plots of land in addition to
operating their looms) while tariffs hobbled the export business. Unemployment became widespread. Moreover, only sub-
sistence wages were paid by Silesian employers competing
with manufacturers who operated the new factories and used
mass-production machinery. The ensuing hunger riots broke
out sporadically and were quickly crushed by the Prussian
state. Hauptmann started with historical details, but intensified and enlarged upon them.

At the same time, and in contradiction to the implica-
tion of cautious scholars who have implied that the plight
of the weavers was a remote subject for the author, it must
be observed that the weavers' conditions in 1892 were
not materially better than they had been in 1844. Hauptmann
had documentary sources for his work, but he also wrote
from observation. The impact of his play was decidedly
"contemporary," and both the government's strong opposition
and the German Social Democratic party's equally firm
support of the play indicates that Hauptmann's "historical"
play was still "topical," and that it hit home. A public performance of *The Weavers* was forbidden in Berlin from
March, 1892 until October, 1893, when the *Freie Bühne*
presented it to its subscription audience. And when the
Deutsches Theater presented the play to the general public
for the first time in September, 1894, the Emperor Wilhelm
II removed the judge who had released the play and punished the management by canceling the royal loge at the
theatre. Efforts (secretly inspired by the Ministry for Internal
Affairs) were made to delay and to otherwise keep the play
from the common people in smaller German cities. Protests
against the play were raised in the Prussian parliament and
the *Reichstag,* while conservative newspapers—mouthpieces
for the Prussian state—denounced Hauptmann as a tool of the
"radical" Social Democrats and a wanton instigator of class
conflict.

The impression made by *The Weavers* was undoubtedly
produced in large part by the pathos of the starving weavers
and the excitement of their revolt, but other, less conspicuous,
qualities contributed to the effect. In technical terms, that ef-

fect resulted from what John Howard Lawson in his *Theory and Technique of Playwriting* calls "intense thematic concentration in handling a multiplicity of events and characters." *The Weavers* had epic sweep and was the best modern example of realistic "mass drama" in the European theatre until the Dublin première of O'Casey's *The Plough and the Stars* in 1926. As Lawson observes, "*The Weavers* introduced different groups of people in each act, . . . But the play gives the effect of harmonious and unified construction." The work also gains power from Hauptmann's avoidance of sentimentality; the play is presented as an objectively written chronicle. Yet it forfeits no grain of sympathy, since the unvarnished facts speak for themselves and are in themselves moving.

In *The Weavers*, Hauptmann was able to make the best use of naturalistic objectivity by assuming detachment yet provoking sympathy. He manages to translate economic fact into emotional experience. More than any other prominent playwright of his times, except Bernard Shaw, he succeeded in annexing the subject matter of economics for the formative modern theatre. And, to conclude, he made large drama with simple people just as he made eloquent drama with their broken stammerings. Perhaps the secret of his inadvertent magic, nevertheless, was personal involvement. Young and susceptible to the ardor of the intellectuals of his generation, he chose a subject to which he could warm without self-pity, on the one hand, or condescension, on the other. A natural bond held together "poet and peasant," so to speak—the playwright-artist and the common man. The published play carried the following dedication:

I dedicate this drama to my father Robert Hauptmann. If I dedicate this play to you, dear father, I do so out of feelings with which you are familiar and that do not have to be dissected here.

Your stories about my grandfather, who in his youth sat at the loom, a poor weaver, like those who are depicted here, became the germ of my play. Whether it possesses vitality or is spoiled at the core, it is at any rate the best that "so poor a man as Hamlet is" can offer.

The Weavers, in a translation by Mary Morison was presented for the first time in English in New York, at the Garden Theatre on December 14, 1915, and ran for 87 performances. The large cast included Otto Brahm's leading actor Emanuel Reicher and Augustin Duncan (who staged the play together since Reicher was a German), Arvid Paulson, and Erskine Sanford.

THE WEAVERS
A Play of the Eighteen-Forties

CHARACTERS

DREISSIGER, a fustian manufacturer

FRAU DREISSIGER, his wife

PFEIFER, manager

NEUMANN, cashier

AN APPRENTICE

JOHANN, coachman

A SERVANT GIRL

} in Dreissiger's employ

WEINHOLD, tutor to Dreissiger's sons

PASTOR KITTELHAUS

FRAU KITTELHAUS, his wife

HEIDE, Police Superintendent

KUTSCHE, a policeman

WELZEL, an innkeeper

FRAU WELZEL, his wife

ANNA WELZEL, their daughter

WIEGAND, a cabinetmaker

A TRAVELING SALESMAN

A FARMER

A FORESTER

SCHMIDT, a physician

HORNIG, a ragpicker

OLD WITTIG, a blacksmith

DYE WORKERS

WEAVERS:

BÄCKER

MORITZ JÄGER

OLD BAUMERT

MOTHER BAUMERT, his wife

BERTHA BAUMERT, their daughter

EMMA BAUMERT, their daughter

FRITZ, Emma's four-year-old son

AUGUST BAUMERT, Old Baumert's son

ANSORGE

FRAU HEINRICH

OLD HILSE

FRAU HILSE, his wife

GOTTLIEB HILSE, their son

LUISE, Gottlieb's wife

MIELCHEN, their six-year-old daughter

REIMANN

HEIBER

A BOY, eight years old

A large number of young and old weavers and weaver women.

The events described in the play take place in the 1840's in Kaschbach, Peterswaldau, and Langenbielau, towns at the foot of the Eulen Mountains, in Silesia.

ACT I

(*A large, gray-walled room in* DREISSIGER'S *house at Peterswaldau. In this room the weavers deliver the finished
cloth. On the left are curtainless windows; in the back is
a glass door. At the right is a similar glass door through
which weavers, their wives, and children continuously
come and go. Wooden shelves, on which the cloth is
stored, hide most of the walls. Along the right wall is a
bench on which the weavers who are already in the
room have spread their webs. They step forward in the
order of their arrival and present their goods to*
PFEIFER, *the manager. He stands behind a large table
on which the weavers put the cloth for his inspection.
For his examination he uses dividers and a magnifying
glass. After the inspection is finished, the weaver puts
the web on scales and an office apprentice checks the
weight. After a piece has been accepted the apprentice
puts it on one of the shelves, while* PFEIFER *calls out
the amount of wages to be paid by* NEUMANN, *the
cashier, who sits at a small table.*

*It is twelve o'clock on a sultry day toward the end of
May. Most of the weavers are like people standing at
the bar of justice from which they await, in agonizing
tension, a decision on life or death. All of them seem
oppressed, like the recipients of alms who, in their
progression from one humiliation to another, are aware
that they are only tolerated and, therefore, try to be
as unobtrusive as possible. Their faces also show traces
of their futile, persistent brooding. The men, half
gnome-like, half like schoolmasters, have much in common with each other. Most of them are flat-chested,
coughing, shabby creatures; their faces show a dirty-
gray pallor. They are creatures of the loom, their knees
bent from overlong sitting. At first glance, their women-
folk have fewer typical characteristics. They look di-
sheveled, hunted, overworked, and their clothes are in
tatters; the men, however, display a certain air of
piteous gravity and their clothes are mended. Some of*

29

*the young girls are not unattractive with the waxen
pallor of their skin, their delicate figures and their
prominent and melancholy eyes.*)

NEUMANN (*counting out money*). That leaves sixteen
groschen, two pfennigs.

FIRST WEAVER WOMAN (*about thirty years old, emaciated;
she takes the money with trembling fingers*). Thank you
very much.

NEUMANN (*as the woman does not move to go*). Well?
Something wrong again?

FIRST WEAVER WOMAN (*agitated, imploring*). I need just
a few pfennigs advance—I need it so bad.

NEUMANN. I need a few hundred talers so bad. As if it
mattered what a person needs! (*Already busy paying another weaver, abruptly.*) Only Herr Dreissiger himself can
decide on advances.

FIRST WEAVER WOMAN. Well then, maybe I could talk
with Herr Dreissiger—personal?

PFEIFER (*used to be a weaver himself—the typical traits
are unmistakable—but now he is well-fed, well-groomed,
and well-dressed; he also takes a lot of snuff. He barks.*)
God knows, Herr Dreissiger would really be a pretty busy
man if he wanted to worry about every little thing himself.
That's what we're here for. (*He inspects with dividers and
magnifying glass.*) Heavens, what a draft! (*He wraps a
thick muffler around his neck.*) Close the door when you
come in!

APPRENTICE (*speaking loudly to* PFEIFER). It's like talking
to a wall.

PFEIFER. Finished. Weigh it. (*THE WEAVER puts the
piece on the scale.*) If you only knew your trade a little
better. Uneven again! . . . Can't stand even looking at it.
A good weaver don't wait till doomsday before he straightens the weave.

BÄCKER (*enters. A young, exceptionally strong weaver,
with an easy, almost impudent bearing.* PFEIFER, NEUMANN
and THE APPRENTICE *exchange knowing glances.*) Damn!
Hotter 'n hell again.

FIRST WEAVER (*under his breath*). Feels pretty much like
rain.

OLD BAUMERT (*pushes through the glass door at the right.
Behind the door one sees* THE WEAVERS *crowded together
shoulder to shoulder, waiting.* BAUMERT *has limped to the*

front and put his pack on the bench, close to BÄCKER. *He sits down next to it and wipes the perspiration off his face.*) That sure deserves a little rest.

BÄCKER. Rest is better 'n money.

OLD BAUMERT. Money wouldn't be so bad neither. Good morning, Bäcker!

BÄCKER. Morning, Father Baumert. Got to wait again God knows how long.

FIRST WEAVER. No matter. A weaver can wait an hour, or he waits a day. A weaver ain't nothing, just a thing.

PFEIFER. Quiet back there. I can't hear my own voice!

BÄCKER (*quietly*). Got one of his days again.

PFEIFER (*to* THE WEAVER *standing at the table*). How many times have I told you, you got to clean better 'n that. What a mess! Lumps in here as long as my finger, and straw and all kinds of dirt.

WEAVER REIMANN. A new burling iron is what I should have.

APPRENTICE (*has weighed the piece*). Short weight, too.

PFEIFER. The kind of weavers we got here—shouldn't give out any warp at all. Jesus, in my time! The master I had would have let me have it! Those days, the spinning trade was something different. A man had to know what he was doing. Today you don't have to no more.—Ten groschen for Reimann.

WEAVER REIMANN. But you figure a pound for waste.

PFEIFER. I haven't got the time. That's it. (*Turns to* WEAVER HEIBER.) What have you got?

WEAVER HEIBER (*puts down his piece. While* PFEIFER *inspects it,* HEIBER *moves up close to him and talks eagerly in an undertone.*) Begging your pardon, Herr Pfeifer, just thought I'd ask you kindly if you wouldn't be good enough perhaps and do me a favor and don't deduct my advance this time.

PFEIFER (*measuring with his dividers and examining, jeers*). Well, this is a fine thing. Half the weft must have got left on the bobbin, huh?

WEAVER HEIBER (*talking as before*). I'd sure make it up next week. Last week I had to do two days' work on the estate, and my woman's home sick . . .

PFEIFER (*putting the piece on the scales*). A real sloppy piece of work again. (*Already beginning to inspect another piece.*) What a selvage that is! Here it's broad and here it's narrow. Here the weft is pulled together like nobody's business and there it's spread wide as my hand. And hardly seventy threads of weft to the inch. What happened to the rest of the yarn? Is that honest? That's really something!

(WEAVER HEIBER, *suppressing his tears, stands by, humiliated and helpless.*)

BÄCKER (*to* BAUMERT, *under his breath*). Those bastards wouldn't mind if we'd buy some yarn on our own.

FIRST WEAVER WOMAN (*had stepped back only a little from the pay table and, from time to time, stared around looking for help without budging. She now gets up her courage and turns once more to the cashier, imploringly.*) I almost could . . . I just don't know . . . if you don't give me no advance this time . . . Oh Jesus, Jesus!

PFEIFER (*calls across*). What Jesusing that is! Just leave Jesus alone. Don't usually seem so concerned about Jesus. You'd do better to watch your man so no one sees him behind the tavern window all the time. We can't give advances. We got to keep accounts around here. It's not our money either. We've got to have it later on. Those who stick to the job and know how to work in the fear of God won't never need no advance. And that's it. Period.

NEUMANN. And if a Bielau weaver gets four times as much wages, he spends four times as much and gets into hock to boot.

FIRST WEAVER WOMAN (*speaking out loud as if appealing to the sense of justice of everybody present*). I sure ain't lazy but I sure can't go on like this. And two miscarriages . . . And what's my man? . . . he's only half. He's been to the shepherd at Zerlau and he couldn't help him none and so . . . we sure can't do more . . . we sure works as much as we can. Haven't closed an eye for many a week . . . and I'll get going again sure enough, if only I could get that weakness out of my bones. You just got to have a little bit of understanding. (*Fervently coaxing and imploring.*) I'm asking kindly, be a nice man and let me have a couple of groschen, just this once.

PFEIFER (*without letting her interrupt him*). Fiedler, eleven groschen.

FIRST WEAVER WOMAN. Just a couple of groschen so's we can buy some bread. The farmer won't lend no more. And a heap of children . . .

NEUMANN (*under his breath, comically serious to* THE APPRENTICE). The weavers have children every year, every year, every year, tra-la-la.

THE APPRENTICE (*replying in the same manner*). The toad is blind for six whole weeks, six whole weeks, six whole weeks, tra-la-la (*continues humming the tune*).

WEAVER REIMANN (*does not touch the money the cashier has counted out*). It always used to be thirteen-and-a-half groschen for a piece.

PFEIFER (*calls across*). If you don't like it, Reimann, just say the word. The world is full of weavers. Specially weavers like you. Give full weight and get full wages.

WEAVER REIMANN. Short weight? That just couldn't be!

PFEIFER. Bring a faultless piece of goods and none of the wages will be missing.

WEAVER REIMANN. There couldn't be too much dirt in this here piece! It just ain't possible.

PFEIFER (*continuing his inspection*). As you weave, so you'll live.

WEAVER HEIBER (*has been hanging around* PFEIFER *to await another opportunity. He, like everybody else, has smiled at* PFEIFER'S *last words; now he steps up and talks to him, as he did before.*) I just wanted to ask you very kindly, Herr Pfeifer, if maybe you would have a pity and not deduct them five groschen this time. My woman she's been in bed all knotted up since Shrove Tuesday; can't do a thing for me, and so I got to pay me a bobbin girl. So . . .

PFEIFER (*taking a pinch of snuff*). Heiber, you ain't the only one I got to take care of. The others want to have a turn, too.

WEAVER REIMANN. That's the way I got the warp, that's the way I put it on the loom, and that's the way it came off again. Can't bring back better yarn than you give me.

PFEIFER. If you don't like it, just don't take no more warp. There are enough people who'd walk their shoes off their feet to get it.

NEUMANN (*addressing* REIMANN). Don't you want the money?

REIMANN. I just can't be satisfied with that.

NEUMANN (*without paying further attention to* REIMANN). Heiber, ten groschen. Deduct five groschen advance, leaves five groschen.

WEAVER HEIBER (*steps up, looks at the money, shakes*

his head as if he were absolutely unable to believe it, then slowly and awkwardly puts the money away). Oh my God, my God. *(Sighing.)* Well, well, well.

OLD BAUMERT *(talking right into* HEIBER'S *face).* Yes sir, Franz, it sure is enough to make you sigh now and then.

WEAVER HEIBER *(talking with difficulty).* Well, I got a sick girl lying home. She should have a bottle of medicine.

OLD BAUMERT. What's wrong with her?

WEAVER HEIBER. Well, it's like this. She's been a miserable little thing from when she was a baby. I just don't know . . . well, I think I can tell you—she was born with it. Kind of unclean all over her . . . like it was coming out through her blood.

OLD BAUMERT. Something wrong everywhere. For the poor there's nothing but one piece of bad luck after another. No stopping it and no help nowheres.

WEAVER HEIBER. What've you got wrapped in that there cloth?

OLD BAUMERT. Just haven't got nothing home no more. So I just had to go and get our little doggie butchered. Not much on him . . . was half starved himself. He was a nice little doggie. I just couldn't kill him myself. Didn't have the heart.

PFEIFER *(has inspected* BÄCKER'S *piece and calls out).* Bäcker, thirteen-and-a-half groschen.

BÄCKER. A lousy hand-out that is, not wages.

PFEIFER. Those who have finished, leave the room, otherwise we can't even move around in here.

BÄCKER *(addressing the people near him without lowering his voice).* A lousy tip, that's what it is. We're supposed to keep the foot on the treadle from early morning to late at night. Stretched across the loom like that for eighteen days so you feel like you're put through a wringer evening after evening, half dizzy from the dust and the heat. What have you finally got for all your work? You've made thirteen-and-a-half groschen.

PFEIFER. No complaining in here!

BÄCKER. You can't tell me to shut up!

PFEIFER *(jumps up shouting).* We'll see about that! *(He rushes toward the glass door and calls into the office.)* Herr Dreissiger, Herr Dreissiger, just a minute, please!

DREISSIGER *(enters. He is in his early forties, a heavy man, asthmatic. With a severe expression on his face.)* What's the matter, Pfeifer?

PFEIFER (*playing dumb*). Bäcker thinks we can't tell him to shut up.

DREISSIGER (*pulls himself up, throws back his head, stares at* BÄCKER *with quivering nostrils*). Oh, I see. Bäcker! (*To* PFEIFER.) Is that he? (THE EMPLOYEES *nod*.)

BÄCKER (*arrogantly*). Yes sir, Herr Dreissiger! (*Pointing to himself*.) That's him—(*Then, pointing to* DREISSIGER) and that's him.

DREISSIGER (*indignantly*). How does this man dare!

PFEIFER. He's feeling a little too good! He'll go dancing on ice until one day it cracks under him.

BÄCKER (*brutally*). Oh, you penny-counter—just shut your trap. When your mother was riding round on her broomstick one moonless night she must've fallen for Lucifer; that's how you turned out such a devil.

DREISSIGER (*losing his temper, screams*). Shut up! Shut up immediately or . . . (*He is shaking, takes a few steps forward.*)

BÄCKER (*resolutely awaiting him*). I'm not deaf. I can still hear all right!

DREISSIGER (*controls himself, asks in a calm, business-like manner*). Wasn't this fellow one of them?

PFEIFER. He's a Bielau weaver. They're always around when somebody's up to some mischief.

DREISSIGER (*shaking*). This I can tell you: if it happens once more, if once more a gang of drunks, a gang of louts marches past my house like last night—singing that vile song . . .

BÄCKER. I suppose you mean "Blood Justice"?

DREISSIGER. You know very well what I mean. I just tell you—if I hear it once more I'll have one of you picked out and, on my honor—I'm not joking now—I'll turn him over to the Prosecutor. And if I find out where this abominable song . . .

BÄCKER. That's a beautiful song that is!

DREISSIGER. One more word and I'll get the police this minute. I'm not going to fiddle around. We'll get you boys in line all right. I've shown bigger men than you where to get off.

BÄCKER. Oh, I believe that! A real boss knows how to finish off two, three hundred weavers before breakfast! He won't even leave a few lousy bones. Them's got four stomachs like a cow, and teeth like a wolf! No fooling around with them!

DREISSIGER (*to his employees*). That man will not get one single piece of work from us any more.

BÄCKER. Oh well, whether I starve to death at the loom or in a ditch really don't matter.

DREISSIGER. Get out! Get out this minute!

BÄCKER (*firmly*). First my wages.

DREISSIGER. How much do we owe this man?

NEUMANN. Twelve groschen and five pfennigs.

DREISSIGER (*quickly takes the money from the cashier and throws it on the pay table so that a few coins roll on the floor*). There . . . there . . . and now out of my sight!

BÄCKER. First I want my wages.

DREISSIGER. There are your wages; and if you don't hurry up and get out now . . . it's just twelve o'clock . . . my dyers are just on their lunch hour . . !

BÄCKER. My wages belong right here in my hand. This is where my wages belong. (*He taps the palm of his left hand with the fingers of his right.*)

DREISSIGER (*to* THE APPRENTICE). Pick it up, Tilgner.

(APPRENTICE *picks up the money and puts it into* BÄCKER'*s hand.*)

BÄCKER. Got to do things right. (*Without hurrying he puts the money into an old bag.*)

DREISSIGER. Well? (*Since* BÄCKER *still does not move, impatiently.*) Do you need any help? (*A commotion has started among the thick crowd of weavers. Someone heaves a long, deep sigh. Then someone falls. Everybody is now interested in the new excitement.*)

DREISSIGER. What's going on over there?

SEVERAL WEAVERS AND WEAVER WOMEN. Somebody's keeled over . . . It's a weak little boy . . . Has he got consumption? . . What is it?

DREISSIGER. What do you mean . . . keeled over? (*He moves closer.*)

AN OLD WEAVER. He's just lying there. (*They make room. A* BOY, *about eight years old, is lying on the floor as if dead.*)

DREISSIGER. Does somebody know the boy?

OLD WEAVER. He ain't from our village.

OLD BAUMERT. Almost looks like Heinrich's boy. (*He looks closer.*) Yes sir, that's Heinrich's little Gustav.

DREISSIGER. Where do the people live?

OLD BAUMERT. Well, up our way—in Kaschbach, Herr Dreissiger. He goes around making music, and by day he hangs over the loom. Nine children they got, tenth is on the way.

SEVERAL WEAVERS AND WEAVER WOMEN. Them's really poor people. Rains right into their house.—Two shirts she's got for them nine boys.

OLD BAUMERT (*touching* THE BOY). Well, son, what's the trouble? Wake up now!

DREISSIGER. Give a hand getting him up. What incredible stupidity to let a sickly child walk all the way down here. Bring some water, Pfeifer.

WEAVER WOMAN (*helping him up*). No nonsense now boy, don't die on us!

DREISSIGER. Or brandy, Pfeifer, brandy would be better.

BÄCKER (*has been standing by, forgotten by everybody, and observing the scene. Now, with his hand on the door-knob, he shouts derisively in a loud voice.*) Don't forget to give him something to eat. You'll see how fast he'll come to!   (*Leaves.*)

DREISSIGER. That one will come to a bad end. Grab him under the arm, Neumann. Easy now, easy . . . we'll take him to my room. What is it?

NEUMANN. He's said something, Herr Dreissiger! He's moving his lips.

DREISSIGER. What is it, my boy?

BOY (*barely audible*). I'm hungry!

DREISSIGER (*turns pale*). Can't understand a word.

WEAVER WOMAN. I think he said . . .

DREISSIGER. Well, we'll see. Let's not waste time.—He can lie down on my sofa. We'll find out what the doctor has to say.

(DREISSIGER, NEUMANN *and* THE WEAVER WOMAN *lead* THE BOY *into the office. Among* THE WEAVERS *a commotion starts as among school children when the teacher has left the room. They stretch, they whisper, they shift their weight from one foot to the other, and within a few seconds the talk becomes general and loud.*)

OLD BAUMERT. I can't help feeling Bäcker's right.

SEVERAL WEAVERS AND WEAVER WOMEN. He said something like that. It's nothing new around here that somebody keels over from hunger.—And what's it going to be like come winter if they keep cutting wages.—Pretty bad year for potatoes this year.—Ain't never going to change around here 'til we're all down on our backs.

OLD BAUMERT. Best thing is, to do like that weaver from Nentwich: put a rope around your neck and hang yourself on the loom. Here, take a pinch. I been to Neurode; my brother-in-law works in the factory there where they make snuff. He gave me them little bits.—What you got in your rag there?

OLD WEAVER. Just a little barley. Miller Ulbrich's wagon was rolling along just ahead of me, and one of the sacks had a little tear. Didn't mind it a bit, believe me.

OLD BAUMERT. There's twenty-two mills in Peterswaldau, but not a grain for you and me.

OLD WEAVER. Got to keep your chin up. Something always happens to keep you going another step.

WEAVER HEIBER. When you get hungry just go and pray to the fourteen saints, and if you're still hungry put a stone in yer mouth and suck it. Ain't that right, Baumert?

(DREISSIGER, PFEIFER and THE CASHIER return from the office.)

DREISSIGER. Wasn't anything of importance. The boy's already perked up quite a bit. (*Walks up and down excitedly, puffing.*) Still, it's unforgivable carelessness. That child is like a leaf that the first wind will blow away. It's quite incredible that people . . . how parents can be so foolish. Burden him down with two pieces of fustian and send him on a trip of a good seven miles. It's really unbelievable! I'll have to make it a rule not to accept goods brought by children. (*Again he walks up and down in silence.*) At any rate, I don't want this sort of thing to happen again. Who's responsible in the end? We manufacturers, of course. We're responsible for everything. If one of these little kids gets stuck in the snow in winter and falls asleep, right away one of those writers comes chasing around, and after a couple of days the horror tale is all over the newspapers. The father, the parents who sent the child out . . . oh no, they couldn't be responsible of course! Get the manufacturer, he's the scapegoat. The weaver always gets a pat on the back, and the manufacturer gets the blows: he's a man without a heart, hard as stone, a dangerous character who's open to the bites of all those newspapers curs. He lives high on the hog and

pays the weavers starvation wages.—That a man like that
has his troubles, too, his sleepless nights, that he runs risks
the worker doesn't even dream of, that his head sometimes
swims from all the dividing, adding, multiplying, calculating,
and checking, that he's got to think all the time, to consider
all sides; and that he's got to fight for his life, as it were, and
to compete, that there isn't a day without trouble and
losses—all that is conveniently and politely ignored. And
who in the world doesn't try to hang on to the manufacturer's
coattails, who wouldn't like to suck his blood and just
live off him! Oh no, I wish you could be in my boots for
a while; you'd have a bellyful of it soon enough. (*After
pausing for a moment to collect himself.*) And how that no-
good tramp, that Bäcker carried on in here! Now he'll go
and trumpet all over the place what a heartless man I am.
How, for the puniest reasons I fire the weavers without
the slightest compunction. Is that true? Am I that heartless?

MANY VOICES. No, no, Herr Dreissiger!

DREISSIGER. Well, I don't think so. And here these bastards run around singing vicious songs about us manufacturers, talking about hunger all the time but always with
enough left to drink liquor by the quart. Why don't they go
and stick their noses some place else? They ought to go take
a look and see how the linen weavers are getting along. *They*
can really talk about distress. But you here, you fustian
weavers, you're so well off you should quietly thank God.
And I ask the old, hard-working, skilled weavers here: can a
worker who does his job make a living working for me, or not?

VERY MANY VOICES. Yes, yes, Herr Dreissiger!

DREISSIGER. Well, there, you see. A guy like Bäcker, of
course, can't. But let me tell you: keep these fellows under
control. If things go too far, I'm going to quit. I'll liquidate
the business, and then you can look out for yourselves. Then
just go and see where you can find work. His Honor, Herr
Bäcker, sure isn't going to give you any.

FIRST WOMAN (*has sidled up to* DREISSIGER *and with ser-
vile humility flicks some dust off his coat*). You got a
little dirty there, Herr Dreissiger.

DREISSIGER. Business is just terrible. That much you know
yourselves. I'm losing money instead of making it. If I see
to it that my weavers have some work regardless, I should
hope that they appreciate it. I've got thousands of bolts of
merchandise lying around, and even today I don't know if I'll
ever sell them.—Now, I've heard that quite a few weavers

around here are completely out of work, and so . . . well, Pfeifer can explain all the details to you.—It's like this: to show my good intentions—of course I'm in no position to distribute hand-outs, I'm not rich enough for that, but up to a point I can give the unemployed an opportunity to make at least a little money. That I take a tremendous risk doing this, that's my lookout, of course.—I simply figure that if a man can earn enough for a piece of bread and pot cheese every day it's better than having nothing to eat at all. Isn't that right?

MANY VOICES. Yes, yes, Herr Dreissiger!

DREISSIGER. So, I want to give work to another two hundred weavers. Pfeifer will explain to you what the conditions are. (*He turns to go.*)

FIRST WEAVER WOMAN (*steps into his path, starts talking to him, hastily, imploringly and insistently*). Dearest Herr Dreissiger, I just wanted to ask very kindly, Sir, if perhaps . . . I've had two miscarriages . . .

DREISSIGER (*abruptly*). Talk to Pfeifer, my good woman, I'm already late. (*He leaves her without paying her any further attention.*)

WEAVER REIMANN (*now also steps into his path. In a tone of hurt pride and accusation.*) Herr Dreissiger, I've really got something to complain about. Herr Pfeifer has . . . well, I always got twelve-and-a-half groschen for a piece . . .

DREISSIGER (*interrupts him*). That's the manager sitting over there. Talk to him, that's the right department.

WEAVER HEIBER (*stops* DREISSIGER). My dearest Herr Dreissiger—(*stammering in his confused haste*). I just wanted to ask you kindly if maybe you could . . . if maybe Herr Pfeifer could . . . could . . .

DREISSIGER. Just what it is you want?

WEAVER HEIBER. The advance I got last, last time, I mean when . . .

DREISSIGER. That's Pfeifer's business, Pfeifer's business. I really can't . . . talk it over with Pfeifer. (*He escapes into his office. The supplicants look at each other helplessly. One after the other, they step back, sighing.*)

PFEIFER (*resuming his inspection*). Well, Annie, what have you got?

OLD BAUMERT. How much are you going to pay for a piece then, Herr Pfeifer?

PFEIFER. Ten groschen a piece.

OLD BAUMERT. Well, I'll be damned!

(*Commotion among* THE WEAVERS, *whispering and muttering.*)

CURTAIN

ACT II

(*Kaschbach, the Eulen Mountains; a small room in the house of* WILHELM ANSORGE. *The room is narrow and less than six feet high from the broken floorboards to the smoke-blackened ceiling. Two young girls,* EMMA *and* BERTHA BAUMERT, *sit at looms.* MOTHER BAUMERT, *an almost-paralyzed old woman, sits on a stool by the bed, a spooling wheel in front of her. Her son,* AUGUST, *a twenty-year-old idiot with a small body and long, spider-like limbs, sits on a footstool; he, too, is spooling yarn. The pink light of evening penetrates weakly through the two small windows in the left wall which are partly covered with paper and plugged with straw. The light shines on the long, flaxen hair of the girls, on their bare, meager shoulders, their thin waxen necks, and on the folds in the backs of their coarse shirts which, together with short skirts of the roughest kind of linen, constitute their only clothing. The warm glow falls full on the old woman's face and on her throat and chest. Her face is so gaunt that it seems to consist only of bones covered by the wrinkles and folds of a bloodless skin. Her eyes, sunk deep into their sockets, are reddened and watery from wool dust, smoke, and working by candle-light; the skin of her long, goitrous neck hangs in folds. Her breast is covered with faded shawls and rags.*

Part of the right wall—with the stove and stove bench, a bed, and several garish pictures of saints—also receives some light. Rags are drying on the stove bar; behind the stove is a pile of old, useless trash. Some battered pots and other cooking utensils stand on the bench; potato peels are spread on paper to dry. Hanks of yarn and yarn winders hang from the rafters. Small) *baskets filled with bobbins stand near the looms. On the back wall there is a door without a lock. Next to it, a bunch of willow twigs leans against the wall. Close by stand several broken bushel baskets. The room is filled with the noise of the looms, the rhythmic, heavy thumping of the batten, which shakes the floor and the walls, and the swishing and snapping of the hurrying shuttles. Intermingled with this noise is the deep, monotonous humming of the spooling wheels, a sound like the buzzing of a swarm of huge bumblebees.)*

MOTHER BAUMERT (*in a whining, exhausted voice, as the girls stop and bend over the web*). You got to tie again?

EMMA (*the older of the girls, twenty-two years of age, while she is tying the broken threads*). Some yarn this is!

BERTHA (*fifteen years old*). This is the damnest warp!

EMMA. Where can he be this late? He's been gone since nine.

MOTHER BAUMERT. That's just it! Where can he be, girls?

BERTHA. Just don't worry, Mother!

MOTHER BAUMERT. Oh, it's a fright every time.

(EMMA *continues weaving.*)

BERTHA. Wait a minute, Emma!

EMMA. What's the matter?

BERTHA. Thought I heard somebody coming.

EMMA. Must be Ansorge coming home.

FRITZ (*a small, barefooted boy, four years old and in rags, comes in crying*). Mama, I'm hungry.

EMMA. Wait a while, Fritzie, wait a while. Grandpa'll be home in a minute. He'll bring bread and barley for coffee.

FRITZ. I'm so hungry, Mama!

EMMA. Now, now. Don't be silly. He'll be here soon. He'll bring some nice bread and barley coffee. And when we're through, mother'll take the potato peels to the farmer, and he'll give her a nice pitcher of buttermilk for her little boy.

FRITZ. Where'd Grandpa go?

EMMA. To the manufacturer's, that's where he went; to deliver a web.

FRITZ. To the manufacturer's?

EMMA. Yes, yes, Fritz; to Dreissiger, down in Peterswaldau.

FRITZ. Does he give him bread?

EMMA. Yes, he gives him money, and then he can buy bread.

FRITZ. Does he give a lot of money to Grandpa?

EMMA (*sharply*). Oh, stop it, boy, stop gabbing. (*She continues weaving, as does* BERTHA. *Soon they stop again.*)

BERTHA. August, go ask Ansorge if he won't come light up.

(AUGUST *goes,* FRITZ *accompanies him.*)

MOTHER BAUMERT (*overpowered by a childish fear, almost whining*). Children, children, where is that man?

BERTHA. Maybe he stopped in at Hauff's.

MOTHER BAUMERT (*crying*). If only he didn't go to a tavern!

EMMA. Oh, nonsense, Mother. You know Father ain't like that.

MOTHER BAUMERT (*the multitude of fears assailing her has brought her almost beside herself*). Well, tell me, what are we going to do now? If he should have . . . if he comes home . . . if he should have drunk it all up and doesn't bring nothing home? There ain't a handful of salt in the house, not a piece of bread, and we could do with a shovel of coal . . .

BERTHA. Never mind, Mama. The moon's out. We'll go over to the woods. We'll take August along and get us a few sticks.

MOTHER BAUMERT. Sure, so the forester will come and get you by the neck!

ANSORGE (*an old weaver of gigantic build; he bows low to get into the room, pushes his head and trunk through the door. His hair and beard are unkempt.*) What is it?

BERTHA. If you would give us some light!

ANSORGE (*softly, as if talking near a sick-bed*). But it's still light.

MOTHER BAUMERT. Now you'll let us sit in the dark, too.

ANSORGE. I got to figure for myself, too.

(*He withdraws.*)

BERTHA. There you have it; that's how stingy he is.

EMMA. Now we can sit and wait until he's good and ready.

FRAU HEINRICH (*enters. A woman of thirty, pregnant. Her tired face tells of torturous worries and fearful anticipations.*) Good evening, all.

MOTHER BAUMERT. Well, Heinrich, what news have you got?

FRAU HEINRICH (*limping*). I got a piece of glass in my foot.

BERTHA. Come on, sit down. I'll see if I can't get it out.

(FRAU HEINRICH *sits down;* BERTHA *kneels in front of her and busies herself with the splinter.*)

MOTHER BAUMERT. How're things home, Heinrich?

FRAU HEINRICH (*in a desperate outbreak*). It just simply don't go at all no more. (*She fights in vain against her tears. She weeps silently.*)

MOTHER BAUMERT. For the likes of us, it'd be best if God showed some understanding and took us out of this world.

FRAU HEINRICH (*losing control of herself, shouts under tears*). My poor children are starving! (*She sobs and whimpers.*) I don't know what to do no more. Do what you want, you just chase around 'til you drop. I'm more dead than alive, but it don't help. Nine hungry mouths, that's what I got to fill. And with what, with what? Last night I had a piece of bread, wasn't even big enough for the two little ones. Who do I give it to? All shouting at me: Me, Mummy! Me, Mummy! . . . No, no. And this is while I can still get around! What's going to happen when I got to lie down? The few potatoes we had the flood's taken. Just haven't got nothing to eat no more.

BERTHA (*has removed the piece of glass and washed the wound*). Let's tie a rag 'round it; (*To* EMMA) go find one!

MOTHER BAUMERT. We ain't no better off, Heinrich.

FRAU HEINRICH. At least you got your girls. You got a man who can work; but mine—last week he broke down again. He was twisting and turning so bad I was frightened to death . . . didn't know what to do with him. And when he gets one of them attacks he's down on his back for a week.

MOTHER BAUMERT. Mine ain't worth nothing no more either. He's starting to give out. He's got it in his chest and in his back. And broke we are, too, not a penny left. If he don't bring a few groschen home tonight, nobody knows what's going to happen.

EMMA. That's right, Heinrich. It's come so far with us . . . Father had to take Ami. Had to get'm killed just so we could get something into our stomachs for a change.

FRAU HEINRICH. You couldn't spare just one handful of flour?

MOTHER BAUMERT. Not that much, Heinrich; haven't even got a grain of salt left in the house.

FRAU HEINRICH. Well, then I just don't know. (*She gets up, stops and thinks.*) I just don't know no more!—Then . . . I just can't help it. (*She shouts, in furious anger and terror.*) I'd be glad if it was pig's feed! But with empty hands I just can't come home. I just can't. God forgive me, but I just don't know what else I can do. (*She quickly limps out, using only the heel of her left foot.*)

MOTHER BAUMERT (*shouts after her, warning*). Heinrich, don't you do nothing foolish!

BERTHA. She ain't going to harm herself. Don't you worry about that.

EMMA. That's how she always carries on. (*She sits down at the loom again and weaves for a few seconds.*)

(AUGUST *enters, lighting his father's way with a candle;* OLD BAUMERT *is weighed down with a pack of yarn.*)

MOTHER BAUMERT. Jesus, man, where have you been this long?

OLD BAUMERT. Well, don't start biting right away. Just give a man a chance to catch his breath.—Take a look who I got along!

MORITZ JÄGER (*comes through the door, stooping. He is of medium height, red-cheeked, a strapping reservist; he wears his Hussar's cap at a jaunty angle, a clean shirt with a collar, and clothes and shoes that are neither torn nor mended. Once in the room, he comes to attention and gives a military salute. Smartly.*) Evening, Aunt Baumert!

MOTHER BAUMERT. Well, well, you're back home? And you didn't forget us? Well, sit down. Come here and sit down.

EMMA (*wipes the dirt off a wooden chair with her skirt and pushes* JÄGER *toward it*). Evening, Moritz! Come to see how the poor people live for a change?

JÄGER. Tell me, Emma—I just couldn't believe it! You got a little boy almost big enough to enlist. Where the devil did you get him?

BERTHA (*takes the little food her father has brought, puts some meat in a pan which she puts into the oven while* AUGUST *lights a fire*). You know that weaver, Finger, don't you?

MOTHER BAUMERT. That's the one who used to stay with us right here in this room, you know. He was willing to take her all right, but then he was already pretty weak in the chest. I'd warned the girl often enough. But would she listen? Now he's been dead and forgotten for a long time, and she's got to see how to bring up the boy by herself. —Tell me now, Moritz, how's it been going with you?

OLD BAUMERT. Don't worry 'bout him, Mother. For him bread grows on trees. He's got the laugh on all of us. He's brought back clothes like a duke's, a silver watch, and—to top it off—ten talers in cash.

JÄGER (in a stance of cocky self-importance, a boasting, roguish grin on his face). Can't complain. I didn't have it too bad in the army.

OLD BAUMERT. Was a captain's orderly, he was. Just listen, he talks like gentle folks.

JÄGER. I got so used to fancy talk, I just can't talk different no more.

MOTHER BAUMERT. You don't say! A good-for-nothing like you was and now you got such a lot of money. Used to be good for absolutely nothing; couldn't even spool one little bobbin without stopping. Had to get out all the time; setting traps for titmice and making slings for robins; you'd always rather do that. Well, it's true, ain't it?

JÄGER. That's the truth, Aunt Baumert. And I didn't catch only robins, I caught swallows, too.

EMMA. No good our saying over and over again: swallows are poison.

JÄGER. That didn't bother me. And how's it been going with you, Aunt Baumert?

MOTHER BAUMERT. Oh, Jesus, the last four years it's been pretty bad, pretty bad.—I got these pains. Just look at these fingers. I just don't know: do I have rheumatism, or what? Oh, I'm so miserable! Can't move a limb. Nobody believes what I suffer.

OLD BAUMERT. It's real bad with her. She ain't going to last long.

BERTHA. In the morning we dress her, in the evening we undress her. And we feed her like a baby.

MOTHER BAUMERT (continues in a pitiful, whining tone). I got to have help for everything. I'm more'n sick, I'm a burden. How often did I ask dear God that He should call me. Oh, Jesus, it's too much for me. I don't know . . . maybe people think . . . but I'm used to work—since I was a tot.

Always could do my share, and now all of a sudden (*She tries in vain to get up*) it just won't work no more. I got a good husband, and good children too, but if I'm to stand by and look on . . . Look at them girls! Hardly no blood left in them. A color like a sheet. It just keeps on and on with this treadmill, even if they don't get nothing for it. What little they get from life! All year they don't move from the bench. Not even a dress they got to show for it—so they could cover themselves and go among people once in a while or go to church and get some encouragement. Look like they was cut off the gallows, the girls do—young girls of fifteen and twenty!

BERTHA (*at the stove*). That's some smoke again!

OLD BAUMERT. Yes, just look at that smoke. Do you think that'll ever change? It's ready to topple any time now, that stove. And we just got to sit and watch it cave in—and breathe the smoke! And the coughing! If you cough, you cough, and if it catches up with you and you kick the bucket, nobody even asks.

JÄGER. That's up to Ansorge, ain't it? He's got to take care of that, don't he?

BERTHA. He'd just make a face. He grumbles enough as it is.

MOTHER BAUMERT. He thinks we take up too much room anyway.

OLD BAUMERT. And if we'd start complaining, out we'd go. He ain't seen no rent for almost half a year.

MOTHER BAUMERT. And a single man like him—he could be a little more friendly at least.

OLD BAUMERT. He ain't got nothin' either, Mother. He's pretty bad off, too, even if he don't make no fuss about it.

MOTHER BAUMERT. He's got his house at least.

OLD BAUMERT. Now, Mother, how you talk. Hardly a splinter of this here house belongs to him.

JÄGER (*sitting down, brings a short pipe with pretty tassels out of one pocket, and out of the other he takes a quart bottle of brandy*). Things can't go on like this much longer, around here. I'm amazed seeing what it's like among the people here. In the towns even the dogs live better than you.

OLD BAUMERT (*eagerly*). Ain't that the truth now! You know that, too, huh? And if you say a word, all you get for an answer is: Times is bad.

ANSORGE (*enters, holding in one hand a small earthen-*

ware bowl of soup, in the other a half-finished bushel basket). Welcome home, Moritz! So you're back!

JÄGER. Thanks a lot, Father Ansorge.

ANSORGE (*pushing his bowl into the oven*). Let me see . . . why, you look almost like a count!

OLD BAUMERT. Show him your pretty watch. And he's brought home a new suit and ten talers in cash.

ANSORGE (*shaking his head*). Well, well, well!

EMMA (*putting the potato peelings into a little bag*). I'll be going with the peels now. Maybe it'll be enough for a little skimmed milk.   (*She goes.*)

JÄGER (*while everybody looks at him with an expression of great interest and admiration*). Just think how often you made it hot for me. You'll find out, you always said, you'll find out when you get into the army. Now you see it went pretty well. After six months I had my first stripe. You've got to be willing to work, that's the trick. I polished the sergeant's boots, I groomed his horse, I got'm his beer. I was quick as a weasel. And I was sharp; I tell you, my stuff had to shine. I was the first in the stables, the first at reveille, the first in the saddle; and when we went on the attack—Squadron, forward! Holy mackerel! Lordy, Lordy! And watching out—like a pointer! I always thought, this is it, you got to do it yourself. And then I pulled myself together, and it worked. And finally I got so that the captain up and says of me—in front of the whole squadron, mind you—that's what a Hussar should be like. (*Silence. He lights his pipe.*)

ANSORGE (*shaking his head*). So you were pretty lucky, huh? Well, well, um, hum. (*He sits down on the floor, the willow branches at his side, and continues weaving the basket which he holds between his legs.*)

OLD BAUMERT. Let's hope you bring your good luck to us! —Well, are we supposed to have a drink with you?

JÄGER. Sure thing, Father Baumert, and when this is gone, there's more. (*He slams a coin on the table.*)

ANSORGE (*so surprised he has a silly grin on his face*). My, my, what goings-on . . . a roast in the oven, there's a quart of liquor—(*He drinks from the bottle.*)—to you, Moritz! Well, well, well! (*From now on the bottle circulates.*)

OLD BAUMERT. If we could at least have a little roast like this on the Holy Days; as it is, we ain't even gettin' to look at a piece of meat for months and months; just have to wait until another little doggie runs into the house like this one did four weeks ago, and that don't happen so often in one lifetime.

ANSORGE. Did you have Ami butchered?

OLD BAUMERT. He would have starved to death anyways . . .

ANSORGE. Well, well, well!

MOTHER BAUMERT. And he was such a nice, friendly little dog.

JÄGER. Is everybody around here still so eager for a dog roast?

OLD BAUMERT. Oh, Jesus, if we only had enough of it.

MOTHER BAUMERT. Well, now, a little piece of meat ain't bad at all.

OLD BAUMERT. You've lost your taste for things like that, huh? Just stay with us, Moritz; it'll come back!

ANSORGE (*sniffing*). Well, well, well! That's really something good; smells just lovely.

OLD BAUMERT (*sniffing*). The real thing, you might say.

ANSORGE. Now tell us what you think, Moritz. You know what it looks like out in the big world. Are things going to change for us weavers, or what?

JÄGER. I hope so.

ANSORGE. Up here, we can't live and we can't die neither. Believe me, it's real bad with us. You fight it to the last, but in the end you've got to give in. Misery eats the roof over your head and the ground under your feet. Before, when a man could still work at the loom, you could just about make ends meet, with worries and rough sledding, it's true, but you could just barely make out. Now, for God knows how long I haven't been able to hunt up a piece of work. Weaving baskets, that's finished too; just enough to keep the little bit of life that's left going for a while. I weave 'til late at night, and when I finally fall into bed, I've made one groschen and five pfennigs, slaving all day. You're educated; now you tell me yourself, can you live on that with prices going up all the time? Three talers I got to cough up for house taxes, one taler for property tax, three talers for interest. I can figure I'll make fourteen talers. Leaves seven talers for me, and that's got to last the whole year; that's to be enough for cooking, and heating, and clothing, and shoes, and patches and thread for mending, and a roof over your head, and what not. No wonder a man can't pay the interest!

OLD BAUMERT. Somebody ought to go to Berlin and tell the King how it is with us.

JÄGER. That wouldn't do much good, neither, Father Baumert. There's been enough talk about it in the newspapers. But the rich, they manage to turn and twist the story so . . . they bedevil the best Christians.

OLD BAUMERT (*shaking his head*). They just haven't got that much courage in Berlin!

ANSORGE. Tell me, Moritz, is that really possible? Ain't there no law against it? If you sweat and slave until the skin comes off your hands and still you can't pay the interest, can the farmer take my house? He's a farmer and he wants his money! I don't know what's going to happen. If I should have to get out of the house . . . (*Fighting down his tears.*) I was born here, my father sat here at the loom for more'n forty years. How often did he tell Mother: Mother, when I ain't here no more, hold on to that house, hold tight. That house I fought for, he said. Every nail in it is a night I worked, every beam's a year of dry bread. You'd think . . .

JÄGER. They'll take the last thing you got, they'll do it all right.

ANSORGE. Well, well, well! But if it comes to that, I wish they'd carry me out so I wouldn't have to walk out in my old days. It's a little thing—dying! My father didn't mind dying much either.—Just at the very end, he got a little scared. But when I crawled into bed with him he got quiet again. Just think, at that time I was a boy of thirteen. Tired, that I was; and so I fell asleep next to the sick old man—I didn't know no better—and when I woke up he was already cold.

MOTHER BAUMERT (*after a pause*). Stick your hand in the oven, Bertha, and give Ansorge his soup.

BERTHA. Here it is, Father Ansorge!

ANSORGE (*eating, with tears in his eyes*). Well, well, well!

(OLD BAUMERT *has started eating the meat from the pan.*)

MOTHER BAUMERT. Now, Father, you ought to be able to wait. Give Bertha a chance to serve proper-like.

OLD BAUMERT (*chewing*). It's two years ago I went last time to take Holy Communion. Right after that I sold the Communion suit. And the money went for buying a bit of pork. Since then I never eaten a piece of meat till tonight.

JÄGER. What do we need meat for! The bosses eat it for us. They wade in fat up to here. And if you don't believe it, just go on down to Bielau and Peterswaldau. Your eyes'll pop: one mansion next to the other, and all of them belong to the bosses. One palace next to the other. With glass windows and towers and iron fences. Oh no! They don't know it's bad times. They got enough for roasts and cakes, for carriages and coaches, for governesses and God-knows-whatnot. They're just itching with greed. They hardly know what to do with their money, so cocky they are.

ANSORGE. Used to be different in my time. Then the bosses gave the weavers enough to live on. Today, it's them who spend it all. But I say the reason is the gentlefolks don't believe in God no more, or in the Devil neither. They don't know commandments and punishment. So, they go and grab our last crumb of bread; and they cripple us and pinch the last bit of food they can get away from us. They're the cause of all our misery. If only the bosses were decent people, there wouldn't be no bad times for us.

JÄGER. Now you listen to this. I'll read you something real nice. (*He takes a few sheets of paper from his pocket.*) Look here, August, you run over to the tavern to get another quart. What's the matter, August? What's so funny?

MOTHER BAUMERT. Don't know what gets into the boy. He's always happy. Laughs all the time no matter what happens. Get going now, go on! (AUGUST *leaves with the empty bottle.*) What do you say, Old Man, you know what's good, eh?

OLD BAUMERT (*still chewing; stimulated by food and drink he is now quite courageous*). Moritz, you belong to us. You know how to read and write. You know what the weavers are up against. Your heart beats for us poor weavers. You go ahead and take a hand in this here situation . . .

JÄGER. If that's all . . . I wouldn't mind. It sure would be a pleasure to make them brutes of bosses dance to our music for once. Wouldn't mind at all. I'm pretty easy to get along with, but if I get my dander up and get mad, I could take Dreissiger in one hand and Dietrich in the other and knock their heads together so the sparks fly. If we'd decide and stand together we could make quite a noise for them bosses. And for that we wouldn't need no king and no government; we'd just up and say: this is what we want and that's the way we want it done, and you'd see; pretty soon they'd sing a different tune. They just got to see we got some pluck and they'll soon pipe down. I know that lot: they're cowards, the bastards.

MOTHER BAUMERT. That's the truth. I sure ain't a bad woman. It's always been me who said: let them rich people be—them's got to live, too. But now . . .

JÄGER. For all I care, the devil can take'm all. They deserve it.

BERTHA. What happened to Father?

(OLD BAUMERT *has quietly left.*)

MOTHER BAUMERT. Don't know what could have happened to him.

BERTHA. I wonder, maybe he ain't used to meat no more.

MOTHER BAUMERT (*excited, crying*). That's it, that's it! He can't even keep it down. Now he'll spit it out again—the little bit of good food he got into his stomach.

OLD BAUMERT (*returns crying with rage*). Oh no, that's too much. That's the end. You finally got a little bit of something good to eat, and you can't even keep it down. (*He sits down on the oven bench, weeping.*)

JÄGER (*in an outburst of fanaticism*). And still there are people, judges, not far from here, stuffed bellies who ain't got nothing to do all year round but steal a day away from our Lord. And those kind claim the weavers could make out well enough if only they wasn't so lazy!

ANSORGE. Them's not human beings. Monsters, that's what they are.

JÄGER. Never mind now, he's got what he asked for. Me and Red Bäcker, we got it started. And before we left, we even sang "Blood Justice" for him.

ANSORGE. Oh Jesus, is that the song?

JÄGER. Yes sir, here it is.

ANSORGE. It's called the "Dreissiger Song," ain't it?

JÄGER. Just wait, I'll read it to you.

MOTHER BAUMERT. Who's thought up the song?

JÄGER. Nobody knows. Listen now. (*He reads, spelling slowly like a schoolboy, stressing poorly, but with unmistakably strong feeling. Many emotions vibrate in his reading: despair, pain, furor, hate and a craving for vengeance.*)

In our town we have a court
Where lynch law is the order;

All sentences are of one sort,
It's not a court, it's murder.

Here men go slowly to their deaths,
Here men in torment languish,
Countless the sighs; their dying breaths
Bear witness to their anguish.

OLD BAUMERT (*shaken to the depth of his being by the words of the song, has only with difficulty resisted the temptation to interrupt* JÄGER. *Now his emotions gain the upper hand; stammering, with tears and laughter, to his wife.*) "Here men in torment languish." Whoever's written that knows the truth. "You are a witness" . . . How did it go? "Countless the sighs" . . . is that it? "Countless the sighs, their dying breaths" . . .

JÄGER. "Bear witness to their anguish."

OLD BAUMERT. You know the sighs we heave, each day and every day, standing up and lying down.

(ANSORGE *has stopped working and, deeply moved, just sits, completely overwhelmed.* MOTHER BAUMERT *and* BERTHA *constantly wipe their eyes.*)

JÄGER (*continues reading*).

The Dreissigers our hangmen are
Their servants do as they're bidden,
They rack their victims near and far
And never keep them hidden.

Scoundrels you all, you devil's brood . . .

OLD BAUMERT (*shaking with fury, stamps his foot*). "Devil's brood," that's it all right!

JÄGER (*reads*).

You hounds of hell, you cancer.
You eat the poor man's scanty food,
And curses are your answer.

ANSORGE. Yes sir, that's well worth a curse.

OLD BAUMERT (*making a fist, threatening*). "You eat the poor man's little food!"

JÄGER (*reads*).

> It does no good to beg and pray,
> For no one hears our moaning.
> "If you don't like it," so they say,
> "Go home and do your groaning."

OLD BAUMERT. How was that? "No one hears our moaning." Every word, every single word . . . it's the truth like in the Bible. It does no good to beg and pray!

ANSORGE. Well, well, well! No, nothing does any good.

JÄGER (*reads*).

> Just think of this degrading lot,
> These wretches' fate is rotten.
> At home they have an empty pot.
> Is pity all forgotten?
>
> Pity! Oh, it's a noble word
> But strange to you man-eaters.
> Of your aim all of us have heard:
> To bleed and to defeat us.

OLD BAUMERT (*jumps up, almost delirious in his rage*). "To bleed and to defeat us." That's it. "To bleed and to defeat us." Here I am, Robert Baumert, Master Weaver from Kaschbach. Who can stand up and say . . . I've been a good man all my life, and now look at me! What good does it do me? What do I look like? What have they made of me? "Here men in torture languish." (*He holds out his arms.*) Here, touch it, nothing but skin and bones. "Scoundrels you are, you devil's brood!" (*He collapses, crying, on a chair, overwhelmed by despair and anger.*)

ANSORGE (*throws his basket into a corner; he rises, shaking all over with rage and stammers*). And it's got to change, I say, it's got to change right now. We ain't going to stand for it no more! We ain't going to stand for it, no matter what happens!

CURTAIN

ACT III

*(The taproom in a tavern at Peterswaldau. This is a large
room; the open-beam ceiling is supported by a wooden
center column around which a table is built. To the
right of the column, in the back wall, is the entrance
door, part of it hidden from view. Through the door,
one can see into the large storeroom which contains
barrels and brewing utensils. Inside the taproom, to the
right of the door in the corner, is the bar: a wooden
partition as high as a man, with shelves for bar utensils.
Behind it is a cupboard with rows of liquor bottles.
Between the partition and the cupboard is a narrow
aisle for the bartender. In front of the bar is a table
covered with a multicolored cloth. A pretty lamp hangs
above the table and several cane chairs stand around
it. Not far from the table, on the right-hand wall, is a
door marked "Wine Room" which leads into the room
reserved for the more prominent citizens. Still further
toward the right front stands an old grandfather clock.
To the left of the entrance door, along the back wall,
stands a table with bottles and glasses. Still further, in
the corner, is the huge tile stove. On the left wall, below
three small windows, there is a long bench. In front
of the bench there are three wooden tables, each
placed with the narrow end turned toward the wall.
At the sides of the tables are shorter benches with
backs; at the other narrow ends are single wooden
chairs. The large room is painted blue. Among the
posters, pictures, and colored prints hanging on the
walls is a portrait of the King, Friedrich Wilhelm IV.*

WELZEL, *a genial colossus in his fifties, is behind the
bar drawing beer from a barrel into a glass.* FRAU
WELZEL *is ironing near the stove. She is a stately,
neatly-dressed woman of not quite thirty-five.* ANNA
WELZEL *is a seventeen-year-old, pretty girl with beautiful reddish-blond hair. She is nicely dressed and sits
behind the table with the colored cloth, busily embroidering. She looks up from her work for a moment*

when she hears from afar the sounds of a funeral hymn sung by schoolchildren. MASTER WIEGAND, *the cabinetmaker, sits at the same table. He wears his working garb and has a glass of Bavarian beer in front of him. It is obvious that this is a man who knows the important requirements of making one's way in the world: shrewdness, speed, and ruthless aggressiveness. A traveling salesman sitting at the table around the column is busy eating a chopped steak. He is of medium height, well-fed, bloated, gay, lively, and impudent. He wears modish clothes. His traveling accouterments—bag, sample case, umbrella, overcoat, and blanket—are placed on chairs next to him.)*

WELZEL (*bringing a glass of beer to the traveling salesman, aside to* WIEGAND). Seems the devil is loose in Peterswaldau today.

WIEGAND (*in a sharp, trumpet-like voice*). Well, it's delivery day up at Dreissiger's.

FRAU WELZEL. But usually there isn't such a commotion.

WIEGAND. Well, could be it's because of them two hundred new weavers he wants to take on.

FRAU WELZEL (*keeps on ironing*). Oh yes, that must be it. If he wants two hundred there'll be six hundred coming. Seems we got plenty of them.

WIEGAND. Oh Jesus, yes, we got enough of them. And even if they're badly off, they never die out. They put more children into the world than we got use for. (*The hymn is heard more clearly for a moment.*) And to top it all, there's that funeral. You know Weaver Fabich died.

WELZEL. Took him long enough. He's been running around like a ghost for a long time.

WIEGAND. You said it, Welzel. Never in my life did I glue together such a tiny casket as his; such a weeny, little thing. What a small little body that was, not even ninety pounds it weighed.

THE SALESMAN (*chewing*). I don't quite understand . . . wherever one looks, no matter what newspaper, one reads the most gruesome stories about the misery of the weavers. One gets the idea that the people around here are all three-quarters dead from starvation. And then you see a funeral like this one! I just got to the village. A brass band, the schoolteacher, the schoolchildren, the pastor and a whole rat-tail of people behind them; by God, it's like the funeral of the Emperor of China. Well, if people have enough money to pay for that! (*He drinks some beer. After putting his glass down again, with frivolous levity.*) Isn't that so, Fräulein? Isn't that the truth?

(ANNA *with an embarrassed smile continues embroidering.*)

SALESMAN. That's surely going to be a pair of slippers for your dad.

WELZEL. Oh no! I wouldn't put my feet into things like that.

SALESMAN. Now, listen! I'd give half my fortune if those slippers were for me.

FRAU WELZEL. He just don't understand things like that.

WIEGAND (*after clearing his throat a few times, pushing his chair back and forth and making several false starts*). You have made a peculiar remark about that funeral, Sir. Now tell me, young woman, that's a pretty small funeral, isn't it?

SALESMAN. Well, in that case, I ask myself . . . That must cost a fantastic amount of money. Where do the people get all that money?

WIEGAND. Begging your pardon, Sir, but that's one of those things where the poor people here are quite unreasonable. With your permission, they have such an exaggerated idea when it comes to the due respect and the duties that the blessed departed survivors deserve. If it's by chance one of the blessed departed parents, well then there's such a superstition, the nearest relatives and testators scratch together their last pennies, and what the children don't have they borrow from the nearest magnate. And so they get over their ears into debt; they owe His Eminence the Pastor, and the sexton, and everybody else standing around there. And then there's the drink and the food and that sort of thing. No, no, I'm all for respectiveness in children, but not so that the sorrowful survivors are oppressed by their debts for the rest of their lives.

SALESMAN. Wait a minute; the pastor should talk them out of it, shouldn't he?

WIEGAND. Begging your pardon, Sir, here I must advocate that each little parish has to maintain its churchly house of God and its warden of souls, the reverend. At such a large funeral the clergy has fine advantages. The more numerous the people at such a burial, the richer flows the offer-

tory. Those who know the working conditions here can say
with irrelevant assurance that the pastors condone quiet fu-
nerals only with repugnance.

HORNIG (*enters. A small, bow-legged old man, with a pull-
rope around his shoulder and chest. He is a ragpicker.*)
Morning, everybody. Gimme a shot. Hey, young woman, got
something in the way of rags? Fräulein Anna! Beautiful
hair ribbons, shirt bands, garters I got in the cart, beautiful
pins, hairpins, hooks and eyes. Give you everything for a
few rags. (*In a changed tone of voice.*) Out of them rags
they make beautiful white paper, and then the boy friend
writes a nice letter on it.

ANNA. No thanks. I don't want any boy friend.

FRAU WELZEL (*putting a hot core into the flatiron*).
That's the way the girl is. She don't want to hear a word
about marrying.

SALESMAN (*jumps up, apparently pleasantly surprised,
steps in front of the table at which* ANNA *is sitting and holds
out his hand to her*). That's the girl, Fräulein, do like me!
Agreed! Give me your hand! We won't get married either one
of us.

ANNA (*red as a beet, takes his hand*). Well, you're married already, aren't you?

SALESMAN. God help me, no. I just pretend. You think because I wear a ring? Ha, I've put it on only to protect my at-
tractive personality from unfair attacks. But I'm not afraid
of you. (*He puts the ring in his pocket.*) Seriously, tell
me, Fräulein, don't you want to get just a little bit married,
ever?

ANNA (*shakes her head*). Oh, leave me alone!

FRAU WELZEL. That one isn't going to get married, or at
least it would have to be something very special.

SALESMAN. Well, why not? A rich Silesian nobleman married his mother's chambermaid and Dreissiger, that rich
manufacturer, married an innkeeper's daughter just like you.
She wasn't half as pretty as you, Fräulein, and now she
rides in a fine carriage with a footman in livery. Why not?
(*He walks up and down, turns in circles and shifts from one
leg onto the other.*) I think I'll have a cup of coffee.

(ANSORGE *and* OLD BAUMERT *enter, each with a bundle, and
quietly and humbly sit down at the front table with*
HORNIG.)

WELZEL. Welcome, Father Ansorge! Come down to see us for a change?

HORNIG. Did you finally make it? Really crawled out of your smoky nest?

ANSORGE (*clumsily and obviously embarrassed*). Yes, I've gone and taken a web again.

OLD BAUMERT. He's going to work for ten groschen.

ANSORGE. I wouldn't never have done it, but basket-weaving is finished, too.

WIEGAND. Always better'n nothing. And he's doing it so you at least got something to do. I know him very well, Dreissiger. A week ago I took his storm windows out. We talked about it then. He's doing it for pure charity.

ANSORGE. Well, well, well!

WELZEL (*putting a brandy in front of* THE WEAVERS). Here it is. Tell me something, Ansorge. How long is it since you had a shave? The gentleman over there would like to know.

SALESMAN. Now, landlord, I didn't say that. The master weaver only attracted my attention because of his dignified appearance. One doesn't see men of such gigantic cast every day.

ANSORGE (*scratches his head in embarrassment*). Well, well, well!

SALESMAN. Such primeval men of nature are pretty rare these days. We have become so civilized . . . but I still take pleasure in the primeval. Those bushy eyebrows! That wild beard . . .

HORNIG. Now look here a minute, Sir; I want to tell you something: with them people there just ain't enough for a barber; and a razor they can afford even less. If it grows, let it grow. They can't waste nothing on looking pretty.

SALESMAN. But please, my good man, I didn't mean to . . . (*Quietly to the innkeeper.*) Is it permitted to offer the hairy one a glass of beer?

WELZEL. Heavens no, he won't accept nothing. He's got funny ideas.

SALESMAN. All right, so I won't. May I, Fräulein? (*He sits down at her table.*) I can assure you, I noticed your hair the minute I came into the room; this subtle brilliance, this softness, this fullness! (*He kisses the tips of his fingers to express his enchantment.*) And this color—like ripe wheat. If you'd come to Berlin, with your hair, you'd have the town at your feet! *Parole d'honneur,* with hair like that you'd be admitted at court in no time. (*Leaning back to regard the hair.*) Splendid, simply splendid!

WIEGAND. That's where she got her nice nickname.

TRAVELER. What's she called?

ANNA (*in constant silent laughter*). Oh, don't listen to him!

HORNIG. "Fox" they call you, don't they?

WELZEL. That's enough! Don't get the girl completely mixed up! They've put enough bees in her bonnet as it is. Today she wants a count, and tomorrow it's nothing less than a duke.

FRAU WELZEL. Man, don't you run the girl down! It's no crime for people to want to get on in the world. Thank God, not everybody thinks like you; that would really be too bad; then nobody'd get ahead . . . everybody'd just stay where he is. If Dreissiger's grandfather had thought like that, he'd have stayed the poor weaver he was, most likely. Now they're rich. Old Tromtra, too, was nothing but a poor weaver, and now he's got twelve estates and he's even been given a title.

WIEGAND. The truth is the truth, Welzel; in this matter your wife is on the right track. That I'll vouch for. If I'd thought like you, where would my seven journeymen be now?

HORNIG. You know how to go after it, even envy's got to admit that. Even when a weaver is still on his feet, you already got his coffin ready.

WIEGAND. If you want to get ahead you got to stick with it.

HORNIG. Oh yes, you're sticking with it all right. You know better than the doctor when Death comes to get a weaver's child.

WIEGAND (*hardly smiling any more, suddenly furious*). And you know better than the police which of the weavers are tipplers and which have a nice ball of yarn left over every week. You come for rags and you take a roll of weft yarn, too, if they twist your arm.

HORNIG. And your clover grows in the graveyard. The more of us who go to sleep on wooden planks, the more you like it. When you look at all them children's graves you tap your belly and say to yourself: it's been a good year. The little blighters have dropped like June bugs from the trees. That's another quart a week, for me.

WIEGAND. That don't make me a thief, not by a long shot.

HORNIG. No, you just bill a rich manufacturer twice, or take a few spare boards from Dreissiger's new house when the moon ain't shining.

WIEGAND (*turning his back to him*). Oh, go on jabbering

if you like; but don't talk to me.—(*Suddenly starting again.*)
Lying Hornig!

HORNIG. Graveyard snooper!

WIEGAND (*to everybody*). He can put a hex on cattle.

HORNIG. Watch out, I can tell you, or I'll make my sign.

(WIEGAND *blanches.*)

FRAU WELZEL (*had left the room and now returns to serve coffee to* THE SALESMAN). Would you rather I serve the coffee in the small room?

SALESMAN. What do you think? (*With a melting glance to* ANNA.) Here I'll sit until I die.

A YOUNG FORESTER AND A FARMER (*enter, the latter with a whip. Both.*) Good morning. (*They remain standing at the bar.*)

THE FARMER. Ginger schnapps for both of us.

WELZEL. Welcome to both of you! (*He pours the drinks, both take the small glasses, clink, drink and put them down on the bar.*)

SALESMAN. Well, Forester, had a good march?

FORESTER. It was all right. I'm over from Steinseifersdorf.

(FIRST *and* SECOND OLD WEAVERS *come and sit down with* ANSORGE, OLD BAUMERT *and* HORNIG.)

SALESMAN. Excuse the question, are you one of Count Hochheim's foresters?

FORESTER. I'm with Count Keil.

SALESMAN. Of course, of course, that's what I meant to say. It's too complicated around here with all those counts and barons and excellencies. You need the memory of an elephant. What do you use the ax for, Forester?

FORESTER. Took it from some wood thieves.

OLD BAUMERT. His Highness, he's pretty particular about a few pieces of firewood.

SALESMAN. Well, I beg your pardon, but that would really go too far if everybody went to get . . .

OLD BAUMERT. With your permission, here it's like everywhere else with the little and the big thieves; there are some have quite a lumber business; they get rich selling stolen lumber. But if a poor weaver . . .

FIRST OLD WEAVER (*interrupts* BAUMERT). We ain't allowed a twig! But His Lordship, he's getting sharper all the time; he's pulling our skins right over our ears anyhow. There's protection fees to pay, spinning fees, fees in kind, and you got to run errands for free and do field work whether you want to or not.

ANSORGE. It's like this: what the manufacturer leaves, the nobleman gets it.

SECOND OLD WEAVER (*sitting down at the next table*). I've told it to His Highness himself. With your kind permission, Your Highness, I told him, this year I just can't do that many days of field work. I just can't do it! And why? You'll excuse me, but the water has ruined everything. The flood has taken the little field I had. I got to work day and night to keep alive. What a storm! Man, oh man. I just stood there wringing my hands. All that good soil just washing down the hill and into the house! And that good, expensive seed. Oh Jesus, Jesus, I just shouted to the clouds for a week, and for a week I just cried until I could hardly see the road no more . . . and afterwards I had to push eighty heavy barrows full of soil up the hill again.

THE FARMER (*roughly*). You're doing some gruesome complaining. What heaven sends, you've got to accept. And if you're not doing so well who's to blame but yourselves? When business was good what did you do? Lost everything gaming and drinking. If you'd saved something then you'd have a few pennies laid up now and you needn't go stealing yarn and wood.

FIRST YOUNG WEAVER (*with some companions in the hallway, talks loudly through the door*). A farmer is always a farmer, even if he sleeps until nine.

FIRST OLD WEAVER. That's the way it is: the farmer and the nobleman pull at the same rope. If a weaver wants a place to live the farmer tells him: I'll give you a little hole in the wall to live in. You'll pay me a nice rent and help me harvest the hay and wheat, and if you don't like it it's your lookout to find another place. If you go to another one he does the same thing.

OLD BAUMERT (*bitingly*). We're like an apple; everybody comes and takes a bite.

FARMER (*excited*). Oh, you starved bastards, what are you good for? Can you press the plow down into the soil? Can you plow a straight furrow or hand a bunch of oats up to the wagon? You're good for nothing but to laze around and lie with the women. Dirt, that's what you are. You're a big help! (*Meanwhile he has paid and leaves.* THE FORESTER *follows him, laughing.* WELZEL, THE CABINETMAKER *and* FRAU WELZEL *are laughing aloud;* THE SALESMAN *laughs quietly to himself. When the laughing subsides, silence reigns.*)

HORNIG. Them peasants are like bulls . . . as if I didn't know what misery there is! In the villages up here, the things you see! Four and five of them lying naked on a bundle of straw.

TRAVELER (*in a quiet, reproving tone*). I beg your pardon, my good man. Opinion about the misery in the mountains is pretty divided; if you can read . . .

HORNIG. Oh, I can read straight down the page, just as well as you. No, no, I should know, I've been around enough among the people. When you've had that pull-rope around your back for forty years you should know something. What happened to Fuller? The children playing around with the neighbor's geese in the dung heap. They died, them folks, naked, on the flagstones in the house. Stinking sizing they ate in their fear of death. Hunger killed them, hundreds and hundreds.

TRAVELER. If you know how to read you ought to know that the Government has made a thorough investigation and that . . .

HORNIG. We know that, we know how that works: comes a gentleman from the Government who knows everything better than if he'd seen it. He trots around in the village for a bit, down at the lower part of the brook where the nicest houses are. He don't want to dirty his nice, polished boots. So he thinks, well, it's going to look the same all over, and he's up and into his carriage and off he goes home. And then he writes to Berlin there really wasn't no distress. But if he'd had just a tiny bit of patience and climbed up the villages to where the brook comes in, and over to the other side of the brook, or even off the road where them little shacks are . . . them old swallow nests stuck to the hillside, so black sometimes and so broken-down they ain't worth a match to set fire to . . . then maybe he'd report to Berlin different. Should have come to me, them gentlemen from the Government who wouldn't believe there was misery around here. I would have shown them something. I would've opened their eyes for 'em in all them hungry holes.

(*The "Weaver Song" is heard outside.*)

WELZEL. There they're singing it again, that devil's song.

WIEGAND. They're turning the whole village upside down.

FRAU WELZEL. It's really as if something was in the air.

(JÄGER *and* BÄCKER *enter noisily arm in arm, leading a group of* YOUNG WEAVERS *into the hallway and from there into the taproom.*)

JÄGER. Squadron halt! Dismount! (*The new arrivals approach different tables already occupied by* WEAVERS *and start talking to them.*)

HORNIG (*calling to* BÄCKER). Tell me, what's going on that you're running around in a mob like that?

BÄCKER (*significantly*). Maybe something will be going on, ain't that so, Moritz?

HORNIG. That'd be something. Don't start a fuss now.

BÄCKER. Blood's already started flowing. Want to see? (*He rolls up one sleeve and shows him freshly bleeding tattoo marks on his bare upper arm. Many of* THE YOUNG WEAVERS *at other tables do the same.*)

BÄCKER. We've been to Barber Schmidt's getting tattooed.

HORNIG. Ain't that something. No wonder there's such a racket in the streets. When young louts like that jabber all over the village . . !

JÄGER (*assuming a swaggering air, in a loud voice*). Might as well give us two quarts to start, Welzel! I'll pay. You think maybe I ain't got the dough? Wait awhile! If we had a mind to we could drink liquor and sip coffee until tomorrow morning just as good as any traveling salesman. (*Laughter among* THE YOUNG WEAVERS.)

SALESMAN (*in comic surprise*). Talking to me? (THE LANDLORD, HIS WIFE, *and* DAUGHTER, WIEGAND *and* THE SALESMAN *laugh.*)

JÄGER. Ain't talking to your uncle!

SALESMAN. If you don't mind my saying so, business seems to be pretty good.

JÄGER. Can't complain. I sell ready-to-wear. I go fifty-fifty with the manufacturer. The more the weavers are hungry, the better I eat. The greater his troubles the more my bread doubles.

BÄCKER. Atta boy, Moritz, well said.

WELZEL (*has brought the corn liquor. Going back to the bar he stops and turns with his usual stolidness and in all his bulk to face* THE WEAVERS *once more. Composed but with emphasis.*) Leave that gentleman alone. He didn't do you no harm.

VOICES OF YOUNG WEAVERS. We don't do him none either.

(FRAU WELZEL *has exchanged a few words with* THE SALESMAN. *She takes his cup with the rest of his coffee and carries it into the next room.* THE SALESMAN *follows her amid the laughter of* THE WEAVERS.)

VOICES OF YOUNG WEAVERS (*singing*). The Dreissigers our hangmen are, Their servants do their bidding . . .

WELZEL. *Psht*, quiet. Sing that song wherever you want but I won't stand for it in my house.

FIRST OLD WEAVER. He's right; stop that singing.

BÄCKER (*shouts*). But we'll march past Dreissiger's house one more time. He's got to hear our song again.

WIEGAND. Don't go too far now, so he won't take it wrong.

(*Laughter and shouts of "Hear, hear!"*)

OLD WITTIG (*a gray-haired blacksmith, without cap, in his leather apron and wooden clogs, sooty as he came out of his shop, comes in and waits at the bar for a glass of brandy*). Just let 'em act up a little. Dogs that bark don't bite.

VOICES OF OLD WEAVERS. Wittig, Wittig!

WITTIG. This is him. What d'you want?

VOICES OF OLD WEAVERS. Wittig is here.—Wittig, Wittig! —Come over, Wittig, we got room for you!—Come over here, Wittig!

WITTIG. I'd better be careful sitting with a bunch like you.

JÄGER. Come, have a drink with us.

WITTIG. Oh, keep your liquor. If I want a drink I'll pay for it. (*He takes his glass and sits down with* BAUMERT *and* ANSORGE. *Tapping* ANSORGE'S *stomach.*) What food do the weavers eat? Sauerkraut and lice for meat.

OLD BAUMERT (*ecstatically*). But what if they ain't happy with that no more?

WITTIG (*feigning surprise, stares stupidly at the weaver*). Well, well, well—tell me, is that you, Heinerle? (*Bursting with laughter.*) Folks, I'm dying with laughter. Old Baumert's going to start a rebellion! That does it: next it's the turn of the tailors and then the bah-bah sheep will be getting rebellious and at last the mice and rats. Oh my God, that's going to be a fine dance! (*Completely helpless with laughter.*)

OLD BAUMERT. Look here, Wittig, I'm still the same as I've always been. I'm still saying it'd be better if it would work out peacefully.

WITTIG. Dirty, it'll work out, but not peacefully. Where did anything like that ever work out peacefully? Did it work out peacefully in France? Did Robspier maybe hold hands with the rich? That was just: *allay*, off with you! Up to the guilyoutine! That's the way it's got to work, *allong sangfang*. Roast duck never flys right out of the blue into your open mouth.

OLD BAUMERT. If I only had halfways enough to get along . . .

FIRST OLD WEAVER. We're fed up to here, Wittig.

SECOND OLD WEAVER. A man hardly dares go home no more. If you sweat or if you loaf . . . you're hungry both ways.

FIRST OLD WEAVER. At home you go completely crazy.

ANSORGE. I don't care no more; if it comes, it comes.

VOICES OF OLD WEAVERS (*with increasing agitation*). No rest nowheres.—Just don't have no gumption left for work.— Up our way in Steinkunzendorf you can see a fellow sitting by the brook all day long washing himself, naked like the day he was born. He's gone completely off his rocker.

THIRD OLD WEAVER (*rises, moved by the Spirit, starts "talking in tongues," lifts his finger threateningly*). There is a judgment coming! Do not seek the company of the rich and the noble! There is a judgment coming! The Lord of Sebaoth . . . (*Some start laughing. He is pushed down on his seat.*)

WELZEL. Just one little glass and he gets fuzzy in the head.

THIRD OLD WEAVER (*rises again*). For O, they do not believe in God, nor in hell nor in heaven . . . They are mocking religion . . .

FIRST OLD WEAVER. That's enough, that's enough!

BÄCKER. You leave that man pray his sermon. There's some might take it to heart.

MANY VOICES (*tumultuously*). Let him talk, leave him alone!

THIRD OLD WEAVER (*with raised voice*). Therefore Hell opened wide its soul and its mouth gaped without measure,

so that descended all those who bend the right of the poor
and use force in their dealings with the wretched, so speaks
the Lord. (*Confusion. Suddenly the* OLD WEAVER *begins reciting like a schoolboy.*)

> And yet how strange,
> if one but thinks with care,
> that people could despise
> the linen weaver's ware!

BÄCKER. But we're fustian weavers! (*Laughter.*)

HORNIG. The linen weavers are still worse off. They slink
around in the mountains like ghosts. You fellows here still
have enough pluck to talk back.

WITTIG. You don't think by any chance the worst is over
around here? That little bit of starch they still got in their
bones the bosses will take out of them soon enough.

BÄCKER. He's even said it: the weavers'll work for a slice
of bread and a lump of pot cheese before we're through.
(*Uproar.*)

SEVERAL OLD AND YOUNG WEAVERS. Who's said that?

BÄCKER. That's what Dreissiger says about the weavers.

A YOUNG WEAVER. That swine should be hung up by his
rear end.

JÄGER. You just listen to me for a spell, Wittig, you've
always talked a lot about the French Revolution. You've
always jabbered a lot. Maybe there'll be a chance pretty
soon when a guy can show what he's made of: if he's a loud-
mouth or an honest man.

WITTIG (*infuriated*). Just one more word, young fellow!
Did you ever hear bullets whistle? Have you ever been a
sentry in enemy country?

JÄGER. Oh, don't get mad. We're friends after all. I didn't
mean nothing.

WITTIG. The hell with your friendship. You bloated oaf!

(POLICEMAN KUTSCHE *comes in.*)

SEVERAL VOICES. *Psht, Psht,* police!

(*The hissing noise continues for an extraordinarily long
time, until finally complete quiet reigns.*)

KUTSCHE (*who takes his place at the center column while everybody preserves deep silence*). A small corn, please. (*Again complete silence.*)

WITTIG. Well, Kutsche, want to see that everything's all right with us?

KUTSCHE (*without paying any attention to* WITTIG). Hello there, Master Wiegand.

WIEGAND (*still in the corner near the bar*). Good morning, Kutsche.

KUTSCHE. How's business?

WIEGAND. Thanks for asking.

BÄCKER. The superintendent's afraid we'll upset our stomachs from all the money we earn. (*Laughter.*)

JÄGER. That's true, Welzel, ain't it? We've all been eating pork and sauce and sauerkraut and dumplings, and now we're busy drinking our champagne. (*Laughter.*)

WELZEL. Just the other way around would be more like it!

KUTSCHE. And even if you had champagne and roast, you wouldn't be content by a long ways. I haven't got no champagne neither, but I manage all right all the same.

BÄCKER (*alluding to* KUTSCHE's *nose*). He waters his beet-red beak with brandy and beer. That makes it blossom so nicely. (*Laughter.*)

WITTIG. A cop like that's got a hard life: one day he's got to put a starved beggar boy in the coop, then he's got to seduce a pretty weaver girl, then he's got to get stewed to the gills and beat up his wife so she comes running to the neighbors all scared to death; and then to trot around on a horse like that, and to hug the pillow until nine in the morning. It ain't an easy life!

KUTSCHE. Go ahead, jabber! The day'll come soon enough when you'll talk your head off. Everybody knows what kind you are anyway. Even the Commissioner knows your seditious mouth. I know somebody who crawls around in the bars and drinks and drinks till wife and child are in the poorhouse and he himself's in jail, who'll stir up trouble and stir up trouble till at last he gets what's coming to him.

WITTIG (*with a bitter laugh*). Who knows what's going to happen? With that last one you may be right. (*Suddenly furious.*) But if it comes to that I'll know who I got to thank for it . . . who's been gabbing to the bosses and to the Count and who's been backbiting and slinging mud at me so I don't get no work . . . not one little job . . . who's got the farmers up in arms against me and the millers so I don't get no

single horse to shoe all week long and no wheel to fix a
tire for. I know who that is. Once I pulled that miserable
wretch from his horse because he went to work on a small,
silly boy who hooked a couple of green pears with a horse-
whip. And I tell you . . . you know me . . . if you get me into
jail you better make your will. If I just get wind of something like that, I'll take what I can lay my hands on . . .
if it's a horseshoe or a hammer, a wheel spoke or a bucket
. . . and I'll go after you and if I've got to pull you out
of bed away from your wife, I'll pull you out and crack
your skull—so help me. (*He has jumped up and is ready to
jump on* KUTSCHE.)

OLD AND YOUNG WEAVERS (*holding him back*). Wittig,
Wittig, you're going crazy!

KUTSCHE (*has automatically risen; his face is white.
While he speaks the following words he keeps moving toward the door. The closer he gets to the door, the more
courageous he becomes. The last words are spoken from the
door and a moment later he has disappeared.*) What do you
want from me? I've got no business with you! I got to
talk to the weavers here. I didn't do nothing to you. You
don't concern me. But to you weavers I've got something
to say: the police superintendent forbids you singing that
song—the Dreissiger song or whatever you call it. And if
that singing in the street don't stop immediately, he'll see
to it that you get a lot of time and rest in the hoosegow.
There you can sing as long as you like and enjoy your bread
and water. (*He leaves.*)

WITTIG (*shouting after him*). He can't forbid a damn
thing. And if we shout so that the windows rattle, and if
they hear us way over in Reichenbach, and if we sing so
that all their houses tumble down on the bosses' heads and
the helmets dance on the skulls of all the police chiefs, nobody's got nothing to say about that!

BÄCKER (*makes a sign and all start singing*).

> In our town we have a court
> Where lynch law is the order;
> All sentences are of one sort,
> It's not a court, it's murder.

(THE LANDLORD *tries to stop them but nobody hears him.*
WIEGAND *stops his ears with his hands and runs out.*
THE WEAVERS *rise and, while they sing the next lines,*

follow WITTIG *and* BÄCKER, *who have given the signal to leave.*)

> Here men go slowly to their death,
> Here men in torment languish,
> Countless the sighs; their dying breaths
> Bear witness to their anguish.

(*The majority of* THE WEAVERS *are already in the street when they sing the following lines; only a few young men are still in the room paying their bills. At the end of the following line the room is empty except for* WELZEL, HIS WIFE *and* DAUGHTER, HORNIG *and* OLD BAUMERT.)

> Scoundrels you all, you devil's brood,
> You hounds of hell, you cancer,
> You eat the poor man's scanty food,
> And curses are your answer.

WELZEL (*calmly clears the tables*). They're really wild today.

(OLD BAUMERT *is about to leave.*)

HORNIG. Tell me, Baumert, just what's going on?

OLD BAUMERT. They want to go to Dreissiger to see that he adds a little to the wages.

WELZEL. And you go along with crazy stuff like this?

OLD BAUMERT. Look, it's like this, Welzel, I can't help it. Sometimes it's like this: the young fellows *can* go, but an old man's just *got* to go.

HORNIG (*getting up*). I'd be surprised if it didn't turn out bad.

WELZEL. Are the old geezers completely losing their heads?

HORNIG. Well, after all, everybody's got his dream!

CURTAIN

ACT IV

(Peterswaldau.—The living room in the house of DREISSIGER.
*It is luxuriously decorated in the frosty taste of the first
half of the century. The ceiling, the stove, and the doors
are white; the wallpaper is lead-gray and has a regular
pattern of small flowers in straight rows. The furniture
is of mahogany, upholstered in red, richly decorated,
and carved; cupboards and chairs are of the same wood.
The furniture is arranged as follows: on the right, between two windows with cherry-red damask curtains, is
a drop-front secretary. On the opposite wall is the sofa
and, close by, an iron safe. In front of the sofa are a
table, easy chairs, and other chairs. On the back wall is
a cupboard containing guns. All the walls are partly
hidden by bad pictures, in gilt frames. Above the sofa
is a mirror in a heavily gilt rococo frame. A single
door on the left leads to the hall, an open double door
in the back to a sitting-room crammed with the same
cold splendor. Two ladies are seen in the sitting-room,
FRAU DREISSIGER and FRAU KITTELHAUS, the pastor's
wife; they are busy looking at pictures. Also visible,
engaged in conversation, are* PASTOR KITTELHAUS *and
the tutor,* WEINHOLD, *who is a student of theology.)*

KITTELHAUS *(a small, friendly man, and* WEINHOLD *enter
the front room, both smoking and pleasantly chatting. The
pastor looks around and, seeing no one, shakes his head in
surprise.)* It isn't at all surprising, Herr Candidate; you are
young. When we oldsters were your age we had perhaps not
identical, but at least similar ideas. Yes, certainly similar.
And, in a way, it's a wonderful thing—youth—and all these
beautiful ideals. Too bad they are fleeting—fleeting like sunshine in April. Just get to my age! After preaching the Word
to people from the pulpit for thirty years, fifty-two times a
year—not even counting the holidays—one becomes of ne-
cessity a little more sedate. Think of me when you have
reached that point, Herr Candidate.

WEINHOLD *(nineteen years, pale, meager, tall, with sim-*

ple, long, blond hair. He is very restless and nervous in his movements.) With all due deference, Herr Pastor . . . I'm not quite sure . . . There are after all great differences in character.

KITTELHAUS. My dear Herr Candidate, you may well be one of these restless spirits—(*In a tone of reproof*) and indeed you are. You may attack existing conditions ever so violently, without restraint; nevertheless, all that will calm down. Oh yes, I admit it—we have some colleagues who act rather youthful even at a pretty advanced age. One preaches against the horrors of drinking and founds temperance societies, another is the author of proclamations which are really quite gripping to read. But what do they accomplish? They won't relieve the poverty among the weavers, as far as it exists. The social peace, however, is undermined. No, no, one feels almost constrained to say: cobbler, stick to your last! Keeper of souls, don't turn into a keeper of bellies! Preach the pure Word of God, and for the rest, leave those cares to Him who provides shelter and food for the birds and will not suffer the lily in the meadow to perish.—But now I'd really like to know what has suddenly become of our gracious host.

FRAU DREISSIGER (*enters the front room with* FRAU KITTELHAUS. *She is in her thirties, a pretty woman in a hearty, robust sort of way. A certain discrepancy between her manner of talking and moving and her elegant, expensive dress is obvious.*) You're quite right, Herr Pastor. Wilhelm does it all the time. As soon he gets an idea, off he goes and leaves me there sitting. I've talked about it many a time, but it does no good.

KITTELHAUS. My dear Madam, he's a businessman, after all.

WEINHOLD. Unless I'm wrong, something has happened downstairs.

DREISSIGER (*enters, puffing and excited*). Well, Rosa, is the coffee served?

FRAU DREISSIGER (*sulks*). Oh, the way you've always got to run off.

DREISSIGER (*lightly*). Oh, what do you know!

KITTELHAUS. I beg your pardon, was there any trouble, Herr Dreissiger?

DREISSIGER. I've got trouble every day that our Lord gives us, Herr Pastor. I'm used to it. Well, Rosa? I suppose you are attending to it?

(FRAU DREISSIGER *in ill humor, walks over to the wide, embroidered bell-pull which she tugs vehemently several times.*)

DREISSIGER. Just now . . . (*He strides up and down a few times.*) I wish you had been there, Herr Weinhold! You really would have seen something! Incidentally—come let's start our whist.

KITTELHAUS. Yes indeed, indeed—shake off the dust and troubles of the day and be one of us.

DREISSIGER (*has moved to the window, pushes a curtain aside and looks out. Involuntarily.*) Hoodlums!—Come here a minute, Rosa! (*She walks over.*) Tell me . . . that tall redheaded fellow there . . .

KITTELHAUS. That's Red Bäcker, as they call him.

DREISSIGER. Tell me, is that by any chance the same one who insulted you two days ago? You remember what you told me, when Johann was helping you into the carriage.

FRAU DREISSIGER (*pulls the corner of her mouth up, slowly*). I can't remember.

DREISSIGER. Oh, do quit sulking now! Because I must know! I'm fed up with this insolence. If that's the one, I'll get him to answer for it. (*The "Weavers' Song" is heard.*) Now just listen to that, listen to it!

KITTELHAUS (*extremely angry*). Haven't they stopped that wickedness yet? I really must say, it's about time for the police to intervene! Permit me! (*He walks to the window.*) Now look at that, Herr Weinhold! These are not only young people, there are also a lot of old, steady weavers among them. Men whom I have considered for years as honorable and God-fearing; here they are joining in, take part in this incredible wickedness. They walk right over God's law. Do you really intend to defend these people?

WEINHOLD. Certainly not, Herr Pastor. That is, Herr Pastor, *cum grano salis.* They are just hungry, ignorant people. They just give vent to their dissatisfaction the only way they know. I wouldn't even expect people like that . . .

FRAU KITTELHAUS (*small, thin, faded, resembles an old maid more than an aging matron*). Herr Weinhold, Herr Weinhold! Please!

DREISSIGER. Herr Weinhold, I am very sorry . . . but I did not take you into my house so you could lecture me on humanitarianism. I'll have to ask you to restrict yourself to the education of my boys, and leave the rest of my business to me, to me alone! Is that clear?

WEINHOLD (*stands for a moment stiff and deadly pale, then bows with a forced smile. Quietly.*) Certainly, certainly, that's quite clear. I have seen it coming—and it coincides with my desire. (*He leaves.*)

DREISSIGER (*shouts after him, brutally*). Make it as soon as possible; we need the room.

FRAU DREISSIGER. But Wilhelm, Wilhelm! Please!

DREISSIGER. Are you quite clear in the head? You want to protect a man who defends this mob? Who excuses wickedness like this slanderous song?

FRAU DREISSIGER. But dear, he didn't even . . .

DREISSIGER. Herr Pastor, did he or did he not defend it?

KITTELHAUS. Herr Dreissiger, one has to make allowances for his youth.

FRAU KITTELHAUS. I don't know—that young man comes from such a good and respectable family. His father was a civil servant for forty years and nothing, not the least little bit, has ever been said against him. His mother was so terribly pleased when he found such a nice position as this. And now . . . now he doesn't know the least bit how to take advantage of it.

PFEIFER (*pulls open the hall door and shouts into the room*). Herr Dreissiger, Herr Dreissiger! They got him! They want you to come, they caught him!

DREISSIGER (*quickly*). Has somebody called the police?

PFEIFER. The superintendent is already coming up the stairs.

DREISSIGER (*at the door*). Your servant, Herr Superintendent! I'm delighted you could come.

(KITTELHAUS *gestures to the ladies, trying to explain that it would be better for them to retire. He, his wife, and* FRAU DREISSIGER *disappear in the sitting-room.*)

DREISSIGER (*extremely excited, to the* POLICE SUPERINTENDENT *who has meanwhile entered*). Herr Superintendent, at last I have had one of the principal singers arrested by my dye workers. I couldn't stand idly by anymore. This impudence just has no limits. I am outraged! I have company, and this scum makes bold . . . they insult my wife when she goes out; my boys are no longer safe. I risk seeing my guests pushed around. I assure you, if it is possible in a well-run community continually and publicly to abuse blameless people like myself and my family, and to get away with it . . . well, then . . . then I am sorry, but I have different ideas about law and morality.

SUPERINTENDENT (*about fifty, of medium height, fat, a man with high blood pressure. He wears a cavalry uniform with a long saber and spurs.*) Certainly not, certainly not, Herr Dreissiger. I am at your disposal. Just calm yourself, I am at your complete disposal. It's quite all right . . . In fact, I am delighted you had one of the chief troublemakers arrested. I am glad that this thing is finally coming to a head. There are a few troublemakers around here on whom I have had my eye for a long time.

DREISSIGER. A few young brats, that's right, lazy bums who hate to work, a loose crowd that spends its time day after day in the taverns until they've chased the last penny down their gullets. But I'm determined to clip the wings of these evil-mouthed louts—and for good. And, that's in the public interest, not only in my own.

SUPERINTENDENT. Absolutely! Absolutely, Herr Dreissiger. Nobody can blame you for that. And as far as my powers go . . .

DREISSIGER. One should go after this low-down mob with a bullwhip.

SUPERINTENDENT. That's right. Absolutely right. We have to teach them a lesson.

POLICEMAN KUTSCHE (*comes in and stands at attention. Since the hall door is open, heavy steps are heard coming up the stairs.*) Sir, I wish to report: we've arrested one.

DREISSIGER. Do you want to see the man, Superintendent?

SUPERINTENDENT. Certainly, most certainly. We shall take a very close look at him. Do me a favor, Herr Dreissiger, and remain quite calm. I'll get you satisfaction, or my name isn't Heide.

DREISSIGER. I won't be content with that. That man is going to be turned over to the prosecutor without fail.

JÄGER (*is being brought in by five dyers who have come straight from work, their faces, hands and clothing smeared with dye. The prisoner wears his cap askew, shows an impudent gaiety and is, as a result of all the liquor he has consumed, in high spirits.*) Oh, you lousy bastards! Workers you call yourselves? Comrades? Before I'd do a thing like that—before I'd lay hands on a fellow worker I think my hand would wither! (*On a signal from the* SUPERINTENDENT,

KUTSCHE *directs* THE DYERS *to take their hands off their victim.* JÄGER *now stands free and cocky, while all the doors are being guarded.*)

SUPERINTENDENT (*barks at* JÄGER). Cap off, you lout! (JÄGER *takes off the cap, but very slowly and without losing his ironic smile.*) What's your name?

JÄGER. Who's asking? *

(*These words cause a stir among the people in the room.*)

DREISSIGER. Now that's really something!

SUPERINTENDENT (*changes color, about to flare up but masters his rage*). We'll see about that! What's your name, I asked you! (*When he gets no reply, storming.*) Talk, you dog, or you get twenty-five lashes!

JÄGER (*completely serene and without as much as batting an eye at the furious talk, over the heads of the others to a pretty* SERVANT GIRL *who was about to serve coffee and now stands stock-still, her mouth wide open at the sight of the unexpected scene*). Tell me now, Ironing-Board Emily, how did you wind up with this crowd? Better see how you get out of here. Maybe a wind'll blow 'round here one of these days that'll blow the whole kit and caboodle away overnight.

(THE GIRL *looks at* JÄGER, *blushes when she realizes* JÄGER *is talking to her, puts her hands in front of her eyes and runs out, leaving the dishes where they are. There is a commotion among the others.*)

SUPERINTENDENT (*almost losing control of himself, to* DREISSIGER). As old as I am, such incredible impudence I have never . . .

(JÄGER *spits on the floor.*)

DREISSIGER. Man, you aren't in a pig sty here! You understand?

SUPERINTENDENT. My patience is at an end. For the last time, what's your name?

---

* In the original, the Superintendent addresses Jäger with the familiar "Du"; Jäger's reply, in which he uses the same form of address, is the equivalent of "Did we ever lie in a ditch together?"

KITTELHAUS (*has, during this last scene, been looking through the sitting-room door which had been ajar; at the latest turn of events he comes out shaking with excitement, and intervenes*). His name is Jäger, Herr Superintendent. Moritz, isn't it? Moritz Jäger. (*To* JÄGER.) Now just tell me, Jäger, don't you recognize me?

JÄGER (*seriously*). You're Pastor Kittelhaus.

KITTELHAUS. Yes, your shepherd, Jäger! The same one who accepted you into the Community of Saints when you were a small baby. The same one from whose hands you received the Lord's supper for the first time. Do you remember? Here I have been trying, and trying hard, to put the Word of God close to your heart. Is this your gratitude?

JÄGER (*dismally, like a cowed schoolboy*). And I put a taler on the plate.

KITTELHAUS. Money, money . . . Do you believe perhaps that this vulgar, miserable money . . . Keep your money, I'd like that better. What nonsense! Behave yourself like a good Christian! Think of what you promised! Keep God's commandments, be good and be pious!—Money, money . . .

JÄGER. I'm a Quaker, Herr Pastor, I don't believe in nothing no more.

KITTELHAUS. What? Quaker! Don't talk nonsense! Make sure you improve yourself and leave undigested words out of it! They are devout people, not heathens like you. Quaker! Of all things!

SUPERINTENDENT. With your permission, Herr Pastor. (*He steps between him and* JÄGER.) Kutsche! Tie his hands!

(*Wild shouting from outside:* "JÄGER, *out!* JÄGER, *out!*")

DREISSIGER (*somewhat frightened like the others, has automatically stepped close to the window*). What's the meaning of this?

SUPERINTENDENT. Oh, I know what they want. They want to have this scoundrel back. But I don't think we'll oblige. Do you understand, Kutsche? He goes to jail.

KUTSCHE (*rope in hand, hesitates*). Respectfully, Sir, we may have some trouble. There is a damned big crowd down there. A real rabble, Sir. There's Bäcker, there's the blacksmith . . .

KITTELHAUS. Kindly permit me—to avoid making things worse than they are already, wouldn't it perhaps be better,

Herr Superintendent, if we tried to do this peaceably? Perhaps Jäger would promise to come along quietly or something . . .

SUPERINTENDENT. What? It's my responsibility! I couldn't possibly take a chance on that. Go to it, Kutsche! No fuss!

JÄGER (*puts his hands together and holds them out, laughing*). Tighter, tighter, as tight as you can. It won't be for long! (KUTSCHE, *assisted by* THE DYERS, *ties him.*)

SUPERINTENDENT. And now forward, march! (*To* DREISSIGER.) If you are concerned, you can ask six of the dyers to accompany me. They can take him in the middle, I'll ride ahead, and Kutsche follows. If anybody gets in the way, we'll beat him down.

(*Shouting from below:* "Cock-a-doodle-doo! Bow-wow!")

SUPERINTENDENT (*menacingly toward the window*). Rabble! I'll cock-a-doodle-doo and bow-wow you! Forward! March! (*He leads the way out, his saber drawn, the others follow with* JÄGER.)

JÄGER (*shouts on the way out*). And no matter how proud Her Highness Frau Dreissiger thinks she is, she's still no better than us. She's served my father his three pfennigs' worth of booze hundreds of times. Squadron left! March!

(*Laughs out loud and leaves.*)

DREISSIGER (*after a pause, seemingly calm and collected*). What do you think, Herr Pastor? Shall we finally get to our game of whist? It seems all the obstacles have now been overcome. (*While lighting a cigar, he gives several short bursts of laughter; when the cigar is lit he laughs out loud.*) I'm beginning to think this business is really funny. That scum! (*In a nervous burst of laughter.*) It's really incredibly ridiculous. First that fuss with Weinhold at table. Five minutes later he takes his leave. Gone and forgotten. Then this business. And now let's continue our game.

KITTELHAUS. Yes, but . . . (*A roar from below.*) Yes, but . . . You know, that crowd makes an awful lot of noise.

DREISSIGER. Let's simply retire to the other room. We'll be undisturbed there.

KITTELHAUS (*shaking his head*). If I could only figure out what has gotten into these people. I must agree with Weinhold to this extent: at least until recently I also thought the weavers were a humble, patient and easily controlled people. Don't you agree, Herr Dreissiger?

DREISSIGER. Of course they were patient and easily controlled; certainly they used to be orderly, nice people. As long, that is, as those do-gooders didn't get mixed up in it. Now they have been told for a long time in what terrible misery they are living. Just think of it . . . all those societies and committees for the relief of the weaver's suffering. At long last, the weavers themselves believe it, and now they've gone stark mad. Somebody had better get them straightened out again! Now that they've started there's no end to the grumbling. They don't like this and they don't like that. Now they want everything painted pink. Nothing but the best will do.

(Suddenly a surging chorus of "Hurrays" is heard.)

KITTELHAUS. So, with all their humane compassion, all they have achieved is making, literally overnight, howling wolves out of patient lambs.

DREISSIGER. Not at all. If you look at the thing dispassionately, you can even detect some good in it. Events like this will perhaps not remain unnoticed in the leading circles. Perhaps they will be convinced that it can't go on like this much longer, that something will have to be done if our local industry is to be saved from complete ruin.

KITTELHAUS. Well, tell me, what's the cause of this enormous depression?

DREISSIGER. Abroad they have barricaded themselves behind high import duties. We are cut off from the best markets there, and at home the competition is also murderous; we are abandoned by everybody, absolutely everybody.

PFEIFER *(stumbles in, out of breath and pale)*. Herr Dreissiger, Herr Dreissiger!

DREISSIGER *(already at the door to the sitting-room and about to leave, turns around, irritated)*. Well, Pfeifer, what's the matter now?

PFEIFER. No, no . . . leave me alone!

DREISSIGER. What's happened now?

KITTELHAUS. You are frightening us. Why don't you talk?

PFEIFER *(still has not recovered)*. Hey, leave me alone! Oh no! No, not that! The authorities . . . well, they got something coming.

DREISSIGER. For God's sake, what's gotten into you? Has somebody broken his neck?

PFEIFER (*almost crying with fear, blurts out*). They've freed Moritz Jäger, they've beaten up the superintendent and chased him away, they've beaten up the policeman and chased him away. Without his helmet . . . the saber broken . . . oh my God!

DREISSIGER. Pfeifer, you must be crazy.

KITTELHAUS. That would be revolution!

PFEIFER (*sitting on a chair, shaking all over, whimpering*). Herr Dreissiger, it's getting serious! It's getting serious, Herr Dreissiger!

DREISSIGER. Well, that whole police force can go . . .

PFEIFER. Herr Dreissiger, it's getting serious!

DREISSIGER. Oh, shut up, Pfeifer! Damn it all!

FRAU DREISSIGER (*comes from the sitting-room with* THE PASTOR'S WIFE). But this is really too much, Wilhelm. Our whole, nice evening has been spoiled. Now Frau Kittelhaus says she'd rather go home.

KITTELHAUS. My dear Madam, perhaps it would really be best today . . .

FRAU DREISSIGER. But Wilhelm, you really should do something drastic about it!

DREISSIGER. Why don't you go and tell them! Why don't you go! Go on! (*Stopping in front of* THE PASTOR, *blurts out.*) Am I really a tyrant? Am I really a slave driver?

COACHMAN JOHANN (*comes in*). Ma'am, I've got the carriage ready. Herr Weinhold has already put Jorgel and Karlchen in. If it gets too bad, we're ready to go.

FRAU DREISSIGER. Why, if what gets too bad?

JOHANN. Well, I don't know for sure . . . I just thought . . . It's just that the crowd's getting bigger and bigger. And they've chased away the policeman and the superintendent.

PFEIFER. It's getting serious, Herr Dreissiger, it's getting serious!

FRAU DREISSIGER (*with mounting fear*). Well, what's going to happen? What do the people want? They can't attack us, can they, Johann?

JOHANN. Ma'am, there are some bad eggs among them.

PFEIFER. It's getting serious, terribly serious!

DREISSIGER. Shut up, you ass! Are the doors barricaded?

KITTELHAUS. Do me a favor . . . do me a favor . . . I've

come to a decision . . . do me the favor . . . (*To* JOHANN.)
What do these people want?

JOHANN (*embarrassed*). More wages is what they want, the
stupid bastards.

KITTELHAUS. Good, fine.—I'll go out and do my duty. I'll
talk to them seriously.

JOHANN. Herr Pastor, Herr Pastor! Better let it be. There's
no use talking.

KITTELHAUS. My dear Herr Dreissiger, one more word. I
want to ask you to put some men behind the door and have
them lock it behind me.

FRAU KITTELHAUS. You really want to do that, Joseph?

KITTELHAUS. Yes, I do. Of course, I do. I know what I am
doing. Don't worry, the Lord will protect me.

(FRAU KITTELHAUS *presses his hand, steps back and wipes
tears from her eyes.*)

KITTELHAUS (*amid the incessant, dull rumbling of the
large crowd below*). I'll pretend . . . I'll pretend I am quietly
going home. I want to see if my spiritual office . . . if there
is not enough respect left in these people . . . I do want to
see . . . (*He takes his hat and cane.*) Forward then, in the
name of God.

(*He leaves.* DREISSIGER, PFEIFER *and* JOHANN *follow him.*)

FRAU KITTELHAUS. Dear Frau Dreissiger—(*She breaks out
in tears and throws her arms around* FRAU DREISSIGER's *neck.*)
If only nothing happens to him!

FRAU DREISSIGER (*bemused*). I really don't know, Frau
Kittelhaus, I've a feeling . . . I really don't know how I feel.
Things like this just don't happen. If that's the way it is . . .
it's almost like wealth was a crime. You see, if somebody
had told me that, I don't know, Frau Kittelhaus, maybe in
the end I'd rather have stuck with the little I had.

FRAU KITTELHAUS. Dear Frau Dreissiger, there are troubles in store and disappointments no matter how you live.

FRAU DREISSIGER. Sure, sure, that's what I tell myself, too.
And if we've got more'n some others . . . by Jesus, we didn't
steal it. Every penny's been earned honestly. It just can't
be possible that people just come and attack you. Is it my
husband's fault that business is bad?

(*Tumultuous shouting is heard from below. While the two
   women are still looking at each other, pale and frightened,* DREISSIGER *rushes into the room.*)

DREISSIGER. Rosa, put something on and hop into the carriage; I'll be with you in a minute. (*He hurries to the safe,
opens it and takes out some valuables.*)

JOHANN (*enters*). Everything ready! But hurry up now
before they're at the back gate, too.

FRAU DREISSIGER (*in a panic, throws her arms around the
neck of* THE COACHMAN). Johann, dearest Johann, save us!
Save us, best, best Johann! Save my boys, oh, oh . . .

DREISSIGER. Be reasonable now, let go of Johann!

JOHANN. Ma'am! But Ma'am! Don't worry! Our horses are
in good shape. Nobody'll catch up with 'em. If somebody
don't make room, he'll get run over.   (*He leaves.*)

FRAU KITTELHAUS (*in helpless fear*). But my husband?
What about my husband? Herr Dreissiger, my husband!

DREISSIGER. Frau Pastor, he is all right, Frau Pastor. Don't
worry, he's all right.

FRAU KITTELHAUS. Something terrible has happened to
him! You just don't want to tell me. You won't tell me.

DREISSIGER. Oh, never mind. They'll be sorry. I know exactly who it was. Such nameless, shameless impudence has
to be punished. A parish that manhandles their shepherd . . .
to the devil with them! Mad dogs, that's what they are, wild
animals who'll be treated accordingly. (*To* FRAU DREIS-
SIGER, *who stands as if in a trance.*) Now get going—move.
(*Banging is heard at the front door.*) Don't you hear? That
rabble's gone raving mad. (*The smashing of windows is
heard from downstairs.*) They've completely lost their minds!
There's nothing else to do. We got to hurry and get out of
here.

(*A chorus of shouts:* "PFEIFER, *come out!* PFEIFER, *come
   out!*")

FRAU DREISSIGER. Pfeifer! Pfeifer! They want Pfeifer!

PFEIFER (*rushes in*). Herr Dreissiger, there are some at
the back gate, too. The front door won't last another minute.
Wittig the smith is banging a bucket against it like a
madman.

(*The shouting from below becomes louder and clearer:*

"PFEIFER, *come out*, PFEIFER *come out!*")

(FRAU DREISSIGER *races out of the room as if pursued,
    followed by* FRAU KITTELHAUS.)

PFEIFER (*listens; his face changes color; he understands
the meaning of the shouts and is now gripped by maddening
terror. He speaks the following at a frantic speed, crying,
whimpering, begging, and whining in rapid succession. At
the same time he floods* DREISSIGER *with childish endear-
ments, pats his cheeks and arms, kisses his hands and finally
clings to him like a man drowning, encumbering and fetter-
ing him without letting him go.*) Oh, my dearest, finest,
most gracious Herr Dreissiger, please don't leave me behind!
I've always served you faithfully; and I've always treated
them folks right. I couldn't give them more wages than the
scale. Please, don't leave me! They'll kill me! If they find me
they'll batter me to death. Oh God, Oh God! My wife, my
children . . .

DREISSIGER (*trying in vain to disentangle himself from*
PFEIFER's *clutches, as he leaves the room*). At least, let go
of me, man! We'll see! We'll see how things'll work out.

(*Leaves with* PFEIFER.)

(*For several seconds the room is empty. In the sitting-
room window glass is shattered. A loud crash reverberates
through the house, a roar of "hurray" is heard, then there is
complete silence. After several seconds quiet and cautious
footsteps are heard on the stairs to the second floor, accompanied by quiet and shy exclamations. To the left!—Upstairs!—Sht!—Slowly, easy now!—Don't slip now!—Damn,
what have I got here!—Hurry up!—We're going to a wedding!
—You go in!—You go!*)

(YOUNG WEAVERS, BOYS *and* GIRLS, *appear in the hall door;
    they don't dare to enter, and everyone tries to push the
    other into the room. After a few seconds their shyness
    is gone, and the poor-looking, thin and often sickly
    figures in ragged or mended clothing spread out in*
    DREISSIGER's *room and the sitting-room. At first they
    are curious and only look shyly at everything; then they
    begin to touch everything. Some girls try out the sofa;
    some form groups and admire themselves in the mirror.*

Some climb on chairs to get a closer look at the pictures and to take them down; there is a constant stream of miserable-looking figures from the hall into the room.)

AN OLD WEAVER (*enters*). No, no, leave me out of things like that. They've even started tearing things apart down there. That's crazy! There's no rhyme or reason for that. In the end it'll go bad. If you keep a clear head you'll keep out of this. I'll be careful. I won't have no part in sinful doings like this.

(JÄGER, BÄCKER, WITTIG *with a wooden bucket,* OLD BAUMERT *and a number of young and old* WEAVERS *rush in as if on a chase, shouting in hoarse voices, all at the same time.)*

JÄGER. Where did he go?

BÄCKER. Where is the slave driver?

OLD BAUMERT. If we're to eat grass he'll eat sawdust.

WITTIG. If we find him we'll string him up.

FIRST YOUNG WEAVER. We'll take him by a leg and throw him out the window, down on the stones, so he'll stay for good.

SECOND YOUNG WEAVER (*enters*). He's gone!

EVERYBODY. Who's gone?

SECOND YOUNG WEAVER. Dreissiger.

BÄCKER. Pfeifer too?

VOICES. Look for Pfeifer, look for Pfeifer!

OLD BAUMERT. Here, little Pfeifer, here! There's a weaver here you can starve! (*Laughter.*)

JÄGER. If we can't get at him, that beast of a Dreissiger . . . he'll be poor at least.

OLD BAUMERT. He's got to be as poor as a church mouse. We'll make him poor. (*Everybody rushes to the sitting-room door, with the intention of demolishing everything they find.)*

BÄCKER (*runs ahead, then turns and stops the others*). Stop! Listen to me! When we've finished here we'll really get going. From here we'll go down to Bielau to look after Dietrich—he's got the mechanical looms. All the trouble comes from the factories.

ANSORGE (*comes in from the hall. After taking a few steps, he stops, looks incredulously around, shakes his head, hits his forehead with the palm of his hand and says.*) Who am

I? Anton Ansorge, the weaver. Has he gone mad, that Ansorge? Must be; things are turning around like a spinning wheel. What's he doing here? He'll do what he feels like. Where is he, Ansorge? (*He hits his forehead several times.*) I've gone crazy. I ain't responsible for nothing. I ain't right in the head. Go away, go away! Go away, you rebels! Head gone, legs gone, arms gone! If you take my shack, I'll take your shack. Let's go to it! (*With a howl he goes into the sitting-room. The others follow him laughing and shouting.*)

CURTAIN

ACT V

(*Langenbielau.—OLD HILSE's small weaving room. At the left is a small window, in front of it a loom. At the right a bed, pushed close to it a table. In the corner to the right is the stove with a bench. Sitting around the table on a foot stool, on the corner of the bed, and on a wooden stool are OLD HILSE, his old, blind and almost deaf WIFE, his son, GOTTLIEB, and the latter's wife, LUISE. They are saying their morning prayers. A spooling wheel with a bobbin stands between the table and the loom. All sorts of old spinning, spooling, and weaving equipment is stored on top of the smoke-darkened ceiling joists. Long strands of yarn hang down. All kinds of trash lies around. The very narrow, low, and shallow room has a door in the rear wall; it is open and leads to the hall. On the opposite side of the hall, another door, also open, leads into a second small weaver's room, much like the first one. The hall has a stone floor, the plaster is cracked; a rickety wooden stair leads up to an apartment in the attic. A laundry tub standing on a stool is partly visible; ragged-looking pieces of clothing and cheap household utensils lie around in a jumble. All the rooms receive their light from the left.*)

OLD HILSE (*a bearded, heavy-boned man, now worn and bent by age, work, sickness, and fatigue. He is a war veteran and has only one arm. He has a pointed nose, his face is pale and his hands tremble; he appears to consist just of skin, bones, and sinews and has the deep-set, sore-looking eyes typical of the weavers.—He, his* Son *and* Daughter-in-Law *rise and he prays.*) Dear God, we can't hardly thank you enough that in your graciousness and goodness you've had pity on us this night, too. That we haven't suffered no grief this night, Lord, that's how far your mercy goes, and we're poor, beastly, sinning children of Man, not worth that your foot stamps us out, that's how sinful and all bad we are. But you, dear Father, you want to look at us and accept us because of your Son, our Lord and Savior, Jesus Christus. Jesus' blood and righteousness, that's my ornament and my dress of honor. And if we become timid under your blows now and then, when the oven that's to purify us burns a little too terribly hot, don't hold it against us too much, forgive us our trespasses. Give us patience, heavenly Father, so after this suffering we can partake of your eternal bliss. Amen.

Mother Hilse (*has been straining, bent forward, to hear, weeping*). Oh dear, oh dear! Father, you do such beautiful praying every time.

(Luise *walks to the washtub;* Gottlieb *goes into the room across the hall.*)

Old Hilse. Where's the girl?

Luise. Gone over to Peterswaldau—to Dreissiger's. She's spooled a few bobbins again last night.

Old Hilse (*speaking very loud*). Well, Mother, now I'll bring you your little wheel.

Mother Hilse. Yes, sure, go ahead and bring it.

Old Hilse (*putting the spooling wheel in front of her*). Look here, I'd be glad to do it for you.

Mother Hilse. No . . . no . . . what'd I do with all that time?

Old Hilse. I'll wipe your fingers a little so the yarn won't get greasy, all right? (*He wipes her hands with a rag.*)

Luise (*by the washtub*). When did we have something greasy to eat?

Old Hilse. If there's no fat, we'll eat dry bread—if there ain't no bread, we'll eat potatoes—if there ain't no potatoes neither, we'll eat dry mash.

Luise (*sneering*). And if there's no black flour we'll do

like the Wengler woman down below: we'll go see where the
flayer has buried a dead horse, and we'll dig it up, and
then we've got carrion to live on for a few weeks. That's
what we'll do, huh?

GOTTLIEB (*from the back room*). What in hell are you
jabbering about?

OLD HILSE. Watch that godless talk! (*He walks over to
the loom.*) You could help me for a bit, Gottlieb—got to
thread a few strings.

LUISE (*from the washtub, calls*). Gottlieb, you should
help your father. (GOTTLIEB *comes. The old man and his son
start the slow job of putting up the threads, which consists
of pulling the threads of the warp through the eyes of the
combs, or shafts, of the loom. They have hardly begun when
HORNIG appears in the hall.*)

HORNIG (*in the door*). Good luck with your work!

OLD HILSE AND HIS SON. Thank you a lot, Hornig!

OLD HILSE. Tell me something, when do you sleep anyway? By day you go trading and by night you stand guard.

HORNIG. I just don't get no sleep no more—none at all!

LUISE. Welcome, Hornig!

OLD HILSE. Bringing good news?

HORNIG. Fine news there is, Master. Over in Peterswaldau
they've risked the devil and have chased Dreissiger and all
his folks out of the place.

LUISE (*with signs of emotion*). Hornig's lying again in
broad daylight!

HORNIG. This time he ain't, young woman! This time he
ain't!—Got some nice aprons for the kids in the cart.—No,
no, it's the truth. They've chased them out. Last night he
got to Reichenbach and, do you know, they didn't even
want to keep 'em there—for fear of the weavers. So he's
gone packing to Schweidnitz.

OLD HILSE (*holds the threads of the warp carefully near
the shaft, while his son uses a wire hook to pull them
through one of the eyes from the other side*). Now, that's
enough, Hornig, time to hold up.

HORNIG. May I never move from this spot with my bones
in one piece! Why, most every child knows it.

OLD HILSE. Tell me now, am I crazy or are you crazy?

HORNIG. Now then—what I told you is as true as the
Amen in church. I wouldn't tell you if I hadn't stood right
close by and seen it all. With my own eyes, just as I see you,
Gottlieb. They've torn up the manufacturer's house, from

the cellar to the ridge beam. From the attic windows—out it went, all the china, down the roof. And how many bolts of fustian d'you think are in the brook? The water can't get through, that's how many; it's been running over the sides. And real sulfur-blue it looked from all that indigo they've thrown out of the windows. Them sky-blue clouds of dust just kept powdering down. No, no, they've really torn the place up. Not only in his house . . . in the dye rooms, in the warehouse! The banister knocked to pieces, the floor boards ripped up, the mirrors bashed in, sofa, chairs, everything torn and ripped and cut and mashed and kicked and axed— damn it, believe me, it's worse than a war!

OLD HILSE. And that was weavers from 'round here? (*He shakes his head slowly and incredulously. Curious neighbors have come to the door, listening.*)

HORNIG. Who else? Don't I know them all by name? I took the commissioner through the house. So I talked with a lot of them. They was as nice as always. They just attended to their business, slowly—but they made a good job of it. The commissioner talked with them, too. And they was as humble as always. But let up they didn't. The finest furniture got axed, as if they was getting paid for the job.

OLD HILSE. You took the commissioner through the house?

HORNIG. Sure! What would I be afraid of? Them people know me like they know a wooden groschen. I don't have no trouble with nobody. I'm good friends with everybody. As sure's my name's Hornig I been through the house. And you can just believe me, I got all soft around here—and the commissioner he shown it too—it touched him real close. And why? You didn't hear one single word, so quiet did they do it. It made you feel quite solemn to see them poor hungry bastards finally take their revenge.

LUISE (*beginning to tremble with excitement, at the same time wiping her eyes with her apron*). That's the way, that's what's got to happen!

VOICES OF THE NEIGHBORS. There's enough slave drivers 'round here, too.—Right across the street there's one. —That one's got four horses and six carriages in the stables and his weavers go hungry to pay for it.

OLD HILSE (*still incredulous*). And how did it start over there?

HORNIG. Who knows? Who knows? One says one thing, another something else.

OLD HILSE. What do they say?

HORNIG. Well, they say Dreissiger said: the weavers can eat grass if they're real hungry. That's all I know.

(Commotion among those in the room and among the neighbors who angrily pass the news on to each other.)

OLD HILSE. Listen now, Hornig. You could tell me for instance: Father Hilse, you're going to die tomorrow. That may well be, I'd say, why not?—Or you could tell me: Father Hilse, the King of Prussia is going to stop by to see you tomorrow. I'd say: All right. But that weavers, men like myself and my son, should have done things like that—never! I won't believe it, never and never.

MIELCHEN *(a pretty girl of seven with long, flaxen hair, skips into the room carrying a little basket. She holds a silver soup spoon up to her mother.)* Mummy! Look what I got! You can buy me a dress with it!

LUISE. Who's chasing you, girl? *(With increasing excitement and tension.)* Now what did you pick up this time, tell me? You're quite out of breath, too. And the bobbins are still in your basket. What's this all about?

OLD HILSE. Girl, where did you get that spoon?

LUISE. She's found it maybe.

HORNIG. That's worth at least two or three talers.

OLD HILSE *(beside himself)*. Get out, girl, get out! Get out immediately! Are you going, or do I have to get a stick? And that spoon you're taking back where you got it! Out! You want to make thieves out of all of us, eh? Brat, I'll learn you to steal! *(He looks for something to beat her with.)*

MIELCHEN *(hanging on to her mother's skirts, cries)*. But Grandpa, don't hit me, we just f-f-found them! All the b-b-bobbin girls got some.

LUISE *(in eager expectation, yet anxiously, blurts out)*. There you see, she just found it. Where did you find it?

MIELCHEN *(sobbing)*. In Peterswaldau—we found them—in front of—of Dreissiger's house.

OLD HILSE. There you see! That's a fine how-d'you-do. You hurry up now or I'll help you move!

MOTHER HILSE. What's going on?

HORNIG. I'll tell you, Father Hilse. Tell Gottlieb to put his coat on and take that spoon over to the police.

OLD HILSE. Gottlieb, put your coat on!

GOTTLIEB *(already getting up, eagerly)*. So I'll go over to the stationhouse, and I'll say: Don't hold it against her, a child that age don't understand what she's doing so I'm bringing the spoon back.—Stop crying, girl!

(*Her* MOTHER *takes the crying girl into the back room and closes the door. Then she returns.*)

HORNIG. That spoon's worth three talers at least.

GOTTLIEB. Give me a cloth, Luise, so it won't get scratched. What a beautiful expensive thing, that! (*He wraps the spoon, tears in his eyes.*)

LUISE. If we kept it we'd have food for weeks.

OLD HILSE. Hurry up, get moving! Hurry as fast as you can. That'd be something! That's all I need! Hurry up and get that devil's spoon out of my house.

(GOTTLIEB *leaves with the spoon.*)

HORNIG. Well, I'd better be on my way, too.

(*He leaves the room, stops to talk for a few seconds with the people in the hall, then disappears.*)

SURGEON SCHMIDT (*a round, quick-silvery little man with a wine-red, shrewd face, enters the hall*). Morning, folks! Fine story that is. Nice people you are! (*He wags his finger threateningly.*) Pretty sly, that's what you are. (*Standing in the doorway to the front room without entering.*) Good morning, Father Hilse! (*To a woman in the hall.*) Well, Mother, how's the rheumatism? Better, eh? There you see! Father Hilse, I thought I'd come take a look how things are going with you. What the devil's the matter with mother?

LUISE. Oh, Herr Doctor, the veins in her eyes are dried up, she can't see nothing no more.

SURGEON SCHMIDT. That's the dust and working by candle-light does it.—Tell me, can you figure it out? The whole town is on the way over here from Peterswaldau. This morning I get into my carriage, thinking of nothing in particular, nothing at all. And then I hear the strangest things. What the devil's got into these people, Hilse? They rage like hungry wolves. Start a revolution, a rebellion; get mean and pillage and plunder . . . Mielchen! Where's Mielchen? (MIELCHEN, *her face still red from crying, comes in, pushed forward by her mother.*) There, Mielchen, put your hand in my coat pocket. (MIELCHEN *does so.*) The ginger snaps are for you. Hey, not all of them at one time! And first a song! "Fox, you've" . . . well? "Fox you've stolen . . . our . . . goose . . ." You wait and I'll tell everybody what you did: you called the sparrows sitting on the pastor's fence "hedge shitters." And they told the deacon about it. Now isn't that incredible? About fifteen hundred people are moving along there. (*Bells ring in the distance.*) Listen, in Reichenbach they're ringing the storm bells. Fifteen hundred people. The world's coming to an end. It's down-right scary!

OLD HILSE. So they're really on the way over here to Bielau?

SURGEON SCHMIDT. Sure, sure, I drove through, right through the middle of that mob. Best thing to do would have been give every one of them a powder. There they walked along, one after the other, gray like misery itself, and giving out with that singing almost turns a somersault; it almost strangles you. My Friedrich on his driver's seat was weeping like an old woman. We had to go buy us a stiff drink as soon as we'd passed them. I wouldn't like to be a manufacturer right now, even if my wheels were rolling on rubber tires. (*Distant singing.*) Listen to that! As if somebody was drumming with his knuckles on a cracked old kettle. Children, it won't be five minutes till they're here. Good-by, folks! Don't do nothing foolish. The soldiers are following right after. Don't lose your heads now! That crowd from Peterswaldau have lost theirs. (*Bells ring close by.*) Heavens, now our bells are starting, too, that'll drive the people completely out of their wits. (*Walks upstairs.*)

GOTTLIEB (*returns. Still in the hall, out of breath*). I've seen them, I've seen them. (*To a woman in the hall.*) They're here, Auntie, they're here! (*In the doorway.*) They're here, Father, they're here! They got beanpoles and pokers and axes. They're already at Dietrich's house up on the hill making a terrible racket. They're getting some money from him too, I think. Oh Jesus, what's going to happen 'round here? I won't look at it. So many people! What a crowd! If they go and take a running start—oh my God, my God, the bosses are going to get it!

OLD HILSE. What did you run like that for? You're going to carry on so you'll get your old trouble again and be flat on your back flailing your arms.

GOTTLIEB (*with almost joyous excitement*). I sure had to run—they were going to hold me. They were all shouting. I should hold out my hand, too. Godfather Baumert was there, too. He says to me: go to it, get your five groschen, you're one of them poor starvelings, too. He even says: go tell your father! Tell him to come and give us a hand paying the bosses back for all our starving. (*With passion.*) Times are changing, he says; things are going to be different for us weavers. We should all come and help make it happen. We're all going to have our half-pound of meat on Sundays and on the Holy Days a blood sausage and sauerkraut, he says. Things are really going to look different, he says.

OLD HILSE (*with suppressed anger*). And that calls himself your godfather? And asks you to take a hand in such godless labors? Don't you have nothing to do with them things, Gottlieb! The devil's got his hand in this. It's Satan's work they're doing.

LUISE (*overcome by a passionate excitement, sharply*). Yes, Gottlieb, go over in the corner behind the stove, take a soup spoon and put a bowl of buttermilk on your lap; put on a little dress and start saying your prayers—that's the way your father likes it!—And that calls himself a man?

(*Laughter among the people in the hall.*)

OLD HILSE (*shaking with suppressed fury*). And you call yourself a good wife, eh? I'll tell you something, for once and proper. You call yourself a mother with that evil tongue of yours? You want to teach your girl what's right and egg your husband on to crime and outrage?

LUISE (*loses all self-control*). You and all your fancy talk . . . there's never been enough even for a child to eat his fill. All four of them . . . there they were in muck and rags. Not a single dry diaper, never. I call myself a mother, all right, I'll tell you! And that's just why I wish all them bosses to hell and the devil himself in their gaping jaws! Yes, because I am a mother.—Can I ever keep such a little thing alive? I've cried more than I've breathed from the minute one of them little things came into the world till death felt sorry for them and took them. You—you didn't give a hoot! You were praying and singing while I walked till my feet got bloody just to get one little bowl of buttermilk. How many hundred nights did I spend racking my brains how I could cheat the graveyard one single time and keep the child. What crime did they commit, eh? And to come to such a miserable end! And over there, at the Dietrichs', they bathe them in wine and wash them in milk.

Oh no, if it starts here, ten horses won't hold me back! And I can tell you, if they storm Dietrich's house I'm going to be the first one, and God have mercy on anybody trying to stop me. I'm fed up—and that's a fact.

OLD HILSE. You're lost. Nobody can help you.

LUISE (*in a frenzy*). Nobody can help you! Weaklings, that's what you are. Rubber-kneed cowards you are, not men. Mealy-mouthed rabbits . . . I could spit at you! Milksops who get scared when they hear a baby's rattle. Idiots who say thank you half a dozen times when they get a kick in the pants. There ain't enough blood in your veins even to blush. A whipping is what you need . . . to beat some spirit into your lazy bones.   (*She leaves quickly.*)

MOTHER HILSE. What's the matter with Luise, Father?

OLD HILSE. Oh, nothing, Mother. What should be the matter with her?

MOTHER HILSE. Tell me, Father, am I just hearing things, or is that the bells ringing?

OLD HILSE. Must be a funeral, Mother.

MOTHER HILSE. And still no end for me. Why don't I die, Father? (*Pause.*)

OLD HILSE (*drops his work, straightens up, solemnly*). Gottlieb, your wife has told us quite a lot. Gottlieb, look at me! (*He opens his shirt.*) Here I had one of them things as big as a thimble. And the King knows where I lost my arm. It wasn't mice that nibbled it off. (*He walks back and forth.*) Your wife—nobody even thought of her when I was already spurting my blood around for my country by the quart. That's why I let her jabber as much as she wants. It's all right by me. I don't care one bit. Afraid? Me, afraid? Who should I be afraid of, I'd like to know. Of that handful of soldiers who are after the rebels maybe? Huh, if that was all! No, no, maybe I'm a little weak in the back, but if it's got to be, I have bones like ivory. I'd gladly take on a couple of puny bayonets.—And—if it really went bad? I'd gladly turn in. They wouldn't have to ask me twice to die. Better today than tomorrow. No, no. Let it come! After all, what do you leave behind? About losing that old torture box I wouldn't shed a tear. That little heap of fear and slaving we call life —I'd be happy to let it go.—But then, Gottlieb, then comes something else—and if you gamble that away, then you're really lost.

GOTTLIEB. Who knows what comes after we're dead? Nobody's seen it.

OLD HILSE. I'm telling you, Gottlieb, don't doubt the one thing we poor people have got. Why should I have sat here treading the loom, busier'n a bee for forty years and more? And why would I have quietly watched how them people across the street live . . . in pride and luxury coining gold from my hunger and my worries? Why? Because I have hope. I've got something—despite all this poverty. (*Pointing out of the window.*) You got your share here, I got mine over in the other world: that's what I've been thinking. And you can draw and quarter me—I'm that certain. We've been promised. There'll be a judgment; but not we will be the judges; no, "Vengeance is mine, speaks the Lord, our God."

A VOICE (*through the window*). Come out, weavers!

OLD HILSE. As far as I'm concerned you can do what you like! (*He climbs into the loom.*) Me—you'll have to leave here.

GOTTLIEB (*after a short fight with himself*). I'll go and work. Let come what may. (*Leaves. The "Weavers' Song" is heard nearby, sung by hundreds of voices; it sounds like a dull, monotonous lamentation.*)

VOICES OF THE NEIGHBORS (*in the hall*). Look! Heavens! Now they're coming like ants.—Where do all them weavers come from?—Make room, I want to see, too.—Just look at that beanstalk fellow walking out front.—Jesus, now they're coming thick all right.

HORNIG (*steps among the people in the hallway*). Why, that's some show, ain't it? Something like that you don't see every day. Come on up to Dietrich's up on the hill! They've got another show going on up there that's real nice. He don't have no house no more, no factory no more, no wine cellar no more, no nothing no more. The bottles they drink . . . don't even take time to pull out the corks. One, two, three, off with the necks, whether they cut their mouths on the glass or not. Some are running around bleeding like stuck pigs.—Now they're going to take care of the Dietrich down here.

(*The crowd has stopped singing.*)

VOICES OF THE NEIGHBORS. They don't look all that mean.

HORNIG. Never mind! Just you wait! They're just taking a good look at this here opportunity. Just look how they're getting a bead on that palace from every angle. Look at that little, heavy-set fellow—he's got a horse pail along. That's the blacksmith from Peterswaldau, fearsome little man he is. He cracks the thickest doors like pretzels, believe you me. If he gets one of the bosses between his hands, he'll finish him right off!

VOICES OF NEIGHBORS. Bang—there goes one!—That stone went right through the window!—Now old Dietrich's getting scared.—He's hanging a sign out.—A sign? What's it say?—Can't you read?—The hell I can't read!—Well, read then!—"You will all get satisfaction," "You will all get satisfaction."

HORNIG. He might as well have skipped that one. That won't help much. Them fellows have their own ideas. They're after the factory. Them mechanical looms are what they want to get rid of. That's what's ruining the hand-weavers . . . even a blind man can see that. No, no, the Christians are really on the march today. No manager and no councillor's going to make them see reason—and a sign least of all. If you'd seen them on the job you'd know what's up.

VOICES OF NEIGHBORS. Lord, what a crowd.—What are they up to?—(Quickly.) Are they coming across the bridge?—(Apprehensively.) Are they coming over this way? (In great surprise and fear.) They're coming here, they're coming for us.—They're getting the weavers out of their houses.

(They all flee and the hallway is empty. A group of rebels, dirty, dusty, their faces flushed with liquor and exertion, wild, weary, their clothes torn, pushes into the hallway with the shout: "Come out, weavers!!" They spread out into the different rooms. BÄCKER and a few YOUNG WEAVERS, armed with clubs and sticks, enter OLD HILSE's room. When they recognize OLD HILSE they stop short, slightly cooled off.)

BÄCKER. Father Hilse, stop slaving! Whoever feels like it can sit there and polish your bench with his butt. You won't have to kill yourself working no more. We'll take care of that.

FIRST YOUNG WEAVER. You won't have to go to bed hungry. —not one more day!

SECOND YOUNG WEAVER. The weavers'll have a roof over their heads and a shirt on their backs again.

OLD HILSE. What the devil are you doing here with sticks and axes?

BÄCKER. We'll break them on Dietrich's back.

SECOND YOUNG WEAVER. We'll heat them red and stuff 'em down the bosses' gullets so for once they'll get an idea how hunger burns.

THIRD YOUNG WEAVER. Come along, Father Hilse! We don't give no quarter.

SECOND YOUNG WEAVER. Nobody took pity on us. Neither God nor man. Now we'll take what's coming to us.

OLD BAUMERT (*enters, a little shaky on his feet, carrying a freshly-killed rooster under his arm. He opens both arms wide.*) Brother of mine—we're all brothers! Come into my arms, my brothers! (*Laughter.*)

OLD HILSE. So that's what you look like now, Willy?

OLD BAUMERT. That you, Gustav? Gustav, you poor starved creature, come into my arms. (*Deeply moved.*)

OLD HILSE (*growls*). Leave me alone.

OLD BAUMERT. Gustav, that's how it is. You've got to be lucky. Gustav, take a look at me. What do I look like? You've got to be lucky! Don't I look like a count? (*Tapping his paunch.*) Guess what's in this belly. A nobleman's meal is in this belly. You've got to be lucky. Then you get champagne and roast hare.—I'll tell you something: we've all been making a mistake . . . help ourselves, that's what we've got to do!

EVERYBODY (*in confusion*). Help ourselves, hurray!

OLD BAUMERT. Once you've had that first bite of good food, right away you start feeling it work in you. Jesus Christ, you feel powerful . . . strong like a bull. And the strength . . . why, it flows through your limbs and out again so you don't even see where you're hitting. God damn it, that feels good!

JÄGER (*in the door, armed with an old cavalry saber*). We've made some pretty nice attacks.

BÄCKER. We've learned our business pretty well by now. One, two, three and we're inside the house and right away we're at it like wild fire so everything just crackles and trembles and the sparks fly like in a smithy.

FIRST YOUNG WEAVER. We really ought to have a nice, little fire for once.

SECOND YOUNG WEAVER. We're going to Reichenbach and burn the roofs right over them rich peoples' heads.

JÄGER. That's just what they'd like. So they get all that insurance money! (*Laughter.*)

BÄCKER. From here we'll go to Freiburg and visit Tromtra.

JÄGER. We ought to go after the bureaucrats for a change.

I've read it . . . all the misery comes from the bureaucrats.

SECOND YOUNG WEAVER. Soon we'll go on to Breslau. More and more people are joining up.

OLD BAUMERT (*to* HILSE). Well, take a swig, Gustav!

OLD HILSE. No, I never touch liquor.

OLD BAUMERT. That was in the old world; today we're in a different world, Gustav!

FIRST YOUNG WEAVER. Ain't every day we're at a fair. (*Laughter.*)

OLD HILSE (*impatiently*). You hell-hounds, what do you want in my house?

OLD BAUMERT (*somewhat taken aback, excessively friendly*). Now look here, I just wanted to bring you this here little rooster. You could cook Mother a nice soup!

OLD HILSE (*perplexed, almost friendly*). Oh, go on, tell Mother about it.

MOTHER HILSE (*having strained to listen, her hand on her ear, now waves him off*). Leave me alone, I don't like chicken soup.

OLD HILSE. You're right, Mother. Me neither. That kind least of all. And I'll tell you something, Baumert! When old people babble like babies, the devil turns handsprings with joy. And just remember, all of you remember this: I and you, we got nothing in common. I didn't ask you here. Under the law and with justice you got no business here.

A VOICE. Who's not with us is against us.

JÄGER (*brutally threatening*). You got things all wrong. Listen here, Old Timer, we're no thieves.

A VOICE. We're hungry, that's all.

FIRST YOUNG WEAVER. We want to live, that's all. That's why we cut the rope we were hanging on.

JÄGER. And that was right! (*Shaking his fist in front of the old man's face.*) Just one more word! And this'll explode —right on target.

BÄCKER. Quiet, quiet everybody! Leave the old man alone. Father Hilse, this is the way we think: rather dead than start the old life all over again.

OLD HILSE. Haven't I lived that life for over sixty years?

BÄCKER. That don't matter. It's got to change.

OLD HILSE. Sure, on Never-never Day.

BÄCKER. What we can't get in peace we'll take by force.

OLD HILSE. By force? (*Laughs.*) Well, then just get ready for your funeral. They'll show you who's got the force. Hmph—just wait, young fellow!

Jäger. You mean because of the soldiers? We've been soldiers, too. With a couple of companies we can cope any day.

Old Hilse. With your mouth, I can believe that. And even if you do, you chase away two, and ten come back.

Voices (*through the window*). Soldiers are coming! Look out! (*Suddenly everybody is silent. For a moment a faint sound of fifes and drums is heard. Into the silence a short, involuntary shout.*) God damn it! I'm taking off! (*General laughter.*)

Bäcker. Who's talking about taking off? Who was that?

Jäger. Who's afraid of a few lousy helmets? I'll lead you. I've been in the army. I know that game.

Old Hilse. And what are you going to use for guns? Them clubs, huh?

First Young Weaver. Leave him alone, the old fool. He ain't quite right in the head.

Second Young Weaver. He's a little crazy, all right.

Gottlieb (*has stepped unnoticed among the rebels and grabs the one who was speaking*). Is that the way to talk to an old man?

First Young Weaver. Leave me alone, I didn't say nothing bad.

Old Hilse (*intervenes*). Oh, let him squawk. Don't touch him, Gottlieb. He'll find out soon enough who's crazy around here, him or me.

Bäcker. Coming along, Gottlieb?

Old Hilse. I should say not.

Luise (*comes running into the hallway, shouts into the room*). Oh, don't stop for them. Don't waste time with them prayerbook heroes. Come on out to the square! You got to come to the square. Uncle Baumert, come on . . . as fast as you can! The major is talking to the people from his horse. He's telling them to go home. If you don't come fast it'll be all over.

Jäger (*leaving*). A fine, brave husband you've got.

Luise. Me? A husband? I don't have no husband!

(*In the hallway some are singing:*)

> Once there was a little man,
> Heigh, diddle!
> He wanted a great big lusty woman,

Heigh, diddle, diddle,
Heigh, diddle dum dum!

WITTIG (*has come down from upstairs, horse bucket in hand, ready to go out; he stops for a moment in the hall-way*). Forward everybody who ain't a coward! Hurray! (*He rushes out. A group of people, LUISE and JÄGER among them, follow him with shouts of "Hurray".*)

BÄCKER. Keep well, Father Hilse, we'll talk again. (*Turns to go.*)

OLD HILSE. That I don't believe. I ain't going to live an-other five years. And it'll be that long before you get out.

BÄCKER (*stops in surprise*). Out from where, Father Hilse?

OLD HILSE. From prison! What did you think?

BÄCKER (*laughing out wildly*). That'd be all right by me. At least they give you enough bread there, Father Hilse!

(*Leaves.*)

OLD BAUMERT (*had been sitting on a stool, dully brood-ing; now he gets up*). It's true, Gustav, I'm a little drunk. But I'm still clear enough in the head. You got your opinion about this thing and I got mine. I say, Bäcker's right: if it ends in chains and ropes, still better in prison than at home. You're taken care of; you don't starve. I'd rather stay out of this. But you see, Gustav, a man's got to breathe just once in his life. (*Moves slowly toward the door.*) Good luck, Gustav. Should something happen, say a prayer for me, you hear?   (*Leaves.*)

(*None of the rebels remains on the stage. The hallway slowly fills again with curious neighbors. OLD HILSE is busy tying the warp. GOTTLIEB has taken an ax out from behind the stove and unthinkingly tries its edge. Both GOTTLIEB and the OLD MAN are disturbed but re-main silent. From outside one hears the hum and roar of a large crowd.*)

MOTHER HILSE. Tell me, Father, the floor's shaking so—what's going on? What's going to happen? (*Pause.*)

OLD HILSE. Gottlieb!

GOTTLIEB. What do you want?

OLD HILSE. You leave that ax alone.

GOTTLIEB. And who'll cut the wood? (*He leans the a* *against the stove.—Pause.*)

MOTHER HILSE. Gottlieb, you listen to what Father tel you.

A VOICE (*sings outside the window*).

Stay at home, my little man,
Heigh, diddle!
You got to clean each pot and pan
Heigh, diddle diddle,
Heigh, diddle dum dum!

(*Moves on.*)

GOTTLIEB (*jumps up shaking his fist*). You louse, don't ge me mad!

(*A volley cracks.*)

MOTHER HILSE (*with a start*). Oh, Jesus Christ! Is i thundering?

OLD HILSE (*his hand on his chest, praying*). Oh, dea God, protect the poor weavers! Protect my poor brothers

(*There is a short silence.*)

OLD HILSE (*to himself, moved*). There's blood flowing now.

GOTTLIEB (*has jumped up the moment he heard the volle and gripped his ax; he is pale and hardly able to contro his excitement.*) Is a man still supposed to knuckle under

A WEAVER GIRL (*calls into the room from the hallway*) Father Hilse, Father Hilse, get away from the window Upstairs a bullet came right through the window into ou room.   (*Disappears.*)

MIELCHEN (*shows her laughing face through the window*) Grandpa, Grandpa, they've been shooting their rifles. A few of them fell. One, he's turning around and around and around. And another one's kicking like a sparrow when you tear his head off. Oh, and so much blood was flowing!

(*She disappears.*)

A WEAVER WOMAN. They've killed a few.

AN OLD WEAVER (*in the hallway*). You watch out ... now hey'll go at the soldiers.

SECOND WEAVER (*completely bewildered*). No, just look at them women, look at them women! Lifting up their skirts! Spitting at the soldiers!

A WEAVER WOMAN (*calls into the room*). Gottlieb, just ook at your wife! She's got more pluck'n you, she's jumping around in front of them bayonets like she was dancing!

(*Four men carry a wounded man through the hallway. Silence. Then one hears distinctly a voice saying.*) That's weaver Ulbrich. (*After a few seconds, the same voice again.*) That'll be the end for him, more'n likely; he got a bullet right into his ear. (*Men are heard stamping up the wooden stairs. Suddenly, from the outside.*) Hurray, hurray!

VOICES IN THE HALLWAY. Where did they get the stones from?—Now you better beat it!—From the new road.—Bye—bye, soldiers.—Now it's raining paving stones.

(*The screams of fear and the shouting spread from the street into the hallway. With a shriek of terror the door of the house is banged shut.*)

VOICES IN THE HALLWAY. They're loading again.—They're going to shoot another volley.—Father Hilse, get away from that window!

GOTTLIEB (*runs for the ax*). What? What? Are we mad dogs? Do they want us to eat powder and lead instead of bread? (*Ax in hand, he hesitates for a moment; to* OLD HILSE.) Do I have to stand by while they're shooting my wife? I won't stand for it! (*Rushing out.*) Watch out now, I'm coming out! (*Leaves.*)

OLD HILSE. Gottlieb, Gottlieb!

MOTHER HILSE. Where did Gottlieb go?

OLD HILSE. To the devil he's gone!

VOICE (*from the hallway*). Away from the window, Father Hilse!

OLD HILSE. Not me! Not if you all go completely mad! (*To* MOTHER HILSE, *in growing ecstasy.*) This is where my Heavenly Father put me. Ain't that so, Mother? Here we stay and do what we have to do—even if the snow catches fire. (*He starts weaving. A volley is heard. Hit,* OLD HILSE *rises up high, then falls forward across the loom. At the*

same time increasing shouts of "Hurray" are heard. The
people who had been standing in the hallway now rush out
with shouts of "Hurray." MOTHER HILSE *asks several*
times.) Father, Father, what's the matter with you? *(The*
uninterrupted shouts of "Hurray" gradually disappear in the
distance. Suddenly, MIELCHEN *runs into the room.)*

MIELCHEN. Grandpa, Grandpa, they're chasing the soldiers out of the village, they've stormed Dietrich's house,
they're doing just as they did over at Dreissiger's. Grandpa?
(Suddenly frightened, she watches closely, puts her finger
into her mouth and gingerly steps closer to the dead man.)
Grandpa?

MOTHER HILSE. Come on now, Father!—Say something!
You're scaring me!

CURTAIN

PREFACE TO *The Beaver Coat*

The Beaver Coat, written by Hauptmann in the summer and fall of 1892, had its première at the *Deutsches Theater* on September 12, 1893. It was a very successful production, and curiously, in contrast with *The Weavers,* it did not encounter official opposition because the censor considered the play contrived—instead of recognizing himself and the German bureaucracy in Hauptmann's portrait of the witch-hunting super-patriot von Wehrhahn.

Comedy without poetry tends to date, and is, moreover, rarely exportable. It is not surprising that *The Beaver Coat* has had hardly any success on the English-speaking stage, and that even a valiant "off-Broadway" group went down to defeat when it presented the play (in the old Ludwig Lewissohn translation) at the Greenwich Village Mews on March 28, 1956. Brooks Atkinson, reviewing the production in *The New York Times,* judged that the play was "hardly more than a curiosity now," and a reviewer for the *New York Post,* Frances Herridge, ventured that "its spoofing of village justice and bureaucratic stupidity in Imperial Germany has little relevance today." The latter suggested that the play "is of interest mainly as a superbly drawn historic cartoon." Contradictions creeping into the critics' evaluation, such as the statement that "Hauptmann has etched with bold, sharp lines a number of amusing characters," suggested that *The Beaver Coat* could not be lightly dismissed even by reviewers remote from the scene Hauptmann submitted to comic scrutiny and satiric treatment.

For those familiar with German officialism and its hold upon the populace the satire on Hauptmann's heel-clicking Dogberry, von Wehrhahn (literally, "Fighting Cock"), certainly had "relevance." The hoodwinking of Prussian officialdom continued to be a good subject for comedy in Central Europe in later years—during the period of the Weimar Republic when Carl Zuckmayer wrote his anti-militaristic satire *The Captain of Koepenick*, notably popular in Germany, and more precariously during the later storm-trooper rule of Hitler. But *The Beaver Coat* is not exclusively a satire. It is a picaresque folk-comedy, rich in texture and replete with flavorsome dialect in the original text. And it is, at the same time, an outstanding character-comedy in the naturalistic vein, chiefly as a result of Hauptmann's characterization of his scrubwoman heroine Mrs. Wolff, which has been invariably recognized as masterly.

The sequel to this play, *Der rote Hahn* or *The Conflagration* (1901), which had an excellent revival in 1956, revolves around Mrs. Wolff's last exploits. Less well regarded than *The Beaver Coat*, the sequel nevertheless constitutes an independent work which presents a deteriorating social scene, and throws light on the earlier work. It is clear that comedy for Hauptmann was not altogether motivated by the desire to entertain. In the days of his liberal associations, he grounded comedy in responsible observation, and used comic exposure as a strategy of protest. His strongly naturalistic view of human nature is best expressed by Mrs. Wolff in her cynical dog-eat-dog philosophy (she might almost be the elder sister of Mrs. Peachum in Brecht's *Threepenny Opera*): "People like us must grasp at every kind of muck. We are always told to be good. But how does one start being that?" Earlier she has declared with the cynical realism of the underdog that everyone cheats his way through life, and that whoever doesn't succeed is said to be lazy, while whoever succeeds is sure to be evil.

THE BEAVER COAT

A Thieves' Comedy in Four Acts

CHARACTERS

Von Wehrhahn, Police Superintendent
Krueger
Dr. Fleischer
Philipp, his son
Motes
Frau Motes, his wife
Frau Wolff, washerwoman

Julius Wolff, her husband

Leontine
Adelheid } their daughters

Wulkow, a bargeman
Glasenapp, clerk in von Wehrhahn's office
Mitteldorf, a bailiff

The action takes place somewhere in the neighborhood of Berlin in the late 1880's.

ACT I

(*A small, narrow kitchen with blue walls and a low ceiling. At the right is a window and a crude, wooden, outside door. In the rear wall is an empty door frame through which one sees a second room. It contains a high, neatly made bed. Above it hang some cheap photographs in even cheaper frames, prints of oil portraits the size of calling cards, etc. A soft-wood chair stands with its back toward the bed. In the left-hand corner of the kitchen is the stove. Kitchen utensils hang from a frame above it. Scattered about are several stools, an old kitchen bench, etc.—It is winter and the moon is shining. On the stove burns a tallow candle in a tin candlestick. LEONTINE WOLFF, asleep on a stool near the stove, rests her head and arms on top of the stove. She is a seventeen-year-old, pretty, blonde girl and is wearing the working clothes of a servant girl. A thick woolen shawl is tied over her blue calico jacket.—For a few seconds there is silence. Then someone is heard trying to unlock the door from the outside, but the key is in the lock on the inside. Then a knock is heard at the door.*)

FRAU WOLFF (*still unseen on the outside*). Adelheid! Adelheid! (*Silence. Then she knocks on the window.*)

LEONTINE (*talking in her sleep*). No—no! I'm not a slave!

FRAU WOLFF. Open up, girl, or I'll come through the window! (*She bangs hard on the window.*)

LEONTINE (*waking up*). Oh, it's you, Mom! I'm coming! (*She unlocks the door.*)

FRAU WOLFF (*without putting down the sack she is carrying on her shoulder*). And what are you doing here?

LEONTINE (*sleepily*). Evening, Mom!

FRAU WOLFF. And how did you get in, eh?

LEONTINE. Well, the key was on top of the goat shed as usual. (*Short silence.*)

FRAU WOLFF. And what do you want here, girl?

LEONTINE (*with a silly pout*). Don't you want me home at all no more?

FRAU WOLFF. Do me a favor and don't start fussing, huh? That's just what I need! (*She lets the sack drop from her shoulder.*) Don't you have any idea what time it is? Off with you now and get home to your people.

LEONTINE. And if I did get back a little late for once—so what!

FRAU WOLFF. Now you just watch yourself, understand? Get going or there's going to be trouble.

LEONTINE (*whining and obstinate*). I ain't going back, Mom!

FRAU WOLFF (*surprised*). You ain't going . . . (*Ironically.*) Well, what do you know about that!

LEONTINE. Well, do I have to be a slave for them people all the time?

FRAU WOLFF (*has been busy trying to get a piece of venison out of the sack*). Oh, so you got to slave for them Kruegers? Why, you poor child! Don't come to me with things like that! A girl like a wrestler! Give me a hand, get a hold of the bottom of the sack. You couldn't be no clumsier if you tried! Don't come to me with stories like that! I ain't going to learn you to loaf! (*Between both of them, they manage to hang the venison on the door frame.*) But now I'm telling you for the last time . . .

LEONTINE. I ain't going back to them people. I'd just as soon go drown myself, Mom!

FRAU WOLFF. Hope you don't catch cold.

LEONTINE. I'll jump into the river!

FRAU WOLFF. Just make sure you let me know when, so I can give you a push and make sure you don't miss the water!

LEONTINE (*shouting, excited*). Well, do I have to stand for that . . . carrying firewood into the shed in the evening, two whole yards of it?

FRAU WOLFF (*pretending surprise*). No, it ain't possible! They ask you to carry wood! Heavens, what people!

LEONTINE. . . . and twenty talers for the whole year? And freeze my hands off for that? And not even enough herrings and spuds to eat?

FRAU WOLFF. Don't start making speeches now, girl. Here's the key. Go get yourself some bread. And after you've had enough, on your way you go, understand? The plum jam's on the top shelf.

LEONTINE (*takes a large loaf of bread from the drawer and cuts herself a slice*). Gustie, the one who works for the Schulzes, you know, she gets forty talers and . . .

FRAU WOLFF. Don't be in such an awful hurry! You ain't going to stay with them people forever. They didn't hire you for all eternity. As far's I'm concerned, till the first of April. Until then you stay put! Got your Christmas present in your pocket and now you want to quit? Them's no manners!—And me meeting them people all the time.—I ain't going to stand for nothing like that!

LEONTINE. You mean because of these rags I got on?

FRAU WOLFF. And how about the cash?

LEONTINE. Sure, that's a pile! Six whole marks!

FRAU WOLFF. That's money, too. Never you mind!

LEONTINE. But if I can make more money?

FRAU WOLFF. Hmph, gabbing maybe!

LEONTINE. No, with the sewing machine. I can go to Berlin and sew coats. Emily Stechow's been doing it since New Year's.

FRAU WOLFF. Don't talk to me about that little bitch! Just let me get my hands on that one! I'll show her something! That'd be something for you, wouldn't it? Tramping around all night with fellers. Oh no, girl . . . just the thought of it! I'd beat you till you'd forget to get up.—There's your father, watch out now!

LEONTINE. If Pop beats me up I know what I'll do.

FRAU WOLFF. Stop squawking! Go feed the goats instead. Haven't milked them tonight either. And give the rabbits some hay.

LEONTINE (*tries to get out of the house as quickly as possible, runs into her father in the door and says in passing*). Evening!

(JULIUS WOLFF, *the father, is a shipwright, tall, with slow movements and stupid eyes, about forty-three years old. He puts the two oars which he has been carrying over his shoulder in the corner, and puts down his carpenter's tools without saying a word.*)

FRAU WOLFF. Did you see Barge-Emil?

(JULIUS *growls*.)

FRAU WOLFF. Can't you talk? Yes or no. Is he coming over?

JULIUS (*testily*). Go ahead! Yell a little louder!

FRAU WOLFF. Oh, you're so brave! And you forgot to shut the door.

JULIUS (*closes the door*). What's wrong with Leontine again?

FRAU WOLFF. Oh, nothing.—What's Emil got loaded this time?

JULIUS. Bricks again. What's he supposed to have? What's the matter with that girl again?

FRAU WOLFF. Half a barge load or a full load?

JULIUS (*flying into a rage*). What in hell's the matter with that girl again, I want to know!

FRAU WOLFF (*even louder*). What Emil's got in his barge is what I want to know! Half a load or a full load?

JULIUS. Ah, go away, a full load.

FRAU WOLFF. *Psst,* Julius. (*Frightened, she closes the shutters.*)

JULIUS (*stares at her, frightened. After a few seconds of silence, in a low voice.*) That's a young forester from Rixdorf.

FRAU WOLFF. Go hide under the bed, Julius! (*After a pause.*) If only you wasn't so terrible dumb. Blowing up like that. You don't understand things like that. Just let me worry about the girls. That's not in your jurisfriction. That's in my jurisfriction. If they was boys that'd be different. I wouldn't tell you what to do with them. Everybody's got his own jurisfriction.

JULIUS. Keep her out of my way, then.

FRAU WOLFF. So you want to beat her to a pulp, eh, Julius? Better forget about that! Don't think for a minute I'd let you . . . let you cripple that girl! That girl could be our fortune! If you only had some brains for them things!

JULIUS. Let her look after herself then!

FRAU WOLFF. Don't worry about that, Julius. Could be you're going to be surprised. That girl's going to live on the best floor in the house some day and we'll be happy if she knows us. What did the doc tell me the other day? "Your daughter's such a beautiful girl," he says, "she could go far on the stage."

JULIUS. Why don't she hurry up and go there, then.

FRAU WOLFF. You just don't have no education, Julius. No, not a trace of it. If it hadn't been for me, what would have become of them girls? I've given them some education. Education, that's the most important thing nowadays. And you don't get it just like that. One thing after another, slowly but surely. Now she's got to learn something about housekeeping first of all. Then if she's got a mind to she can go to Berlin. For God's sake, she's still much too young for the stage! (*During this conversation there has been repeated knocking at the door.*)

ADELHEID (*voice is heard from outside*). Mom, Mom, open up! (FRAU WOLFF *opens the door for her and she comes in. She is a tall schoolgirl of fourteen, with a pretty child's face. Her eyes, however, betray early depravity.*) Why don't you open up, Mom? My hands and feet are frozen stiff.

FRAU WOLFF. Don't start talking a lot of rubbish. Go make a fire in the stove instead. That'll warm you up. And where've you been all this time if I may ask?

ADELHEID. Well, I've been getting Pop's boots.

FRAU WOLFF. And that took you two hours?

ADELHEID. But I only left at seven!

FRAU WOLFF. So you left at seven? Now it's half-past ten. You didn't know that, did you? So you've been away for three and a half hours, and that ain't so much, huh? Now you listen to me, young lady. If you stay out that long once more, and with that lousy cobbler Fielitz at that—you better watch out! Something's going to pop!

ADELHEID. Am I supposed to hang around the house all the time?

FRAU WOLFF. You just keep your mouth shut now and don't say another word!

ADELHEID. Just because I go over to Fielitz' for a little while . . .

FRAU WOLFF. Are you going to be quiet? You're telling me about Fielitz! He's nothing to be proud of. His trade ain't just mending shoes, you know. If somebody's done time twice . . .

ADELHEID. That's not true . . . That's all a pack of lies. He's told me it is, Mom!

FRAU WOLFF. The whole village knows it, you silly goose! A pimp, that's what he is.

ADELHEID. He even goes and talks to the superintendent.

FRAU WOLFF. Sure he does. So he can tell him stories. An unformer he is on top of everything.

ADELHEID. What's that, an unformer?

JULIUS (*from the other room where he has gone*). Just one more word! (ADELHEID *blanches; quickly and silently she starts to make a fire in the stove.*)

(LEONTINE *enters.*)

FRAU WOLFF (*cuts open the venison, takes out the heart, the liver, etc. and hands them to* LEONTINE). Quick now, wash that! And don't say a word or lightning will strike. (LEONTINE, *visibly cowed, starts working. The girls whisper to each other.*)

FRAU WOLFF. Eh, Julius? What are you doing in there? You've forgotten all about it, eh? And only this morning I told you. That board that's come off.

JULIUS. What board?

FRAU WOLFF. You don't remember, huh? That board back on the goat shed. The wind must've torn it loose last night—get going and nail it on, understand?

JULIUS. Aw, that roof'll still be there in the morning.

FRAU WOLFF. Oh no, you don't! None of that! We ain't going to start that sort of business here! (JULIUS *has come back into the kitchen and grumbles.*) There, take the hammer! Here's your nails! Get going now!

JULIUS. You're crazy.

FRAU WOLFF (*calling after him*). If Wulkow comes, how much do you want?

JULIUS. Well, twelve marks at least! (*Leaves.*)

FRAU WOLFF (*contemptuously*). Twelve marks! (*Pause.*) Hurry up now so's Pop gets something to eat!

ADELHEID (*looking at the venison*). What's that, Mom?

FRAU WOLFF. A stork! (*Both girls laugh.*)

ADELHEID. A stork? Does a stork have horns? Oh, I know, a deer, that's what it is!

FRAU WOLFF. So if you know why do you ask?

LEONTINE. Did Pop shoot it, Mom?

FRAU WOLFF. Just go on now and shout all over the village that your father's shot a deer!

ADELHEID. Catch me doing that! We'd get the cops!

LEONTINE. I'm not afraid of Officer Schulze. He's tickled me under the chin once.

FRAU WOLFF. Just let him come. We've done nothing bad. If a deer is wounded and just about to croak and nobody finds him, the ravens'll eat him. Whether we eat it or the ravens, it's going to be eaten one way or the other. (*Short pause.*) How was that now: firewood you had to carry in?

LEONTINE. . . . and with this freezing cold! Two yards of logs! And if a person's dog-tired—and at half-past nine at night!

FRAU WOLFF. So now all that nice wood's lying around on the street?

LEONTINE. Sure, right by the garden gate. That's all I know.

FRAU WOLFF. Now—suppose somebody went and stole that wood? Then what, tomorrow morning?

LEONTINE. I don't know. I won't be there.

FRAU WOLFF. Are the logs dry—or green?

LEONTINE. Oh, nice dry logs! (*Yawns several times.*) Oh, Mom, I'm all worn out. I've just been working my head off today. (*She sits down, obviously tired.*)

FRAU WOLFF (*after a short silence*). Well, if you want to, stay here tonight. I've changed my mind. Tomorrow morning we'll see.

LEONTINE. There's nothing left of me, Mom! My clothes just hang on me.

FRAU WOLFF. Hurry up now and get some sleep; up to the bedroom you go, so we don't have no trouble with Pop. He don't understand nothing of things like this.

ADELHEID. Pop always talks so—uneducated.

FRAU WOLFF. He just hasn't learned no education. And with you it would have been no different, if I hadn't learned you some education. (*Holding a pot on the stove, to* LEONTINE.) Come on now, put it in! (LEONTINE *puts the pieces of meat she has washed into the pot.*) There, now go to sleep!

LEONTINE (*goes into the back room, but is still visible*). Mom, that Motes fellow has left from Kruegers'.

FRAU WOLFF. Didn't want to pay the rent, huh?

LEONTINE. It was one hell of a lot of trouble getting it, says Herr Krueger. But he's turned him out all the same. A liar and a windbag he is, he says. And always so uppity with Krueger, he says.

FRAU WOLFF. If that had been me, I wouldn't have put up with him that long.

LEONTINE. Just because Herr Krueger used to be a cabinetmaker, Motes always looks down on him so. And he's been quarreling with Dr. Fleischer, too.

FRAU WOLFF. Well, who'd start a fight with him . . . I'd like to know! Them people wouldn't hurt a fly.

LEONTINE. The Fleischers won't even let him into the house no more.

FRAU WOLFF. That'd be a nice place for you, with them people.

LEONTINE. They treat their servants as if they were their own children.

FRAU WOLFF. And his brother . . . he's in Berlin, cashier at the theater.

WULKOW (*has knocked at the door several times; now shouts in a hoarse voice*). Are you going to let me in?

FRAU WOLFF. Sure, sure! Why not? Come on in!

WULKOW (*enters; he is a barge captain on the river Spree, almost sixty years old, and walks with a stoop. He has a yellowish-gray beard that reaches from one ear to the other and under his chin so that his weatherbeaten face is left clear.*) A pleasant evening, everybody.

FRAU WOLFF. Here he is again, so's he can cheat Frau Wolff a little.

WULKOW. That . . . I wouldn't even try no more.

FRAU WOLFF. Well, that's how it's going to wind up again.

WULKOW. Just the other way 'round, that'd be more like it.

FRAU WOLFF. How about that!—Well, here he is. Well, don't he beat all?

WULKOW. Just tell Julius to watch out. They's all in a stew about poachers.

FRAU WOLFF. What are you going to pay? That's what I want to know. All this jabbering's going to get us no-wheres.

WULKOW. I'm telling you. I've just come from Gruenau. Heard it for sure. They've shot Fritz Weber; his pants are full of buckshot.

FRAU WOLFF. What you are going to pay, that's what we're talking about.

WULKOW (*feeling the venison*). And I got four bucks lying around already.

FRAU WOLFF. They won't sink your barge.

WULKOW. I should hope not! But if I get stuck here, then what? After all, I got to get the beasts up to Berlin. It was bad enough today working on the river. And if it keeps freezing like this all night I'll be stuck in the morning.

I'll be sitting nicely in the ice with my boat and have them beasts around my neck.

FRAU WOLFF (*seems to change her mind*). All right, girl, just run down to Schulze quickly and tell him Mother's got something to sell.

WULKOW. Did I say I wasn't going to buy it?

FRAU WOLFF. Don't matter to me who buys it.

WULKOW. But I want to buy it.

FRAU WOLFF. If you don't like it you can leave it.

WULKOW. I'm going to buy that piece. How much do you want?

FRAU WOLFF (*touching the venison*). That buck here weighs at least some thirty pounds. At least that, I can tell you. Eh, Adelheid! You were there. We could hardly get it hung up on the nail, could we?

ADELHEID (*who had not been present*). I've even wrenched something here, lifting it.

WULKOW. Well, thirteen marks ought to pay for it. And that way I ain't making even ten pfennigs for myself.

FRAU WOLFF (*pretends complete surprise; the next moment she starts doing something else and, as if she had completely forgotten WULKOW's presence, seems to notice him again*). Oh yes, I meant to wish you a good trip!

WULKOW. No, I just can't give more'n thirteen.

FRAU WOLFF. Why don't you forget about it!

WULKOW. I just can't pay more than that. Like I'm telling you. I'm doing it just so I keep my customers. Lightning may strike me down, sure as I'm standing here, I don't make that much on this whole deal. And if I'd say fourteen, I'd have to add: that's one mark out of my pocket. But I don't mind; just so you see I'm willing. Fourteen marks!

FRAU WOLFF. That's all right. Never mind. We'll sell that buck before tomorrow morning anyways.

WULKOW. Hope nobody'll see it hanging there so nice and pretty! That'd be kind of expensive!

FRAU WOLFF. That buck was dead when we found it.

WULKOW. Sure, in the snare! I'll believe that!

FRAU WOLFF. Don't you start that tune! That won't get you nowheres. You want people just to give you their last shirt, huh? We slave till we're out of breath, take a bath in the snow for hours, not to speak of all the risks we take in that pitch-dark night. That's no fun!

WULKOW. Too bad I got them other four already. Otherwise maybe I'd say fifteen marks.

FRAU WOLFF. No, Wulkow. We just can't do business today. You can go take a walk now. Here we've been slaving to get across the lake . . . and almost got stuck in the ice. Couldn't go forward or back. No, we ain't going to give that away for nothing.

WULKOW. As if I was going to make a million on the deal! Running a barge is pretty rough going. And pushing stolen goods ain't no mint neither. And if you get nabbed I'll get it in the neck, too. Almost forty years I've been working. And what have I got to show for it? Rheumatism! When I get out of bed in the morning I cry like a pup. For years I've been wanting to buy me a fur coat. All the doctors have told me I should, because I'm suffering so! Never been able to buy one, Frau Wolff. Not to this day sure as I'm standing here!

ADELHEID (*to her mother*). Hear anything from Leontine?

WULKOW. All right, so I'll say sixteen! Sixteen marks!

FRAU WOLFF. No, nothing doing! Eighteen! (*To* ADELHEID.) What did you say?

ADELHEID. Well, Frau Krueger's just bought a fur coat. Almost five hundred marks it cost. A beaver coat.

WULKOW. A beaver coat?

FRAU WOLFF. Who's that who bought it?

ADELHEID. Frau Krueger, for Herr Krueger for Christmas she bought it.

WULKOW. That girl's a servant at the Krueger's, ain't she?

ADELHEID. No, not me. My sister is. I'll never work as a servant.

WULKOW. Ah, if I could only have one like that. I been waiting for something like that for a long, long time. I'd gladly pay sixty talers for it. Rather spend the money on a fur coat than give it to the doctors and druggists. That'd be some fun at least.

FRAU WOLFF. Why don't you just go, Wulkow, walk over to Kruegers and see . . . maybe they're giving it away.

WULKOW. Not likely! But, as I said, I'm very interested in something like that.

FRAU WOLFF. Sure, sure. I wouldn't mind having a fur coat myself.

WULKOW. How do we stand now? Sixteen?

FRAU WOLFF. Nothing doing below eighteen. Not below eighteen, that's what Julius told me. If I came to him with sixteen . . . once he gets something like that in his noodle

. . . (JULIUS *comes back.*) Didn't you say eighteen, Julius?

JULIUS. What did I say?

FRAU WOLFF. Must be one of your hard-of-hearing days! Didn't you tell me, not below eighteen? Not to sell that buck under eighteen?

JULIUS. Did I say that? . . . Oh that, that piece of venison. Oh, sure! That wouldn't be too much.

WULKOW (*taking some money out of his pocket and counting*). We got to come to an end with this. Seventeen marks. All right?

FRAU WOLFF. You're really a louse. Just as I said when you came in: he just walks across that threshold, and he's cheated you already.

WULKOW (*brings out a rolled-up sack that he has kept hidden*). Give me a hand now getting that thing in here. (FRAU WOLFF *helps him put the deer into the sack.*) And if by any chance you hear anything about . . . like a fur coat for instance . . . I might invest something like sixty, seventy talers.

FRAU WOLFF. You must be out of your mind! Where would we get a hold of a fur coat?

MAN'S VOICE (*calling outside*). Frau Wolff! Frau Wolff! Are you still up?

FRAU WOLFF (*is startled, as is everyone in the room; vehemently but under her breath*). Quick, get it out of the way! Quick! Into the other room! (*She pushes everybody into the back room and closes the door.*)

MAN'S VOICE. Frau Wolff! Frau Wolff! Are you already in bed?

(FRAU WOLFF *puts out the candle.*)

THE MAN'S VOICE. Frau Wolff! Frau Wolff! Are you still up? (*The voice moves off singing.*) The morn glows re–ed, the morn glows re–ed, Brings the day—when I'll be de–ad.

LEONTINE. That's only "Morning Glow," Mom!

FRAU WOLFF (*listens for a while, then quietly opens the door and listens again. Finally she is satisfied, closes the door and relights the candle. Then she lets the others in from the back room.*) It was only Mitteldorf, the bailiff.

WULKOW. The hell! Fine friends you got!

FRAU WOLFF. Well, Wulkow, you better get going now.

ADELHEID. Mom, Mino is barking.

FRAU WOLFF. Get going now, Wulkow! Get a move on! And out through the back, through the vegetable garden.

Julius is going to open up for you. Go on, Julius, open the gate for him!

WULKOW. And as I said, if you run across anything . . . like a beaver coat for instance . . .

FRAU WOLFF. Sure, sure! Hurry up now!

WULKOW. If the Spree don't freeze up, in three, four days I'll be back from Berlin. I'll be down there again with my barge.

ADELHEID. By the big bridge?

WULKOW. Where I always tie up. Well, Julius, go on, you shuffle ahead. (*Leaves.*)

ADELHEID. Mom, Mino's barking again.

FRAU WOLFF (*at the stove*). Oh, let him bark. (*A long, drawn-out cry in the distance: "Ferryman, ahoy!"*)

ADELHEID. Somebody trying to get across the Spree, Mom.

FRAU WOLFF. Well, go on down. Pop's down there by the water anyways. *"Ferryman, ahoy!"* Go bring him the oars. But he better let Wulkow get away first.

(ADELHEID *leaves with the oars. For a while* FRAU WOLFF, *busily working, remains alone.* ADELHEID *returns.*)

ADELHEID. Pop's got the other oars down in the boat.

FRAU WOLFF. And who'd want to get across this late?

ADELHEID. I think it's that stupid Motes.

FRAU WOLFF. What? Who did you say?

ADELHEID. It sounded like Motes.

FRAU WOLFF (*vehemently*). Run on down again! Hurry up! Tell Pop to come on up; that idiot Motes can stay where he is. No need for him to come in here sniffing around.

(ADELHEID *goes.* FRAU WOLFF *hides everything that might give away the deer episode. She puts an apron over the pot on the stove.* ADELHEID *returns.*)

ADELHEID. Too late, Mom. I can already hear them talking.

FRAU WOLFF. And who is it?

ADELHEID. Like I told you, Motes.

(FRAU *and* HERR MOTES *appear, one after the other, in the door. Both are of medium build. She is an alert, young woman of about thirty, unpretentiously but neatly dressed. He wears a green hunting coat, his face is healthy and commonplace; he wears a black patch over his left eye.*)

FRAU MOTES (*calling into the room*). My nose is frozen blue, Mother Wolff!

FRAU WOLFF. What do you go traipsing around for in the middle of the night! You got time for walks in the daytime.

MOTES. Nice and warm in here.—Who's got time during the day?

FRAU WOLFF. Well, you!

MOTES. Do you think that I have an independent income?

FRAU WOLFF. I'm sure I don't know what you're living on.

FRAU MOTES. Don't be so grouchy, Mother Wolff. We just wanted to ask for our bill.

FRAU WOLFF. You've asked me more'n once for that.

FRAU MOTES. Well, so we ask once more, what of it? We'll have to pay some day!

FRAU WOLFF (surprised). You want to pay?

FRAU MOTES. Sure. Naturally!

MOTES. Mother Wolff seems surprised. You didn't think we'd run out on you, did you?

FRAU WOLFF. Why, who'd think a thing like that! If you want to we'll settle it right now. Eleven marks and thirty pfennigs it was.

FRAU MOTES. Yes, Mother Wolff, we're coming into money. People will really open their eyes!

MOTES. Smells like roast hare in here, doesn't it?

FRAU WOLFF. Hmph, roast cat more likely! That'd be more like it!

MOTES. I'll just take a look-see! (He is about to lift the cover from the pot.)

FRAU WOLFF (stopping him). No fussing around with my pots!

FRAU MOTES (has suspiciously observed the scene). Mother Wolff, we've found something.

FRAU WOLFF. I didn't lose nothing.

FRAU MOTES. Here, take a look at these! (Shows her two wire snares.)

FRAU WOLFF (undisturbed). That's snares, ain't it?

FRAU MOTES. Found them quite close by, hardly twenty steps from your garden.

FRAU WOLFF. My God, the poaching that's going on around here!

FRAU MOTES. If you really watch carefully, Mother Wolff, you might even catch the poacher.

FRAU WOLFF. Them things are no business of mine.

MOTES. If I ever catch one of those scoundrels I'll box his ears and then turn him in.

FRAU MOTES. Frau Wolff, have you got any fresh eggs?

FRAU WOLFF. What? Now? In the middle of winter? They're pretty rare now.

MOTES (*to* JULIUS *who is just coming in*). Forester Seidel has caught another poacher. They'll take him to court tomorrow. He's got pluck, that guy, that much you have to say. If only I hadn't had that accident, I'd be a head forester by now. Oh, I'd really let them have it, those dogs!

FRAU WOLFF. Quite a few've been sorry they tried.

MOTES. Yes, if somebody's afraid. But I'm not afraid. I've already informed on a few of them. (*Gazing alternately at* FRAU WOLFF *and her husband.*) And I'm just waiting for a few more. But they'll run straight into my arms one of these days. I hope those snare-setters don't think I don't know them. I know them very well!

FRAU MOTES. Did you do some baking, Frau Wolff? We just can't stand the bread the bakers bake.

FRAU WOLFF. I thought you wanted to pay your bill.

FRAU MOTES. I'm telling you, Mother Wolff . . . on Saturday. You know, my husband's been made editor of the *Journal of Hunting and Forestry.*

FRAU WOLFF. Sure, sure. I know what that means, all right.

FRAU MOTES. Yes indeed, Frau Wolff! And we've already moved away from Krueger's!

FRAU WOLFF. Because you *had* to, you moved.

FRAU MOTES. We had to? Honey, just listen to that! (*She gives a forced laugh.*) Frau Wolff says we had to move away from Krueger's!

MOTES (*red with fury*). Some day you'll find out why I moved away. That man is a usurer and a cut-throat.

FRAU WOLFF. I don't know nothing about that. Can't say nothing about that.

MOTES. I'm just waiting to get the evidence. He'd better watch out for me. He and his bosom friend, that Dr. Fleischer! Particularly that one! If I just wanted to, one word would be all that'd be necessary to get that man behind bars. (*From the beginning of his speech he has started to draw back to the door. With his last words he disappears.*)

FRAU WOLFF. Did the men quarrel again?

FRAU MOTES (*assumes a confidential tone*). You can't play around with my husband. If he gets his mind on something, he won't give up. And he's on very good terms with the Superintendent, too.—How about the eggs and the bread?

FRAU WOLFF. Well, five's all I got left; and a piece of bread. (FRAU MOTES *puts the eggs and half a loaf of bread into her basket.*) Are you happy now?

FRAU MOTES. Oh, sure. Of course. The eggs are fresh, aren't they?

FRAU WOLFF. Just as fresh as my hens lay them.

FRAU MOTES (*anxious to catch up with her husband, hurriedly*). Well, good-night then! And next Saturday's money day! (*Leaves.*)

FRAU WOLFF. Sure, sure. That's all right. (*Closes the door. Under her breath.*) Hurry up and get out of here. They owe money to everybody! (*Busy with the pot.*) Ain't none of their business what we eat. Let them look into their own pots. Go to bed now, girl.

ADELHEID. Night, Mom. (*Kisses her.*)

FRAU WOLFF. Ain't you going to give your father a good-night kiss?

ADELHEID. Night, Pop. (*Kisses him; he growls.* ADELHEID *leaves.*)

FRAU WOLFF. Always got to remind her! (*Pause.*)

JULIUS. What do you have to give them people eggs for?

FRAU WOLFF. Do you want me to make that fellow mad at me? You make him mad at you, Julius, and I'm telling you, that fellow's dangerous. He don't do nothing but keep an eagle eye on everybody. Come on, sit down. Eat now. Here's a fork. You just don't understand them things. Better take care of your own business! Leaving the snares right behind the garden! Them were your snares all right, weren't they?

JULIUS (*annoyed*). Well, sure.

FRAU WOLFF. And that stupid Motes had to find them! You ain't going to set no more snares right around the house, you hear? Somebody might get the idea it's us who's setting them.

JULIUS. Oh, stop jabbering. (*Both eat.*)

FRAU WOLFF. Listen, there ain't no more wood neither.

JULIUS. So you want me to go all the way back into the woods, huh?

FRAU WOLFF. Better get it over with.

JULIUS. I can't hardly feel my bones no more. I don't care who goes. Just leave me alone.

FRAU WOLFF. You men always talk so damn big, and then when you got to do something you don't feel so well. I could race you working through a haystack and back again, three times too, all of you. If you don't want to go tonight, tomorrow you'll just have to go whether you like it or not. How's your climbing irons? Are they sharp?

JULIUS. I lent them to Karl Machnow.

FRAU WOLFF (*after a moment's silence*). If only you weren't such a coward! We'd have us a few cords of wood in a hurry! And we wouldn't have to work so hard for it neither. Wouldn't even have to walk very far.

JULIUS. Just let me eat a bite, will you?

FRAU WOLFF (*boxes his head playfully*). Oh, don't be such a miserable grumbler all the time! Just watch, I got something nice for you! (*Gets out a bottle of liquor and shows it to him.*) See that? That's what I brought you. Now you look more cheerful right away, don't you? (*Pours him a glass.*)

JULIUS (*empties the glass; then*). With that damn cold . . . that feels pretty good!

FRAU WOLFF. See? Don't I take care of you?

JULIUS. That was all right, all right. Pretty good! (*Pours himself another glass and drinks it.*)

FRAU WOLFF (*starts splitting wood, eating a bite now and then in between, after a pause*). That Wulkow's a real scoundrel! Always carrying on as if he was *so* poor.

JULIUS. He should talk, that one! With all his business.

FRAU WOLFF. Well, you heard what he said . . . about that beaver coat.

JULIUS. I didn't hear nothing.

FRAU WOLFF (*pretending indifference*). Well, the girl told him about Frau Krueger and how she bought her husband a beaver coat.

JULIUS. Well them people's got the dough.

FRAU WOLFF. Well, and so Wulkow says . . . you heard it, didn't you? If he only could get himself a fur coat like that he'd pay sixty talers or more, he says.

JULIUS. Let him burn his fingers himself.

FRAU WOLFF (*after a brief silence, pouring him another drink*). Eh, you might as well take another one.

JULIUS. Pour away . . . pour away . . . anything . . .

(FRAU WOLFF *gets out a small notebook and leafs through it.*)

JULIUS. How much did we save since July?

FRAU WOLFF. Paid off just thirty talers.

JULIUS. And that leaves . . . that leaves . . . how much?

FRAU WOLFF. Still leaves seventy. That way we just don't

make no progress at all. Fifty, sixty talers at one clip . . . if we could do that, this here plot would soon be paid for. And then we could borrow a hundred or two again and add on two, three nice rooms. As it is we can't take no summer guests. And summer guests, that's what brings in the money.

JULIUS. Well . . . I don't know . . . how . . .

FRAU WOLFF (*determined*). You're just too slow, Julius. Would you've bought the land, heh? Well? And now if we had a mind to sell it we could get double. I just got a different temperature. If only you had my temperature . . .

JULIUS. I'm working . . . but what good does it do?

FRAU WOLFF. Oh working! With that kind of work you don't get very far.

JULIUS. Well, I can't go stealing! You want me to get into trouble?

FRAU WOLFF. Well, you're just stupid and that's the way you'll stay most likely. Nobody's been talking about stealing. Nothing ventured nothing gained. And once you're rich and ride around in a carriage nobody's going to ask where you got your money from. Of course, if you took it from poor people!—But seriously now—if we up and went over to Krueger's and put them two cords of wood on the sleigh and brought them into our shed, them people wouldn't be none the poorer!

JULIUS. Wood? What's that about wood now?

FRAU WOLFF. You just don't think of nothing. They can drive your daughter to her death! They wanted her to carry in wood at ten o'clock at night, and that's why she run away. That you don't care about, of course. Maybe you'd even beat her up and chase her back to them people.

JULIUS. Sure! That's just what I'd do! That'd be a fine thing . . .

FRAU WOLFF. There's got to be some punishment for things like that. If somebody beats me, I say, I hit him back—

JULIUS. Well, did somebody hit the girl?

FRAU WOLFF. She ran away, didn't she? Oh, Julius, I can't do nothing with you. There's the wood—just lying around on the street. Now, if I said, let's go . . . if you treat my children bad, why I'll take your wood—a fine face you'd make.

JULIUS. No, nothing doing . . . what do I care . . . I can do more than eat bread! And I won't stand for things like that . . . I won't stand for them hitting that girl!

FRAU WOLFF. Well? Don't just stand there gabbing. Go get

your rope. Just show them people you got some pluck. In an hour the whole thing will be over. Then we'll go and get some sleep. And tomorrow no need for you to go into the woods. And we'll have wood, more'n we can use.

JULIUS. Well, if they find out . . . I don't give a damn.

FRAU WOLFF. And why should they? Just watch you don't wake up the girls.

MITTELDORF (*outside*). Frau Wolff, Frau Wolff, are you still up?

FRAU WOLFF. Sure, Mitteldorf, come on in! (*She opens the door.*)

MITTELDORF (*enters. He wears a shabby uniform and an overcoat. There is something Mephistophelian in his face. His nose has an alcoholic-red tint. His behavior is gentle, almost shy. His speech is slow, dragging, and his face expressionless.*) Good-evening, Frau Wolff.

FRAU WOLFF. Good-night, you mean.

MITTELDORF. I was here before, a while ago. First I thought I saw some light; then suddenly everything was dark. And nobody answered. Now this time I was quite sure I saw light and so I thought I'd drop by again.

FRAU WOLFF. Well, what is it, Mitteldorf?

MITTELDORF (*sits down and thinks for a while; then*). That's why I came. I got something from the Superintendent's wife.

FRAU WOLFF. She wants me come and do the laundry, huh?

MITTELDORF (*raises his eyebrows in deep thought*). Yes, that's right!

FRAU WOLFF. When does she want me?

MITTELDORF. Tomorrow. Tomorrow morning.

FRAU WOLFF. And you tell me that the night before . . . at twelve o'clock?

MITTELDORF. Tomorrow is laundry day at the Superintendent's.

FRAU WOLFF. But I got to know a few days ahead of time.

MITTELDORF. Sure, sure. Don't get upset now. I just plumb forgot about it. I got so many things in my head, it's easy to forget something like that.

FRAU WOLFF. Well, Mitteldorf, I'll manage. We're friends after all, huh? I know you got a pile of troubles with your eleven children. You don't have to let her bawl you out.

MITTELDORF. If you don't come, Mother Wolff, I'd sure be in Dutch tomorrow morning.

FRAU WOLFF. I'll be there, don't worry. Here, have a drink. You sure can use one. (*She gives him a glass of grog.*) Just had some hot water on the stove. We still got to go out—over to Treptow get some nice fat geese. In the daytime we just ain't got the time. That's the way it is. Poor people just got to work day and night. The rich can spend their time in bed.

MITTELDORF. I got my notice, did you know that? The Superintendent gave me my notice. I ain't snappy enough going after the people.

FRAU WOLFF. What do they want? Are people supposed to be like bloodhounds?

MITTELDORF. I'd just as soon not go home at all. If I do there'd be nothing but fighting; nothing to listen to but complaints.

FRAU WOLFF. Why, just plug your ears!

MITTELDORF. So you go to the tavern a little now and then to forget your troubles. That you ain't supposed to do neither. Nothing you're supposed to do! Now take today: I've been sitting in the tavern a while . . . somebody put up a keg.

FRAU WOLFF. But you ain't going to be scared of a woman! If she calls you names, go ahead and call her names! If she hits you, hit her back.—Come on over here . . . you're taller than me. Get that stuff down from up there. And you get the sleigh ready, Julius. (JULIUS *leaves.*) How often do I have to tell you. (MITTELDORF *gets strings and ropes down from a high shelf.*) Get the big sleigh ready. Just hand them strings to me.

JULIUS (*outside*). Can't see a thing.

FRAU WOLFF. What can't you do?

JULIUS (*stands in the door*). I can't get that sleigh out all by myself. All kinds of stuff's piled all over the thing. And without a light I just can't do it no how.

FRAU WOLFF. Oh, you're really helpless! (*She hurriedly ties kerchiefs around her head and chest.*) Just wait a minute, I'll come and help you. Take the lantern there, Mitteldorf! (MITTELDORF *struggles to get down a lantern and gives it to* FRAU WOLFF.) That's it, thanks. (*She puts the candle into the lantern.*) That goes in here, and now we're ready to go. I'm coming—I'll help you get that sleigh out! (*She goes ahead carrying the lantern.* MITTELDORF *follows. When she reaches the door she turns around and hands* MITTELDORF *the lantern.*) You can hold the light for us just for a moment!

MITTELDORF (*holding the lantern and singing to himself*).
The morn glows re–ed, the morn glows re–ed . . .

CURTAIN

ACT II

(*The office of the Police Superintendent, VON WEHRHAHN; it is a large, bare room; the walls and the ceiling are white, there are three windows in the rear wall. The entrance door is on the left wall. Along the right wall stands a long desk on which books, files, etc., are piled; behind it is the chair for the Superintendent. Near the center window are a table and chair for the clerk. A softwood bookcase filled with books is toward the front on the right, placed so that the books will be handy when the Superintendent sits at his desk. File shelves cover the left wall. In front there are six chairs; they stand with their backs to the audience in a row that starts at the left-hand wall. It is a clear winter morning. The clerk, GLASENAPP, sits at his place and writes. He looks insignificant and wears glasses. The Superintendent, VON WEHRHAHN, enters quickly, carrying a file of documents under his arm. WEHRHAHN is almost forty years old and wears a monocle. He gives the impression of belonging to the landed gentry. As his official dress he wears a black frockcoat, buttoned all the way up, and high boots that are pulled over his trousers. His voice is high-pitched, almost a falsetto, and he expresses himself with military conciseness.*)

WEHRHAHN (*off-hand, as if he were terribly busy*). Morning!
GLASENAPP (*getting up*). Your servant, Herr Superintendent!
WEHRHAHN. Anything happened, Glasenapp?
GLASENAPP (*standing, leafing through some papers*). I wish to report, Herr Superintendent—first, there was—yes! Fiebig, the innkeeper. He is asking for permission, Herr Superintendent, to be allowed to have dance music next Sunday.

WEHRHAHN. Fiebig? Isn't that . . . seems to me, somebody rented his dance hall recently . . . ?

GLASENAPP. To the Liberals. Yes sir, Herr Baron!

WEHRHAHN. The same Fiebig?

GLASENAPP. Yes sir, Herr Baron!

WEHRHAHN. We're going to have to put the bit on him!

(BAILIFF MITTELDORF *enters.*)

MITTELDORF. Your servant, Herr Baron!

WEHRHAHN. Listen—once and for all—when I'm on duty I'm the Superintendent.

MITTELDORF. Yes sir. Yes sir, Herr Ba— . . . Herr Superintendent, I meant to say.

WEHRHAHN. Try to remember that now: that I'm a baron is beside the point. It doesn't matter at all here. (*To* GLASENAPP.) Now please, tell me the rest. Hasn't Motes, the writer, been here?

GLASENAPP. Yes sir, Herr Superintendent.

WEHRHAHN. So. He was here? I'm very curious. I hope he's going to come back?

GLASENAPP. He said he'd be back toward eleven-thirty.

WEHRHAHN. Did he tell you anything by any chance, Glasenapp?

GLASENAPP. He was here in the matter of Dr. Fleischer.

WEHRHAHN. Tell me something, Glasenapp. Do you know this Dr. Fleischer?

GLASENAPP. He lives in Krueger's house; that's all I know.

WEHRHAHN. How long has he been living here?

GLASENAPP. I've been here only since last fall.

WEHRHAHN. That's right; you came at the same time I did, and I've been here about four months.

GLASENAPP (*glancing at* MITTELDORF). I think he must have been here about two years.

WEHRHAHN (*to* MITTELDORF). You wouldn't know anything about that, of course?

MITTELDORF. At your service, sir; he's been here since the fall before last.

WEHRHAHN. What? Did he move here at that time?

MITTELDORF. At your service, sir; from Berlin, Herr . . . Superintendent.

WEHRHAHN. Do you know this individual pretty well, then?

MITTELDORF. I just know his brother is the cashier at a theater.

WEHRHAHN. I don't care about his brother. What does he do? What's his occupation? Who is he?

MITTELDORF. Well, I don't think I know too much about that. Only that he's sick, people say. Seems he's got diabetes.

WEHRHAHN. I don't care whether he is sick or not. As far as I'm concerned he can spit molasses if he feels like it. What does he do?

GLASENAPP (*shrugs his shoulders*). A scientist he calls himself.

WEHRHAHN. *Sci—sci*entist, not scentist!

GLASENAPP. The bookbinder, Hugk, has got some of his books. Every week he gives him some for binding.

WEHRHAHN. I'd like to see what that man reads, some time.

GLASENAPP. The postman thinks he must read twenty newspapers. Some even Democratic, too.

WEHRHAHN. Tell Hugk to come and see me.

GLASENAPP. Right away?

WEHRHAHN. No, any time. Tomorrow, the day after . . . He might as well bring some of those books along. (*To* MITTELDORF.) You seem to be asleep all day long—or does that man have good cigars perhaps?

MITTELDORF. But—Herr Superintendent!

WEHRHAHN. Never mind. I'll take a look at those people. My predecessor here . . . he's just let things go to pot completely. Well, we'll get it straightened out after a while. —For anybody connected with the police to take gratuities from anybody is contemptible! To you, that's Chinese, of course. (*To* GLASENAPP.) Motes didn't say anything definite, did he?

GLASENAPP. No, not exactly anything definite. He said, Herr Superintendent would know . . .

WEHRHAHN. I just know in general. I've had an eye on that man for some time. Dr. Fleischer, I mean. Herr Motes just confirmed that I was completely right in sizing the man up.—What kind of a reputation does Motes have? (GLASENAPP *and* MITTELDORF *look at each other.* GLASENAPP *shrugs his shoulders.*) Borrows all over the place, does he?

GLASENAPP. He says he has a pension.

WEHRHAHN. A pension?

GLASENAPP. Well, he got shot in the eye.

WEHRHAHN. That would be money paid as damages, then.

GLASENAPP. Begging your pardon, sir. I think there's been

plenty of damage, but as for the money, nobody's seen any of it.

WEHRHAHN (*amused*). Anything else of importance?

GLASENAPP. Just—little things, sir. A removal notice.

WEHRHAHN. All right, all right. Did you ever hear that Fleischer talks a lot?

GLASENAPP. No, I don't remember that I did.

WEHRHAHN. Because that's what I've been told. That he makes illegal speeches about important personages. Well, we'll see about all that. Now we got to get down to work. Well, Mitteldorf, anything you want to say?

MITTELDORF. Seems something was stolen last night.

WEHRHAHN. Stolen? Where?

MITTELDORF. At Krueger's.

WEHRHAHN. What's been stolen?

MITTELDORF. Firewood.

WEHRHAHN. Last night? Or when?

MITTELDORF. Last night.

WEHRHAHN. And who told you that?

MITTELDORF. Well Herr . . .

WEHRHAHN. Come on now! Who told you?

MITTELDORF. It was . . . Herr Fleischer who told me.

WEHRHAHN. What? You talk to that man?

MITTELDORF. Herr Krueger himself told me, too.

WEHRHAHN. That man's a permanent complainer. Every week he writes me at least three letters. Somebody cheated him, or somebody broke his fence, or somebody moved the boundary marker on his property. Just a lot of annoying trifles.

MOTES (*enters. He laughs nervously and almost continuously, while he talks.*) Your servant, Herr Superintendent, your servant!

WEHRHAHN. Well, here you are. Delighted you could come. Perhaps you could tell me right away: seems something was stolen from Krueger?

MOTES. I don't live there anymore.

WEHRHAHN. And you didn't hear anything about it, Herr Motes?

MOTES. Yes, I've heard something—but nothing very definite. When I passed by his house just now, they were looking for traces in the snow.

WEHRHAHN. Is that right? Dr. Fleischer is helping him? So those two are pretty good friends, eh?

MOTES. Like two brothers. Hand-in-glove, sir.

WEHRHAHN. Now, as for this man, Fleischer. That's what I'm primarily interested in. Please, sit down!—I can tell you, I didn't close an eye all night. Couldn't sleep at all because of this business. You wrote me a letter that's got me all upset. That's a matter of temperament, of course. My predecessor here, it wouldn't have bothered him one bit—oh no! But I, I've decided definitely you might say to push through to the heart of the matter. What I am supposed to do here is to survey and to clean up. The garbage that has accumulated here under the protection of my worthy predecessor! Peculiar people, political outcasts, enemies of King and country! I'll make those people squirm!—Now then, Herr Motes. You are an author?

MOTES. I write about such subjects as hunting and forestry, yes, sir.

WEHRHAHN. Then you probably write in journals for hunting and forestry? Incidentally, can you live on that?

MOTES. If one has contacts as I have them, Herr Baron, yes, thank God, I make quite a nice living.

WEHRHAHN. You studied forestry, did you?

MOTES. Yes, sir, I attended the Forestry Academy. Studied at Eberswalde. Then, just before my exam, this accident happened . . .

WEHRHAHN. Yes of course, you're wearing an eye patch.

MOTES. I lost my eye hunting, Herr Baron. Got buckshot into my right eye. I never did find out who did it. So, I had to break off my career.

WEHRHAHN. You don't get a pension, then?

MOTES. No, sir. But I've managed to get along. Fortunately, by now my name is pretty well known.

WEHRHAHN. Hm. Do you know my brother-in-law by any chance?

MOTES. Chief Forester von Wachsmann? Yes, indeed. I have quite a correspondence with him. And we belong to the same club, The Association of Pointer Breeders.

WEHRHAHN (*fairly sighing with relief*). Is that so. So you know him? I'm delighted to hear that. That makes things much easier, sets the tone for mutual understanding and confidence. The road is clear, Herr Motes!—Now, in your letter you wrote me you have had an opportunity to observe Dr. Fleischer. Tell me a little what you know about him.

MOTES (*clearing his throat*). When I . . . when I went to live in Krueger's house about a year ago, Herr Baron, I didn't have the faintest idea with what sort of people I would be thrown into contact.

WEHRHAHN. You didn't know either Krueger or Fleischer?

MOTES. No, sir. And the way things are in a home, there isn't a chance to keep apart.

WEHRHAHN. What sort of people used to come to the house?

MOTES (*with a significant gesture*). Oh, *that* sort!

WEHRHAHN. I understand.

MOTES. Every Tom, Dick, and Harry! Democrats, Liberals . . .

WEHRHAHN. Were there regular meetings?

MOTES. Every Thursday, as far as I know.

WEHRHAHN. We shall pay a little attention to that!—Do you still see these people?

MOTES. In the end, I just couldn't stand it any more, sir.

WEHRHAHN. Pretty disagreeable, huh?

MOTES. I absolutely loathed them.

WEHRHAHN. All these subversive goings-on, the impudent mocking of high personages, you just couldn't stand that any more?

MOTES. I stayed because I thought, who knows, perhaps it would be good for something.

WEHRHAHN. Finally, though, you did give notice?

MOTES. Yes, Herr Baron, finally I moved away.

WEHRHAHN. And now you've decided . . .

MOTES. I considered it my duty.

WEHRHAHN. . . . to inform the authorities. I think that's very honorable. So he said something—we'll draw up a statement later, of course—he said something concerning a personage that stands high in the esteem of all of us.

MOTES. Exactly, sir. That's what he did.

WEHRHAHN. You would be prepared to state this under oath, if necessary?

MOTES. Yes indeed, sir, I would.

WEHRHAHN. That's what you would have to do.

MOTES. Yes sir, Herr Baron.

WEHRHAHN. It would be best, of course, if we could find a second witness.

MOTES. I could look around, Herr Baron. Only the man throws his money around in a way . . .

WEHRHAHN. Oh, just wait a minute, there's Krueger coming now. I'd rather finish with him first. At any rate, I'm most grateful for your energetic help. One really has to rely on that if one wants to accomplish anything these days.

KRUEGER (*enters, excited and in a hurry*). Dear God! Good morning, Herr Superintendent.

WEHRHAHN (*to* MOTES). If you will excuse me for a moment! (*Arrogantly inquiring, to* KRUEGER.) And what do you want?

(KRUEGER *is a small man, somewhat hard of hearing, almost seventy. He walks with a slight stoop, the left shoulder a little lower than the right, but is otherwise still quite active; he underlines his words with vigorous gestures. He wears a fur cap which he carries in his hand, a brown winter overcoat and a thick wool muffler around his neck.*)

KRUEGER (*bursting with annoyance, shouts*). I've been robbed, Herr Superintendent! (*Catching his breath, he wipes the perspiration off his forehead with his handkerchief and looks at the* SUPERINTENDENT's *mouth as people who are hard-of-hearing are wont to do.*)

WEHRHAHN. Robbed? Is that so?

KRUEGER (*already irritated*). Yes sir, robbed! I've been robbed! They've stolen two yards of firewood.

WEHRHAHN (*looking around with the trace of a smile, unimpressed*). Nothing like that seems to have happened around here in quite a while.

KRUEGER (*his hand at his ear*). What? Nothing's happened! Good God! Do you think I'm here just to while away the time?

WEHRHAHN. You don't have to get insulting. What's your name by the way?

KRUEGER (*taken aback*). My name?

WEHRHAHN. Yes, your name.

KRUEGER. You still don't know my name? It seems to me I've had the pleasure of meeting you before.

WEHRHAHN. Sorry. I just can't remember. Wouldn't matter in this case anyway.

KRUEGER (*resigning himself*). My name is Krueger.

WEHRHAHN. Living on your income?

KRUEGER (*vehemently, ironically and quickly*). Yes indeed. Living on my income. I also own some houses.

WEHRHAHN. Do you have any identification?

KRUEGER. I-Identification? My name is Krueger. There's no point in making a lot of fuss about it. I've been living here for thirty years. Any child on the street can tell you who I am.

WEHRHAHN. I don't care a bit how long you've been living here. All I want is some proof of your identity. Do you know this gentleman, Mr. Motes? (MOTES *half rises with an angry face*.) Oh, yes, I understand. Please remain seated. What do you say, Glasenapp?

GLASENAPP. Yes sir. Your servant. This is Herr Krueger. He lives here.

WEHRHAHN. All right. Now—you say some wood has been stolen?

KRUEGER. Yes. Wood. Two cords of pine logs.

WEHRHAHN. Did you have the wood in the shed?

KRUEGER (*getting violent again*). That's something else again. That's a separate complaint.

WEHRHAHN (*turning to the others, with a quick and ironical laugh*). Another one?

KRUEGER. What did you say?

WEHRHAHN. Nothing. Just continue your story. So the wood was not in the shed?

KRUEGER. The wood was in the garden. That is—it was in front of the garden.

WEHRHAHN. In other words, it was on the street?

KRUEGER. It was on my property, outside the garden fence.

WEHRHAHN. So that anybody could get at it without any trouble?

KRUEGER. That's the fault of the servant girl. She was supposed to bring the wood into the shed last night.

WEHRHAHN. And she forgot all about it?

KRUEGER. She refused—she simply refused to do it. And when I insisted she simply ran away. I'll sue her parents for that. I demand full damages.

WEHRHAHN. That, you can handle any way you want. But it probably wouldn't do you much good.—Do you have any suspicions?

KRUEGER. No. Everybody around here is a thief.

WEHRHAHN. Please, try not to generalize. You really have to give me some clue.

KRUEGER. I'm not going to accuse anybody—just like that.

WEHRHAHN. Who lives in your house besides yourself?

KRUEGER. Dr. Fleischer.

WEHRHAHN (*pretending to be in deep thought*). Dr. Fleischer—Dr. Fleischer—Dr. Fleischer? Isn't that the man who . . .

KRUEGER. ... has an enormous knowledge. He is a great scholar.

WEHRHAHN. And the two of you are—intimate friends?

KRUEGER. That's my business who my intimate friends are. That's got nothing to do with what we are talking about, it seems to me.

WEHRHAHN. How am I going to find out anything about this business? You have to give me a hint at least.

KRUEGER. I have to? Good God! I have to? So here I am, simply reporting that two cords of wood have been stolen from me . . .

WEHRHAHN. You must have some idea at least. *Somebody* must have stolen the wood.

KRUEGER. Wha—? Yes, I'm sure it wasn't I. That's certain.

WEHRHAHN. But my dear man . . .

KRUEGER. Krueger is my name.

WEHRHAHN (*giving in, apparently bored*). Ah well. —All right. Glasenapp, prepare the deposition.—Now, what's that story about the servant girl, Herr Krueger? The girl ran away?

KRUEGER. That's just what she did. Back to her parents.

WEHRHAHN. Do the parents live here?

KRUEGER. What's that about—beer?

WEHRHAHN. I am asking you whether the parents live here in the village?

GLASENAPP. She's the daughter of the washerwoman, Frau Wolff.

WEHRHAHN. Frau Wolff? The one who's doing our laundry today, Glasenapp?

GLASENAPP. Yes, sir.

WEHRHAHN (*shaking his head*). Extremely curious! Such a hard-working, decent woman. (*To* KRUEGER.) Is that right? Frau Wolff's daughter?

KRUEGER. I'm telling you: the daughter of the washerwoman, Wolff.

WEHRHAHN. And did the girl come back?

KRUEGER. She hasn't come back yet.

WEHRHAHN. Well, let's call Frau Wolff. Eh, Mitteldorf! I hope you aren't too tired—just run over across the yard and tell Frau Wolff to come here right away. Please, sit down, Herr Krueger.

KRUEGER (*sitting down, sighs*). Good God! What a life!

WEHRHAHN (*in a subdued tone to* MOTES *and* GLASENAPP). I'm really curious what this is going to be. Something must be wrong here. I'm really setting great stock in that woman. She works like four men. My wife says that she'd have to have two women to do the laundry if Frau Wolff didn't do it.—She's got pretty sound ideas, too.

MOTES. She's got notions to see her daughters on the stage . . .

WEHRHAHN. Oh well, she may well have a little foolishness in her, too. But that doesn't reflect on her character. What have you got there, Herr Motes?

MOTES. Wire snares. I'm going to give them to Forester Seidel.

WEHRHAHN. Oh, let me take a look at them. (*He holds one in his hands and studies it attentively.*) Hm, that'll slowly throttle an animal all right.

(FRAU WOLFF *enters,* MITTELDORF *behind her. She is drying her hands that are still wet from washing the laundry.*)

FRAU WOLFF (*frankly, pleasantly, with a quick glance at the snares*). Here I am. What's up? What you want me for?

WEHRHAHN. Frau Wolff, do you know this gentleman?

FRAU WOLFF. And which gentleman, may I ask? (*Pointing one finger at* KRUEGER.) This one? That's Herr Krueger. I should know him, I should think. Good-morning, Herr Krueger.

WEHRHAHN. Your daughter works at Herr Krueger's house?

FRAU WOLFF. Who? My daughter? Sure. Leontine. (*To* KRUEGER.) I should say did work—after all she ran away from you.

KRUEGER (*furiously*). That, indeed, she did!

WEHRHAHN (*interrupting*). Now, just a minute!

FRAU WOLFF. Just what did you two fight about?

WEHRHAHN. Frau Wolff, now listen to me! Your daughter has to go back to the Kruegers.

FRAU WOLFF. Oh no! We're going to keep her home now.

WEHRHAHN. That won't be as easy as you think. If necessary, Herr Krueger has the right to ask the police for assistance. In that case, we'd have to bring your daughter back.

FRAU WOLFF. It's just that my husband's got the idea into his head. Just won't let her leave! And once my husband got something in his noodle . . . God, you men get so awful furious sometimes!

WEHRHAHN. Never mind that now, Frau Wolff. How long has your daughter been home?

FRAU WOLFF. Since last night.

WEHRHAHN. Fine. Since yesterday. Seems she was supposed to carry firewood into the shed and refused to do it.

FRAU WOLFF. What? Refused? That girl don't refuse no work. I'd show her all right!

WEHRHAHN. You heard what Frau Wolff said.

FRAU WOLFF. That girl's always been willing. If she'd refused to give me a hand just once . . .

KRUEGER. She refused to carry in the wood.

FRAU WOLFF. Why, sure—lugging wood, at near eleven o'clock at night, who'd ask a child like that . . .

WEHRHAHN. The important thing, Frau Wolff, is that the wood stayed outside, and was stolen last night. Now . . .

KRUEGER (exploding). You are going to replace that wood, Frau Wolff!

WEHRHAHN. We'll see about that. Just a minute!

KRUEGER. Every last penny's worth you are going to replace!

FRAU WOLFF. What do you know about that! Them's new tricks they are! Did I steal your blasted wood?

WEHRHAHN. Just let the man calm himself a little.

FRAU WOLFF. Eh, if Herr Krueger starts with stuff like that . . . pay for the wood and things like that . . . he's talking to the wrong person. I'm always kind enough to everybody. Nobody can't say nothing about that. But if I got to—why not?—I'm going to speak my piece and no bones about it. I'm doing my duty and that's all. Nobody in the whole village can't say nothing about that. But I ain't going to let nobody walk all over me!

WEHRHAHN. Please keep calm, Frau Wolff. There's no reason at all to get excited, just keep calm. After all, we're not strangers. Nobody is going to deny that you're a hard worker and a very decent woman. Tell me now, what do you have to say about it?

KRUEGER. She has nothing to say about it!

FRAU WOLFF. Is that so? Now I've seen everything! Isn't that girl my daughter? And I've nothing to say about it? I'm not that stupid! You don't know Mother Wolff! I'm not going to keep quiet for nobody, not for the Superintendent, and much less for you, believe you me!

WEHRHAHN. I can well understand that you're upset, Frau Wolff, but it would really be much more useful if you'd stay calm.

FRAU WOLFF. Here I've been working for them people,

doing their laundry for ten years. Always got along just fine with them. And now all of a sudden they come up with things like that? I'm not going to work for you no more and that's a fact!

KRUEGER. I'm sure you won't have to. There are lots of women who can do the laundry.

FRAU WOLFF. And the fruit and vegetables from your garden?—Better find somebody else to peddle them for you!

KRUEGER. Don't worry, we will.—Why didn't you just take a good stick and chase your daughter back to us?

FRAU WOLFF. Me stand by and watch my own daughter being exploited and abused?

KRUEGER. And just who's been abusing your daughter if I may ask?

FRAU WOLFF (to WEHRHAHN). Just nothing but skin and bones she is, that girl.

KRUEGER. Then she'd better not stay out dancing half the night.

FRAU WOLFF. I suppose she's been sleeping like a log all day?

WEHRHAHN (speaking to KRUEGER over FRAU WOLFF's head). Just where did you buy that firewood?

FRAU WOLFF. Well, is this thing going to drag on much longer?

WEHRHAHN. Why do you ask, Frau Wolff?

FRAU WOLFF. Because of the laundry. Can't get that done if I'm standing around here all day.

WEHRHAHN. I can't worry about that, Frau Wolff.

FRAU WOLFF. Oh? And your wife? What's she going to say? You better go talk to her about it, Herr Superintendent.

WEHRHAHN. We'll be finished in a minute.—You can tell us, Frau Wolff. After all, you know everyone in the village. Who do you think might have done it? Who just might have stolen that wood?

FRAU WOLFF. I wouldn't know a thing about that, sir.

WEHRHAHN. You didn't notice anything suspicious?

FRAU WOLFF. I wasn't even home last night. Had to go over to Treptow to buy geese.

WEHRHAHN. About what time was that?

FRAU WOLFF. Shortly after ten. Mitteldorf here was there when we left.

WEHRHAHN. And you didn't see a load of wood going by anywhere?

FRAU WOLFF. Not that I know.

WEHRHAHN. And you, Mitteldorf, you didn't notice anything?

MITTELDORF (*after thinking for a while*). I didn't observe nothing suspicious.

WEHRHAHN. Of course not. Just as I thought. (*To* KRUEGER.) So where did you buy the wood?

KRUEGER. Why do you want to know that, I'd like to know.

WEHRHAHN. I think you better leave that to me.

KRUEGER. From the Forest Administration, naturally.

WEHRHAHN. That isn't so natural at all. There are, for instance, wood dealers. Take me, I buy my wood at Sandberg's. Why couldn't you have bought your wood from a dealer? It's cheaper most of the time.

KRUEGER (*impatiently*). I don't have time for these questions, Herr Superintendent!

WEHRHAHN. You don't have time? You haven't got time? Did you come to see me or the other way round? Do I take up your time, or are you wasting mine?

KRUEGER. That's your job. That's what you're here for.

WEHRHAHN. What? Do you think I'm here to brush your shoes?

KRUEGER. And did I steal silver spoons? Don't talk to me like a sergeant! I won't stand for it!

WEHRHAHN. This is really the end . . . Don't you shout at me!

KRUEGER. You are shouting, sir!

WEHRHAHN. I'm shouting because you're half deaf.

KRUEGER. You shout all the time, you shout at everybody who comes to your office.

WEHRHAHN. I don't shout at anybody! Quiet now!

KRUEGER. You think you are God knows what around here. Pestering everybody in the village . . .

WEHRHAHN. You haven't seen anything yet! Just wait until I really start being unpleasant.

KRUEGER. That doesn't impress me one bit. You're just dying to be somebody, that's all. Just blowing yourself up, that's all. Playing the king . . .

WEHRHAHN. I *am* king around here!

KRUEGER (*laughing heartily*). Ha, ha, ha, ha. Never mind, as far as I'm concerned you're nobody. You're simply a Police Superintendent. And you got to learn be one first, at that.

WEHRHAHN. Mister, if you don't keep quiet this minute . . .

KRUEGER. You'll have me arrested, is that it? I wouldn't ad-

vise you to do that. That could really become dangerous
for you.

WEHRHAHN. Dangerous? You? (*To* MOTES.) Did you hear
that? (*To* KRUEGER.) You can go and agitate and scheme all
you want, you and your delightful friends, you're not going to
budge me.

KRUEGER. Good God! Agitate against you? I? You aren't
anywhere near important enough to me. If you don't change
your methods, believe me, it won't take long until you've
caused so much trouble you'll be completely impossible
around here.

WEHRHAHN (*to* MOTES.) One just has to take his age
into account!

KRUEGER. I request that you take my deposition.

WEHRHAHN (*digging among his papers*). Please be good
enough to report the facts in writing. I don't have time
just now.

(KRUEGER *is dumfounded, looks at* WEHRHAHN, *then turns
violently and leaves the room without a word.*)

WEHRHAHN (*after an embarrassed silence*). People always come with these silly trifles! Bah! (*To* FRAU WOLFF.)
You better get back to your laundry.—I can tell you, my dear
Motes, they really make it difficult to do a job. If one wasn't
dedicated to his work, one would be sorely tempted sometimes just to throw in the towel. But, for myself, the watch-
word is . . . Courage! Stay at your post! After all, what is it
we are fighting for? The nation's most noble aspirations!

CURTAIN

ACT III

(FRAU WOLFF'S *house, about eight o'clock in the morning. The water for coffee is boiling on the stove.* FRAU
WOLFF *is sitting on a footstool and counting money,
using the seat of a chair as a table.* JULIUS *comes in
carrying a rabbit he has just killed.*)

JULIUS. For God's sake, put that money away!

FRAU WOLFF (*absorbed in her calculations, rudely*). Oh, why don't you shut up! (*Silence.*)

(JULIUS *throws the rabbit on a stool; unable to make up his mind what to do next he touches one object after another and finally starts polishing his boots. A hunting horn is heard in the distance.*)

JULIUS (*listens, frightened and excited*). Are you going to put that money away?

FRAU WOLFF. Leave me alone, Julius. Just let Motes blow his stupid horn. He's over in the woods and don't think about nothing.

JULIUS. We'll all wind up in the jug because of you!

FRAU WOLFF. Stop talking rubbish. The girl's coming.

ADELHEID (*enters, obviously just out of bed*). Morning, Mom!

FRAU WOLFF. Sleep well?

ADELHEID. You was out last night, wasn't you?

FRAU WOLFF. You must have been dreaming, girl; now get going and bring in some wood. Get moving!

(ADELHEID *playing ball with an orange, goes to the door.*)

FRAU WOLFF. Where did you get that orange?

ADELHEID. Schoebel, the grocer gave it to me.

(*Leaves.*)

FRAU WOLFF. You're not supposed to take no presents from that fellow!—Come over here, Julius, and listen to me. I got fifty-nine talers here. Always the same with that Wulkow. Always has to cheat you out of one at least: sixty he was going to pay he said.—I'm going to put that money in this here bag, understand? You go get a pick-ax, and dig a nice hole in the back of the goat shed. But make sure it's under the feed box so it's nice and dry, and that's where you put the bag, see? And put a flat stone on top. Don't dawdle now!

JULIUS. I thought you was going to pay off something to Fischer.

FRAU WOLFF. Just go and do as I tell you. And don't stand there jabbering all day, understand?

JULIUS. Don't you get me mad or you'll be sorry! I'm not

going to stand for that . . . having the money stay around the house.

FRAU WOLFF. So where would you put it?

JULIUS. Just take it over to Fischer. That's what you said we was going to do . . . pay off something.

FRAU WOLFF. You are the stupidest fool I ever laid eyes on! If you didn't have me you'd really be lost.

JULIUS. Just go . . . yell your head off!

FRAU WOLFF. Sure I have to shout when you're being that stupid! Don't talk so much rubbish and I won't have to shout. If we up and take that money to Fischer, you just watch what happens next.

JULIUS. That's what I've been saying all along . . . damn this whole business! What am I going to get out of sitting in the klink?

FRAU WOLFF. About time you shut up!

JULIUS. Can't you scream any louder?

FRAU WOLFF. No reason for me to go buy another mouth. You're carrying on something awful just about . . . I don't know, about this here little business. Just take care of yourself and don't worry about me!—Did you throw that key into the river yet?

JULIUS. Have I been down to the water?

FRAU WOLFF. About time you got going. Do you want them to find you holding on to that key? (JULIUS *turns to go.*) Hey, just a minute, Julius! Give me that key!

JULIUS. Now what?

FRAU WOLFF (*taking the key*). None of your business. I'll take care of that. (*She puts the key into her clothing, puts coffee into the grinder and starts to grind.*) Go get your work done in the shed now. Then you can come and have coffee.

JULIUS. If I'd only known before! (JULIUS *leaves.* ADELHEID *enters, carrying a load of firewood in her apron.*)

FRAU WOLFF. Where did you take that wood from?

ADELHEID. Well, from that pile of new wood.

FRAU WOLFF. You ain't supposed to touch them new logs.

ADELHEID (*drops the wood in front of the stove*). It sure won't matter if some of that's used.

FRAU WOLFF. And what do you know about that? What's the big idea? You better get dry behind the ears first!

ADELHEID. I know where that's from!

FRAU WOLFF. What do you mean, girl?

ADELHEID. I mean the wood.

FRAU WOLFF. Don't talk rubbish. We bought that at an auction.

ADELHEID (*playing ball with her orange*). Oh, sure! If only it was true!—That's been lifted!

FRAU WOLFF. What was that?

ADELHEID. Lifted! If that ain't Krueger's wood! Leontine even told me.

FRAU WOLFF (*boxes her ears*). That's what I got to say to that! We're no thieves. Go on do your homework. And properly, understand? I'll come and look at what you've done.

ADELHEID (*goes into the other room*). I think I'll go skating.

FRAU WOLFF. And your confirmation class? Forgot all about it, eh?

ADELHEID. That's only on Tuesday.

FRAU WOLFF. It's tomorrow, if you don't mind. Just make sure you learn your Bible lessons. You'll recite them for me later on.

ADELHEID (*is heard yawning loudly in the other room; then she says*). To his disciples Jesus spake, You can use your fingers to eat your cake.

(JULIUS *enters*.)

FRAU WOLFF. Well, did you do the job proper, Julius?

JULIUS. You can do it yourself if you don't like the way I do it.

FRAU WOLFF. Sure would be best if I did. (*She pours coffee into cups both for* JULIUS *and herself, puts the cups, bread and butter on the chair*.) There, have some coffee!

JULIUS. I only hope Wulkow got away all right.

FRAU WOLFF. Why wouldn't he, with that thaw we're having?

JULIUS. You call that a thaw?

FRAU WOLFF. So it's freezing a bit. That's no reason for him to get stuck. He's quite a ways up the canal by now, more than likely.

JULIUS. I only hope he isn't still down by the bridge!

FRAU WOLFF. I don't care where he is.

JULIUS. That Wulkow, one of these days he's really going to get nabbed, believe me.

FRAU WOLFF. That's his look-out.

JULIUS. Sure. Only he'd get all of us in trouble. Just let them find that fur coat on his barge.

FRAU WOLFF. Fur coat? What are you talking about?

JULIUS. Krueger's fur coat, what do you think?

FRAU WOLFF. Don't talk so much trash, understand? You'll put your foot in your mouth yet, gabbing about everybody's business!

JULIUS. So that don't concern me none, huh?

FRAU WOLFF. The hell it concerns you. It's none of your business, I'm telling you. I'm taking care of that. You ain't even a man; an old woman that's what you are. Here's some money for you, now get out of my way. Why don't you go over to Fiebig and bend your elbow for a while? I don't mind if you have yourself a real gay Sunday. (*Knocking at the door.*) Come in, come in, whoever it is.

(DR. FLEISCHER *enters with his five-year-old son. He is twenty-seven, has black hair, a beard and mustache that are just as black, deep-set eyes and a soft voice. He wears a suit cut in the style of the "reform clothing" movement led by Jäger. His continual concern for the boy is touching.*)

FRAU WOLFF (*delighted*). Oh, there's Philipp paying us a visit for a change! That's real nice. I'm real flattered! (*She takes the child and takes off his overcoat.*) Come, take off your overcoat. It's warm in here, you won't be cold.

FLEISCHER (*concerned*). I think there is a draft, Frau Wolff. I'm positive there's a draft.

FRAU WOLFF. Who's going to be such a softie! A little draft won't hurt the boy.

FLEISCHER. Heavens, no! You don't know him! That boy'll catch cold in a second. Move around, Philipp. Keep moving around.

(PHILIPP *wiggles his shoulders in disapproval, and squeals.*)

FLEISCHER. Yes, Philipp, you see, otherwise you'll get sick. Just walk up and down slowly.

PHILIPP (*stubbornly*). I don't want to!

FRAU WOLFF. Oh, let him be.

FLEISCHER. Good-morning, Frau Wolff.

FRAU WOLFF. Good-morning, Dr. Fleischer. Coming to see us again? It's been a long time.

FLEISCHER. Good-morning, Herr Wolff.

JULIUS. Good-morning, Herr Fleischer.

FRAU WOLFF. Well, make yourself at home. Sit down.

FLEISCHER. We really don't mean to stay long.

FRAU WOLFF. Well, if we've such nice visitors first thing in the morning, we're sure going to have a good day today. (*Kneeling in front of the boy.*) Isn't that right, little fellow, you're going to bring us luck, huh?

PHILIPP (*excitedly*). I've been to the zoo, and I saw storks and they bited each other with their gold beaks.

FRAU WOLFF. No, is that right? You're telling me stories. (*Cuddles and kisses the boy.*) Boy, oh boy, I could eat you. Herr Fleischer, I'm keeping that boy. He's my boy. You're my boy, aren't you? How's your mommy, huh?

PHILIPP. She's fine. And she sends her love, and you should come and do the laundry tomorrow morning.

FRAU WOLFF. Well, what do you know. What a boy. He can give you real messages already. (*To* FLEISCHER.) Well, aren't you going to sit down for a minute?

FLEISCHER. The boy's been nagging me, he wants to go in a boat. Do you think we could?

FRAU WOLFF. Why, sure. There's no ice on the Spree. The girl can row you around a piece.

FLEISCHER. He just won't give up. He's simply got it into his head.

ADELHEID (*appears in the door from the other room, waves to* PHILIPP). Come on, Philipp, I'll show you something nice.

(PHILIPP *lets out a scream in protest.*)

FLEISCHER. Now, Philipp, don't be naughty!

ADELHEID. There, look at this nice orange!

(PHILIPP *beams, takes a few steps toward* ADELHEID.)

FLEISCHER. All right, go on, but no begging!

ADELHEID. Come on, we'll eat it together. (*She takes a few steps toward the child, takes him by the hand, holds the orange in front of him with the other hand, and both go peacefully into the other room.*)

FRAU WOLFF (*looking after the boy*). Ah, what a boy! I just keep looking at him all the time. I don't know, when I see a boy like that . . . (*She wipes her eyes with a corner of her apron.*) . . . I just feel like crying.

FLEISCHER. Didn't you have a boy?

FRAU WOLFF. Sure. But what good does it do you? Can't

bring him back to life.—So, there you are . . . them's the facts of life.

FLEISCHER. One just can't be careful enough with children.

FRAU WOLFF. You can be as careful as you like. What's going to happen is going to happen. (*Pause. Shaking her head.*) What have you been doing to Motes?

FLEISCHER. I? Nothing. What am I supposed to have done to him?

FRAU WOLFF. Oh, nothing special.

FLEISCHER. How old is your daughter now?

FRAU WOLFF. She'll be finishing school come Easter. How about it? Do you want her, Herr Fleischer? Wouldn't mind a bit having her work in your house.

FLEISCHER. Why not? That wouldn't be a bad idea at all.

FRAU WOLFF. A strong girl she's gotten to be. She's still pretty young but work—I tell you she can work like a horse. Sometimes she's a little bitch, sometimes she just don't know what's good for her. But she's not dumb! You know what I think sometimes? She's almost a genius!

FLEISCHER. Hm, hm, that may well be.

FRAU WOLFF. Just let her once recite something for you, a poem or what not. I can tell you, Doctor, it makes your flesh creep. You call her in some time when you got company from Berlin. You always got all kinds of poets and what not coming to see you. She's got pluck, that one . . . off she goes. She just recites too beautiful!—(*In a changed tone.*) But now let me give you some advice. You won't be mad at me, though, huh?

FLEISCHER. I never get mad about a piece of good advice.

FRAU WOLFF. First of all: don't keep giving away so much stuff! Nobody'll even say thank you. Ingratitude's all you get.

FLEISCHER. But I'm not giving away an awful lot, Frau Wolff.

FRAU WOLFF. Never mind, I know. And don't talk so much. You only get people suspicious. Right away they say: he's a Demicrat. Just watch what you're saying.

FLEISCHER. What do you mean?

FRAU WOLFF. Go ahead and think what you want. But talking, that's something else again; better watch out. Suddenly you're sitting in the klink and don't even know how you got there.

FLEISCHER (*turns pale*). Oh, but that's nonsense, Frau Wolff!

FRAU WOLFF. No, I'm telling you. It's serious.—And then, just watch that fellow!

FLEISCHER. What fellow?

FRAU WOLFF. Well, the one we've been talking about.

FLEISCHER. You don't mean Motes?

FRAU WOLFF. I'm not mentioning no names. You must have done something to him, didn't you?

FLEISCHER. I don't even see him anymore.

FRAU WOLFF. See? Just as I thought!

FLEISCHER. But nobody can blame me for that, Frau Wolff!

FRAU WOLFF. I'm not blaming you.

FLEISCHER. That would be a fine thing! To be friends with a swindler, a notorious swindler!

FRAU WOLFF. That he is. There you're right.

FLEISCHER. Now he's moved to Frau Dreier—Cake-Dreier, they call her. That poor woman better watch out. If she's got anything at all she'll lose it for sure. With a fellow like that ... practically a jail-bird ...

FRAU WOLFF. Well, sometimes he talks ...

FLEISCHER. Is that right? About me? I'd really like to know what he says.

FRAU WOLFF. Seems you've been saying something bad about some high person or something.

FLEISCHER. Oh? You don't know anything definite, do you?

FRAU WOLFF. Him and Wehrhahn, they put their heads together an awful lot. But you know what? I'll tell you something. Why don't you go and see Mother Dreier? The old hag's smelling a rat anyways. First they talked to her so nice and sweet, and now they're ready to take her last shirt.

FLEISCHER. Oh for heaven's sake! This is all just a lot of foolishness.

FRAU WOLFF. You just get yourself over there to the Dreier woman ... that won't do no harm. She told me some story, she did. Seems he's tried to get her to perjure herself. You'd have that fellow right in your pocket, wouldn't you?

FLEISCHER. Well, I might take a walk over there. But really, I don't care a hoot about the whole thing. That'd really be just dandy if a fellow like that ... just let him try! —Philipp, Philipp! Where are you? We have to go.

ADELHEID'S VOICE. We're looking at some nice pictures.

FLEISCHER. By the way, what do you think of that story?

FRAU WOLFF. What story?

FLEISCHER. Haven't you heard?

FRAU WOLFF (*uneasily*). No, I told you. (*Impatiently.*)

Go on, Julius, so you'll be back for lunch. (*To* FLEISCHER.) He's killed a rabbit this morning. Aren't you gone yet, Julius?

JULIUS. Just let me find my cap! All right?

FRAU WOLFF. I just can't stand people taking a whole year to do something. Always thinking, tomorrow is another day. With me, things got to move!

FLEISCHER. At the Kruegers's there's been a . . .

FRAU WOLFF. That's enough! Don't mention that name to me! I'm so damn mad at that man . . . he's really insulted me something awful. The way the both of us used to get along, and then he up and talks bad of me in front of all them people. (*To* JULIUS.) Well? Are you going or aren't you?

JULIUS. I'm going. Just keep your shirt on. Good-morning, Herr Fleischer!

FLEISCHER. Good-by, Herr Wolff!   (JULIUS *leaves.*)

FRAU WOLFF. As I was telling you . . .

FLEISCHER. Yes, you two had quite a fight about that stolen firewood, didn't you? He's been sorry about that ever since.

FRAU WOLFF. That one sorry!

FLEISCHER. No, Mother Wolff, it's true! And after this business now he's even more sorry. He really thinks very highly of you. It would really be better if you made up.

FRAU WOLFF. If he had come and talked to me, reasonable-like—all right. But run to the police right off . . . now really!

FLEISCHER. They just don't have much luck, poor old people. First, a week ago, the firewood, and now the fur coat . . .

FRAU WOLFF. What? Tell me about that piece of news!

FLEISCHER. There's been another robbery.

FRAU WOLFF. Robbery? No fooling!

FLEISCHER. Yes, a brand new fur coat.

FRAU WOLFF. You want to know something? I'm not going to stay around here much longer! What a gang! It just isn't safe no more! Tut-tut. Some people! It's incredible!

FLEISHER. You can imagine the hullabaloo!

FRAU WOLFF. Can't blame them, can you?

FLEISCHER. And pretty expensive that coat was, too. Mink, I believe.

FRAU WOLFF. Would that be something like beaver, Herr Fleischer?

FLEISCHER. It may even have been beaver. They'd been awfully proud of it. And still—I couldn't help laughing to myself. If something like that happens it's always just a bit comical.

FRAU WOLFF. You're really cruel, you know that? That's nothing to laugh about, Herr Fleischer!

FLEISCHER. Well, you don't think I don't feel sorry for the man, do you?

FRAU WOLFF. I just can't understand people like that! I simply can't get it through my head . . . how they simply go and take things that belongs to other people!—No, no. I'd rather work until I drop dead.

FLEISCHER. Do you think you might sort of keep your ears open a little? I believe that fur coat's still in the village.

FRAU WOLFF. You got any suspicions?

FLEISCHER. There was a woman . . . she did the Kruegers' laundry, I believe . . .

FRAU WOLFF. The Mueller woman?

FLEISCHER. Is that the one with the big family?

FRAU WOLFF. That's the one . . . children she's got a heap of, but steal . . . no! Maybe a little filching, that could happen, but steal?

FLEISCHER. Krueger's fired her, of course.

FRAU WOLFF. But they ought to be able to find out about a thing like that, for goodness' sake! That's just plain impossible! Oh, if only I was the Police Superintendent! That man's really too stupid! A real ass! I can see more with my eyes closed than him with both eyes wide open and that glass eye he's wearing to boot!

FLEISCHER. Yes, I wouldn't be surprised if you were right there.

FRAU WOLFF. I can tell you, I wouldn't have no trouble stealing his chair from under his rear end if I had to.

FLEISCHER (*laughs, gets up and calls into the next room*). Come on, Philipp, come now! We have to go. Good-by, Mother Wolff!

FRAU WOLFF. Put something on, Adelheid, and go take them for a little boat ride.

ADELHEID (*comes in, buttoning the last buttons at the neck of her dress; she leads* PHILIPP *by the hand*). I'm ready. (*To* PHILIPP.) Come here, I'll take you on my arm.

FLEISCHER (*worried, helping to dress the child*). Let's button him up well! He catches cold so easily. And it's going to be windy out on the river.

ADELHEID. I'll go on ahead and get the boat ready.

FRAU WOLFF. How're you feeling these days?

FLEISCHER. Much better, thank you, since I've been living out here.

ADELHEID (*calling from the door*). Mom, here's Herr Krueger!

FRAU WOLFF. Who's there?

ADELHEID. Herr Krueger.

FRAU WOLFF. Not possible!

FLEISCHER. Oh yes, he said he'd drop by this morning.

(*Leaves.*)

FRAU WOLFF (*glancing quickly at the pile of wood, starts with great determination to clear it away*). Come on, girl, give me a hand getting that wood out of the way!

ADELHEID. Why, Mom? Oh yes, of course! Because of Herr Krueger!

FRAU WOLFF. Of course, that's why, you silly goose! Is that the way a proper house should look? Is that right for a Sunday morning? What's Herr Krueger going to think of us! (KRUEGER *appears, sweating and puffing.* FRAU WOLFF *shouts in his direction.*) Don't look around, Herr Krueger! The house is in a terrible mess!

KRUEGER (*blurts out*). Good-morning, good-morning! Never mind. You go out to work all week long, so the house can't very well be spic and span on Sunday. You're a good woman. You're an honest woman, Frau Wolff! Let's just forget what happened between us!

FRAU WOLFF (*so moved that she has to wipe her eyes with the corner of her apron now and then*). I never had nothing against you. I always liked to work for you. But then you got so mad I couldn't help myself. But I'm sure sorry about it.

KRUEGER. Well, come on back then and do our laundry! Where is your daughter, Leontine?

FRAU WOLFF. She's out . . . taking some cabbage over to the postmaster.

KRUEGER. You let us have the girl back! We'll give her thirty talers instead of the twenty she's been getting. We've always been satisfied with her. Let's forget and forgive! (*He holds his hand out and* FRAU WOLFF *shakes it.*)

FRAU WOLFF. This whole business . . . that wasn't necessary at all. She's still a silly little girl. And we old people have always gotten along just fine.

KRUEGER. Well, thank God, that's finished! (*Catching his*

breath.) So far at least, everything's all right. Now—tell me something. You know what's happened to me this time. What do you think?

FRAU WOLFF. You know . . . no, I'd better not say anything.

KRUEGER. Now we got this Herr von Wehrhahn there. Harassing honest citizens, chicanery, bothering people—he's great at that. What that man doesn't stick his nose into!

FRAU WOLFF. Only when we need him, he don't seem to have it.

KRUEGER. I'm on my way to his office now to make a report, and I'm not going to stop until this thing's cleared up.

FRAU WOLFF. You mustn't let them get away with it, Herr Krueger!

KRUEGER. Frau Wolff, if I have to turn everything upside down, I'm going to get my fur coat back!

FRAU WOLFF. It's about time they really started to clean up this place, so we can get some peace. They're liable to steal the roof from over your head!

KRUEGER. For Heaven's sake, just think! Two robberies in two weeks! Two cords of logs just like you got there. (*He picks up a piece of wood.*) And good, expensive wood, Frau Wolff!

FRAU WOLFF. No . . . it's enough to get you so angry you get blue in the face! That's really some gang, that is! A damn shame, that's what it is! What next!

KRUEGER (*furiously waving the piece of wood in the air*). And if I have to spend a thousand talers to do it, I'll find those thieves! They'll all wind up in prison!

FRAU WOLFF. God knows, that'd really be a relief!

CURTAIN

ACT IV

(*The* POLICE SUPERINTENDENT's *office.* GLASENAPP *sits at his table.* FRAU WOLFF *and* ADELHEID *are waiting for the* SUPERINTENDENT. *The girl holds a small, cloth-wrapped package in her lap.*)

FRAU WOLFF. He's taking his time again today.

GLASENAPP (*keeps on writing*). Patience! Patience!

FRAU WOLFF. If he's this late again, he won't have no time for us today, neither.

GLASENAPP. Good God! What you have to tell him can't be very important anyway. There are a lot more important things we have to do here.

FRAU WOLFF. Hmph, fine things they are, too, I bet.

GLASENAPP. That's no way to talk! That's not the way to behave here!

FRAU WOLFF. Oh . . . don't blow yourself up like that. The girl's here because Krueger sent her.

GLASENAPP. That fur coat business again, huh?

FRAU WOLFF. Sure. So what?

GLASENAPP. The old geezer's really got himself something to talk about this time. Now he really can go to it—the old bowlegged complainer.

FRAU WOLFF. Complainer yourself! Better see that you find out something about this business!

MITTELDORF (*appears in the door*). He wants you to come over, Glasenapp. Wants to ask you something, the Superintendent does.

GLASENAPP. Oh, these interruptions all the time! (*He throws his pen on the table and leaves.*)

FRAU WOLFF. Morning, Mitteldorf!

MITTELDORF. Good-morning!

FRAU WOLFF. What's the Superintendent doing all this time?

MITTELDORF. Scribbling whole sheets full he does, Mother Wolff. Important stuff, I can tell you. (*Confidentially.*) And you know, something's in the air. Can't tell you what it is, but there's something in the air . . . that's for sure. Just watch, you'll see something. There's going to be some uproar, and when it starts roaring, Mother Wolff . . . it'll really roar! No, like I told you, I don't understand nothing about them things. It's all new to me. Everything's new. And about that new-fangled stuff I don't understand nothing. Something's going to happen. It can't go on like this. The whole place's got to get cleaned up. The old Superintendent, the one we used to have, the one who died . . . why, he was just a bum compared with this one. Eh, I could tell you some stories! I haven't got the time, though. The baron's waiting for me. (*He starts to leave but, on reaching the door, he turns back once more.*) It's going to roar, Mother Wolff, you can believe me! (*Leaves.*)

FRAU WOLFF. Well, if it didn't get him at last! (*Pause.*)

ADELHEID. What was that I'm supposed to say? I forget.

FRAU WOLFF. What did you say to Herr Krueger?

ADELHEID. Well, that I found this here package.

FRAU WOLFF. Right. That's all. You don't have to say no more here, neither. Now don't be shy! Speak up! Usually you know pretty well how to wag your tongue.

WULKOW (*enters*). Good-morning, everybody!

FRAU WOLFF (*stares at* WULKOW, *flabbergasted; after a pause*). I can't believe it! Wulkow—has something snapped up there? What do you think you're doing here?

WULKOW. Why—my wife just had a little one.

FRAU WOLFF. What did she have?

WULKOW. A little girl. So I damn well had to come and get her registered!

FRAU WOLFF. And I thought you were way up along the canal.

WULKOW. I wouldn't mind if I was, Frau Wolff! If it was up to me that's exactly where I'd be. I started off right away. But when I come up to the locks . . . no soap. But ice, and plenty of it! I wait for the river to let go of me . . . I wait for two days and two nights . . . and finally—this thing with my wife starts. So I couldn't do nothing but turn back.

FRAU WOLFF. So you got your barge down at the bridge again?

WULKOW. Sure. Where else?

FRAU WOLFF. Oh, go away!

WULKOW. I only hope nobody's smelled nothing yet.

FRAU WOLFF (*to* ADELHEID). Go get ten pfennigs' worth of thread at the store.

ADELHEID. I'll get it on the way home.

FRAU WOLFF. You're going now, and don't argue!

ADELHEID. As if I was a baby! (*Leaves.*)

FRAU WOLFF (*vehemently*). So you were tied up at the locks, huh?

WULKOW. For two whole days. I'm telling you.

FRAU WOLFF. You go get yourself framed—in a nice gold picture frame! Oh, aren't you smart . . . wearing that fur coat in broad daylight!

WULKOW. Me? Wear the fur coat?

FRAU WOLFF. Sure you were wearing it. And in broad

daylight, too. So as the whole place can get a good look at that nice new fur coat you got.

WULKOW. Oh that . . . that was out where the canal runs right through the middle of the fields.

FRAU WOLFF. Sure! About a quarter of an hour away from where we live! My girl saw you sitting out there. She had to row Dr. Fleischer around, and he of course gets suspicious right away.

WULKOW. I don't know nothing about that. And what's more, I don't care.

(*Steps are heard from the hall outside the room.*)

FRAU WOLFF. Shh, just watch yourself now, Wulkow!

GLASENAPP (*hurries in, apparently imitating the manner of the* SUPERINTENDENT. *In an arrogant tone, he asks* WULKOW). And what do you want?

WEHRHAHN (*still outside in the hall*). What is it you want, girl? You've come to see me? All right, come in. (WEHRHAHN *lets* ADELHEID *enter ahead of himself.*) Haven't got much time, though. Oh, you're the little Wolff girl? Well, sit down then. What have you got there?

ADELHEID. It's about this package. I . . .

WEHRHAHN. Just a minute now. (*To* WULKOW.) And what do you want?

WULKOW. I want to report a birth.

WEHRHAHN. Oh, registry work. Get the books, Glasenapp! No, first I want to get done with this other thing here. (*To* FRAU WOLFF.) What's the matter with your daughter? Did Krueger slap her again?

FRAU WOLFF. No, he hasn't gone that far yet.

WEHRHAHN. Well? What's wrong then?

FRAU WOLFF. It's about this here package . . .

WEHRHAHN (*to* GLASENAPP). Hasn't Motes come yet?

GLASENAPP. No, not yet.

WEHRHAHN. Can't understand that. Well now, my girl, what is it?

GLASENAPP. It's about the stolen fur coat, sir.

WEHRHAHN. Oh that! I won't have time for that today. I just can't do everything at once. (*To* FRAU WOLFF.) She can report to me tomorrow.

FRAU WOLFF. She's tried to talk to you a couple of times already.

WEHRHAHN. So she'll try for the third time tomorrow.

FRAU WOLFF. Only . . . Herr Krueger keeps after her all the time.

WEHRHAHN. How does Krueger get into this?

FRAU WOLFF. The girl's shown him the package.

WEHRHAHN. What kind of a rag is that, anyway? Let me take a look!

FRAU WOLFF. It's got something to do with that fur coat business. That is . . . that's what Herr Krueger thinks.

WEHRHAHN. Well? What's in that rag?

FRAU WOLFF. A green vest's in it. One of Herr Krueger's.

WEHRHAHN. And you found that?

ADELHEID. Yes, I found it. Yes, sir.

WEHRHAHN. And where did you find it?

ADELHEID. When I was walking to the station with Mom. I was just walking along, and then . . .

WEHRHAHN. Never mind. (*To* FRAU WOLFF.) Leave the package here for the time being, and we'll talk about it tomorrow.

FRAU WOLFF. As far as I'm concerned that's fine—but . . .

WEHRHAHN. And who would object?

FRAU WOLFF. It's just . . . Herr Krueger's so terribly anxious about it.

WEHRHAHN. Herr Krueger! Herr Krueger! I don't care one bit about what Herr Krueger thinks. That man is getting to be a pest. One can't rush things like this. After all, he's put up a reward, and we put a notice about it into the official journal, so . . .

GLASENAPP. The way he figures, we're still not doing enough.

WEHRHAHN. What does that mean: not doing enough? We have a statement of the facts in the case. Then he was suspicious of his washerwoman—and we searched her house. What else does he want? If he'd only keep quiet!—Well, as I told you, I think I'll have time for you tomorrow.

FRAU WOLFF. It don't matter to us. We'll be back.

WEHRHAHN. All right then, tomorrow morning.

FRAU WOLFF. Good-by!

ADELHEID (*curtsies*). Good-by!

(FRAU WOLFF *and* ADELHEID *leave*.)

WEHRHAHN (*leafing through his files, to* GLASENAPP). I'm really curious how this is going to work out. Herr Motes has agreed to bring a witness. He thinks that Frau Dreier, the old cake-hag, was standing close by one time when Fleischer made one of his disrespectful remarks. Tell me, about how old is that Dreier woman?

GLASENAPP. Oh—pushing seventy, sir.

WEHRHAHN. A little gone already, huh?

GLASENAPP. Well, that depends. She's still got her wits about her.

WEHRHAHN. I can't tell you, Glasenapp, what a satisfaction it would be for me really to clamp down on this bunch. Just so they get an idea with whom they are dealing. Who wasn't at the Emperor's birthday celebration? Fleischer, of course. That man is capable of absolutely anything. He can make that stupid sheep's face as long as he wants! We know them anyway, these wolves in sheep's clothing. They wouldn't hurt a fly, but when they feel like it they blow up entire cities. They're going to find it a little too hot for comfort around here, though!

MOTES (enters). Your servant!

WEHRHAHN. Well? How are you doing?

MOTES. Frau Dreier will be here about eleven.

WEHRHAHN. This affair is going to stir up quite a bit of dust. There's going to be a lot of screaming. Wehrhahn sticks his nose everywhere. Well, thank God, I am prepared. After all, I'm not here just to have a good time, and my superiors didn't put me here just for fun. Perhaps these people think that a Police Superintendent is just a glorified bailiff. Hah, in that case somebody else could take my place. But the gentlemen who appointed me to this position know very well who I am. They know very well how serious my convictions are. I look upon my office as a sacred calling. The report to the prosecutor is ready. If I send it off today we can have the warrant for his arrest here the day after tomorrow.

MOTES. They'll really jump on me now.

WEHRHAHN. You know that my uncle is a Lord-in-Waiting. I'll have a word with him about you. Good God! There comes Fleischer! What does he want? Did he smell a rat by any chance? (There is a knock at the door. WEHRHAHN shouts.) Come in!

FLEISCHER (enters, pale and excited). Good-morning! (No answer.) I would like to make a report in connection with the recent theft.

WEHRHAHN (*with the policeman's penetrating gaze*). You are Dr. Joseph Fleischer, aren't you?

FLEISCHER. Absolutely correct. My name is Joseph Fleischer.

WEHRHAHN. And you want to make a report?

FLEISCHER. Yes, with your permission. Because I have noticed something that may help to track down the thief of the fur coat.

WEHRHAHN (*drums on the table with his fingers and, affecting an expression of surprise, looks around trying to elicit a smile. Bored.*) And what did you notice that's so terribly important?

FLEISCHER. Of course, if you aren't in the least interested in what I have to report before I even start . . . in that case I prefer . . .

WEHRHAHN (*quickly, arrogantly*). What would you prefer?

FLEISCHER. I would prefer to remain silent.

WEHRHAHN (*turns silently, as if he did not understand, to* MOTES; *then, changing his tone, off-handedly*). I'm really quite busy. I would ask you to be brief.

FLEISCHER. I am busy, too, but I considered it my duty . . .

WEHRHAHN (*interrupting him*). You considered it your duty. That's just wonderful. Now please tell me what you know.

FLEISCHER (*overcoming his repugnance*). Yesterday I went boating. I had Mrs. Wolff's boat. And her daughter was sitting up front rowing.

WEHRHAHN. Is that really essential?

FLEISCHER. Yes, in my opinion it is.

WEHRHAHN (*impatiently drumming with his fingers*). All right, all right! Let's get on with it.

FLEISCHER. We went up pretty close to the locks. A river barge was tied up there. The ice was piled up at that spot. He had probably gotten stuck there.

WEHRHAHN. Hm, is that so! That's really not overwhelmingly interesting. What's the point of this whole story?

FLEISCHER (*restraining himself as best he can*). I must admit that this method . . . Here I am coming to you of my own free will, to volunteer my services to the authorities . . .

GLASENAPP (*impudently*). The Superintendent really hasn't got the time. As few words as possible, please. Say what you have to say but say it briefly.

WEHRHAHN (*vehemently*). To the point! To the point! What do you want?

FLEISCHER (*with distaste*). I am anxious to see this matter cleared up. And in the interest of old Herr Krueger I shall . . .

WEHRHAHN (*bored, yawns*). The sun's blinding me. Close the curtains, please!

FLEISCHER. There was an old bargeman on that barge, probably the owner.

WEHRHAHN (*as before, yawns*). Yes, most likely.

FLEISCHER. This man sat on deck wearing a fur coat which from a distance looked like beaver.

WEHRHAHN (*as before*). I might have thought it was marten.

FLEISCHER. I approached as closely as possible and so I could see pretty well. He was a bedraggled, dirty bargeman, and that fur coat just didn't look as if it had been made for him. It was brand-new, too . . .

WEHRHAHN (*appears to recover consciousness*). I'm listening, I'm listening. And so? And then? What else?

FLEISCHER. What else? That's all.

WEHRHAHN (*appears to come to life again*). I thought you wanted to report something. You mentioned something was very important.

FLEISCHER. I have told you what I came to tell you.

WEHRHAHN. You have told us a story about a bargeman who wore a fur coat. Now it so happens that bargemen sometimes wear fur coats. That's really not great news.

FLEISCHER. You may think about that one way—or another. Under the circumstances I consider I have finished.

(*Leaves.*)

WEHRHAHN. Did you ever see anything like that? On top of everything, that man is hopelessly stupid! He must have gone out of his mind! I have a beaver coat myself, and that doesn't make me a thief by a long shot.—For heaven's sake, what is it now? Isn't there going to be one minute's peace today? (*To* MITTELDORF *who is standing at the door.*) Don't let anybody else in! Herr Motes, I wonder if you would be good enough to go over to my private apartment. We'll be able to talk there without all these constant interruptions.—Krueger again? How many times . . . he's got ants in his pants, that man! If he continues to bother me, I'll have to throw the old idiot out on his ear one of these days!

(KRUEGER *appears in the doorway, accompanied by*
FLEISCHER *and* FRAU WOLFF.)

MITTELDORF (*to* KRUEGER). You can't see the Superintendent, now, Herr Krueger!

KRUEGER. Oh no? Can't see him, indeed! Never mind that!
(*To the others.*) Come on in, we'll see about this. (KRUEGER
steps into the room, followed by the others.)

WEHRHAHN. A little more quiet, please! Can't you see that
I'm busy?

KRUEGER. Go ahead! We can wait. And when you get
through you'll be busy with us!

WEHRHAHN (*to* MOTES). So—please wait in my apartment.
And if you see Frau Dreier outside, please tell her that I
want to see her there, too. You can see yourself—it's absolutely impossible to get anything done here.

KRUEGER (*pointing to* FLEISCHER). This gentleman here
has something from Frau Dreier, too. He can even give it to
you in writing.

MOTES. Your servant! Your servant!   (*Leaves.*)

KRUEGER. He'll never be anything else, either!

WEHRHAHN. Keep your observations to yourself if you
don't mind!

KRUEGER. I'll say even more! That man is a swindler!

WEHRHAHN (*pretends not to have heard the remark; to*
WULKOW). Now then, what is it? I'll take care of you first
now. Oh yes, the books, Glasenapp!—No, never mind. I want
to get rid of him first. (*To* KRUEGER.) All right, I'll take
care of you first.

KRUEGER. I would most urgently ask you to do that.

WEHRHAHN. Let's forget about that "urgent"! But what
do you wish to request?

KRUEGER. Request—nothing! I don't want to request anything! I'm here to ask for what I consider is my right.

WEHRHAHN. And what right is that?

KRUEGER. The right I'm talking about, Herr Superintendent,
is the right of a citizen to have the assistance of the authorities in recovering stolen property.

WEHRHAHN. Did anyone deny you that right?

KRUEGER. Oh no! Indeed not! That would be quite pre-
posterous, wouldn't it? But I notice that nothing is done,
nothing happens! There is no progress!

WEHRHAHN. Do you think everything can be done in . . .
just like that?

KRUEGER. No, I don't believe that at all, sir. I probably wouldn't have come here if I did. But I have evidence, sir, that you are not doing anything about my case.

WEHRHAHN. I think I would be amply justified in cutting you short right now. It is really beyond the extent of my duties to listen to this sort of thing. However—for the moment—proceed!

KRUEGER. Cut me short? Oh no! That you can't do at all, sir! As a Prussian citizen I have certain rights. And if you should try to cut me short, we would have an opportunity to continue our conversation elsewhere! You're not taking any interest in my case whatsoever!

WEHRHAHN (*seemingly undisturbed*). All right, go ahead and prove it!

KRUEGER (*pointing to* FRAU WOLFF). This woman here came to see you because her daughter had found something. Although she is a poor woman and has to work, she didn't mind the time and trouble to come here. You turned her away once, and today she came again, and . . .

FRAU WOLFF. Well—the Superintendent just didn't have no time.

WEHRHAHN. Go on!

KRUEGER. I certainly will. I haven't finished by far. What did you tell this woman? You simply told her you didn't have the time to talk about the case. You didn't even question her daughter! So, you don't know one single thing, nothing at all about the entire incident!

WEHRHAHN. I must ask you to restrain yourself a little.

KRUEGER. I'm restrained, sir . . . very, very restrained. I'm far too restrained! Otherwise I'd react quite differently to something like this. What kind of an investigation is this? This gentleman here, Herr Fleischer, comes to you to report something that he has noticed. He has noticed a bargeman wearing a beaver coat and . . .

WEHRHAHN (*holding up one hand*). Sh, just a minute! (*To* WULKOW.) You're a bargeman, aren't you?

WULKOW. Yes sir, I've been shipping on the river for thirty years.

WEHRHAHN. Are you nervous? You have a peculiar twitch there.

WULKOW. I just got a little frightened just now.

WEHRHAHN. Do river bargemen often wear fur coats?

WULKOW. Sure. Sure, there's quite a few who got fur coats.

WEHRHAHN. The gentleman over there has seen a barge-man standing on deck wearing a fur coat.

WULKOW. Nothing strange about that, Herr Superintendent. There's lots of them got real nice fur coats. Even got one myself.

WEHRHAHN. There you are! This man has a fur coat himself!

FLEISCHER. But surely not a beaver coat.

WEHRHAHN. Well, you didn't see that very clearly, you said yourself.

KRUEGER. What? Does this man have a beaver coat?

WULKOW. There's heaps have the finest beaver coats you ever saw, I can tell you. And why not? They got the cash to buy them.

WEHRHAHN (savoring his triumph, pretends complete nonchalance). Well!—Now then—please go on, Herr Krueger. This was just a little detour. I only wanted to demonstrate to you the value of this supposed "observation." As you see, this man has a fur coat himself. (Again violently.) And we wouldn't dream of accusing him of theft on the basis of this evidence! That would be positively absurd!

KRUEGER. What's that? I didn't understand a word of any of this.

WEHRHAHN. In that case I'll have to talk a little louder. And while I'm at it, I'd like to tell you something else. Not as an official, but simply as one human being to another. A man of honor should be a little more careful about choosing the people in whom he places his confidence! He shouldn't bring people as witness who . . .

KRUEGER. Do you mean my friends?

WEHRHAHN. Yes indeed, I mean your friends!

KRUEGER. You'd better be a little careful yourself in that respect! People like that Motes you're so chummy with, people like that I have thrown out of my house!

FLEISCHER. That individual who's waiting in your apartment now . . . I've shown him the door!

KRUEGER. He's swindled me out of the rent he owes me.

FRAU WOLFF. There's not too many around here he hasn't swindled out of some money. He's been cheating just about everybody, left, right, front, and center; with some it's a few groschen, some a few marks, some a few talers—and even gold pieces!

KRUEGER. That man has developed a regular system of taxation!

FLEISCHER (*pulls a paper from his pocket*). And now he's really ready for the prosecutor. (*He puts the paper on the table.*) I'd be very much obliged if you would read this!

KRUEGER. Frau Dreier has signed the paper herself. He's tried to get her to commit perjury!

FLEISCHER. She was supposed to be a witness against me!

KRUEGER (*touching* FLEISCHER's *arm*). This is an honest man! And that scoundrel has been plotting to get him into all kinds of trouble. And you—you give that creature a helping hand!

(WEHRHAHN, KRUEGER, FLEISCHER *and* GLASENAPP, *all talk at once.*)

WEHRHAHN. I'm at the end of my patience! Any business you have to settle with that man doesn't concern me. I'm not interested. (*To* FLEISCHER.) And you be good enough to get that scrap of paper out of my sight!

KRUEGER (*alternately to* FRAU WOLFF *and to* GLASENAPP). And that's a friend of the Superintendent's! He's his authority! A fine authority he is! A trigger man . . . that's what I call him.

FLEISCHER (*to* MITTELDORF). I don't have to account to anybody. What I do and what I don't do is my own business. Who my friends are—that's my concern. And what I think and what I write is my own affair.

GLASENAPP. I can't hear myself think any more, Herr Superintendent, there's such a racket. Do you want me to call the sergeant? I can quickly run over and get him. Mitteldorf!

WEHRHAHN. Quiet, please! (*Silence is restored. To* FLEISCHER.) Take that scrap of paper away, will you please?

FLEISCHER (*takes the paper*). That scrap of paper, as you call it, is going straight to the prosecutor's office!

WEHRHAHN. Please yourself. (*He gets up and takes* FRAU WOLFF's *package out of the bookcase.*) Let's get finished with this thing now. (*To* FRAU WOLFF.) Now then—where did you find this?

FRAU WOLFF. It wasn't me who found it, sir.

WEHRHAHN. Well, who did find it then?

FRAU WOLFF. My daughter, the younger one.

WEHRHAHN. So why didn't you bring her along?

FRAU WOLFF. But she was here, sir. And I can go and get her again in a minute.

WEHRHAHN. No, that would take much too long. Didn't the girl tell you anything about it?

KRUEGER. You told me she found it on the way to the station, didn't you?

WEHRHAHN. In that case the thief has probably gone to Berlin. We'll have a tough time finding him there.

KRUEGER. I don't agree at all, Herr Superintendent. Herr Fleischer has an idea about that and I think he's quite right. This whole business, with this package, is nothing but a fraud to lead us on the wrong track.

FRAU WOLFF. Uhuh, that could be, too. That's quite possible.

WEHRHAHN. Now listen, Frau Wolff. Usually you're not dumb at all. Any stolen goods . . . off they go to Berlin. That fur coat had already been sold in Berlin before we even knew it was stolen.

FRAU WOLFF. No—no, sir, I can't help it but I don't quite agree with you there. If the thief's in Berlin, what does he have to lose a package like this for?

WEHRHAHN. Well, usually one doesn't lose things intentionally.

FRAU WOLFF. Why, just take a look at this here package. There's everything nicely wrapped together: the vest, the key, the piece of paper . . .

KRUEGER. I'm convinced the thief is right here in the village.

FRAU WOLFF (*supporting* KRUEGER). That's exactly right, Herr Krueger!

KRUEGER (*now completely convinced*). I'm absolutely sure of it!

WEHRHAHN. I regret very much, but I don't share your opinion. I have too much experience . . .

KRUEGER. What? Experience? Hm!

WEHRHAHN. Certainly. On the basis of this long experience I can say that this possibility deserves hardly any consideration at all.

FRAU WOLFF. Ah-ah, Herr Superintendent! One should never close the door all the way!

KRUEGER (*pointing to* FLEISCHER). After all, he saw a bargeman . . .

WEHRHAHN. Oh no! Not that story again! I would have to use twenty policemen and search homes every day in the week . . . I'd have to search everybody's home!

FRAU WOLFF. In that case, sir, please start with me!

WEHRHAHN. Now isn't this utterly ridiculous? No, no, gentlemen. That way is never going to work. That way we'll never get anywhere. You'll just have to let me handle this! I have some suspicions—but I still want to watch a little closer for a while. There are some most peculiar characters around here on whom I've had my eye for quite a time. Early in the morning they go to Berlin, heavy baskets on their backs, and in the evening they come back—empty!

KRUEGER. That's what the vegetable women do. They carry the vegetables on their backs.

WEHRHAHN. Not only the vegetable women, Herr Krueger! That's probably the way your fur coat took a trip, too!

FRAU WOLFF. Yes—that's possible, too, of course. Nothing's impossible in this world.

WEHRHAHN (to WULKOW). Now then—you wanted to register ...

WULKOW. A baby girl. Yes sir.

WEHRHAHN (to KRUEGER). I'll do my best.

KRUEGER. I won't rest, Herr Superintendent, until I get my fur coat back.

WEHRHAHN. We'll do everything we can. Maybe Frau Wolff could keep her ears open a little, huh?

FRAU WOLFF. I'm not much good at that sort of thing. But that business better get cleared up! Heavens, there's just nothing safe no more.

KRUEGER. You're absolutely right, Frau Wolff, absolutely! (To WEHRHAHN.) I wish you'd take a very careful look at that package. There's some handwriting on that piece of paper that might well lead to the thief. The day after to-morrow I'll take the liberty of dropping by again, Herr Superintendent, so I can get the latest news. Good-day!

(*Leaves.*)

FLEISCHER. Good-day!   (*Leaves.*)

WEHRHAHN (to WULKOW). How old are you?—Good-day, good-day!—Those two have a screw missing. (*Again to* WULKOW.) What's your name?

WULKOW. August Philipp Wulkow.

WEHRHAHN (to MITTELDORF). You walk over to my apartment. Motes is sitting there waiting for me. Tell him I'm sorry but I'm too busy this morning.

MITTELDORF. You don't want him to wait?

WEHRHAHN (*short*). No, tell him not to wait.

(MITTELDORF *leaves.*)

WEHRHAHN (*to* FRAU WOLFF). Do you know Motes?

FRAU WOLFF. As far as he's concerned, I'd rather not say. I couldn't tell you much good about him.

WEHRHAHN (*sarcastically*). You could tell me lots of nice things about Fleischer, though!

FRAU WOLFF. That's really not too bad a fellow.

WEHRHAHN. Are you trying to be just a little cagey?

FRAU WOLFF. No, you know I'm no good at that. I'm always straightforward, Herr Superintendent. You know that. If I didn't always open my trap and say what I think, I'd be a lot further ahead.

WEHRHAHN. Well, saying what you think has never done you any harm with me.

FRAU WOLFF. No, Herr Superintendent, not with you. You can stand a little frank talk. One really don't have to watch out and hide things from you.

WEHRHAHN. So in one word, you think Fleischer is a respectable citizen.

FRAU WOLFF. Yes sir, that's what he is.

WEHRHAHN. You remember what you said just now!

FRAU WOLFF. And you, too!

WEHRHAHN. All right, we'll see. (*He stretches, gets up and starts walking up and down to get the stiffness out of his legs. To* WULKOW.) This is our washerwoman—the hardest working woman you ever saw. She thinks everybody is like her. (*To* FRAU WOLFF.) Unfortunately, though, that's not the way the world is made. You just look at the outside of people. We look a little deeper! (*He takes a few steps, then stops in front of her and puts his hands on her shoulders.*) It's certainly true when I say that Frau Wolff is an honest woman. And it's just as sure that Dr. Fleischer is a very dangerous man. One's as true as the other!

FRAU WOLFF (*shakes her head in resignation*). Well . . . I don't know . . .

CURTAIN

PREFACE TO *Hannele*

It is a slight exaggeration to say that in *Hannele* or *The Ascension of Hannele* (*Hannele's Himmelfahrt*) Hauptmann made a definite break with the Naturalistic school of playwriting. But Hauptmann did anticipate his later ventures in poetic and symbolic drama when he combined his oppressive picture of life in a rural workhouse with the deliriums of a child-suicide. In her delirious state, Hannele, the stepdaughter of a brutish peasant, transfigures her miserable condition into fairy-tale fantasy. In the play, poverty is background rather than foreground. Moreover, misery is dissolved into fantasy—with a lapse into sentimentality that would be intolerable but for the possibility of accepting Hannele's delusion as a more or less authentic blending of fragments of folk-fancy, religious education, and life-experience. The pathos of her life is contrasted with her fantasy, and the childish vision which transforms her sympathetic schoolmaster into Christ is contrasted with the savagery of the réal world. Although *Hannele* first won favor as a poetic drama, it owes its survival to the prose of reality that forms, so to speak, the banks that keep Hauptmann's flow of sentiment within bounds and prevent his dramatic talent from drowning in a sea of saccharinity. Here the "unpoetic" Hauptmann saved the "poetic" Hauptmann, for Naturalism was still a source of strength at this stage in Hauptmann's career.

On February 1, 1894, *Hannele*, under the title of *L'Assomption de Hannele Mattern*, was staged by André Antoine at his *Théâtre Libre*. Antoine's staging methods, however, were better suited to this play's continuously naturalistic predecessor, *The Weavers*. It was the last important work to be produced by the *Théâtre Libre* under Antoine's management, and it is symbolic of the course of theatre in

Europe that this should be so, since the play stands between the naturalistic and the symbolist styles of drama.

Hannele, twice produced professionally in London before World War I, had a historic production by the Liverpool Repertory Company in the spring of 1913 when the play was staged by Basil Dean with Gertrude Lawrence, whom the historian Ernest Short described at fourteen as "a vivacious little minx, wearing a peaked military cap and a black satin coat." Another member of the cast was the young Noel Coward, who appeared as an angel in the dream scene and later played one of the school children, wearing a blue smock. *Hannele* continued to provide tidbits of theatrical history in English. A student actor at Piscator's Dramatic Workshop of the New School in New York, Marlon Brando, played the role of the schoolmaster Gottwald in a production associated with the present editor's "March of Drama" series of lecture-demonstrations in the early 1940's. *Hannele* was first presented in New York at Miner's Fifth Avenue Theatre on May 1, 1894; and, subtitled a "Dream Poem," it was revived by Harrison Grey Fiske for his wife, the celebrated Mrs. Fiske, in the season of 1909–10 (April 11, 1910) at the Lyceum Theatre. The translation, by Mary J. Saffird, was supplemented with "metrical passages" by Percy Mackaye. The cast was headed by Mrs. Fiske and Holbrook Blinn. Arthur Schnitzler's ingenious one-act "grotesquerie" *The Green Cockatoo* was used as a curtain-raiser for this production—one of a number of productions by Mrs. Fiske and her husband which gave the New York stage its greatest series of plays before the career of the Theatre Guild in the 1920's. The play was also revived in New York under the full title of *The Assumption of Hannele* in the season of 1923–24 with Eva Le Gallienne and Basil Rathbone.

HANNELE

A Dream Poem in Two Acts

CHARACTERS

HANNELE
GOTTWALD, a teacher
SISTER MARTHA, a deaconess*
TULPE
HEDWIG
PLESCHKE } inmates of a poorhouse
HANKE
SEIDEL, a woodcutter

BERGER, Police Superintendent
SCHMIDT, a bailiff

DR. WACHLER

In her fever, Hannele sees the following apparitions: Bricklayer Mattern, her father; The Woman, her dead mother; a large black angel; three angels of light; the Deaconess; Gottwald and his pupils; Pleschke, Hanke, and other inmates of the poorhouse; Seidel; four youths in white; The Stranger; numerous small and large angels; the village tailor; mourners; women, etc.

* "Diakonissinnen," or deaconesses, are members of a German Protestant Order devoted to the care of the sick.

ACT I

(*A room in the poorhouse of a mountain village. The walls are bare; in the center there is a door, at the left a window as small as a peephole. In front of the window stands a wobbly table and a bench. To the right is a cot with a straw mattress. Along the rear wall is a stove with a bench and a second cot with a straw mattress and some rags on it.—It is a stormy night in December. TULPE, an old, ragged, beggar woman, is sitting at the table singing from a hymn book by the light of a tallow candle.*)

TULPE (*sings*). Abide, O dearest Jesus,
　　　　　　　Among us Thy grace
　　　　　　　That Satan may not harm us . . .

(HEDWIG, *nicknamed* HETE *enters; she is a dissolute woman of about thirty; she wears her hair in bangs. Around her head she wears a thick shawl; under her arm she carries a bundle; she is scantily and poorly dressed.*)

HETE (*blowing into her hands, without letting go of the bundle*). Oh Jesus, Jesus, what weather! (*She drops the bundle on the table, blows into her hands and hops from one torn shoe to the other.*) Haven't had wild weather like this for many a year.

TULPE. What've you got?

HETE (*grinds her teeth and whimpers with pain, sits down on the bench by the stove and tries to take off her shoes*). Geeze, my toes! Burn like fire they do.

TULPE (*has meanwhile opened the knots of the bundle which reveals a loaf of bread, a small package of chickory, a small paper bag of coffee, a pair of stockings, etc.*). Should be a little something left over for me, too.

169

HETE (*has been so busy taking off her shoes, that she has paid no attention to* TULPE; *now she descends on her possessions like a vulture and gathers them together*). Tulpe! (*One foot bare, the other still in a shoe, she hobbles with her things to the cot at the rear.*) I'm supposed to walk for miles, huh? And freeze every bone in my body so you can pocket the stuff, huh?

TULPE. Shut your mouth, you old tramp! I wouldn't touch your pile of junk . . . (*She gets up, closes the hymn book and dusts it carefully with her skirt.*) . . . that stuff you been begging.

HETE (*stowing away her things under the straw mattress*). Who's been begging more in her life, you or me? You never done nothing else as old as you are. Everybody knows that.

TULPE. You've done a lot of other things, too, haven't you? The Pastor's told you what he thinks of you. This I'll say, when I was a young chicken like you, I sure thought a little more of myself.

HETE. Sure, that's why you went to jail!

TULPE. That's where you'll wind up, without even half trying. If I just happen to meet the cop once I'll tell him a thing or two. Just don't get so snooty, girl, I tell you.

HETE. Why don't you send the cop to me while you're at it. Got a few things to tell him myself.

TULPE. What's that to me? Tell him what you like.

HETE. Who stole that overcoat, huh? From Innkeeper Richter's little boy? (TULPE *pretends spitting at* HETE.) Damn you, Tulpe! Just for that you won't get nothing at all.

TULPE. See if I care! Wouldn't take nothing from you anyways.

HETE. Sure, because you won't get nothing.

(PLESCHKE *and* HANKE *are practically blown into the hall by the storm which is once again battering the house.* PLESCHKE *is laughing loudly. He is a half-childish old man with a goiter, dressed in rags.* HANKE, *a young, ne'er do-well, is swearing. Both are visible through the open door as they shake the snow off hats and clothing. Each of them is carrying a bundle.*)

PLESCHKE. Thunder and lightning, thunder and lightning! Pushes you around like the devil. This old wreck of a poorhouse, it'll fall—fall—fall apart sure enough one of—one of these days.

(*Seeing the two men,* HETE *thinks for a moment, then pulls her things out from under the mattress and runs past the men, out of the room and up the stairs.*)

PLESCHKE (*calling after* HETE). What are you running away for—running away for? We won't—won't—won't do you no harm. Ain't that so, Hanke? Ain't that so?

TULPE (*at the stove, busy with a pot of potatoes*). That woman ain't quite right in the head. Thinks we'll steal something from her.

PLESCHKE (*entering*). Oh Jesus, Jesus! Man, oh man! That's a good one. —Evening! Good—good-evening! Devil, what a weather! Fell down—fell down—flat on my face, flat on my face.

(*With bent knees he limps to the table, puts his bundle on it and turns his shaky head with its white hair and watering eyes toward* TULPE. *He is still gasping for air after the exertion: he coughs and flaps his arms to warm himself. Meanwhile* HANKE, *too, has entered the room. He puts his beggar's sack next to the door, and, shaking with cold, starts immediately to stuff dry twigs into the stove.*)

TULPE. Where've you been?

PLESCHKE. Me? Me? Where've I been? Far, far away. Walked all over the Upper Village.

TULPE. Bringing something home?

PLESCHKE. Sure, sure, nice things, nice things—I got. At the teacher's I got—I got—a fiver, yeah—and up at the tavern —up—at the tavern—I got—I got a pot with soup—pot with soup—a pot with soup—I got.

TULPE. Going to warm it right away. Gimme it. (*She pulls the pot from his bundle, puts it on the table and keeps digging.*)

PLESCHKE. A piece—a piece of sausage I got—I got, too. The butcher—butcher Seipelt—gave it—gave it to me.

TULPE. And how much money you got?

PLESCHKE. Three groschen, yeah three groschen I think it is.

TULPE. Better give it to me. I'll keep it for you.

HETE (*coming back*). Pretty dumb you are, giving everything away. (*She walks over to the stove.*)

TULPE. Mind your own business!

HANKE. Don't you know they're going to get married?

HETE. Oh, no!

HANKE. So naturally he's got to bring something home to the bride. That's the way it's got to be if it's like that.

PLESCHKE. You can make a fool—make a fool—of anybody you like. But leave alone, alone—leave alone an old man like me.

HETE (*aping* PLESCHKE's *stammering*). Old Pleschke—old Pleschke—can hardly—can hardly—can hardly talk no more. Soon he won't—soon he won't—won't—won't—won't be able to get out a single word—single word.

PLESCHKE (*going after her with his stick*). Now beat—beat—beat it!

HETE. Run away—from you, huh?

PLESCHKE. Now beat it!

TULPE. Just let her have it.

PLESCKE. Now beat it!

HANKE. Stop being an ass.

TULPE. You shut up!

(*While* HANKE *is busy defending* HETE, *she takes advantage of his inattention to grab something with lightning speed from his sack and to run away with it.* TULPE *has noticed it and is shaking with laughter.*)

HANKE. Don't see nothing to laugh about.

TULPE (*still laughing*). Oh that's too funny, it's killing me!

PLESCHKE. Oh, Jesus, Jesus, just look at that!

TULPE. Just take a look at your stuff. Could be there's a little less now.

HANKE (*turns around, realizes he has been made a fool of*). Bitch! (*He runs after* HETE.) If I get a hold of you! (*They are heard tramping up the stairs, and running overhead; then there are suppressed screams.*)

PLESCHKE. Devil of a girl—devil of a girl! (*He roars with laughter.* TULPE, *too, is overcome with laughter. Suddenly, the front door is heard banging loudly. Both abruptly stop laughing.*) Huh, what's that?

(*Violent blasts of wind batter the house. Sleet drives against*

*the window. For a moment there is silence. Then the
teacher,* GOTTWALD, *appears. He is thirty-two years old
and has a black beard. He is carrying* HANNELE MAT-
TERN *in his arms. She is about fourteen. Her long, red
hair hangs down over the teacher's shoulders and she
whimpers steadily. Her face is buried in the teacher's
neck and her arms are hanging down, limp and lifeless.
She is scantily clad and wrapped in shawls. Very carefully* GOTTWALD *lets her slide down on the cot at the
right, paying no attention to anybody.* SEIDEL, *a woodcutter, follows, carrying a lantern, his saw and ax
and a bundle of wet rags. He is wearing an old hunter's
hat set at a bold angle on his graying head.*)

PLESCHKE (*staring stupidly and surprised*). Eh, eh, eh, eh!
What's—what's going on here? What's going on here?

GOTTWALD (*putting blankets and his own overcoat on the
girl*). Heat some bricks, Seidel, quickly!

SEIDEL. Get a move on! Hurry up! A few bricks! Hey
you! Get going!

TULPE. And what's the matter with her?

SEIDEL. Never mind, stop asking questions. (*Quickly
leaves with* TULPE.)

GOTTWALD (*trying to soothe* HANNELE). Never mind now,
never mind! Don't be afraid. Nothing's going to happen to
you.

HANNELE (*through chattering teeth*). I'm so afraid! I'm
so afraid!

GOTTWALD. But you don't have to be afraid of anything.
Nobody is going to do you any harm.

HANNELE. My father, my father . . .

GOTTWALD. He isn't here.

HANNELE. I'm so afraid that father will come.

GOTTWALD. But he isn't coming. Believe me, please!

(*Somebody comes running down the stairs in a great hurry.*)

HETE (*holding up a grater*). Just take a look: that's the
kind of thing people give Hanke!

(HANKE *chasing after her, finally reaches her, tries to pull
the grater away from her, but she quickly throws it
into the middle of the room.*)

HANNELE (*sits up in terror*). He's coming, he's coming!

(*Half-rising, she stares in the direction of the noise, her head inclined forward, an expression of terrible fear on her pale, sick, and sad little face. HETE has torn away from HANKE and has fled into the back room. HANKE comes in to pick up the grater.*)

HANKE. I'll get even with you! You bitch!

GOTTWALD (*to HANNELE*). It's all right, Hannele. (*To HANKE.*) And what do you want?

HANKE (*surprised*). Me? What do I want?

HETE (*putting her head through the door*). Thief, thief!

HANKE (*menacingly*). Quiet, you! I'll show you!

GOTTWALD. Please be quiet! The child is sick.

HANKE (*picks up the grater and puts it into his pocket; somewhat intimidated he steps back*). Well, what's the matter?

SEIDEL (*comes back bringing two bricks*). Here are two for now.

GOTTWALD (*touches the bricks to see if they are warm*). Is that hot enough?

SEIDEL. They'll warm her some. (*He puts one of the bricks at the girl's feet.*)

GOTTWALD (*pointing to another spot*). The other one over here.

SEIDEL. She hasn't warmed up yet.

GOTTWALD. She's shaking with cold.

(*TULPE enters behind SEIDEL; HETE and PLESCHKE are behind her. Several other inmates of the poorhouse, rather doubtful looking characters, appear in the door. All are curious; they whisper to each other, but gradually become bolder and move closer.*)

TULPE (*standing next to the bed, with arms akimbo*). Hot water and brandy if there's any around.

SEIDEL (*pulls out a brandy flask; PLESCHKE and HANKE do the same*). There's a little left.

TULPE (*already at the stove*). Gimme.

SEIDEL. Any hot water?

TULPE. Jesus, hot enough to steam an ox.

GOTTWALD. And put a little sugar in it, if you have any.

HETE. Where are we supposed to get sugar from?

TULPE. You got some. Don't play dumb!

HETE. Me? Sugar? Oh no. (*She gives a forced laugh.*)

TULPE. You brought some home. I seen it in your bundle before. Don't have to go lying.

SEIDEL. Well, get going, get it.

HANKE. Hurry up, Hete, hurry up!

SEIDEL. Don't you see the girl needs it?

HETE (*stubbornly*). What's that to me.

PLESCHKE. Go! Go get that sugar!

HETE. There's plenty at the grocer's.   (*She sidles out.*)

SEIDEL. Get a move on, now, or I'll box your ears. Maybe that's what you need—and you won't come back for seconds either.

PLESCHKE (*has left the room for a moment, comes back*). That's—that's—that's the way she is, that girl, that's the way she is.

SEIDEL. I'd show her where to get off, all right. If I was running the Town Hall I'd take a nice willow stick and before you know it she'd be working. A girl like that, young and strong, why does she have to hang around the poorhouse?!

PLESCHKE. I've found—a small piece—small piece—small piece of sugar here—sugar here—sugar here.

HANKE (*sniffing the aroma of the grog*). Wouldn't mind being sick myself once in a while.

SCHMIDT (*enters with a lantern. Urgently, but in a confidential tone*). Make room, the Superintendent's coming.

(BERGER, *the Police Superintendent, enters. He is unmistakably a reserve officer. He has a small mustache and a pleasant, youthful face, but his hair is already quite gray. His entire appearance has just a touch of elegance. He wears a long overcoat, a brimmed hat at a jaunty angle, carries a walking stick and there is something jovial in his manner.*)

THE INMATES. Good-evening, Superintendent! Good-evening, Captain!

BERGER. Evening! (*He takes off his hat and overcoat and puts them down together with his stick. With a sharp gesture.*) Now, out of here everybody! (SCHMIDT *pushes the inmates out of the room and into the back room.*) Good-evening, Herr Gottwald. (*Shakes his hand.*) Well, how's it going?

GOTTWALD. Well, we pulled her out of the water.

SEIDEL (*steps up*). Begging your pardon, Captain! (*By force of habit he gives a military salute putting his hand to his forehead.*) I had something to do in the smithy—wanted to have a band put around my ax. And as I step out of the smithy, now—down there at the Jeuchen smithy—now there's this pond, might almost call it a lake. (*To* GOTTWALD.) Well, it's true. It's almost that big. And maybe you know, Chief, there's a spot there where it never freezes over . . . it never, never freezes over. When I was still a small boy . . .

BERGER. Well? What happened?

SEIDEL (*saluting again*). Well, just as I come out of the smithy—the moon just came out a tiny little bit—I hear this whimpering. First I think I'm dreaming. But right away I see something on the pond. And it keeps moving toward that open spot. I shout—and it's already gone. Well, you can imagine, I up and back to the smithy, take a board—don't say nothing to no one—and around to the pond. Down with the board on the ice and one, two, three I got her, by the scruff of her neck, you might say.

BERGER. Well done, Seidel. Usually all I hear is stories of fighting, bloody noses, broken legs! This at least is different for once. And so you brought her here right away?

SEIDEL. Teacher Gottwald . . .

GOTTWALD. I just happened to walk by. Came from the teachers' meeting. So I took her to my house first of all. My wife quickly dug up a few things so we could get her dry at least.

BERGER. And what's behind this story?

SEIDEL (*hesitatingly*). Well, it's Bricklayer Mattern's stepdaughter.

BERGER (*taken aback for a moment*). Whose? That scum!

SEIDEL. Her mother died six weeks ago. The rest everybody knows. She's been scratching and kicking just because she thought I was her father.

BERGER (*murmurs*). That scoundrel!

SEIDEL. Now he's sitting in the tavern again, down in the village, drinking since yesterday without stopping for breath. They're giving him as much as he wants down there.

BERGER. We'll spoil his pleasure all right, the dog! (*He bends over the bed to talk to* HANNELE.) Now, my girl, tell me, why are you whimpering so? You don't have to look at me as if I scare you. I won't do you any harm. Well, what's your name?—What do you say? I can't understand you. (*He straightens up.*) I think the girl's a little stubborn.

GOTTWALD. She's only frightened.—Hannele!

HANNELE (*very softly*). Yes.

GOTTWALD. You have to answer the Superintendent.

HANNELE (*shivering*). Dear God, I'm so cold.

SEIDEL (*brings the grog*). Here, come, drink a little!

HANNELE (*as before*). Dear God, I'm so hungry.

GOTTWALD (*to the* SUPERINTENDENT). And if you give her something she won't eat it.

HANNELE. Dear God, it's hurting so much.

GOTTWALD. Where does it hurt you?

HANNELE. I'm so afraid.

BERGER. Who's hurting you, then? Who? Now talk, girl.—I don't understand one word, child. That doesn't help me at all.—Now listen to me, little girl! Did your stepfather treat you badly? Did he beat you, I mean?—Did he lock you in? Throw you out of the house, something like that?—Good God . . .

SEIDEL. That girl's a quiet one all right. Would have to get real bad before she'd say something. She's silent—like a lamb, you might say.

BERGER. I just have to know something definite. Then perhaps I can catch the beast!

GOTTWALD. She is terribly afraid of that man.

SEIDEL. That's an old story with that one. Everybody, just everybody knows that, you might say. You can ask whoever you want. That the girl's still alive, that's what I'm surprised about. Seems impossible, you might say.

BERGER. What did he do to her?

SEIDEL. Well, all sorts of things, you might say. Nine o'clock at night he'd chase her out of the house—even in weather like we got today—so she'd bring some money home. For him to go and guzzle it up, of course. And where would a girl like that find five groschen? So, many a time she spent half the night outdoors.—Because if she got home and no money—people came running from all around, that's how she screamed—howled, you might say.

GOTTWALD. The mother at least gave her a little support.

BERGER. Well, in that case I'll put the guy behind bars right away. He's been on my list of drunkards for a long time. Come on now, girl, look at me.

HANNELE (*imploringly*). Oh, please, please, please!

SEIDEL. Won't be easy to get something out of her.

GOTTWALD (*softly*). Hannele!

HANNELE. Yes.

GOTTWALD. Do you know who I am?

HANNELE. Yes.

GOTTWALD. And who am I?

HANNELE. The—teacher—Gottwald.

GOTTWALD. Right. You see, I've always been good to you, haven't I? Now you might as well tell me . . . you were down at the pond by the smithy, weren't you? . . . Why didn't you stay home? Well? Why didn't you?

HANNELE. I'm so afraid.

BERGER. We'll go into the corner. You can tell the teacher when you're all alone with him.

HANNELE (*shyly and mysteriously*). He called me.

GOTTWALD. Who called?

HANNELE. Our dear Lord Jesus.

GOTTWALD. From where—did the Lord Jesus call you?

HANNELE. From the water.

GOTTWALD. From where?

HANNELE. Well, from down in the water.

BERGER (*changing his mind, puts on his overcoat*). What we need here most of all is a doctor. He'll still be in the "Sword," I think.

GOTTWALD. I also sent over to the Sisters. The child definitely needs a nurse.

BERGER. I'll go and talk to the doctor. (*To* SCHMIDT.) And you get me the sergeant. I'll wait for him at the "Sword." Good-night, Herr Gottwald. We'll get the fellow before the night is over. (*Leaves with* SCHMIDT. HANNELE *falls asleep.*)

SEIDEL (*after a pause*). The devil he'll put him in the klink.

GOTTWALD. And why not?

SEIDEL. He knows why. After all, who's the girl's father?

GOTTWALD. Ah, Seidel, that's only gossip.

SEIDEL. Well, you know, that fellow used to live it up!

GOTTWALD. The lies people can spread around! You can't believe the half of it.—If only the doctor would come soon!

SEIDEL (*in a low voice*). I don't think that girl's going to get up again.

(DR. WACHLER *enters; he is a serious man of about thirty-four.*)

DR. WACHLER. Good-evening!

GOTTWALD. Good-evening!

SEIDEL (*helps him take off his fur coat*). Good-evening, Doctor!

DR. WACHLER (*warming his hands at the stove*). I'd like to have another candle. (*In the back room someone plays a hand organ.*) They must have gone crazy in there.

SEIDEL (*is already at the open door of the back room*). Be a little quiet! (*The noise stops;* SEIDEL *disappears in the back room.*)

DR. WACHLER. Herr Gottwald, isn't it?

GOTTWALD. Yes, my name is Gottwald.

DR. WACHLER. She tried to drown herself, I understand.

GOTTWALD. She probably didn't know any more what to do. (*Short pause.*)

DR. WACHLER (*steps over to the bed and looks at* HANNELE). She talks in her sleep, doesn't she?

HANNELE. Millions of little stars. (DR. WACHLER *and* GOTTWALD *watch her. Moonlight falls through the window upon the group.*) Why do you keep pulling at my bones? Ow, ow! It hurts so much.

DR. WACHLER (*carefully opens her shirt at the throat*). It seems her whole body is covered with marks.

SEIDEL. That's how the mother looked when she was lying in her coffin.

DR. WACHLER. Pitiful, pitiful!

HANNELE (*in a changed tone, obstinately*). I don't want to . . . I don't want to . . . I don't want to go home. I got to go—to Mother Holle—into the well. Leave me alone, Father. Ush, what a stench! You've been drinking brandy again. —Listen to the trees rustle!—This morning there was a storm in the mountains. If only there won't be a fire!—If the tailor doesn't carry a stone in his pocket and an iron in his hand the storm will blow him all over the mountains. Listen how it's blowing!

(SISTER MARTHA, *a deaconess, enters.*)

GOTTWALD. Good evening, Sister.

(SISTER MARTHA *nods.* GOTTWALD *walks over to the deaconess who is preparing everything necessary for her nursing work, and talks with her in the background.*)

HANNELE. Where is my mother? In heaven? Oh, oh, so

far! (*She opens her eyes, looks around in surprise, passes her hand across her eyes and says in a voice that is hardly audible.*) Where—am I—now?

DR. WACHLER (*bending over her*). With good people.

HANNELE. I'm thirsty.

DR. WACHLER. Water! (SEIDEL, *who has brought a second candle, goes to get water.*) Does it hurt you anywhere? (HANNELE *shakes her head.*) No? Well, what do you know? Perhaps things are not too bad.

HANNELE. Are you the doctor?

DR. WACHLER. Yes.

HANNELE. Then—I'm sick, am I?

DR. WACHLER. A little sick, but not too bad.

HANNELE. Do you want to get me better?

DR. WACHLER (*quickly starting to examine her*). Does it hurt here? Here? Does this hurt you? This? Here?—You don't have to look at me as if you were frightened, I won't hurt you. How is this? Any pains here?

GOTTWALD (*returns to the bed*). Answer the doctor, Hannele!

HANNELE (*with a tear-choked voice, fervently imploring*). Oh, dear Herr Gottwald!

GOTTWALD. Now you listen to what the doctor says and answer him nicely.

(HANNELE *shakes her head.*)

GOTTWALD. And why not?

HANNELE. Because—because I want so much to go to my mother.

GOTTWALD (*moved, strokes her hair*). Now, there—you'll be all right.

(*Short pause.*)

(THE DOCTOR *straightens up, draws a deep breath and thinks for a moment.* SISTER MARTHA *has taken the second candle from the table and holds it for him.*)

DR. WACHLER (*beckons to* SISTER MARTHA). Please, Sister!

(*He steps to the table and in a low voice gives her instructions.* GOTTWALD *takes his hat and waits, glancing now toward* HANNELE, *now toward the doctor and the deaconess.*

Dr. Wachler *finishes his quiet conversation with* The Sister.) I'll probably be back. And I'll have the medicine sent over. (*To* Gottwald.) Seems he's been arrested at the tavern.

Sister Martha. At least that's what I've just heard.

Dr. Wachler (*putting on his fur coat, to* Seidel). Perhaps you'll come with me to the pharmacy.

(The Doctor, Gottwald, *and* Seidel, *ready to leave, quietly say good-by to* The Sister.)

Gottwald (*urgently*). What do you think of her condition, Doctor?

(*All three of them leave.* The Deaconess *remains alone with* Hannele. *She pours milk into a small pot. Meanwhile* Hannele *has opened her eyes and watches her.*)

Hannele. Do you come from the Lord Jesus?

Sister Martha. What did you say?

Hannele. Do you come from the Lord Jesus?

Sister Martha. Don't you recognize me, Hannele? I'm Sister Martha, you remember? You came to see us, remember, and we prayed together and sang beautiful songs, didn't we?

Hannele (*nods happily*). Oh yes, beautiful songs!

Sister Martha. And now I'll take care of you, in God's name, until you are well again.

Hannele. I don't want to get well.

Sister Martha (*bringing the little pot with milk*). The doctor says you are to take a little milk so you will get strong again.

Hannele (*refuses*). I don't want to get well.

Sister Martha. You don't want to get well? Why not think about it for a little while. Come, I'll tie up your hair. (*She does so.*)

Hannele (*cries silently*). I don't want to get well.

Sister Martha. But why not?

Hannele. I would like so much—so much—to go to heaven.

Sister Martha. That's not in our power, my dear child. We have to wait until God calls us. But if you repent your sins . . .

Hannele (*eagerly*). Oh, Sister, I repent them so much.

Sister Martha. And believe in the Lord Jesus . . .

Hannele. I believe so firmly in our Savior!

Sister Martha. . . . then you can wait confidently and

peacefully.—I'll straighten out your pillows now, and then you'll sleep.

HANNELE. I can't sleep.

SISTER MARTHA. Try anyway.

HANNELE. Sister Martha!

SISTER MARTHA. Well?

HANNELE. Sister Martha, are there sins—are there sins that won't be forgiven?

SISTER MARTHA. You go to sleep now, Hannele! Don't get excited!

HANNELE. Oh please—please tell me!

SISTER MARTHA. Yes, there are such sins. There are. The sins against the Holy Ghost.

HANNELE. If I have committed one . . .

SISTER MARTHA. Oh, nonsense! That's only really bad people. Like Judas, who betrayed the Lord Jesus.

HANNELE. But it could—it could have happened.

SISTER MARTHA. You go to sleep now.

HANNELE. I'm so afraid.

SISTER MARTHA. There is no reason at all.

HANNELE. But if I have committed a sin like that!

SISTER MARTHA. But you have not committed such a sin.

HANNELE (clings to THE SISTER and stares into the darkness). Oh, Sister, Sister!

SISTER MARTHA. Quiet, quiet now.

HANNELE. Sister!

SISTER MARTHA. What is it?

HANNELE. He'll be here in a minute, don't you hear?

SISTER MARTHA. I don't hear anything at all.

HANNELE. It's his voice—outside. Listen!

SISTER MARTHA. Whom are you talking about?

HANNELE. My father, my father—there he is.

SISTER MARTHA. But where?

HANNELE. There, at the foot of the bed.

SISTER MARTHA. That's only a coat hanging there, and a hat. We'll take this ugly stuff away—and take it over to Father Pleschke. I'll get some cold water while I'm out, and then I'll make you a cold compress. Will you stay alone just for one little moment? But stay quite, quite still!

HANNELE. Oh, I'm so silly. It was only a coat and hat, wasn't it?

SISTER MARTHA. Quite, quite still! I'll be back right away. (She leaves but has to turn back since the hall is pitch dark.) I'll put the candle out here in the hall. (Warn-

HANNELE *once more by affectionately wagging her finger.*)
Quite, quite still. (*Leaves.*)

(*It is almost completely dark. Immediately, the shape of
BRICKLAYER MATTERN appears at the foot end of HAN-
NELE's bed. He has the red, ravaged face of a drunkard;
his hair is unkempt and on his head perches an old soldier's cap without its peak. In his left hand he carries his
bricklayer's tools; he has a strap wrapped around his
right hand and during the entire scene he remains
tense, as if he were ready to start beating HANNELE at
any moment. A pale glow emanates from the apparition, throwing a circle of light around HANNELE's bed.*)

(HANNELE *terrified, covers her face with her hands, groans,
twists, turns and makes soft, whimpering sounds.*)

THE APPARITION (*in a hoarse voice, almost choking with
rage*). What's happened to you? Where have you been,
girl? What have you been doing? I'll teach you. I'll show
you, you'll see. What did you tell the people? I beat you
and abuse you? Huh? If that's true you ain't my child. Up
with you, get up! You don't matter none to me. I can throw
you out in the street any time.—Get up and make a fire! Are
you going? Out of charity and kindness I've kept you in my
house. And now you want to loaf on top of it. Well? Get
going or I'll beat you until, until . . .

(HANNELE *struggles to get up with her eyes closed, drags
herself over to the stove, opens the door and collapses
in a faint.*)

(*At the same moment* SISTER MARTHA *enters carrying the
candle and a pitcher of water; the hallucination of*
MATTERN *disappears. She stops, sees* HANNELE *lying in
the ashes and, in sudden alarm, cries,* "Lord Jesus!"
She puts the candle and pitcher down, runs to HAN-
NELE *and lifts her from the floor. Her cry has attracted
the inmates of the poorhouse.*)

SISTER MARTHA. I just had to go out to get some water,
and she got out of bed. Please, Hedwig, give me a hand!
HANKE. Better watch out, Hete, or you'll break every bone
in her body.

PLESCHKE. I think something's—something's happened—to the girl—to the girl, Sister!

TULPE. Maybe—the girl—is bewitched.

HANKE (loudly). She's just about finished, that's what I say.

SISTER MARTHA (with HEDWIG's help has put HANNELE back to bed). Perhaps you are right, my good man, but please, you understand, don't you: we shouldn't keep getting the sick girl excited!

HANKE. We ain't making that much noise.

PLESCHKE (to HANKE). You're—you're a dope—a dope, now you know it, that's what—that's what you are. A sick —a sick—a sick child—anybody knows that—has got to have —to have rest.

HETE (imitating him). A sick—a sick—a sick . . .

SISTER MARTHA. I really must ask you, urgently and most kindly ask you . . .

TULPE. The Sister is right; hurry up and get out of here.

HANKE. We'll go all by ourselves soon's we're ready.

HETE. Are we supposed to sleep in the chicken coop?

PLESCHKE. You'll find room—you'll find room, you'll know where to go.

(All the poorhouse inmates leave.)

HANNELE (opens her eyes, still frightened). Is—is he gone?

SISTER MARTHA. The people are gone. You didn't get frightened, Hannele, did you?

HANNELE (unchanged). Is father gone?

SISTER MARTHA. But he hasn't been here.

HANNELE. Oh yes, Sister, oh yes, he has.

SISTER MARTHA. You must have been dreaming.

HANNELE (praying with deep sighs). Oh, dear Lord Jesus! Oh, dear Lord Jesus! Oh, nicest, best little Lord Jesus! Please take me to you, please take me! (Changed.)

> Oh, if only He came,
> Oh, if only He'd take me
> So I could escape
> The eyes of the world.

I'm quite certain, Sister, I know . . .

SISTER MARTHA. And what do you know?

HANNELE. He's promised me. I'll go to heaven, he's promised me.

SISTER MARTHA. Hm.

HANNELE. Do you know who?

SISTER MARTHA. Well?

HANNELE (*talking secretively into* THE SISTER'S *ear*). Dear Lord—Gottwald.

SISTER MARTHA. And now you go back to sleep, Hannele. —You know what?

HANNELE. Sister, Teacher Gottwald is a handsome man, isn't he? His name is Heinrich. Heinrich is a beautiful name, isn't it? (*Tenderly.*) You dear, sweet Heinrich! Sister, do you know what? We'll get married, we two. Oh yes, the two of us: Teacher Gottwald and I.

> And after they'd become betrothed
> The two went off together;
> In a darkened room their bed was clothed
> With linen and snow-white feathers.

He's got a beautiful beard. (*In ecstasy.*) On his head the clover blooms! Listen—he's calling me. Don't you hear him?

SISTER MARTHA. Sleep now, Hannele, go to sleep. Nobody is calling.

HANNELE. That was Herr—the Lord Jesus. Listen! Listen! Now he is calling again: "Hannele!" Quite loud: "Hannele!" very, very clearly. Come, you come with me.

SISTER MARTHA. When God calls me, I'll be ready.

HANNELE (*struck again by the moonlight, stretches her head as if she were smelling sweet perfume*). Don't you notice anything, Sister?

SISTER MARTHA. No, Hannele.

HANNELE. The scent of lilacs? (*In an ever-increasing happy ecstasy.*) But listen! Listen! What can that be? (*From faraway a sweet voice is heard.*) Are they angels? Don't you really hear anything?

SISTER MARTHA. Of course, I hear it. But you know, you really must turn on your side now; lie quite still and sleep until tomorrow morning.

HANNELE. Can you sing that, too?

SISTER MARTHA. Sing what, my little one?

HANNELE. "Sleep, little one, sleep!"

SISTER MARTHA. Would you like to hear it?

HANNELE (*lies down and caresses* THE SISTER'S *hand*). Mother dear, sing it for me! Dear Mother, sing it for me!

SISTER MARTHA (*puts out the candle, leans over the bed*

and speaks, barely hinting at the tune, accompanied by the distant music).

> Sleep, little one, sleep!
> In the garden walks a sheep.

(*Now she sings while it becomes completely dark.*)

> In the garden walks a little lamb
> He walks upon the little dam,
> Sleep, little one, sleep!

(*A dim twilight fills the miserable room. The ghost-like figure of A* WOMAN *sits on the edge of the bed, bent forward, supporting herself with her bare, thin arms. She is barefoot; her long, white hair falls loosely from her temples down to the blanket. Her face is emaciated and worn with grief; her eyes have sunk deep into their sockets and, although they are closed tight, seem to gaze at the sleeping girl. She speaks with a monotonous voice, as if talking in her sleep. Her lips move silently as if to form the words before speaking them. She seems able to tear the sounds from the depth of her breast only after a struggle. Aged before her time, she has hollow cheeks, a wasted body; she is very poorly dressed.*)

WOMAN. Hannele!

HANNELE (*also with closed eyes*). Mummy, my darling Mummy, is it you?

WOMAN. Yes, I have washed the feet of our Savior with my tears and dried them with my hair.

HANNELE. Do you bring me good news?

WOMAN. Yes.

HANNELE. Have you been far away?

WOMAN. I have traveled through a hundred thousand miles of darkness.

HANNELE. Mother, what do you look like?

WOMAN. Like the children of the world.

HANNELE. Lilies-of-the-valley are growing in your mouth. Your voice is like music.

WOMAN. It is not a pure tone.

HANNELE. Mother, dearest Mother, how you shine in your beauty!

WOMAN. The angels in heaven are many hundred times more beautiful.

HANNELE. Why aren't you as beautiful as they?

WOMAN. I suffered for your sake.

HANNELE. Mother dear, stay with me!

WOMAN (*rises*). I must go.

HANNELE. Is it beautiful where you are?

WOMAN. There are wide, wide meadows, sheltered from the wind, shielded from storm and hail; they are in God's care.

HANNELE. Do you rest when you are tired?

WOMAN. Yes.

HANNELE. Do you have food to eat when you are hungry?

WOMAN. I still my hunger with fruit and meat. When I am thirsty, I drink golden wine. (*She draws back.*)

HANNELE. Are you going, Mother?

WOMAN. God calls.

HANNELE. Does God call loudly?

WOMAN. God calls me loudly.

HANNELE. My whole heart is scorched, Mother!

WOMAN. God will cool it with roses and lilies.

HANNELE. Will God redeem me?

WOMAN. Do you see the flower I hold in my hand?

HANNELE. It's a primrose, the Key-to-Heaven.*

WOMAN (*puts the flower into* HANNELE's *hand*). You shall keep it, as a token from God. Farewell!

HANNELE. Mother dear, stay with me!

WOMAN (*retreating*). For a short time, you will not see me, but beyond that short time, you will.

HANNELE. I'm afraid.

WOMAN (*retreating still further*). As the wind blows the powdery snow on the mountaintops, so God will persecute your tormentors.

HANNELE. Don't leave me!

WOMAN. The children of heaven are as the blue lightning in the night.—Sleep!

(*Gradually it gets dark again. At the same time, one hears the lovely voices of little boys singing the second stanza of the song "Sleep, Little One, Sleep."*)

My little one, sleep tight,
Guests will come tonight.

(*Suddenly, a green-gold light fills the room. The luminous*

* The German word for "primrose" is, literally translated, "Key-to-Heaven."

figures of THREE ANGELS *become visible, beautiful winged youths wearing wreaths of roses on their heads; they finish the song, reading from long sheets of music which hang down on both sides of their hands. Neither* THE DEACONESS *nor* THE WOMAN *are visible.*)

> To visit you we come from far
> Your guests beloved angels are,
> Sleep, little one, sleep!

HANNELE (*opens her eyes, stares at* THE ANGELS, *enchanted and surprised*). Angels! (*Her astonishment grows, she is delighted but still doubtful.*) Angels!! (*Finally, with exuberant joy.*) Angels!!! (*Short pause.*)

(THE ANGELS *now speak, one after the other, to the accompaniment of music.*)

FIRST ANGEL.   The gold of the hills in the sunshine
                Was never granted to you;
                The billowing green of the valleys,
                Was never unfolded for you.
SECOND ANGEL.   The golden fruit of the cornfields
                Has never blunted your hunger's pain,
                The milk of the cows in the pasture
                Has never foamed in your jug.
THIRD ANGEL.   No flowers and blossoming bushes,
                Abounding with sweetness and perfume,
                Of purple and heavenly blueness,
                Have ever bordered your path.

(*Short pause.*)

FIRST ANGEL.   We bring the first greeting of welcome,
                To you through the darkness and night;
                On feathered white wings we bring you
                The first faint breath of bliss.
SECOND ANGEL.   We bring on the hem of our garments
                The first, sweet fragrance of spring.
                Our blossoming lips are the mirror
                Of the first, rosy light of the dawn.
THIRD ANGEL.   Our feet are aglow with the splendor
                Of the brilliant, green light of our home;

Our eyes are ablaze with the image
Of the walls of the City of God.

CURTAIN

ACT II

*(The scene is the same as it was before the apparition of
the angels.* THE DEACONESS *sits by* HANNELE's *bed.
She relights the candle and* HANNELE *opens her eyes.
Her vision seems to persist; her face has an expression
of ecstatic, heavenly joy. As soon as she recognizes*
THE SISTER *she begins to talk, bubbling with delight.)*

HANNELE. Sister! Angels! Sister Martha, angels!—Do you
know who was here?

SISTER MARTHA. Hm. Are you awake again?

HANNELE. Guess who was here! Well? (*Eagerly.*) Angels!
—Angels! Real angels! Angels from Heaven, Sister Martha,
you know—angels with long wings.

SISTER MARTHA. Well, if you had such a beautiful
dream . . .

HANNELE. Oh no! Now she says I've been dreaming. And
what do you think this is? Look at it! (*She seems to be
holding a flower in her hand and showing it to* SISTER
MARTHA.)

SISTER MARTHA. And what have you got there?

HANNELE. Well, look at it!

SISTER MARTHA. Hm.

HANNELE. Here, look at it!

SISTER MARTHA. Oh, yes.

HANNELE. Just smell it!

SISTER MARTHA (*bends over and pretends to smell a
flower*). Hmm, it smells beautifully.

HANNELE. No, not so close. You'll break it.

SISTER MARTHA. I am sorry. But what is it really?

HANNELE. Why, a primrose, the Key-to-Heaven; don't
you know it?

SISTER MARTHA. Oh yes, of course!

HANNELE. No . . . you don't really . . . Why don't you bring the candle! Quick, quick.

SISTER MARTHA (*holding up the candle*). Oh yes, now I see it.

HANNELE. Beautiful, isn't it?

SISTER MARTHA. You are really talking far too much. We'll have to be quite still now, or the doctor will be mad at us. He's sent you some medicine, too. And we'll take that just as we are supposed to.

HANNELE. Oh, Sister. Why are you so worried about me? And you don't even know what has happened. Well? Just tell me if you know. Who's given me that flower? Well? The golden primrose-key? Well, who? And what does the key fit? Well?

SISTER MARTHA. You tell me all about it tomorrow morning. Then you'll be nicely rested, fresh and well . . .

HANNELE. But I am well. (*She sits up and puts her feet on the floor.*) You see? I am quite well, Sister!

SISTER MARTHA. No, Hannele! You really mustn't do that. You really shouldn't do that.

HANNELE (*gets up, pushes* THE SISTER *back, takes a few steps*). You've got to let me . . . You've just got to let me . . . I must go. (*Startled, she stares at something.*) Oh, heavenly Saviour!

(AN ANGEL *dressed in black, with black wings appears. He is tall, strong, and handsome and carries a long, sinuate sword, the hilt of which is wrapped in black crepe. He sits near the stove, silent and serious, and looks at* HANNELE *with a steady, calm gaze. White, dreamlike light fills the room.*)

HANNELE. Who are you? (*No reply.*) Are you an angel? (*No reply.*) Did you come to see me? (*No reply.*) I am Hannele Mattern; did you come to see me?

(*No reply.* SISTER MARTHA *has been standing with folded hands, in pious humility. Now she slowly leaves the room.*)

HANNELE. Did God take away the words from your tongue? (*No reply.*) Do you come from God? (*No reply.*) Are you my friend? Or do you come as an enemy? (*No reply.*) Did you hide a sword in the folds of your garment?

(*No reply.*) Brr, I'm cold. A biting cold comes from your
wings. A chill comes from you. (*No reply.*) Who are you?
(*No reply. A sudden terror overwhelms her. With a cry she
turns, as if someone were behind her.*) Mother, dear
Mother! (*A figure in the garments of the deaconess, but
more beautiful and younger than she, with long, white wings,
enters the room.* HANNELE *presses close to the apparition
and seizes her hand.*) Mother, Mother, somebody is here!

DEACONESS. Where?

HANNELE. Over there—there!

DEACONESS. Why are you shivering so?

HANNELE. I'm afraid.

DEACONESS. Don't be afraid, I am with you.

HANNELE. My teeth are chattering with fear. I can't help
it. He's so horrible!

DEACONESS. Don't be afraid. He is your friend.

HANNELE. Who is it, Mother?

DEACONESS. Don't you know him?

HANNELE. Who is it?

DEACONESS. Death.

HANNELE. Death. (HANNELE *looks at the black angel in
respectful silence.*) Does it have to be?

DEACONESS. It is the gate, Hannele.

HANNELE. Does everybody have to pass through the gate?

DEACONESS. Everybody.

HANNELE. Are you going to be rough, Death? He doesn't
answer. He doesn't answer any of my questions, Mother!

DEACONESS. The Word of God is loud in your heart.

HANNELE. I have often longed for you with all my heart.
Now I'm afraid.

DEACONESS. Prepare yourself.

HANNELE. For Death?

DEACONESS. Yes.

HANNELE (*after a pause, timidly*). Do I have to lie in my
coffin in these rags?

DEACONESS. God will clothe you. (*She brings out a small
silver bell and rings it. Without a sound—as do all those
appearing subsequently—a small hump-backed village* TAILOR
*enters; he is carrying a bridal gown, a veil and bridal
wreath over his arm, and in his hands a pair of glass
slippers. He walks with a comical, swinging gait, bows silently before* THE ANGEL, *then before* THE DEACONESS *and
finally, even deeper than before, in front of* HANNELE.)

TAILOR (*still repeating his bows*). Fräulein Johanna

Katherina Mattern. (*He clears his throat.*) Your father, His Highness the Count, has deigned to order the bridal garments from me.

DEACONESS (*takes the gown from* THE TAILOR *and puts it on* HANNELE). Here, I'll help you put it on, Hannele.

HANNELE (*excited and delighted*). Oh, how it rustles!

DEACONESS. It's white silk, Hannele.

HANNELE (*looks down on herself in rapture*). Everybody will be surprised to see me in my coffin so beautifully dressed.

TAILOR. Fräulein Johanna Katherina Mattern. (*He clears his throat.*) The whole village knows about it. (*Clears his throat.*) What luck you have in death, Fräulein Hanna! (*Clears his throat.*) Your gracious father . . . (*Clears his throat.*) . . . His Highness the Count . . . (*Clears his throat.*) . . . has been to see the Mayor . . .

DEACONESS (*puts the bridal wreath on* HANNELE'*s head*). Bow your head now, bride of heaven!

HANNELE (*trembling with childish delight*). Do you know something, Sister Martha, I am looking forward to death . . . (*Suddenly doubtful about* THE SISTER.) It is you, isn't it?

DEACONESS. Yes.

HANNELE. You are Sister Martha, aren't you? Oh, no. Aren't you my mother?

DEACONESS. Yes.

HANNELE. You are both?

DEACONESS. The children of heaven are one in God.

TAILOR. With your permission, Princess Hannele. (*Kneels down before her, the slippers in his hands.*) These are the smallest slippers in the whole realm. All the others have big feet: Hedwig and Agnes, Liese and Martha, Minna and Anna, Käthe and Grete. (*He has put the slippers on her feet.*) They fit! They fit! We have found the bride! Fräulein Hannele has the smallest feet of them all.—If you should require my services again! Your servant, your servant! (*With profuse reverences, he retires.*)

HANNELE. I can hardly wait, Mother dear.

DEACONESS. Now you won't have to take any more medicine.

HANNELE. No.

DEACONESS. Soon you'll feel as fresh and gay as a brook trout, Hannele.

HANNELE. Yes.

DEACONESS. Come now, lie down on your death bed.

(*She takes* HANNELE's *hand, gently leads her to the cot, and*
HANNELE *lies down on it.*)

HANNELE. Now I'll find out at last what dying is all about.
DEACONESS. Yes, you will, Hannele.
HANNELE (*lying on her back, keeping her hands folded
as if they were holding a flower*). I have a token.
DEACONESS. Hold it tight to your breast.
HANNELE (*again afraid, glances timidly at* THE ANGEL).
Does it really have to be?
DEACONESS. It has to be.

(*From far away come the sounds of a funeral march.*)

HANNELE (*listening*). Now they are playing for the funeral, Master Seyfried and his musicians. (THE ANGEL *rises.*)
Now he is getting up. (*The storm outside increases.* THE
ANGEL *has arisen; slowly and solemnly he approaches*
HANNELE.) Now he is coming closer. Oh, Sister; Mother! I
can't see you any more. Where are you? (*Beseeching* THE
ANGEL.) Be quick, black, silent spirit! (*Groaning as if in a
nightmare.*) It presses on me, presses on me—like—like a
stone. (THE ANGEL *slowly lifts his broad sword.*) He wants—
he wants—to destroy me. (*In terrible fear.*) Help me, Sister!
DEACONESS (*steps between* THE ANGEL *and* HANNELE *with
authority and puts both her hands on* HANNELE's *heart.
Imposing and forceful, she declares with great solemnity*).
He may not do it.—I am protecting your heart with both of
my consecrated hands.

(THE BLACK ANGEL *disappears. Silence.* THE DEACONESS
folds her hands and looks at HANNELE *with a gentle
smile; then she loses herself in thought, moving her
lips in silent prayer. The music of the funeral march
has continued during the entire scene. A noise of many
pattering small feet is heard. A moment later, the figure
of* TEACHER GOTTWALD *appears in the center door.
The funeral march stops.* GOTTWALD *is dressed in black
funeral attire and holds a bouquet of beautiful bluebells
in his hand. He reverently removes his top hat and, as
soon as he has entered, he turns and gestures for silence. Behind him are his schoolchildren, boys and
girls in their best clothes. Responding to the teacher's
gesture, they stop their whispering and keep very quiet.*

They do not dare to cross the threshold. With a solem
expression, GOTTWALD *now approaches* THE DEACO
ESS, *who is still praying.*)

GOTTWALD (*softly*). Good day, Sister Martha!

DEACONESS. Herr Gottwald! God's greetings!

GOTTWALD (*looks at* HANNELE *and shakes his head*
grief and pity). Poor little thing!

DEACONESS. But why are you so sad, Herr Gottwald?

GOTTWALD. Because she has died after all.

DEACONESS. We need not be sad about that; she h
peace, and I don't begrudge her that peace.

GOTTWALD (*sighing*). Yes, she is well. At last all he
misery and grief are gone.

DEACONESS (*lost in contemplation of her*). How beautift
she looks!

GOTTWALD. Yes, you are beautiful! Now that you are dead
you've really begun to bloom.

DEACONESS. Because she was such a pious girl God ha
made her so beautiful.

GOTTWALD. Yes, she was good and she was pious. (*H
sighs deeply, opens his hymnal and looks sadly into it.*)

DEACONESS (*also looking into the hymnal*). Let us no
complain. We must be patient and calm.

GOTTWALD. Oh, my heart is heavy.

DEACONESS. Because she has been redeemed?

GOTTWALD. Because my two flowers have faded.

DEACONESS. Where?

GOTTWALD. Two violets that I have in this book. The
are my dear Hannele's dead eyes.

DEACONESS. They'll bloom even more beautifully in God'
heaven.

GOTTWALD. Oh, how much longer shall we have to con
tinue our pilgrimage through this vale of sorrows? (*Sud
denly changed, busy and businesslike, he pulls out som
sheets of music.*) What do you think? I thought first, her
in the house, we might sing: "Jesus Christ, My Sure Defense."

DEACONESS. Yes, that's a beautiful hymn, and Hannel
Mattern believed.

GOTTWALD. And then at the cemetery we'll sing "Let M
Go." (*He turns, steps over to* THE CHILDREN *and says.*) Num
ber 62, "Let Me Go." (*He intones, lightly beating time.*
Let me—go, let me—go, Lord—to me— Thy presence show

(THE CHILDREN *have been singing softly*.) Children, are you sure you're all warmly dressed? Out in the cemetery it's going to be very cold. But come in now. Take a last look at poor Hannele. (THE CHILDREN *come in and group themselves solemnly around the bed*.) Look how beautiful death has made this dear, little girl! She used to wear rags, now she wears a silk dress. She used to run around barefoot, now she has glass slippers on her feet. Soon she'll live in a golden castle and she'll eat roast meat every day.—Here she lived on cold potatoes—and she didn't even have enough of them! You've always called her "Princess Rags"; soon she'll be a real princess. So, if somebody's got to ask her forgiveness for something, now is the time; otherwise she'll tell God about everything, and then it would go bad with you.

A SMALL BOY (*steps forward a little*). Dear little Princess Hannele, don't be mad at me and don't tell God about it—that I always called you "Princess Rags."

ALL THE CHILDREN (*confusedly talking together*). We're all real sorry.

GOTTWALD. Well, I'm sure Hannele will forgive you. Go out into the hall now and wait for me.

DEACONESS. Come, I'll take you to the back room. I'll tell you what you have to do if you want to become beautiful angels like Hannele is going to be very soon. (*She walks ahead,* THE CHILDREN *follow; the door is left ajar*.)

GOTTWALD (*stays alone with* HANNELE. *Deeply moved, he puts the flowers at her feet*.) My dearest Hannele, I've brought you a bunch of these pretty bluebells. (*Kneeling down at the bed, in a trembling voice*.) Don't forget me altogether in your magnificence. (*He sobs, pressing his forehead into the folds of her gown*.) My heart is breaking because we must part. (*Voices are heard;* GOTTWALD *gets up and spreads a cloth over* HANNELE. TWO OLD WOMEN *enter quietly and quickly, dressed for a funeral; in their hands they carry handkerchiefs and yellow-edged hymnals*.)

FIRST WOMAN (*looking around*). Are we the first?

SECOND WOMAN. No, the teacher's here already. Good-day, Teacher!

FIRST WOMAN. Hits you pretty hard, don't it, Teacher? Really was almost too good, that child. Always working, always working.

SECOND WOMAN. Is it true what they say . . . it isn't true, is it? That she took her own life?

THIRD WOMAN (*has joined them*). That'd be a sin agains
the Holy Ghost.

SECOND WOMAN. A sin against the Holy Ghost.

THIRD WOMAN. A sin like that, says the pastor, can neve
be forgiven.

GOTTWALD. Don't you know what the Saviour said? Suffe
little children to come unto me?

FOURTH WOMAN (*has entered*). My, oh my, what weather
We'll probably freeze our feet. Just hope the pastor won'
make it too long. The snow's a yard deep at the cemetery

FIFTH WOMAN (*enters*). You know what? The pasto
won't bless her. He's going to refuse her the holy ground.

PLESCHKE. Did you—did you—did you hear? A grand gentleman—has been—been—to see the pastor—and has said—ha
said, has said that Mattern's Hannele is a saint.

HANKE (*enters quickly*). They're bringing a glass coffin

SEVERAL VOICES. A glass coffin!—A glass coffin!

HANKE. Jesus, that must have cost a pretty penny.

SEVERAL VOICES. A glass coffin! A glass coffin!

SEIDEL. We're going to see a lot of things! An angel's
walked smack through the middle of the village. Tall as
a poplar, believe me. At the pond by the smithy there's
two others sitting. But they're small, like little children.
The girl sort of looks like a beggar girl.

SEVERAL VOICES. The girl looks like a beggar girl.—A
glass coffin they are bringing.—An angel's walked right
through the village.

(FOUR YOUTHS *in white garments bring a glass coffin which
they put down near* HANNELE's *bed. The mourners
whisper, astounded and curious.*)

GOTTWALD (*lifts the cloth covering* HANNELE). Well, you
can look at the dead girl.

FIRST WOMAN (*inquisitively peering under the cloth*).
Her hair, my!—Sure looks like gold.

GOTTWALD (*removes the cloth completely from* HANNELE;
she is bathed in a pale light.) And a silk gown and glass
slippers!

(*All draw back with exclamations of utter amazement, as if
blinded.*)

SEVERAL VOICES. Oh, isn't she beautiful!—Who is that?

—Mattern's Hannele? That's Hannele Mattern?—I don't believe it.

PLESCHKE. The girl—the girl—the girl is a saint. (*The* FOUR YOUTHS *gently and carefully put* HANNELE *into the glass coffin.*)

HANKE. She ain't going to be buried at all, I hear.

FIRST WOMAN. She'll lie in state in the church.

SECOND WOMAN. I don't believe that girl's dead. She looks like life itself.

PLESCHKE. Give me—give me—give me a feather, so we can—so we can hold it in front of her mouth. And see—and see if she's still breathing. (*He is handed a feather which he holds in front of* HANNELE's *mouth.*) Don't move. The girl—the girl's dead all right. Not—not a trace of life in her.

THIRD WOMAN. I'll give her this bunch of rosemary. (*She puts a small bunch of flowers into the coffin.*)

FOURTH WOMAN. My lavender she can take along, too.

FIFTH WOMAN. But where is Mattern?

FIRST WOMAN. Where is Mattern?

SECOND WOMAN. Oh, him—he's sitting in the tavern.

FIRST WOMAN. He don't even know what's happened, does he?

SECOND WOMAN. As long as he's got his liquor—he don't know from nothing.

PLESCHKE. Didn't you—didn't you—didn't you tell him that he's got a—a corpse in the house?

THIRD WOMAN. He should know that himself.

FOURTH WOMAN. I wouldn't want to say nothing, not me. But everybody knows who killed the girl.

SEIDEL. Sure do; the whole village knows that, you might say. A bump like my fist she's got.

FIFTH WOMAN. Where that one puts his foot no grass'll ever grow again.

SEIDEL. We got her dressed all of us and I sure could see something. I'm telling you, a bump like my fist she's got. That's what killed her.

FIRST WOMAN. Mattern's sure enough got her on his conscience.

ALL (*agitated, talking to each other in whispers*). He did it!

SECOND WOMAN. A murderer, that's what he is.

ALL (*furiously but secretively*). A murderer, a murderer.

(*The drunken, screeching voice of* MATTERN *is heard.*)

MATTERN'S VOICE (*sing-song*). A good conscience is the best pillow. (*He appears in the door and screams.*) Girl, girl! You brat! Where are you? (*Slouching by the door frame.*) I'll count to five—I'll wait that long. I won't wait one second longer: one—two—three—and one is—girl, don't get me mad, I tell you. If I go looking for you and I find you, you scum, I'll squash you. (*Becomes aware of* THE MOURNERS, *who maintain dead silence; startled.*) What are you doing here? (*No answer.*) How did you get here?—The devil sent you, huh? Get out of here! Well, are you going? (*He laughs to himself.*) Better wait a while. I know them tricks. Don't mean nothing. Just got a little too much —went to my head. Makes you see things. (*Sings.*) A good conscience is a soft pillow. (*Startled.*) You still here? (*With uncontrollable fury he starts looking for something to use as a weapon.*) I'll take anything I can find . . .

(*A* MAN *enters, wearing a brown, shabby traveling cape and sandals. He is about thirty years old, with long, black hair and a pale face with features like those of* TEACHER GOTTWALD. *In his left hand he carries a broad-brimmed hat; he looks dusty and tired from walking. He interrupts the bricklayer, gently touching his arm.* MATTERN *spins around.*)

THE STRANGER (*looking calmly and seriously into his face, says humbly*). Bricklayer Mattern—God be with you!

MATTERN. Where do you come from? What do you want?

THE STRANGER (*humble and imploring*). My feet are bloody from walking; give me water to wash them with. The hot sun has scorched me; give me wine to refresh myself. I have not had any bread since I started out this morning. I am hungry.

MATTERN. What do I care! Who asked you to tramp around on the roads? Go find some work instead. I have to work.

THE STRANGER. I am a worker.

MATTERN. A tramp, that's what you are. If you work you don't have to go begging.

THE STRANGER. I am a worker without wages.

MATTERN. A tramp, that's what you are.

THE STRANGER (*hesitates; humbly but insistently*). I am a physician—and you may need me.

MATTERN. I ain't sick, I don't need a doctor.

THE STRANGER (*in a voice trembling with emotion*). Bricklayer Mattern, reflect! You need not give me water and I shall cure you nevertheless. You need not give me bread to soothe my hunger, and yet I shall make you well, so help me God.

MATTERN. Why, you get out of here! Get on your way! I got sound bones in my body. I don't need no doctor! Understand?

THE STRANGER. Bricklayer Mattern, reflect! I shall wash your feet. I shall give you wine for your thirst. You shall eat sweet bread. Put your foot on my head, and yet I shall cure you and make you well, so help me God.

MATTERN. Well, let's see if you don't get out of here! And if you can't find the way, I tell you, I'll . . .

THE STRANGER (*somberly, in an admonishing tone*). Bricklayer Mattern, do you know what there is in this house?

MATTERN. Everything that belongs. Everything that belongs here. You don't. Get moving now!

THE STRANGER (*simply*). Your daughter is ill.

MATTERN: No need for a doctor to cure her. What she's sick from is loafing. And I can handle that all right.

THE STRANGER (*solemnly*). Bricklayer Mattern, I come to you as a messenger.

MATTERN. And who gave you a message?

THE STRANGER: I come from the Father—and I return to the Father. Where is His child?

MATTERN. How would I know where she hangs out! His children don't mean nothing to me. He ain't been worrying none about her before.

THE STRANGER (*firmly*). There is a body in your house.

MATTERN (*notices* HANNELE *lying in the coffin; stiffly and silently he walks over and peers into it; he murmurs*). Where did you get them beautiful clothes from? Who bought you that glass coffin?

(THE MOURNERS *whisper to each other, excitedly and secretively. Several times the word* "murderer" *is heard, spoken with bitterness.*)

MATTERN (*quietly, trembling*). But I never treated you bad. I given you clothes and I given you food. (*Arrogantly to* THE STRANGER.) What do you want from me? Don't bother me.

THE STRANGER. Bricklayer Mattern, do you have something to tell me?

(The whispering among THE MOURNERS *is getting more and more excited, more and more furious, the word "murderer, murderer" is heard repeatedly.)*

THE STRANGER. Don't you have anything to regret? Didn't you ever tear her from her sleep at night? Didn't she ever collapse like dead under your blows?

MATTERN *(horrified, beside himself)*. Strike me down! Right here and now! Lightning from heaven shall strike me if it's my fault!

(Faint, bluish lightning and distant thunder.)

EVERYBODY *(talking at once)*. A thunderstorm coming. In the middle of the winter! He's perjured himself. The murderer of his child has perjured himself!

THE STRANGER *(emphatically, kindly)*. Is there still nothing you have to tell me, Mattern?

MATTERN *(miserably afraid)*. Whoever loves his child chastises him. I done nothing but good to this girl. Kept her like my own daughter. And I can punish her if she's no good.

THE WOMEN *(advancing toward him)*. Murderer, murderer, murderer, murderer!

MATTERN. She's lied to me and she's cheated me. Day in, day out she's been stealing from me.

THE STRANGER. Do you speak the truth?

MATTERN. May God punish me . . .

(At this moment a primrose appears in HANNELE's *folded hands; a yellowish-green glow emanates from it.* BRICK-LAYER MATTERN *stares at this apparition, his whole body shaking, completely beside himself.)*

THE STRANGER. Bricklayer Mattern, you are lying.

ALL *(talking at once in the greatest excitement)*. A miracle!—A miracle!

PLESCHKE. The girl—the girl—the girl is a—a saint! Body and soul—body and soul he's sworn away!

MATTERN *(screams)*. I'll hang—myself! *(Holding his head with both hands he rushes out.)*

THE STRANGER *(slowly walks to* HANNELE's *coffin and*

turns to THE MOURNERS; *everybody shrinks back from the man who now stands majestically before them.*) Do not be afraid! (*He bends down and takes* HANNELE's *hand as if examining her.*) This little girl has not died. She is asleep. (*With deep emotion and convincing strength.*) Johanna Mattern, arise!

(*A bright, golden-green light fills the room.* HANNELE *opens her eyes, pulls herself up by* THE STRANGER's *hand, but does not dare to look at his face. She steps out of the coffin and immediately sinks down on her knees before him. Gripped by fear,* THE MOURNERS *flee.* THE STRANGER *and* HANNELE *remain alone. The gray cape has fallen from his shoulders and he now stands in a white-gold garment.*)

THE STRANGER (*softly and tenderly*). Hannele.

HANNELE (*enraptured, bows her head as deeply as possible*). He is here.

THE STRANGER. Who am I?

HANNELE. You.

THE STRANGER. Say my name.

HANNELE (*breathes, trembling with awe*). Holy, holy!

THE STRANGER. I know all your suffering and all your pain.

HANNELE. Oh dear, dear ...

THE STRANGER. Arise.

HANNELE. Your garments are clean. My shame is great.

THE STRANGER (*puts his right hand on* HANNELE's *head*). Thus I take from you all that is base. (*He bends her head up with gentle force and touches her eyes.*) Thus I let your eyes partake of the eternal light. Behold with these eyes suns and ever more suns. Behold with these eyes the eternal day, from dawn to dusk, and from dusk to dawn. Behold with these eyes all the splendor, the blue sea, the blue sky and the green meadows, for ever and ever. (*He touches her ear.*) Thus I let you partake of the rejoicing of all the millions of angels in the millions of heavens of God. (*He touches her mouth.*) Thus I free your tongue from its stammering and put upon it your soul, and my soul and the soul of God the Almighty.

(HANNELE *tries to rise, her whole body trembling. As if weighed down by an immense burden of joy, she is*

*unable to do so. Shaken by deep sighs and violent sobs,
she hides her head on the breast of* THE STRANGER.)

THE STRANGER. With these tears I wash from your soul
all the dust and all the torment of this world. I shall lift
your foot beyond God's stars.

(THE STRANGER, *gently caressing* HANNELE's *head, speaks
the following lines to the accompaniment of soft music.
While he is speaking, the figures of* ANGELS *appear in
the doorway; some are tall, some small, some are boys,
some girls; at first they hesitate, then they become bold
enough to enter. They swing censers and decorate the
room with carpets and flowers.*)

THE STRANGER. A wondrous and beautiful town is bliss.
      In its walls, peace and joy you never will
        miss.

(*The sound of harps is heard, at first softly, in the end full
and loud.*)

      Of marble the houses, with roofs of gold.
      Red wine the silvery fountains hold.
      On its broad, white streets are carpets of
        flowers
      And wedding bells ring from the soaring
        towers.
      The walls, shining green in the dawn's
        early light,
      Are sheathed in red roses—a marvelous
        sight.
      White swans, circling wide high over the
        town,
      Puff out their bright feathers, their rus-
        tling gown.
      Through the blossoming air they fly round
        upon round,
      Through the air atremble with bells'
        brazen sound.
      Their wings sound like harps as they
        solemnly fly
      Their eternal course in the fragrant sky.
      They look down upon Zion, on garden
        and lake,

Green streamers of gossamer trail in their
    wake.
Far below, men and women walk hand
    in hand,
Wearing festive garments, through heav-
    en's land.
The wide sea is filled with the reddest
    red wine;
When they bathe like rubies their bodies
    shine.
Immersed in the foam, engulfed by the
    splendor,
To the transparent purple they wholly
    surrender.
And when joyfully they emerge from the
    flood
They are washed and cleansed by Jesus'
    blood.

(THE STRANGER *now turns to* THE ANGELS *who have meanwhile completed their task. Timidly, yet full of happiness and joy they approach and form a half-circle around*
HANNELE *and* THE STRANGER.)

With linen approach now, heavenly chil-
    dren!
Come close, sweet children, turtle doves!
Wrap this poor body, weak from suffering,
Shaken by cold, by fever scorched.
Tenderly! Pressure must not hurt the flesh.
And gently floating, with your wings ex-
    tended,
The meadows' grass just touching,
You'll lift her sweetly through the moon-
    lit night,
Through flowers' fragrance and the scent
    of paradise,
Until the temple's cooling air receives her.

(*Short pause.*)

Then mix, while she still sleeps on silken
    cushions—

From water of the mountain's gurgling
    brook,
From purple wine and antelope's white
    milk—
A bath to wash away her earthly sickness.
From lilacs break their flower-laden
    branches,
From jasmin also, heavy with the dew of
    night,
And their clear drops, their humid bur-
    den,
Let drip upon her like refreshing rain.
Then take soft silk and dry her limbs
As carefully as lily petals.
From golden vessels pour refreshing wine,
Enriched with juice pressed from the
    ripest fruits.
Bring strawberries to her, still warm with
    sunlight,
And raspberries, their sweet blood over-
    flowing,
Pineapples, too, and velvet-covered
    peaches,
And yellow oranges like setting suns
On silver platters, glistening like mirrors.
Flatter her palate, and her heart may wel-
    come
The riches and the splendor of the morn.
Allow her eyes to feast on stately col-
    umns.
Let flame-red butterflies around her flutter
Above the greenish floor of malachite.
Her feet shall walk on satin carpets
Through beds of tulips and of hyacinths,
Amid the palm trees' broad and trembling
    fronds,
The shining walls reflecting everything.
Show her the fields of glowing poppies
Where Heaven's children play with gold-
    en balls,
Aglitter with the rising sun's first rays;
Let lovely melodies entice her senses.

THE ANGELS (*singing in unison*).
    We carry you yonder in silken silence,

> Hush-a-by, by-by to heavenly rest,
> Hush-a-by, by-by, to heavenly rest.

(*During* THE ANGELS' *song the scene grows darker, and the sound of the singing becomes weaker and more distant. Then the lights brighten and the room in the poorhouse is seen exactly as it was before the apparition.* HANNELE *lies in her bed, once again a poor, sick child.* DR. WACHLER *bends over her with his stethoscope;* THE DEACONESS *holds a candle for him, anxiously looking at his face. Only now the singing stops completely.*)

DR. WACHLER (*straightening up*). You were right.
SISTER MARTHA. Is she dead?
DR. WACHLER (*nods sadly*). Yes, dead.

CURTAIN

PREFACE TO *Drayman Henschel*

In *The Rats*, Hauptmann presents a conversation between an old-fashioned actor-manager, Hassenreuter, and his pupil, a former student of theology, Spitta. The manager reminds him: "You asserted the other day that a barber or a scrubwoman might as fittingly be the protagonist of a tragedy as King Lear or Lady Macbeth." To this challenge, the progressive pupil, obviously a devotee of the new naturalistic theatre, retorts, "Before art, as before the law, all men are equal, sir." At the end of the play in which a scrubwoman is destroyed by the maternal instinct, the student asks, "Won't you admit that a genuinely tragic fatality has been acted here?" and the comically-delineated master replies, "Tragedy is not confined to any class of society, I always told you that."

Much the same doctrine had been propounded more than half a century earlier by Victor Hugo in the famous *Préface* to *Cromwell*. Hugo affirmed the then current revolt against French classicism and his own ultra-romantic penchant for the grotesque which, "as a means of contrast with the sublime," he called "the richest source that nature can offer art." Rejecting conventional "ennoblement," "good taste," and "the graces," Hugo, who is justifiably better remembered for his social novel *Les Misérables* than for his operatic plays, wanted art "to set about doing as nature does, mingling in its creations . . . darkness and light, the grotesque and the sublime . . . the body and the soul, the beast and the intellect." There was no other way, according to Hugo, to reflect reality.

In *Drayman Henschel* Hauptmann went about doing just that, but with a naturalistic disregard of "the sublime" and "the intellect" (in contrast to the instinctual element in life) and without any romantic or sensation-seeking exploitation of the grotesque. Avoiding rhetoric and plot contrivance, fixing his attention instead on the submission to instinct and blind gropings of his characters, Hauptmann managed to create the austere yet moving tragedy—call it, if you will, "*low* tragedy"—of a common man greatly bewildered and put upon in a world devoid of beauty, nobility, or distinction. The only distinction in the play belongs to Henschel by virtue of his inarticulate good will, his troubled conscience—for breaking his vow to his dying wife and marrying their unscrupulous housemaid—and the intensity of his unostentatious suffering.

If Edith Hamilton is correct in asserting that a tragic character is distinguished by his unusual capacity for suffering, Henschel is "tragic" and validates the common man as a possible protagonist of tragedy. And if we should be disposed to interpose objections to using uncommon suffering as the sole criterion, *Fuhrmann Henschel* is nonetheless an excellent example of what naturalists considered to be "naturalistic tragedy"—namely, the presentation of catastrophe in the life of a common man caused by natural forces in an unpoetic, preferably lowly, environment, and under rather ordinary circumstances brought to an extraordinary pitch of crisis.

A deep and sharp conflict agitates *Drayman Henschel* with its contrasts between the noble but bewildered title-character and the feral female, Hanne, who extracts an offer of marriage from Henschel, betrays him, neglects his child by a previous marriage, drives away his friends, and undermines him. "*Henschel*," according to one of Hauptmann's best English critics, Margaret Sinden, "has Hauptmann's insight into character and environment, his ability to give depth and tension to the most everday scenes, and his skill in recording the living language, at their best." In this work, "written with a sure and quiet mastery" and with an effective "slight detachment," though with an ample sympathy for his hero, Hauptmann accepts the tragedy with well-nigh Olympian equanimity. Blaming no one, he holds out no possibility of escape from a fatality compounded of character, desire, will, error, and the crass casualty that obscures the light of understanding because no explanation seems adequate.

Not especially suited for export to English-speaking theatre, this work, which made a strong impression on the German stage when first presented on November 5, 1898,

tands, nevertheless, as a monument to the integrity of
dramatic realism in the European theatre. It should not be
difficult for the sympathetic reader to release the emotional
energy of this play with the help of his imagination.

DRAYMAN HENSCHEL

A Play in Five Acts

CHARACTERS

Drayman Henschel

Frau Henschel

Hanne Schäl, later Frau Henschel

Bertha

Walther, a horse dealer

Siebenhaar, a hotel owner

Little Karl, his son

Wermelskirch, a tavern keeper

Frau Wermelskirch, his wife

Franziska Wermelskirch, their daughter

Hauffe, in Henschel's service

Franz, in Siebenhaar's service

George, a waiter

Fabig, a peddler

Master Hildebrant, a blacksmith

Grunert, a veterinary

Firemen

The time is in the eighteen-sixties, the scene is the Gray Swan Hotel in a Silesian spa.

ACT I

(*A peasant's room in the basement of the Gray Swan Hotel.
The dim light of a late winter afternoon comes through
windows set high in the left wall. Below the windows
stands a bed of polished, yellow softwood.* FRAU
HENSCHEL, *a woman of about thirty-six years, lies sick
in the bed. Her six-months' old daughter lies in a cradle
next to the bed. A second bed stands along the rear
wall. All the walls are painted the same blue, with a
dark stripe setting off the walls from the ceiling. In the
right foreground stands a large, brown tile stove. Around
its exposed sides runs a bench. Split firewood is piled
into the large opening at the bottom of the stove. In
the right-hand wall is a narrow door leading to the
small bedroom.*

HANNE SCHÄL, *a young, strong servant girl, is busily
at work. She has taken off her wooden clogs and has
only thick blue stockings on her feet. She pulls a pot in
which some food is cooking out of the oven, then pushes
it back in. On the bench lie a wooden cooking spoon, a
twirling stick and colanders; next to them stands a
large, bulging earthenware pitcher with a bottle-like
neck that is closed with a cork and, finally, a jug for
getting water from the well. Hanne's skirts are rolled
up. She wears a gray-black bodice that leaves her arms
bare.—Around the upper part of the stove runs a square
bar on which long, "hunting" stockings, diapers,
leather pants with small ribbons, and a pair of water-
proof boots are hung to dry. To the right of the stove
stand a chest and a cupboard, both of them old, painted
pieces of furniture in Silesian peasant style. Through
the open door in the back one looks into the dark,
broad basement passage, at the far end of which is a
glass door with multicolored panes. Behind the door, a*

213

wooden stairway leads upstairs. In the stairwell is a gas
light that shines through the panes in the door.—It is a
stormy day in the middle of February.

FRANZ, *a young fellow in a simple coachman's livery,*
ready to go out, looks into the room.)

FRANZ. Hanne!

HANNE. What do you want?

FRANZ. Frau Henschel asleep?

HANNE. Sure she is. Don't make so much noise!

FRANZ. Oh . . . if she don't wake up from all them doors
banging all over the house! . . . I'm driving over to Waldenburg with the coach.

HANNE. Who's going?

FRANZ. Madam. She's going shopping for birthday
presents.

HANNE. Whose birthday is that?

FRANZ. Little Karl's.

HANNE. Them people's got ideas! Harness the horses
because of that silly boy and drive to Waldenburg in weather
like this!

FRANZ. Well, I got my fur coat.

HANNE. They just don't know how to get rid of their
money. And we sweat!

(*The veterinary,* GRUNERT, *appears at the end of the pas-*
sage; he advances slowly, looking around to orient him-
self. He is a small man in a black sheepskin coat, wool
cap, and high boots. He tries to attract attention by
knocking at the doorframe with the handle of his whip.)

GRUNERT. Isn't Henschel home yet?

HANNE. What's it about?

GRUNERT. I've come about the gelding.

HANNE. Oh, you're the doctor from Freiburg then, huh?
No, Henschel isn't home yet. He went down to Freiburg
with a load. Seems you two should have met.

GRUNERT. Which stable is the gelding in?

HANNE. Well, it's that big chestnut with the blaze. I think
they've put him in one of the visitors' stalls. (*To* FRANZ.)
You run along and show him.

FRANZ. It's just across the yard, straight down, under the
big hall and into the coachmen's room. Ask for Friedrich,
he'll show you. (GRUNERT *leaves.*)

HANNE. Go on! Show him the way!

FRANZ. How's about a couple of pennies for me?

HANNE. Want me to sell my skin for you?

FRANZ (*tickles her*). I'd buy it right away!

HANNE. Franz! Stop that! Do you want the woman to wake up? (*She looks for change.*) You just don't feel right if you can't weedle a few groschen from me! I'm broke.— Here! (*She gives him something.*) And now off with you! (*A bell rings.*)

FRANZ (*startled*). That's the master! See you!

(*Leaves quickly.*)

FRAU HENSCHEL (*wakes up and says weakly*). Girl!— Girl!—Can't you hear, girl?

HANNE (*gruffly*). What's the matter?

FRAU HENSCHEL. You're supposed to come when you're called.

HANNE. I'm listening, but if you don't talk a little louder I just can't hear. Only got two ears!

FRAU HENSCHEL. Getting fresh again, girl?

HANNE (*brutally*). Oh, what the hell!

FRAU HENSCHEL. Is that the way to behave? To kick a sick woman in the teeth like that?

HANNE. And who started? As soon as you wake up you're at it again, riding me. Can't do a thing right no matter what I do and how I do it.

FRAU HENSCHEL. Because you never do what you're told.

HANNE. Why don't you do it yourself then! I slave all day and half the night, but if it's like this I'd just as soon be on my way! (*She lets her skirt down and runs out.*)

FRAU HENSCHEL. Girl!—Hanne! Don't do that to me now! —What did I say now?—Jesus, oh Jesus! What's going to happen when the men come home? They want to eat!— Girl!—Girl! (*She sinks back exhausted, whimpers softly and starts gently rocking the cradle with a ribbon tied to it.*)

(KARL *pushes with difficulty through the glass door in the background. He carries a pot of soup, walks timidly and cautiously to* FRAU HENSCHEL's *bed, and puts the pot on a wooden stool by her side.*)

FRAU HENSCHEL. No really, Karlchen, is that you? And what are you bringing there, eh?

KARL. Soup. Mama sends her love and she says she hopes you'll be better soon. She says she hopes you'll like it, Frau Henschel.

FRAU HENSCHEL. You're really a good boy, Karlchen! You're my best!—And chicken soup! What do you know! —Now you go and tell your mother that I thank her a lot, understand? And don't forget!—And now I'll tell you something, Karlchen. You don't mind doing something for me, do you? Take that rag over there, hop on the bench—all right? —and pull that iron pot a little more up front, will you? The girl's left and she's put it too far back in the oven.

KARL (*willingly looks for the rag, finds it and gets on top of the bench; he looks into the oven and asks*). The black one or the blue one, Frau Henschel?

FRAU HENSCHEL. What's in the blue one?

KARL. Sauerkraut.

FRAU HENSCHEL (*excitedly*). Quick, pull it out! That's going to cook to a pulp!—Oh no, that girl!

KARL (*pulls the pot toward the front*). Is this all right?

FRAU HENSCHEL. Yes, that's fine. Just leave it like that. Come over here a minute, I'll give you a cord for your whip. (*She takes it from the windowsill and hands it to him.*) How's your mother?

KARL. Fine. She went to Waldenburg shopping . . . for me . . . for my birthday.

FRAU HENSCHEL. I'm not well at all, my boy. I think I'll die.

KARL. Oh no, Frau Henschel!

FRAU HENSCHEL. Yes, yes, I know I'm dying, my boy! You can tell your mother if you want to.

KARL. I'm going to get a wool cap, Frau Henschel!

FRAU HENSCHEL. Yes, that's the truth. Come over here . . . be quiet a minute . . . listen . . . do you hear the ticking? Hear how it's ticking in the old wood?

KARL (*whom she holds feverishly by the wrist*). I'm afraid, Frau Henschel!

FRAU HENSCHEL. Don't be afraid! Everybody's got to die. —Hear it ticking, eh? You know what this is? Do you? That's the death watch ticking. (*She sinks back.*) One . . . two . . . oh no! That girl—that girl! (*She lets go of* KARL *and he retreats uneasily toward the door. When he has his hand on the doorknob fear suddenly grips him. He pulls open the door and slams it behind him with such force that the panes*

*attle. A moment later one hears a whip cracking in the
yard. When she hears this noise* FRAU HENSCHEL *sits up
with a start.)*

FRAU HENSCHEL. Father's coming!

HENSCHEL *(still invisible in the passage).* Doctor, what
are we going to do with that animal? *(He and the veterinary,* GRUNERT, *appear in the doorway.)*

GRUNERT. He won't let anybody come near him. We'll
have to put a rope on him.

HENSCHEL *(a man of about forty-five, with an athlete's
build. He wears a fur cap, a sheepskin jacket over his blue
teamster's blouse, green hunting stockings and high water-
proof boots. He carries a whip and a lighted lantern.)* I just
don't know what's wrong with that beast. I get home last
night—had been loading coal over at the Fox Mine—take
the harness off, put the horses in the stable—and right away
he throws himself down and starts kicking all over the place.
(He puts the whip in the corner and hangs up his cap.—
HANNE *returns and starts working where she left off; she is
still furious.)* Light up, girl!

HANNE. One thing after another!

HENSCHEL *(puts out the light in the lantern and hangs it
up).* Heaven knows what's going on: first the woman gets
sick; then a horse falls. It's just as if somebody had it in for
me.—I bought that gelding from Gottfried Walter, around
Christmas time; so after two weeks he's lame. But I'll get
even with him. Two hundred talers I paid.

FRAU HENSCHEL. It's raining, isn't it?

HENSCHEL *(without paying attention).* Yes, Mother, it's
raining.—And cheating his own brother-in-law that way!
(He sits down on the oven bench. HANNE *has lighted a
tallow candle in a tin-plated candlestick and puts it on the
table.)*

FRAU HENSCHEL. You're just too good, Father! You trust
everybody!

GRUNERT *(sits down at the table and writes a prescription).* I'll write down something for you to get from the
pharmacy.

FRAU HENSCHEL. No, if that chestnut goes, too! The Lord
can't want that to happen!

HENSCHEL *(holding his leg out for* HANNE). Come on,
pull the boots off for me!—It's been whistling something
fierce, over from Freiburg way. Seems the wind took half

the roof off the church in the lower village, they say. (*To* HANNE.) That's some heaving you're doing. Aren't you done yet?

FRAU HENSCHEL (*to* HANNE). I can't understand why you can't learn even that! (HANNE *has finished with the first boot, puts it aside and tackles the other one.*)

HENSCHEL. Leave her alone, Mother. You're not much better at it yourself.

HANNE (*succeeds in getting the second boot off and puts it aside, then to* HENSCHEL *in a gruff tone of voice*). Did you bring my apron from Kramsta at least?

HENSCHEL. The things I'm supposed to keep in my head! I'm just glad if I don't forget my own business and get the cases of bottled water to the station. Bother with women's aprons!

GRUNERT. You really aren't famous for that sort of thing!

FRAU HENSCHEL. Good thing that, too!

HENSCHEL (*puts on wooden clogs and gets up; to* HANNE.) Hurry up now! Let's have something to eat! I still have to go down to the smithy tonight.

GRUNERT (*has gotten up, leaving the prescription on the table; he puts pad and pencil away and is about to leave.*) Take it to the pharmacy as soon as you can, will you? To-morrow morning early I'll come and see about him. (HENSCHEL *sits down at the table.*)

HAUFFE (*enters slowly; he wears wooden clogs and leather pants; he, too, carries a lantern in his hand.*) Real lousy weather again!

HENSCHEL. How does it look in the barn?

HAUFFE. He's simply wrecking the whole stall. (*Puts out the light in his lantern and hangs it next to* HENSCHEL'*s.*)

GRUNERT. Good-night, everybody. We'll just have to wait and see. Even we doctors are only human.

HENSCHEL. Sure, sure. We know that all right. Good-night —and watch out . . . see that you stay on the road! (GRUNERT *leaves.*) Now then, Mother, how are you doing?

FRAU HENSCHEL. Oh, I'm all bothered again.

HENSCHEL. And who's bothering you? (HAUFFE *sits down at the table.*)

FRAU HENSCHEL. It's just that I can't do anything . . . nothing at all. (HANNE *puts a dish with dumplings and an-other one with sauerkraut on the table, then takes forks out of the table drawer and puts them on the table.*)

HENSCHEL. That's what the girl's here for.

FRAU HENSCHEL. A girl just don't think much.

HENSCHEL. Well, we got something to eat; it's working out all right.—If only you hadn't gotten up too early you'd be able to be up and dancing by now.

FRAU HENSCHEL. Oh Jesus! Dancing! That'd be something. (HANNE *has set out three plates with a piece of pork on each, now pulls up a stool and sits down herself.*)

HAUFFE. The oats won't last much longer, neither.

HENSCHEL. I bought thirty bags yesterday. And Saturday we'll get a load of hay. Feed's getting more expensive all the time.

HAUFFE. If you want them animals to work they got to eat, too.

HENSCHEL. Sure, but everyone seems to think they live on air.—He even wants to cut the cartage again.

HAUFFE. Told me something like that, too.

FRAU HENSCHEL. Who? The Spa Inspector?

HENSCHEL. Sure, who else. But this time I'm not giving in.

FRAU HENSCHEL. Good heavens, that'd really be the end; what are we supposed to do in bad times like this?

HANNE. The Highway Inspector's been around. Seems he wants you to send some teams tomorrow, over to the big road roller. They're back near Hinterhartau now.

(HERR SIEBENHAAR *comes down the stairs behind the glass door. He is in his early forties, very carefully dressed; he wears a black cloth coat, white vest, light-colored English trousers; elegant in the style of the end of the eighteen-sixties. He is almost bald, with only a neat circle of graying hair remaining. His mustache, however, is full and still dark blond. He wears golden spectacles and when he wants to look closely at something he uses, in addition, a gold pince-nez that he usually puts behind the spectacles. He looks intelligent.*)

SIEBENHAAR (*holding in his right hand a key-ring, and a tin candlestick with an unlit candle, comes close to the open door and looks into the room shielding his sensitive eyes with his left hand.*) Has Henschel come back?

HENSCHEL. Yes sir, Herr Siebenhaar.

SIEBENHAAR. Oh, you're just eating. I have something to do in the cellar. We can talk later.

HENSCHEL. No, no. As far as I'm concerned . . . I've finished.

SIEBENHAAR. Maybe you better come on upstairs then. (*He enters and lights his candle with the one that is on the table.*) I just want to light the candle.—In my office we'll be quite undisturbed.—And how are you, Frau Henschel? Did you like the chicken broth?

FRAU HENSCHEL. No, just think of it! I forgot all about it!

SIEBENHAAR. You don't say.

HANNE (*discovering the pot with the chicken broth*). What do you know! There it is!

HENSCHEL. That's how that woman is! How's she going to get well? She just forgets to eat and drink.

(*Violent blast of wind.*)

SIEBENHAAR. Tell me, what do you think: my wife's driven over to Waldenburg, you know. The weather seems to be getting worse and worse. I'm really worried. What do you think?

HENSCHEL. Probably sounds worse than it is.

SIEBENHAAR. Well, there's no point biting off more than one can chew. Didn't you hear that terrible noise? One of the big windows, you know, on the terrace, in the dining room, has already been blown in by the wind. It's really quite a storm!

HENSCHEL. Isn't that something!

FRAU HENSCHEL. There goes a lot of money again!

SIEBENHAAR (*leaving through the basement passage, turning left*). Only death costs nothing.   (*Leaves.*)

HENSCHEL. Yes, he's got his pile of troubles, too.

FRAU HENSCHEL. I wonder what he wants from you again, Father?

HENSCHEL. Oh, nothing. Who knows? I'll soon find out.

FRAU HENSCHEL. I only hope he don't ask you for money again.

HENSCHEL. Oh, don't talk nonsense, Mother.

HANNE. If them people don't have the money, why does the woman have to buy a hat that costs four talers?

HENSCHEL. You be quiet. Nobody asked you. Stick your nose into the pots, not in other peoples' business.—A house like that, sure needs keeping up. For eight weeks a year some money's coming in, after that he can see how he makes out.

HAUFFE. And he's had to build, too.

FRAU HENSCHEL. That's what really did him in. He shouldn't have done it.

HENSCHEL. Women don't know about things like that. He had to build . . . damn well couldn't do nothing else. Now there are more guests than ever taking the waters . . . wasn't half that many before. But before, they used to spend money, now they want everything for free.—Pour me a drink, will you? I feel like having a glass of corn.

HAUFFE (*slowly folding his penknife and about to get up*). Forty rooms, three banquet halls, and nothing but rats and mice in them. How's he going to raise the interest?

(FRANZISKA WERMELSKIRCH *looks in through the door; she is a vivacious, pretty girl of sixteen. She wears her long, dark hair loose. Her dress is somewhat eccentric: a short, white skirt, a blouse with a low-cut V-neck, and a long, multicolored sash. Her arms are almost bare; around her neck she wears a colored ribbon with a gold crucifix.*)

FRANZISKA (*very eagerly*). Wasn't Herr Siebenhaar here just now?—A pleasant meal, ladies and gentlemen! I just meant to ask whether Herr Siebenhaar has been down here just now?

FRAU HENSCHEL (*gruffly*). How would we know? Hasn't been to see us.

FRANZISKA. He hasn't? And here I thought he had. (*She puts one foot coquettishly on the stove bench to tie a shoe lace.*)

FRAU HENSCHEL. Herr Siebenhaar here, Herr Siebenhaar there. What d'you want from the man all the time?

FRANZISKA. I? Nothing! It's just that he likes goose liver very much. Mama happens to have some and so Papa sent me to tell him. Incidentally, Herr Henschel, do you know something? You might honor us with your presence again one of these days.

FRAU HENSCHEL. Oh no, you just leave Father alone, will you? Don't start that now. He isn't in no mood for the tavern right now.

FRANZISKA. And we have just put a new barrel on tap today!

HENSCHEL (*while* HAUFFE *grins and* HANNE *laughs out loud*). Mother, you mind your own business. You think I'm going to ask permission if I want to go drink a glass of beer? I don't need to ask nobody.

FRANZISKA. And how do you feel, Frau Henschel?

FRAU HENSCHEL. Tomorrow I'm going to put on a sash, too, and start rope dancing.

FRANZISKA. I'm coming along! That's something I can do really well. I've been practicing on the wagon shaft.

HENSCHEL. Now I know at last why all the shafts are bent!

FRANZISKA. You see, that's how it's done, that's the way to balance on a rope. (*Imitating the movements of a rope dancer on the tightrope, she dances out of the room.*) Right leg, left leg, right leg, left leg. Au revoir!   (*Leaves.*)

HAUFFE (*taking his lantern down*). She'll crack pretty soon, that one, if she don't get a man.   (*Leaves.*)

FRAU HENSCHEL. If they'd only keep her working as hard's everybody else! I'd soon get them silly ideas out of her head.

HANNE. She ain't allowed upstairs no more. Madame won't have it.

FRAU HENSCHEL. Right she is, too. I wouldn't stand for it, neither.

HANNE. She's after the Master she is, like a pointer. But darn it, she's really going a bit too far.

FRAU HENSCHEL. Throw them out, that's what he should do—Siebenhaar. With those goings-on with the women and the fellows down there.

HENSCHEL. Oh, don't talk nonsense, Mother!

FRAU HENSCHEL. Well, in the tavern, I mean.

HENSCHEL. They're people just like us. They got to live. You want him to throw them out on the street? Wermelskirch is not a bad fellow.

HANNE. But the woman's an old bitch.

HENSCHEL. So what! If he pays the rent, he's going to stay. And about the girl . . . that won't make no difference, either. (*He has gotten up and bends over the cradle.*) We got a little thing like that here, too, and nobody's going to throw us out on account of her, either.

FRAU HENSCHEL. Of course not! That'd be a fine thing! —She's sleeping all the time. Just don't like waking up.

HENSCHEL. Just not much to her. Now, Mother, don't you die on me, will you? (*Takes his cap from the hook.*) Hanne, I've been fooling you. Your apron is out in the wagon.

HANNE (*eagerly*). Where?

HENSCHEL. In the back. Just go and look. (*Leaves through the middle door;* HANNE *goes into the bedroom.*)

FRAU HENSCHEL. So he brought—her the—apron—after all!

(HANNE *comes out of the bedroom and quickly leaves by the center door.*)

FRAU HENSCHEL. So he brought—her the apron—after all!

SIEBENHAAR (*enters slowly, carrying a candle and his keys as before, and two bottles of red wine.*) All alone, Frau Henschel?

FRAU HENSCHEL. So he brought—her the apron . . .

SIEBENHAAR. It's me, Frau Henschel; I believe you are mistaking me for somebody else.

FRAU HENSCHEL. I believe . . . hardly . . .

SIEBENHAAR. I hope I didn't wake you up. It's me— Siebenhaar!

FRAU HENSCHEL. Of course! Why, of course!

SIEBENHAAR. I just wanted to bring you a little wine. You ought to drink it; it's good for you. Don't you recognize me?

FRAU HENSCHEL. Sure. That'd be something! You are . . . of course . . . you're our Herr Siebenhaar. I'm not that far gone! I sure ought to know you!—I don't know, have I been dreaming, or what?

SIEBENHAAR. That's quite possible. And how is it going now?

FRAU HENSCHEL. Of course, you're Herr Siebenhaar!

SIEBENHAAR. Did you think I was your husband?

FRAU HENSCHEL. I don't know—I just can't—say—really. It just seemed . . .

SIEBENHAAR. It looks as if you aren't very comfortable at all lying like that. I'll straighten out your pillow a bit. Does the Doctor come regularly?

FRAU HENSCHEL (*excited and whining*). I just don't know, they leave me all alone all the time.—No, I know, you're Siebenhaar all right. And do you know something? I'll tell you something; you've always been good to me. You're a good man . . . even if you look cross sometimes! To you I can tell it: I'm so afraid! I always think he wants me to hurry up.

SIEBENHAAR. Hurry up? Doing what?

FRAU HENSCHEL (*bursting into tears*). Dying! I'm not dying fast enough!—Oh . . . what's going to become of Gustel?

SIEBENHAAR. But my dear Frau Henschel! What are you saying!

FRAU HENSCHEL (*sobbing softly*). What's going to happen to Gustel—when I die?

SIEBENHAAR. Frau Henschel, you're a reasonable woman. Now listen to me. If one has to lie in bed, without moving like that, like you have to, unfortunately, you see one gets silly ideas, of course. You just imagine all kinds of silly things. But there you'll have to be quite firm, Frau Henschel. That'd be a fine thing! Such nonsense! Just forget all about it! That's nothing but foolishness.

FRAU HENSCHEL. Oh good God! You don't believe me . . . but I know what I'm talking about.

SIEBENHAAR. That's just what you don't know. Unfortunately, just now you don't and if you think back later you'll laugh about it yourself. I'm quite sure.

FRAU HENSCHEL (*in a passionate explosion*). Didn't he go see her in the bedroom?

SIEBENHAAR (*perplexed and incredulous*). What? Who are you talking about?

FRAU HENSCHEL. Well, Henschel! And the girl!

SIEBENHAAR. Your husband? And Hanne? You know, whoever told you that story is a dastardly liar.

FRAU HENSCHEL. After I'm dead he'll take her for sure.

(HENSCHEL *appears in the doorway*.)

SIEBENHAAR. You must be suffering from hallucinations, Frau Henschel.

HENSCHEL (*kindly and surprised*). What's bothering you, Malchen? Why are you crying like that?

SIEBENHAAR. Henschel! You mustn't leave your wife alone!

HENSCHEL (*has walked over to the bed, tenderly*). Who's hurting you?

FRAU HENSCHEL (*irritated, turns around, her face toward the wall, her back to* HENSCHEL). Oh, leave me alone!

HENSCHEL. What's the matter?

FRAU HENSCHEL (*barking at him through her tears*). Oh, get away from me! (HENSCHEL *is visibly puzzled and looks questioningly at* SIEBENHAAR *who shakes his head and cleans his pince-nez.*)

SIEBENHAAR (*quietly*). Better leave your wife alone just now.

FRAU HENSCHEL (*as before*). In my grave you'd like to see me!

SIEBENHAAR (*to* HENSCHEL *who is about to lose his temper*). Sh, Sh! Do me the favor and keep still.

FRAU HENSCHEL. I got eyes, after all. I'm not blind. You don't have to put it on so thick! I'm no use no more . . . and now you want me to go packing.

HENSCHEL (*forcing himself to remain calm*). Now, what does that mean, Malchen?

FRAU HENSCHEL. Oh yes, just go on pretending!

HENSCHEL (*quite helplessly*). Now, please . . . just tell me . . .

FRAU HENSCHEL. Whatever happens, I won't let you make a fool out of me . . . never . . . even if you try and hide God knows where. I can look through walls; I can see you anyways. Oh no, you don't! You think it's easy to cheat a wife. Not on your life! Just remember, when I die Gustel's going to die with me. I'm going to take her along. I'd rather strangle her than leave her to that damn bitch.

HENSCHEL. Mother, what in God's name's gotten into you?

FRAU HENSCHEL. You want to see me in my grave.

HENSCHEL. You stop that now or I'll get really angry.

SIEBENHAAR (*quietly restraining him*). Easy, Henschel, easy. The woman is sick after all.

FRAU HENSCHEL (*who has heard him*). Sick? And who's made me sick? The two of you: that—bitch and you!

HENSCHEL. What I'd like to know is, who in the world has put all these bees in your bonnet? That girl and me? Damn it all! I'm supposed to have something with her?

FRAU HENSCHEL. Don't you bring her ribbons and aprons?

HENSCHEL (*again perplexed*). Ribbons and aprons?

FRAU HENSCHEL. Yes, ribbons and aprons!

HENSCHEL. Now I've heard everything.

FRAU HENSCHEL. And everything she does is just so nice and so pretty! Do you ever tell her off? She's already behaving like she owned the house.

HENSCHEL. Mother, shut up now, I'm telling you!

FRAU HENSCHEL. You're the one who has to shut up—because you got nothing to say.

SIEBENHAAR (*by the bed*). Frau Henschel, you must pull yourself together. All this is just pure imagination.

FRAU HENSCHEL. You're no better, either. You're doing the same thing! The poor wives, they can suffer for it. They can just lie down and die! (*Softly weeping.*) They can just go and die. (SIEBENHAAR *gives a short, bitter laugh, walks over to the table and starts to uncork one of the wine bottles.*)

HENSCHEL (*sits down on the side of the bed and tries to calm her*). Mother! Mother! Turn around! I want to tell you something. (*He turns her around with gentle force.*) You see, Mother, you've just been dreaming. You just had a bad dream. Just like the dog, he sometimes dreams things. But wake up now! Understand, Mother? You've been making some god-awful speeches here, the biggest wagon would just go to pieces if you tried to load it with all the tripe you've been talking. My head's still turning!

SIEBENHAAR (*has looked for and found a glass which he is now filling*). You've had me on the carpet too!

HENSCHEL. No, I really hope you won't take that wrong. What a woman! A fellow's really got his troubles with a woman like that. You better go and get well now! Or soon you'll be going around telling people I'm a horse thief.

SIEBENHAAR. Here, drink some wine, that'll make you strong again.

FRAU HENSCHEL. If I only knew! (SIEBENHAAR *holds her up while she drinks.*)

HENSCHEL. Know what?

FRAU HENSCHEL (*after she has finished drinking*). Are you going to promise?

HENSCHEL. Anything you like.

FRAU HENSCHEL. If I die, would you marry her?

HENSCHEL. Don't ask such silly questions.

FRAU HENSCHEL. Yes or no?

HENSCHEL. Hanne you mean? (*Jokingly.*) Sure I would!

FRAU HENSCHEL. No, I mean dead serious.

HENSCHEL. Now just listen to this, Herr Siebenhaar. What's a man going to say? You won't die.

FRAU HENSCHEL. But if I die?

HENSCHEL. I wouldn't take her. There you are. Now you know. Just to get it over with.

FRAU HENSCHEL. You promise?

HENSCHEL. Promise what?

FRAU HENSCHEL. That you wouldn't take the girl.

HENSCHEL. Sure, I promise.

FRAU HENSCHEL. Give me your hand on it!

HENSCHEL. I've told you. (*He puts his hand into hers.*) But now that's finished. Leave me alone now with this stuff.

CURTAIN

ACT II

(*A beautiful May morning.—The room is the same as in the first act; the bed which had been occupied by FRAU HENSCHEL is no longer there. The window above the spot where it had been is open. HANNE works at the washtub, her sleeves rolled up; she faces the window. FRANZ enters, carrying a pail he is using for washing the carriage; his shirtsleeves and trousers are rolled up and he wears wooden clogs on his bare feet.*)

FRANZ (*awkwardly joking*). Hanne, I'm coming to pay you a visit. Well now. You got a little warm water for me, huh?

HANNE (*impatiently throws the piece of laundry she has on the washboard back into the tub and walks over to the stove*). Don't bother me all the time.

FRANZ. What's the matter with you? What's wrong?

HANNE (*filling the pail with hot water*). Don't ask so many questions. I haven't got time.

FRANZ. I'm washing the carriage. I'm not loafing, neither.

HANNE (*furious*). Leave me alone, will you? I've told you more than once.

FRANZ. What did I do now?

HANNE. Don't run after me, if you want to know!

FRANZ. Have you forgotten all about . . . the two of us?

HANNE. Nothing, the two of us. What should there be about the two of us? I'm going my way and you go yours. That's the way it is with the two of us and nothing else.

FRANZ. That's sure news to me!

HANNE. Well, it's old stuff to me.

FRANZ. Sure seems like it.—Hanne, what's come between us?

HANNE. Nothing, plain nothing. Just leave me alone.

FRANZ. Have you got something against me? Haven't I been faithful to you?

HANNE. What do I care! That's none of my business. Go ahead and run around with anybody you please. I got no objections.

FRANZ. Since when is that, Hanne?

HANNE. Since Methuselah was a boy.

FRANZ (*touched, almost weeping*). You're lying, Hanne!

HANNE. Don't start that now! That won't get you nowheres with me. Call me a liar! And now once and for all . . . to put a stop to it . . . since you got such a thick skin nothing gets through . . . I just got to talk plainly and tell you right out: it's finished with us!

FRANZ. Do you really mean that?

HANNE. It's finished—finished . . . and don't you forget it!

FRANZ. I won't forget! (*Getting more and more excited, finally weeping more than talking.*) You don't think I'm so stupid I've never noticed until now. I just thought you'd see reason . . .

HANNE. That's just what I did see.

FRANZ. Depends how you look at it. I'm a poor devil, of course, and Henschel, he's got a whole chest full of money. In a way, come to think of it, you've seen reason.

HANNE. You start with that kind of stuff and you've really lost the game!

FRANZ. Well, isn't it true? You're awful anxious to be Frau Henschel, aren't you? Isn't that the truth?

HANNE. That's my business. Don't you worry about it. Everybody's got to look out for himself.

FRANZ. All right then! Suppose I go and look out for myself! Suppose I go to Henschel and tell him: look, Hanne's promised to marry me, everything was settled!

HANNE. Just try, that's all I can say.

FRANZ (*almost crying with pain and anger*). And I'm going to try! You look out for yourself and I for myself. If that's the way you want to be, that's how I'll be. (*Suddenly changed.*) But I don't even want you no more. Even if you throwed yourself on me I wouldn't want no part of you. A woman like that ain't good enough for me!

(*Leaves quickly.*)

HANNE. What do you know! That finally did it.

(*While* HANNE *continues working at the washtub,* WERMEL-
SKIRCH *appears at the end of the hallway. He is in his
fifties; the fact that he used to be an actor is unmistakable. He wears a shabby dressing-gown and mended
slippers. He smokes a long pipe.*)

WERMELSKIRCH (*after standing at the door looking into
the room for a while without being noticed*). Did you hear
him cough?

HANNE. Who?

WERMELSKIRCH. Well, the first summer guest has arrived
upstairs.

HANNE. It's about time, too. It's the middle of May.

WERMELSKIRCH (*comes slowly across the threshold—singing in an undertone, punctuated by simulated coughing*).

> I've got consumption, what a blow!
> Widiwidiwit, boom-boom!
> I'll soon be dead, that's all I know,
> Widiwidiwit, boom-boom!

(HANNE *laughs out loud.*) That really feels good. You
know summer isn't far away.

HANNE. One swallow doesn't make a summer!

WERMELSKIRCH (*makes room for himself on the stove
bench and sits down*). And where's Henschel?

HANNE. He went down to the graveyard today.

WERMELSKIRCH. Oh, of course, today's her birthday.
(*Pause.*) It's really hard on the man.—Tell me, when do you
think he'll be back?

HANNE. I don't know why he even had to drive down
there. We could really use the horses for something else.
And he's taken the new coachman along, too!

WERMELSKIRCH. Shh, Hanne, anger's no good for your ap-
petite.

HANNE. But it's really true! Leaves everything just as it is.
The bus is supposed to leave on time, and the carriage's
still standing there all muddy, and Hauffe—he just never
gets nowheres. That old wreck's as stiff as a broom.

WERMELSKIRCH. Yes, it's beginning; there's a lot to do.
The chef upstairs is starting today. And I notice it in the
tavern, too.

HANNE (*with a short laugh*). You don't look so terribly
busy, though.

WERMELSKIRCH (*taking no offense*). It starts a little later, about eleven o'clock. Then it's full steam ahead and I really get busy.

HANNE. About the steam, that I'll believe: that pipe of yours, won't get cold . . . not likely.

WERMELSKIRCH (*grins, then*). You're rather pointed, Madam! Sharp as a needle! For lunch we'll have . . . let me see now . . . first of all the bass violin, secondly a cello, and then two first and two second violins. Three first, two second, three second, two first . . . oh, I'm getting all mixed up. At any rate, there are ten fellows from the band. What are you laughing about? Do you think I'm telling you stories? How much do you think that bass violin can put away? You'd be surprised! And you think that's no work?

HANNE (*after her laughter has subsided*). Sure, the cook's probably busy enough!

WERMELSKIRCH (*simply*). My wife, my daughter, the whole family—we just have to do an honest job of work all of us.—And at the end of the summer when it's all over, there's nothing to show for all the work.

HANNE. I don't know what you're complaining about. You're doing more business than anyone else in the house. The tavern's never empty, winter or summer. If I was Siebenhaar upstairs there, I'd really charge you some rent! You wouldn't get away with no measly three-hundred talers. Nothing doing under a thousand, and you'd be doing all right at that.

WERMELSKIRCH (*gets up and walks up and down, whistling*). Is there anything else? You've scared me so my pipe's gone out.

(GEORGE *rushes down the stairs behind the glass door carrying a breakfast tray. He is a young waiter, quick and wide-awake. Suddenly he stops, then opens the door and looks down the passage to the right and to the left.*)

GEORGE. Good heavens, where did I get to now?

HANNE (*still at the washtub, laughs*). You went the wrong way. Better turn back!

GEORGE. God knows you can get dizzy around here. Got to be a hunting dog to find your way around in this old box.

HANNE. You're new here, huh?

GEORGE. Sure, just came yesterday. Don't tell me—Lord—this has never happened to me before. I've been in many a hotel, but in this place you really need a guide.

WERMELSKIRCH (*exaggerating* GEORGE'S *accent*). Would you mind telling me, are you by any chance from Dresden?

GEORGE. No, I'm from Meissen.

WERMELSKIRCH. Is that so. Not really. Is that right?

GEORGE. Now, where do you go from here, would you mind telling me?

HANNE (*comes alive in the presence of the waiter, cheerful and coquettish*). Just go back up the stairs. We ain't got no use for swallow-tails down here.

GEORGE. This must be the first floor . . . I mean the best floor in the house, huh?

HANNE. You mean the dog house, don't you? We'll bow-wow you something. This is the floor where the better people live!

GEORGE (*confidential, flirtatious*). You know something, young woman? You come along and show me the way, young woman! With you along I wouldn't be a bit afraid no matter where you lead me. I won't care if it's the basement . . . or even the hay loft!

HANNE. You just stay out of here! You'd be the right one. Got enough windbags around here without you!

GEORGE. Young woman, would you like me to give you a hand with the laundry?

HANNE. Oh no! But if you insist I'll give you a hand getting you on your way! (*She pulls a piece of linen half out of the tub.*) But your beautiful white dicky wouldn't look so nice!

GEORGE. You wouldn't do that, would you? Get me into a mess like that? Now look, we can't do that! Heavens, no! We'd have to talk about that first. Isn't that so, young woman? Of course, naturally. We'll talk about it. As soon as I get time—a little later—another time.

(*He goes up the stairs.*)

WERMELSKIRCH. He won't take the wrong way too often! Siebenhaar will soon show him the quickest way from the dining room to the kitchen.—Hanne, when is Henschel supposed to be back?

HANNE. Oh, around lunch time.—Want me to give him a message?

WERMELSKIRCH. Yes. Tell him—don't forget now!—Tell
him—huh, I send him my best regards.

HANNE. What nonsense! But I think I know.

WERMELSKIRCH. Thoughts are free. My compliments of
the morning!   (*Leaves.*)

HANNE (*alone, energetically washing her laundry*). I only
wish Henschel wasn't so dumb!

(*Kneeling outside the window, the peddler* FABIG *looks
down into the room.*)

FABIG. Young woman! Morning!—How's it going? How're
you doing?

HANNE. And who are you?

FABIG. I'm Fabig, from Quolsdorf. Don't you remember
me? Bring you greetings from your father. He wants me to
tell you . . . maybe I better come in?

HANNE. Never mind! I know. He wants money again. I
got none myself.

FABIG. That's what I told him. He wouldn't believe it,
though. Are you alone, young woman?

HANNE. Why do you ask?

FABIG (*lowering his voice*). Look, I just got a couple of
things I'd like to tell you. Like this, through the window, people are liable to hear.

HANNE. All right, come on in for all I care. (FABIG *disappears from the window.*) He would have to come today—
that fellow! (*She dries her hands.* FABIG *enters. He is poorly
dressed, about thirty-six years old and has a sparse beard. He
is very agile and amusing.*)

FABIG. Good-morning to you, young woman!

HANNE (*irritably*). First of all, I'm not a young woman.

FABIG (*slyly*). Oh that! Won't be long now anyways.

HANNE. That's a damn pack of lies, that is.

FABIG. I just heard people talking . . . I can't help it!
People just talk about it . . . just because Frau Henschel's
dead now . . .

HANNE. All right! Let them talk! I'm doing my work . . .
don't matter to me.

FABIG. That's the spirit. That's just the way I am. You
should hear what they say about me! One place, I'm supposed to have stolen pigeons. Another place a little dog
followed me, and right away people say I stole him.

HANNE. If you got something to tell me, out with it and make it short.

FABIG. Right. You see, that's just what I always say. People always talk too much. If they got some rags to sell or something, there they go talking about it as if they were selling an estate.—Now then, I'll be brief. Young woman, it's about . . . heavens, don't mind me, here I go again, saying the wrong thing! What I meant to say, Fräulein, it's about your daughter.

HANNE (*vehemently*). I ain't got no daughter if you must know. The girl that's with my father, that's my sister's girl.

FABIG. Well, in that case, that's different. It's just that all of us thought it was your girl. Just what's happened to your sister?

HANNE. God knows where she is. She'll be careful all right so nobody can find her. She is gone off and left us take care of the brat.

FABIG. Jesus, oh Jesus, there you see how it goes! Here, I could have sworn on a stack of Bibles . . . and not only me, not me alone . . . just all of us over in Quolsdorf . . . that you're the mother of the little thing.

HANNE. Oh sure, I know who's talking about me. I could name every one of them. They just want to make a whore out of me. If I ever get my hands on them there'll be a payoff, just remember that.

FABIG. Well, that's really too bad. Because you see, it's like this, young woman: the old man, your father that is . . . well, you know how he is! That's the way it is. He just don't even sober up no more. Just goes on boozing and boozing. And now, two years ago, your mother died. Before, why, he could leave the little thing home . . . the girl I mean. Now that's finished, the house is empty. So he just drags her around in all the taverns, from one to the other. It turns your stomach just to look at it.

HANNE (*vehemently*). Is it my fault that he drinks like a fish?

FABIG. Heavens, no. There's nothing anybody can do for him. It's just the girl . . . I just feel sorry for her. If nobody comes and gets her and gives her some care . . . with some good people . . . she won't last long.

HANNE (*stubbornly*). What do I care? I can't take her. I got work enough as it is.

FABIG. Why don't you come over to Quolsdorf one day,

just to take a look for yourself. That'd be the best thing. It's just . . . such a pretty little thing, the girl; hands and feet she's got, my, just like china, so delicate.

HANNE. She's not my child. It's none of my business!

FABIG. Just come on over and see what you can do. It's simply awful to look at. You come into a tavern, no matter what time it is . . . in the middle of the night . . . you see I got to go there because of my business . . . there you see her with the old man, in all that smoke; it's enough to make your heart turn a somersault in your body.

HANNE. They shouldn't give him so much to drink in the taverns. They should take a stick and give him a good thrashing. He'd come to his senses all right.—There's a wagon rolling into the yard. Here's five groschen. Now hurry up, I'll think about it. I haven't got the time now. But if you gab about it all over the taverns, we're not friends no more.

FABIG. Wouldn't think of it! It don't concern me none, if that's your child or your sister's; I'm not going to look up the birth register; and I'm not going to talk myself into trouble neither. But if you want some good advice: best thing would be to tell Henschel right away; he won't kill you.

HANNE (*getting more and more excited as* HENSCHEL's *voice becomes audible*). Oh, all this confounded talk! You can get blue in the face listening. (*Goes into the bedroom.*)

(HENSCHEL *comes in, slowly and very serious. He is wearing a black suit, top hat, and white, knitted gloves.*)

HENSCHEL (*stops and looks at* FABIG, *trying to remember who he is. Simply and quietly*). Who are you?

FABIG (*quickly*). I buy rags, waste paper, furniture, old clothes, just about anything that's around.

HENSCHEL (*after a long glance, pleasant but firmly*). Out you go! (FABIG *leaves, smiling sheepishly.*)

HENSCHEL (*takes off his top hat and wipes his forehead and neck with a colored handkerchief; he then puts the hat on the table and turns toward the bedroom.*) Girl! Where are you?

HANNE. I'm with Gustel, here in the bedroom.

HENSCHEL. That's all right. I can wait. (*He sits down, sighing deeply.*) Oh Lord, Oh Lord! No, no, what troubles!

HANNE (*busily comes into the room*). Dinner will be ready in a minute.

HENSCHEL. I can't eat a thing. I'm not hungry.

HANNE. Eating and drinking keeps body and soul together. I was working for a shepherd once, and he told me more than once: if somebody's got a heartache or something like that, even if he's not hungry, he's got to eat.

HENSCHEL. Well, go ahead and cook your dinner. We'll see.

HANNE. You shouldn't let it get you so. One's got to accept things like that.

HENSCHEL. Has Horand, the printer, been here?

HANNE. Yes, everything's all right. He's printed forty new tickets. They're over there on the chest.

HENSCHEL. There the old grind starts again: every morning, every noon—drive the old bus over to Freiburg and bring sick people back across the mountains.

HANNE. You're doing too much all by yourself. Old Hauffe's really too slow. I can't help it, but I'd pay him off if I was you.

HENSCHEL (*gets up and walks over to the window*). I'm fed up with the whole carting business. As far as I'm concerned it could stop right now. Wouldn't mind a bit. Today or tomorrow, I don't care. I'd take the horses down to the flayer, the wagons we'll chop up for firewood. And for myself, I'll find a strong, little rope.—I'll go up and talk to Siebenhaar for a while.

HANNE. I wanted to tell you something.

HENSCHEL. Well, what is it, eh?

HANNE. Look, this isn't so easy for me. (*Close to tears.*) But my brother, he just needs me so badly. (*Crying.*) I'll just have to go.

HENSCHEL (*dumfounded*). You aren't quite right . . . now listen!

(HANNE *sheds torrents of crocodile tears, her apron in front of her eyes.*)

HENSCHEL. Listen now, girl, you're not going to do that to me just now, are you? That'd be a nice trick! Who'd be keeping house? With the summer coming up you're going to leave me in the lurch?

HANNE (*as before*). I'm just feeling sorry for the girl.

HENSCHEL. If you didn't take care of her who'd do it?

HANNE (*after crying some more, seems to pull herself together, forcing herself to be calm*). Just got to do it myself!

HENSCHEL. Nothing has to be done if one don't want to. But you've never talked about this before? Now all of a sudden there's this brother?—Did I do anything wrong? Don't you like it no more in my house?

HANNE. Oh, it's that gossip ... it just has to stop.

HENSCHEL. What gossip?

HANNE. Oh, I don't know. Maybe it's better just to keep out of the way.

HENSCHEL. If I only knew what you're talking about!

HANNE. I'm doing my work and I get my wages. And I'm not going to let them talk like that. When your wife was still alive I was slaving all day long and I'm not loafing now that she's dead. People can say what they want ... that I'm just making myself pretty, that I just want to get married. No, it's better for me to find work some place else.

HENSCHEL (*relieved*). If that's all, just never mind!

HANNE (*starts doing something to have a pretext for leaving*). No, no. I'm going. I just can't stay.   (*Leaves.*)

HENSCHEL (*calling after her*). Never mind the people. Let 'em talk. What'd happen if all those tongues ... (*He takes off his black coat and hangs it up, sighing.*) That pile of worries isn't getting no smaller.

(SIEBENHAAR *enters slowly; he is carrying a full water bottle and a glass.*)

SIEBENHAAR. Good-morning, Henschel.

HENSCHEL. Good-morning to you, Herr Siebenhaar.

SIEBENHAAR. Am I interrupting?

HENSCHEL. Not a bit. What do you think? Come on in!

SIEBENHAAR (*putting the bottle and the glass on the table*). I have to take the waters again. I'm having the old throat trouble. Well ... Good Lord ... after all, everybody has to die from something.

HENSCHEL. Keep drinking the water. That'll get rid of it.

SIEBENHAAR. Yes, that's what I'm doing.

HENSCHEL. And not from the Mill Spring or the Upper Spring. Our spring is still the best.

SIEBENHAAR. Well, now to something else. (*Lost in thoughts he takes a branch of ivy from the table and plays with it. Suddenly he becomes aware of the ivy, glances quickly at the top hat, then at HENSCHEL and says.*) Today was your wife's birthday?

HENSCHEL. She'd have been thirty-six today.

SIEBENHAAR. Doesn't seem possible.

HENSCHEL. Yes—yes—thirty-six. (*Pause.*)

SIEBENHAAR. Henschel, I think I better leave you alone now. But when you have time, maybe tomorrow, I'd like to talk over some business with you.

HENSCHEL. I'd just as soon we talk about it right now.

SIEBENHAAR. It's about those thousand talers . . .

HENSCHEL. Before you go on, Herr Siebenhaar—you can keep them till winter. Look, why should I lie to you? I don't need them just now. I have no use for them and I know I can trust you.

SIEBENHAAR. Well, Henschel, I'm really very grateful to you. You're doing me a big favor. During the summer money's coming in, you know that; and right now it would really have been very difficult for me.

HENSCHEL. There you are. Suits both of us then. (*Pause.*)

SIEBENHAAR (*pacing up and down*). Yes, sometimes I wonder: I've grown up in this house, yet today, if I could only get a tolerably decent amount for it, I wouldn't mind a bit leaving it.

HENSCHEL. I wouldn't like to leave, that I'll say. I just wouldn't know where to go.

SIEBENHAAR. For you, things have moved ahead, Henschel. The same circumstances against which I had to fight so hard—even to stay in the same spot—made your success; you've moved ahead.

HENSCHEL. Well—for one something goes wrong one place, for the other somewhere else. Who knows which one's better off? You see, the hail battered down my wheat, too, and if it'll ever rise again . . . I just haven't caught my breath yet. (*Pause.*)

SIEBENHAAR. Henschel, there's a time for everything! You simply have to get over it. You'll have to see people, see and hear what's going on, go drink a glass of beer, drown yourself in your business if you want to—but don't keep brooding about the past. Nothing will change it, so you must go forward.

HENSCHEL. That's true. You're right there.

SIEBENHAAR. Certainly! Your wife was the best, the most faithful woman—everybody says the same thing. But you're part of life, Henschel. You're in your best years; you still have a lot to accomplish in the world. Who knows what you still have in front of you? And you don't have to forget your wife for all that. On the contrary. That would be impossible for a man like you anyway; but you'll have to honor her memory in a way that's healthy, sound. This won't help! I've been watching you for quite a while and I'd already decided I'd have to talk to you quite seriously. You're letting it get you down.

HENSCHEL. But what can one do about it? You're right, I don't deny it. But one sure don't know what to do sometimes. If I dive into my business, something's missing everywhere. It's just that four eyes see more than two, and four hands get more work done! All those carriages during the summer! And who keeps things going in the house? It just isn't so easy.

SIEBENHAAR. I thought Hanne was a pretty good worker?

HENSCHEL. Well, you see, on top of everything else, she's given me notice, too. Life is just real hard without a wife. You can't trust nobody. That's what's wrong.

SIEBENHAAR. Why don't you get married again, Henschel?

HENSCHEL. Yes, that would be best.—What can I do without a wife? People like us just can't get along without a wife. I been thinking I'd come upstairs and have a talk with your wife; maybe she could have given me some advice.—The whole thing just came too sudden! Here she dies right in the middle of everything.—To tell you the truth, the carting business isn't what it used to be, neither. Won't be long and we'll get the railroad up here. You see, we'd saved up a little nest egg and thought we'd buy a small tavern, in a couple of years, or so, maybe. And you can't do that sort of thing without a wife.

SIEBENHAAR. No, in the long run that probably wouldn't work. But I'm sure you're not going to be a widower all your life. Apart from everything else, it wouldn't be good for your child.

HENSCHEL. That's just what I'm thinking.

SIEBENHAAR. Of course, I have no business to stick my nose into your private life, but after all, we've been friends for a long time. To wait, Henschel, just because of what people might say, that I think is nonsense. If you are seriously thinking of getting married again, the sooner the better, both for yourself and for the child. Don't rush into it, of course. But once you've made up your mind— To the attack, Prussians! What would you be waiting for? (*After a short pause during which* HENSCHEL *scratches his head.*) Do you already have somebody in mind?

HENSCHEL.—You want to know if I've someone in mind?—
Could be, only I can't take her.

SIEBENHAAR. Why not?

HENSCHEL. You know very well why.

SIEBENHAAR. I? I know very well? What?

HENSCHEL. Just think about it for a minute.

SIEBENHAAR (*shaking his head*). I really don't know.

HENSCHEL. Well, I had to promise my wife.

SIEBENHAAR. —Huh?—Oh, that! You mean the girl?
Hanne? (*Pause.*)

HENSCHEL. I been thinking about it a whole lot. Well,
why not tell you? When I wake up during the night, I just
can't get back to sleep—for a couple of hours sometimes.
I'm always thinking about it. Just can't get rid of it.—She's
a good girl, maybe a little young for an old codger like
me. But she can work as hard as four men. And she's taking care of Gustel. The girl's own mother couldn't do better.
And then, the girl's got a head on her shoulders, even better
than mine. And she can figure, better than me. She'd make a
real good accountant. She's got everything in her head,
down to the last penny, even weeks later. I think she'd
make a fool out of a couple of lawyers, she would.

SIEBENHAAR. Well, if you're so sure of all that . . .

HENSCHEL. I just can't think of a better wife for me!—And
still. I just can't forget it. (*Pause.*)

SIEBENHAAR. Yes—yes, I'm beginning to remember now.
That must have been just before she died.—But I can tell
you quite frankly, I didn't take that so seriously. Your wife
was just very upset; that was part of her illness.—I don't
think that's the most important point. It seems to me, the
most important thing is if Hanne is really right for you.
—She certainly has many assets, no doubt about it. And
many faults—but then, who hasn't? Seems she has a child,
from what I hear.

HENSCHEL. Yes, she's got a child. I've asked around some.
So what? That don't matter to me. I can't expect her to wait
for me! She didn't even know me then. A hot-blooded girl
she is—and that has to come out somehow. When the pears
are ripe they just drop. No, that don't bother me none.

SIEBENHAAR. Well, in that case! Everything else doesn't
matter. Or, it does matter perhaps—I understand quite well
that it disturbs you—but at any rate, one has to get over it.
It would be foolishness, Henschel, to strap yourself to that
idea especially since you really know better.

HENSCHEL. I've told myself the same thing a hundred times. She's always wanted the best for you, I say to myself. My wife, I mean, when she was still healthy. She wouldn't want to stay in my way. Wherever she may be now, she wants me to keep rolling along.

SIEBENHAAR. I'm sure of that, Henschel.

HENSCHEL. Now today I was down to visit her grave.—Your wife had a wreath put there, too.—So I thought, you'll go down there, I thought, and maybe she'll send you a message. Maybe you can settle this thing.—Mother, I thought to myself, please give me a sign. Should I or shouldn't I? Say something, yes or no, and it'll be all right with me. Half an hour I kept standing there; and then I prayed, too. And I explained everything to her—thinking to myself I mean, of course—about the child and the tavern and how I don't know how to get along with my business. But she didn't send me no sign.

(HANNE *comes in, barely glancing at the two men; she immediately gets busy with her work. She puts the stool and the washtub aside and starts working at the stove.*)

SIEBENHAAR (*to* HENSCHEL). God may rest the dead in peace. You're a man, and you are living your own life. You don't need any signs and miracles, Henschel! We can find our own way all right; we can pretty well reason out what we have to do. You go your own way. You're the captain of your ship. Forget all about this stuff and rubbish—throw it overboard! The more I think about it the more convinced I am . . .

HENSCHEL. Well, Hanne, what do you have to say about it?

HANNE. I don't know. I don't even know what you're talking about.

HENSCHEL. Just wait a while. I'll tell you later.

SIEBENHAAR. Well, good-by, Henschel; we'll be talking again. Good luck!

HENSCHEL. Sure hope so.

SIEBENHAAR. I'm not worried about you. You've always been lucky. (*Leaves.*)

HENSCHEL. Touch wood!

HANNE. Better spit three times. Pft-pft-pft. (*Pause.*) I can't help it. You're just too good.

HENSCHEL. Why's that, huh?

HANNE. Everybody's just robbing you, it seems to me.

HENSCHEL. You think he wanted something from me, huh?

HANNE. What else? He ought to be ashamed of himself coming begging to poor people.

HENSCHEL. Hanne, you don't know what you're talking about.

HANNE. I know all right.

HENSCHEL. No, you don't. And how could you? But you'll understand later on. First, I'm going down to the tavern though, and for once I'll buy myself a stein of beer. First time in eight weeks. And after that we'll both eat, and after dinner, you hear, after dinner we'll have a little talk. And then we'll see how things will work out. Or don't you want to?

HANNE. Well, as you say: we'll see.

HENSCHEL. Yes, we'll just have to see.   (*Leaves.*)

HANNE (*continues working without interruption. As soon as* HENSCHEL *is out of earshot, she suddenly stops and dries her hands, hardly able to control her delight and excitement. She pulls off her apron and, without thinking, mutters to herself.*) I'll show you! Just watch me!

CURTAIN

ACT III

(*The same room as in the preceding two acts. It is a November evening. There is a fire in the stove. A candle burns on the table. The center door is closed. From the upper floors of the house one hears muffled dance music.* HANNE, *who is now* FRAU HENSCHEL, *sits at the table knitting. She wears a neat blue cotton dress over which she has knotted a red shawl.* MASTER HILDEBRANT, *the blacksmith, enters. He is small but wiry.*)

HILDEBRANT. Evening, Henschel! Where is your husband?

FRAU HENSCHEL. He went to Breslau. He's getting the three new horses, you know.

HILDEBRANT. Well, he won't be home tonight then, huh?

FRAU HENSCHEL. No, not before Monday.

HILDEBRANT. And today is Saturday. Hm.—We brought

the wagon back. Left it down below the dance hall. We had
to make new tires for all four wheels. Is Hauffe around?

FRAU HENSCHEL. He hasn't been with us for a long
time.

HILDEBRANT. Ugh, what in hell am I saying. Nonsense. I
meant the new man of course. Is Schwarzer around?

FRAU HENSCHEL. He went along to Breslau.

HILDEBRANT. No, no, I sure know about Hauffe. He comes
down to the smithy all the time and gapes while we put
irons on. Hasn't found a place yet, you know.

FRAU HENSCHEL. I hear he's started drinking.

HILDEBRANT. I believe that. Could well be—It's really
rough on the old fellow though. Just nobody wants him no
more.—What's going on up there tonight?

FRAU HENSCHEL. Dance music. They're having a ball up
there.

HILDEBRANT. How about going upstairs—the two of us,
Henschel, huh? Why shouldn't we dance a waltz, too?

FRAU HENSCHEL. Huh, their eyes would pop all right.
—What did you want from Henschel, Master?

HILDEBRANT. You know that chestnut stallion the Superintendent's got. It's plain impossible to shoe the damn beast.
So we thought we'd come ask Henschel to give us a hand. If
he can't make that hellhound stand still the devil can come
and get him. Well, good-night, Henschel!

FRAU HENSCHEL. Good-night, Master! (HILDEBRANT
leaves. FRAU HENSCHEL listens; from the hallway comes a
sliding noise.) What's going on out there? (She gets up and
opens the door.) Who's making all that racket out there?

FRANZISKA (comes in dancing). Make room, make
room, Frau Henschel, I'm in a hurry! (She dances around the
table to the rhythm of the waltz one hears from above.)

FRAU HENSCHEL. Well, that's really the limit! What's gotten into you? Did a mad dog bite you? (Undisturbed,
FRANZISKA continues to dance, singing a waltz tune at the
same time. FRAU HENSCHEL, more and more amused.) For
heaven's sake, you'll have a stroke!—Oh no, girl, you're really
going completely crazy! (The music stops.)

FRANZISKA (drops exhausted into a chair). I could dance
myself to death, Frau Henschel.

FRAU HENSCHEL (smiling). If you carry on like that—I
wouldn't be surprised if you do. I'm getting dizzy just looking at you.

FRANZISKA. Don't you ever dance?

FRAU HENSCHEL. Me? Do I ever dance? Sure, I dance. Happened many a time I went through a pair of new shoes in one night.

FRANZISKA. Come on, dance with me then!

FRAU HENSCHEL. You better go on upstairs and dance with them.

FRANZISKA. Oh, if they'd only let me! You know what? I'm going to sneak upstairs. I'll sneak up to the gallery. Have you ever been up there? On the gallery of the dance hall? Where the sacks of dried prunes are piled up? I'll simply go up there and look down into the hall. Up there I can eat prunes and watch. Any reason why I shouldn't look down?

FRAU HENSCHEL. Maybe Siebenhaar is going to get you down from there.

FRANZISKA. I don't care. I'll simply look down. And if one of them dances with Herr Siebenhaar I'll bombard her with prune pits.

FRAU HENSCHEL. You really got a crush on Siebenhaar, huh?

FRANZISKA. That's because he's the very nicest of them all. (*Music.*) Now they're starting again. That's a polka. (*Resuming her dance.*) Oh, I'd like to dance with Herr Siebenhaar! And before he knew what's happening I'd give him a kiss—just like that.

FRAU HENSCHEL. Me, I'd think he'd be too old for me.

FRANZISKA. But your husband is just as old, Frau Henschel!

FRAU HENSCHEL. You little bitch! My husband is five years younger, understand?

FRANZISKA. He looks much older, though. He looks so old and wrinkled. Pooh! Oh no, I wouldn't like to kiss him.

FRAU HENSCHEL. You get out of here now, or I'll get the broom! Just go ahead and try to run my husband down! Where do you think I'll find a better one? Just wait until you get a little older; you'll find out what it means to have a husband.

FRANZISKA. I'm not going to get married at all! I'll just wait until a fine gentleman comes, best of all a Russian . . . in the summer . . . as a summer guest . . . and I'll ask him to take me along, out into the wide world! I want to see the world, I want to travel to Paris. And I'll write you from there, Frau Henschel.

FRAU HENSCHEL. That I'll believe, that you'll run off some day.

FRANZISKA. I swear I will. You can rely on it. Herr Siebenhaar was in Paris, too—during the revolution. He tells such
lovely stories about it. I'd just love to see a revolution like
that some time . . . It'd be such fun to help build barri-
cades . . .

WERMELSKIRCH'S VOICE. Franziska! Franziska! Where are
you?

FRANZISKA. Sh! Not a word!

WERMELSKIRCH'S VOICE. Franziska! Franziska!

FRANZISKA. Sh! Don't say anything. They want me to
serve up front again. But I despise it, I hate it.

WERMELSKIRCH'S VOICE. Franziska!

FRANZISKA. Let Papa or Mama do it. Or they can get a
waiter. I'm not going to be a barmaid.

FRAU HENSCHEL. That wouldn't be the worst that could
happen to you.

FRANZISKA. Oh, if they were real gentlemen . . . but like
this, nothing but workers, coachmen, and miners. No, thank
you. That's not my line.

FRAU HENSCHEL. If I was in your place I wouldn't think
nothing of it. I'd get myself some nice tips. You could put
aside quite a few pfennigs and save quite a little pile.

FRANZISKA. I don't even accept pfennigs and groschen. And
if Herr Siebenhaar, or the architect, or Dr. Vallentiner gives
me something once in a while, I spend it on candy right
away.

FRAU HENSCHEL. That's just it! No wonder with them parents. Your father and your mother's just the same. You people just don't know what a gold mine you got in that tavern.
You just don't do nothing with it. If you'd really take care
of your business you'd be lending money by now.

FRANZISKA. We're just not as stingy as you.

FRAU HENSCHEL. I'm not stingy; I just don't let the money
slip through my fingers.

FRANZISKA. Everybody says you're a skinflint.

FRAU HENSCHEL. What do I care what people say! Or
you, when it comes to that. Get out of here now, I'm fed up
with your jawing. And don't bother to come back either. I
wasn't one bit homesick for you. Not to see or hear any of
you, that's what I'd like best—any of you, you hear?

FRANZISKA (*already at the door, turns around again, ma-
liciously*). You know what else people say?

FRAU HENSCHEL. I don't care, just get out! And just
watch that people don't start talking about you! Who knows

what you got with Siebenhaar! You know, the two of you, and
so do I. Or he'd have thrown you out a dozen times already,
you and your whole mess. Anyone who knows Siebenhaar
can tell what's up . . . that he didn't do it.

FRANZISKA. Ough! Shame on you! You're disgusting!

(*Leaves.*)

FRAU HENSCHEL. Trash, that's what they are!

(*The center door has remained open. SIEBENHAAR, coming
from upstairs, and GEORGE, coming down the hallway,
meet outside the door. GEORGE is dressed in Viennese
fashion, wearing a hat, a long overcoat, a garish tie and
a thin cane.*)

SIEBENHAAR. What do you want here?

GEORGE. Excuse me, but I want to see Drayman Henschel.

SIEBENHAAR. Henschel isn't home. And I've told you at
least three times, there's no room for you in my house. If you
keep forgetting I'll have to see that your memory is re-
freshed the next time it happens—by the police! Is that
clear?

GEORGE. Herr Siebenhaar, begging your pardon, I'm not
coming to see you. These people live in your house. Besides,
you can't prove one thing that I'd be ashamed of.

SIEBENHAAR. All right, but if I see you in this house once
more I'll have the porter throw you out. So just keep that in
mind!   (*Leaves.*)

GEORGE (*comes into the room, cursing*). That I'd like to
see! We'll see about that!

FRAU HENSCHEL (*closes the door with a bang, hardly
able to control her furious anger at SIEBENHAAR*). I'd like to
see him try it! After all, we're still living here. This is our
room, not his. And it's none of his God damn business who
comes to see us. He don't have nothing to say about that.

GEORGE. We'll see, we'll see. That might cost him a
pretty penny, specially if the police get to hear about it. He's
got himself into the soup once before, with Alfons, the fellow was here two years ago. With me it'll be a little more
expensive, though. Thirty talers damages won't be enough for
me.

FRAU HENSCHEL. Ugh, he don't have that much in his
pocket, damned beggar that he is. Borrowing from Peter to
pay Paul. Nothing but debts all over the place. Won't be long

and he'll be through; then it'll be his turn to get out of the house instead of throwing other people out.

GEORGE (*takes off his overcoat and hangs it up, next to his hat, and brushes off specks of dust from his trousers*). Sure, sure. That's no secret any more. They even talk about it in the tavern. Nobody feels sorry for him, they're all after him. My boss, he just can't stand him nohow. Just mention his name to him and he hits the ceiling. (*He takes a mirror and pocket comb out of his pocket and starts priming.*) "God knows," he says, "that man Siebenhaar! He irks me more than a bagful of fleas."

FRAU HENSCHEL. I believe that! And right he is, too.

GEORGE. Well, Hannchen,—got something nice and warm for me?

FRAU HENSCHEL. Just why didn't you come yesterday like you was supposed to?

GEORGE. Do you think I can skip out just any day? It was hard enough to get away today. Last night things were really hopping until three in the morning.

FRAU HENSCHEL. What was going on?

GEORGE. Meeting of the Fire Company. You know they bought a new pumper for them, so they're planning to give a big party to celebrate. So they had to have a meeting.

FRAU HENSCHEL. They always find some reason to booze. And I'm sitting here all that time, all by myself, waiting all night. Once, I don't know what it was . . . maybe a bird banging into the window . . . anyways I thought it was you. So I go to the window and open it . . . and . . . and after that I was so mad I couldn't sleep half the night! (*She weakly hits the table with her fist.*) I don't know—I'm still mad!

GEORGE. Oh, come now. Why let it spoil the fun? (*He puts his arm around her waist.*) That's nothing. Come on now.

FRAU HENSCHEL (*disengages herself*). No, really! It's the truth! I don't know how it always happens that everything goes wrong. All week Henschel is home, and as soon as he goes away for once I got to sit and watch the time go by.

GEORGE. But what's the matter? We got lots of time today. I thought he's coming back only on Monday?

FRAU HENSCHEL. Who knows? Maybe not.

GEORGE. But why not, that's what I'd like to know.

FRAU HENSCHEL. That man's got to sit home all the time.

Before, it wasn't half as bad. For weeks he'd be away on trips. But now, if he's got to sleep just one night someplace else, he gets all upset. And when he says he's going to be away for three days he's usually back after two.—Listen! I wouldn't be surprised if that's them now. Who else'd be snapping the whip like that out in the yard?

GEORGE (*listens; under his breath*). To hell with it! God damn it! A fellow's hardly gotten warm and now I'm supposed to clear out in a hurry, huh? I'd thought this would be a different sort of an evening! (*He puts on his overcoat and takes his hat from the hook.*)

FRAU HENSCHEL (*grabs the hat away from him*). You stay right here! What do you want to run away for? Do you think I'm scared? Of Henschel? He'd better keep quiet! I don't pay no attention to him. But—if only you'd come yesterday as I told you! Not a soul would have bothered us, not Henschel and not Siebenhaar. Today all hell's broken loose.

(WALTHER, *the horse trader, comes in. He is a good-looking man, powerfully built, not quite forty years old. He wears a woolen cap, a fur jacket, hunting stockings, and high boots; his mittens hang down on strings.*)

WALTHER. Henschel, your husband's down in the yard. Evening! Just thought I'd come up and say good-evening. Got to go right down again and on my horse. We bought some beautiful Belgians. And he's brought you something else, too.

FRAU HENSCHEL. I thought you'd be coming back Monday.

WALTHER. That's just the way it would have been. But we rode the horses only to Kanth, then we had to load them on the train. They'd have broken their necks, that's how bad the ice is on the roads.

GEORGE. Sure is quicker by railway.

WALTHER. Hey, what have we got here? You're making yourself plain invisible! Isn't that our George? What do you know! The fellow looks like a real, honest-to-goodness count, don't he?

GEORGE. It's just that you can make a little more money over at the "Star." I'm just making out an awful lot better over there. Here, I had to wear out all my clothes and in the end I was running around almost naked. Now, at least I can buy a few things again.

WALTHER. Hanne, guess what Henschel's bringing you!

FRAU HENSCHEL. Well, what is it?

WALTHER. Think you'll like it?

FRAU HENSCHEL. We'll see. Depends what it is.

WALTHER. Well, good-by now—or my wife'll take a bite out of me.

FRAU HENSCHEL. Bye now!

WALTHER. Good-night!

GEORGE. I think I'll run along, too. Good-night, Frau Henschel!

FRAU HENSCHEL. Didn't you want to talk to Henschel?

GEORGE. There's no hurry. That can wait.

WALTHER. If you got something to talk over with him, you better wait till tomorrow, George. He's got other things on his mind today. You know what he's bringing you, Hanne?

FRAU HENSCHEL. Oh, I don't know. Don't gab so much.

WALTHER. He's bringing you your daughter!

FRAU HENSCHEL. What is he bringing?—I didn't get what you said.

WALTHER. Well, we were over in Quolsdorf and took her along.

FRAU HENSCHEL. Are you completely drunk, the two of you?

WALTHER. No, no, I'm telling you.

FRAU HENSCHEL. Who did you bring?

WALTHER. He didn't tell me nothing about it. All of a sudden we were over at Quolsdorf sitting in the tavern.

FRAU HENSCHEL. Well? And then what?

WALTHER. We were just sitting there, and then after a little while in comes your father with your little girl.

FRAU HENSCHEL. It's not my girl!

WALTHER. Well, I don't know anything about that. All I know is he's got her outside in the yard. He went over to your dad and said what a pretty girl he had. Then he took her on his arm and patted her. Want me to take you along, he asks her, and she wanted right away.

FRAU HENSCHEL. Well? And my father?

WALTHER. Well, he didn't know Henschel from Adam.

FRAU HENSCHEL. Getting better and better! Is that all?

WALTHER (now addresses GEORGE). Wasn't much else. He just takes her outside and says to the father, I'll just let her sit on the horse for a while. And she just shouts and shouts "ride on a horse, ride on a horse." So he puts her on his great, big Belgian—I had to hand her up to him—and then he says good-by and off he goes.

FRAU HENSCHEL. And my father just stood there taking it all in?

WALTHER. What's he going to do? Even if the whole village had come and tried stopping him—you know, once Henschel gets his hands on something—I wouldn't advise anybody . . . There ain't anybody in the whole district who'd like to pick a fight with him. And your father, he didn't even know what was going on. All of a sudden he screams something God-awful, and roars and swears something terrible. The people . . . why, they just laugh! They know Henschel! And he just says real quiet-like: bye-bye, now Father Schäl. I'm taking her along. Her mother's waiting for her home. Stop boozing, he says, and there'll be room for you too in our house.

GEORGE. Good-by now, I'll come by tomorrow. (*Leaves.*)

FRAU HENSCHEL. And so you think I'm going to keep her here? Never and never! She's not my child. And how will I look in front of everybody? First in Quolsdorf, and now here. As if one didn't slave enough! Day and night, every day with Gustel. And now start that life all over again? Oh, no! He'd better watch out!

(HENSCHEL *appears in the center door; he is also dressed in a fur jacket, high boots, hunting stockings, and leather trousers. He leads a six-year-old girl, in very dirty and tattered clothes, by the hand.*)

HENSCHEL (*alluding to* HANNE's *last words which he has overheard, gaily*). Who's that who'd better watch out?

FRAU HENSCHEL. What do I know.

HENSCHEL. Look, Hanne, look who's coming. (*To the girl.*) Go on, Bertha, say good-evening. Go ahead and say it! Say good-evening, Mother!

(BERTHA *hesitates, finally lets go of* HENSCHEL *who propels her forward, gently pushing her; she walks across the whole room toward* HANNE *who sits, grouchy, on the oven bench.*)

FRAU HENSCHEL (*to the child standing helplessly before her*). And what do you want?

BERTHA. I've been riding on a beautiful horse.

(HENSCHEL *and* WALTHER *roar with laughter.*)

HENSCHEL. All right then, we'll keep her here. Good-evening, Hanne. Well? Are you mad at me?

FRAU HENSCHEL. I thought you said you wouldn't be back before Monday. Now I haven't got a thing to eat in the house for dinner.

HENSCHEL. You'll find some bread and bacon all right. (*He hangs up his cap.*)

FRAU HENSCHEL (*roughly pulling at* BERTHA's *clothes*). How you look!

HENSCHEL. You'll have to buy her some clothes real soon. She's hardly got anything on her. Was a good thing I had plenty of blankets along, or she'd been froze stiff on the way over. (*Hangs up his fur jacket and warms his hands.*) Best thing would be you put her straight in the washtub.

FRAU HENSCHEL (*without thinking*). Best thing would have been you left her where she was.

HENSCHEL. What did you say?

FRAU HENSCHEL. Nothing.

HENSCHEL. I thought you said something. All right—into the tub, and then to bed. Maybe you better look around a bit in her hair. Wouldn't be surprised if she had some uninvited guests. (BERTHA *starts crying.*) What's the matter? Don't pull her like that.

FRAU HENSCHEL. Oh, don't start howling, girl. That's all I need!

HENSCHEL. Be a little nice to her. The girl's grateful for every kind word. All right now, Bertha, you be quiet now!

BERTHA. I want to be with father!

HENSCHEL. You're with mother now, and mother's good to you.—I'm real glad we got her here; sure was about time or we'd have to go looking for her in the graveyard.

FRAU HENSCHEL. Oh, it probably wasn't half as bad as you make out.

HENSCHEL (*perplexed but kindly*). What do you mean? (*Pause.*)

WALTHER. I got to go now. Good luck!

HENSCHEL. No, just wait one minute and we'll first have a glass of grog together.

FRAU HENSCHEL. That'd be fine idea if we'd only some rum in the house.

HENSCHEL. You can go get some from Wermelskirch, can't you?

FRAU HENSCHEL. I don't want nothing to do with them people.

WALTHER. No, no. I got to get home. I really haven't got time. Still got a half-hour to trot. (*To* HANNE.) I wouldn't want to bother you for anything in the world!

FRAU HENSCHEL. Who said you bothered me?

WALTHER (*sullenly*). Nothing. I didn't say a thing. God knows, I don't want any trouble with you. You're a tough one. Good-by now, and good luck!

HENSCHEL. Good-by! And say hello for me to your wife, will you?

WALTHER (*already on the other side of the door*). Will do. Good-night! I'll remember.   (*Leaves.*)

HENSCHEL. Well, didn't I do the right thing?

FRAU HENSCHEL. And what'll I tell the people?

HENSCHEL. You aren't going to be ashamed of your own daughter, are you?

FRAU HENSCHEL. Who says I'm ashamed? It don't matter to me. Seems that's what you want . . . that people talk behind my back. It's as if you'd planned it that way! (*To the child, curtly.*) There, drink some milk! And then off to bed! (BERTHA *drinks.*)

HENSCHEL. Are you going to keep on like this?

FRAU HENSCHEL. Am I doing something wrong?

HENSCHEL. With the girl, I mean.

FRAU HENSCHEL. I'm not going to eat her, don't worry. (*She takes the girl who is crying softly, to the bedroom and puts her to bed.*)

HENSCHEL (*calling after her*). And I didn't bring her to be eaten either. Or else I might as well have left her where she was. (*Short pause.* HANNE *comes back alone.*)

HENSCHEL. If a man only knew how to do the right thing by you. Seems just impossible to get along with women. Here you've always carried on as if . . .

FRAU HENSCHEL (*spiteful, whining*). That's a lie!

HENSCHEL. What's a lie?

FRAU HENSCHEL (*as before*). I've never bothered you about Bertha . . . hardly ever even mentioned her.

HENSCHEL. I didn't say you did. And there's no reason to shout at me! That's just why. You never said nothing, so I thought I'd help you get over your silence.

FRAU HENSCHEL. Couldn't you at least have asked me? Seems one ought to ask before starting something like that.

HENSCHEL. I'll tell you something; today is Saturday. I've hurried up as much as I could so's I'd be home again. I thought you'd have a different kind of welcome for me. But, if it's like this, there's nothing I can do about it. Just leave me alone, you understand?

FRAU HENSCHEL. Nobody's bothering you.

HENSCHEL. You understand? I want my peace and that's all. You've got me that far. I meant well. Gustel is dead. She ain't coming back. Her mother came and got her. So the bed is empty and we're alone. Why shouldn't we take care of the girl? That's the way I feel—and I'm not even her father. So—shouldn't you feel that way—and even more so? You who's her mother?

FRAU HENSCHEL. There you are—already throwing it in my face.

HENSCHEL. If you don't stop it I'm going down to Wermelskirch and I won't be back all night. Are you trying to drive me out of the house?—I always think one day it's going to start getting better; but it's getting worse and worse all the time. I thought once you had your own girl home you'd calm down and get some sense. But if this don't stop . . .

FRAU HENSCHEL. That much I'll tell you: if she stays here and you tell everybody she's my girl . . .

HENSCHEL. Everybody knows! Who am I going to tell the news?

FRAU HENSCHEL. . . . you can count on it: I'll run away.

HENSCHEL. Run then, run—run as fast as you can—as far as you can. You ought to be ashamed of yourself, real ashamed!

CURTAIN

ACT IV

(WERMELSKIRCH'S *tavern, a shallow room with white walls. At the left is a door leading to the living quarters. The rear wall runs straight from the left and then turns, forming a right angle at the center of the room; it continues all the way to the back of the stage. From the corner, it constitutes the left wall of a second room, a sort of hallway. Its rear wall is in the background,*

*its right wall continues unbroken toward the front and
thus forms also the side wall of the front room. It contains a glass door leading to the street and, further toward the front, a window.—Along the back wall of the
large room, at the left, is the bar with square liquor
bottles, the tap, glasses, and other bar accessories. The
chairs and tables are of polished, light-colored cherry
wood. A red curtain separates the shallow front room
from the adjoining deep back room, which also contains tables and chairs and, all the way in the back, a
billiard table. Prints, for the most part depicting hunting scenes, hang on the walls.*

WERMELSKIRCH, *in his dressing-gown and smoking a
long pipe, sits and plays at the upright piano which
stands at the left by the wall. Three volunteer firemen
are playing billiards. At the right, toward the front,
HAUFFE sits at a table brooding over a glass of liquor;
he has visibly deteriorated. FRAU WERMELSKIRCH, a
gypsy-like, sloppy old woman, is washing glasses behind the bar. FRANZISKA is perched on the window
ledge playing with a kitten. GEORGE is standing at the
bar with a glass of beer; he is wearing an elegant spring
suit, patent-leather shoes, kid gloves, and a top hat.)*

WERMELSKIRCH (*plays at the piano and sings*).

> When I the prince was of Arcadia
> I swam in money, gems and gold.

GEORGE (*has been making dance movements to the
music*). Well? Go on, go on!

WERMELSKIRCH (*pretending a cough*). Impossible!—Hoarse
as a frog!—Well, anyway . . . Let's start all over!

> When I the prince was . . . (*coughs*)
> When I the prince was of Arcadia
> I swam in money . . . swam in money . . .

Oh, the hell with it!

GEORGE. Keep going! That was all right! Very nice!

WERMELSKIRCH. I'll cough you something! Just doesn't
work anymore.

GEORGE. I just don't understand you! I think that's real
beautiful chamber music.

WERMELSKIRCH. Chambermaid music—you mean!

GEORGE. All right, what do I care. I can't tell the difference. Well, Fräulein Franziska, what are you laughing about?

FRANZISKA. Because you're wearing such beautiful patent-leather shoes.

GEORGE. Sure, after all, I can't walk around barefoot! Give the man there a glass of beer, too. How about a glass of "Danziger Goldwasser," Fräulein Franziska? Yes, these patent-leather shoes, they're nice all right. Cost four talers of hard money, too. Well, I can afford it. Now I can really afford it. At the "Sword" at least one can make some money. Of course, while I was at the "Star" over there—ugh—I couldn't even dream of buying patent-leather shoes.

WERMELSKIRCH. So you like it better at the "Sword"?

GEORGE. Sure! Such a friendly boss! I've never had it so good in all my life. We're like friends, the two of us—like brothers you might say. I could call him by his first name.

WERMELSKIRCH. That, of course, you could never do with Siebenhaar.

(FRANZISKA *bursts out laughing.*)

GEORGE. There you got it: pride goeth before a fall. Two weeks—or maybe three—then there'll be the auction and I can buy his gold watch.

WERMELSKIRCH. Why don't you buy the whole house!

GEORGE. No, not just yet. With that sort of thing one's got to wait; and besides; it's sold already. Well, your health, gentlemen! Your very good health! And when this is gone, there's more of the same.—What's the buyer's name? Exner? Is that it? The man who bought it? Seems he's just going to bottle the water and sell it. He's going to lease the hotel, it seems.—I'd rent it this minute if I had the money.

HAUFFE. Why, go and see Henschel! He'd give it to you right away!

GEORGE. You know what? That wouldn't be impossible at all.

HAUFFE. No, sure! I know you're in pretty well with his wife.

(FRANZISKA *laughs.*)

GEORGE. And why not? That woman isn't bad at all, you

know! If you know how to handle them, I can tell you, women eat out of your hand.

HAUFFE. Well, if you got the Henschel woman to eat out of your hand you've got it made; you really know your business.

(FABIG enters, a rope around his shoulders. He modestly sits down in a corner.)

GEORGE. That's what I'm telling you! And nobody's going to copy that trick in a hurry! But you have to be on your toes or you can get yourself the most beautiful thrashing.

WERMELSKIRCH. Well, you still have a chance, then! *(SIEBENHAAR enters from the left.)* When Henschel swings his fists he leaves nothing but a cloud of dust. Your servant, Herr Siebenhaar.

SIEBENHAAR *(rather pale)*. Good-morning!

GEORGE. I think I'll go back to the billiard table for a while.

(He takes his glass of beer and disappears in the rear.)

SIEBENHAAR *(sits down at the table next to the piano)*. Weren't you singing a little while ago, Herr Wermelskirch? Please, don't let me interrupt you.

WERMELSKIRCH. What? I? Singing? That's hardly possible! You know, I'm deeply touched. But if you say so it must be true. May I sit down with you? Bring a beer for me, too, Franziska!

SIEBENHAAR. Well, if you think about it: three, four years ago you were as hoarse as can be. You've really recovered remarkably well.

WERMELSKIRCH. But what good is it. You're right. I've recovered quite a bit, but now—who knows what's going to happen.

FRANZISKA *(putting the beer in front of SIEBENHAAR; to WERMELSKIRCH)*. I'll bring yours right away.

SIEBENHAAR *(drinks, then)*. What do you mean, what's going to happen?

WERMELSKIRCH. I don't know exactly . . . I don't really know . . . but you see, all my bones are itching. I think we're going to have a change in the weather. Joking aside, though, I got certain signs—routine for an old comedian.

That time, when the water really started to help me, I thought, no ten horses are ever going to get me away from here, and pronto, not four weeks later my theater was finished. Now I'll have to push these old bones on again, some place else. Who knows where?

SIEBENHAAR. Who knows where! That's the way the world is made. For my part, I can't say I regret it!

WERMELSKIRCH. Of course, you're in your best years. A man like you can find his place anywhere in the world. But for an old dog like me it's different. If I lose my livelihood here, if I get notice that is, what is there left for me to do I'd like to know? I could buy myself a hurdy-gurdy, of course, and Franziska could pass the hat.

FRANZISKA. And I wouldn't mind a bit, Papa!

WERMELSKIRCH. Sure, if it rained gold pieces!

FRANZISKA. No, Papa, how you always talk! You could very well go back on the stage.

WERMELSKIRCH. Not even in a flea circus, my girl.

SIEBENHAAR. Did Herr Exner give you any hint? He told me he was going to leave most things pretty much as they are.

WERMELSKIRCH. Maybe I'm not one of the "most things."

FRAU WERMELSKIRCH (*comes to the table in great excitement*). This I can tell you, Herr Siebenhaar . . . you can really believe me, Herr Siebenhaar . . . I'm an old woman of fifty, and I've seen a lot of things, really a lot of things. But the way we've been treated here—no really, that is . . . I simply don't know . . . that is plain, pure meanness, plain wickedness, pure infamy, that's what I say.

WERMELSKIRCH. Oh, Mother, don't you start now! Go on, be so good as to retreat! Kindly retreat behind your fortifications!

FRAU WERMELSKIRCH. What did our Franziska do to that good-for-nothing woman?

FRANZISKA. Oh—never mind, Mama!

FRAU WERMELSKIRCH. To the contrary, are we supposed to let them walk all over us? Aren't we even allowed to defend ourselves if she tries to take our bread away from us? If she gossips about our daughter? (*To* SIEBENHAAR.) Has the girl ever been forward toward you?

WERMELSKIRCH. Mama, Mama! Come now, Mama! There! Rest a while! You did that part pretty well. Tonight we'll have another rehearsal, though. (*He leads her behind the bar from where her sobs can be heard for a while longer.*)

WERMELSKIRCH (*sits down again*). Basically, she's right. I've also heard some rumors that Henschel's going to rent the tavern. And of course it's that woman who's behind it.

HAUFFE. Who else would be behind it? If there's some trouble somewheres in the village nowadays you needn't even ask who started it. That Henschel woman's got the devil in her.

FABIG. And the tavern she's been ogling for a long time.

SIEBENHAAR (*to* HAUFFE). Hauffe, you're never around any more. Just what's happened to you?

HAUFFE. Huh, what do you think happened? I'm down-and-out and the one who pushed me was that cursed slut. Who else? Never had no trouble with Henschel.

FABIG. Yes, his wife wears the pants all right.

HAUFFE. I'm just not strong enough no more. Sure, I'm kind of getting old. But hang on to her apron strings, no sir, that I won't do! And that's just what she wants—you got to see that . . . how she's carrying on. Always breathing hot down somebody's neck . . . never gets enough.—But when it comes to working, that I can still do. Them young brats she hires, they're so God-awful lazy I can finish a job before they even start.

SIEBENHAAR. I can't help feeling sorry for old Henschel.

HAUFFE. If he likes it, I don't care. But if my bones is getting stiff, he knows why. It don't come from loafing around. And if he's got a whole chest full of gold, a good part of it's from my slaving for him.

SIEBENHAAR. Yes, I remember very well; you were working for Wilhelm Henschel's father too, weren't you?

HAUFFE. Sure, sure I did. And I've fed Wilhelm's horses for eighteen years or more. Hitched them up and unhitched them, went on trips summer and winter, over to Freiburg and up to Breslau and all the way to Bromberg I drove his teams. Many a night I spent on the wagon. Had my hands and ears froze and got me chilblains as big as pears on both feet. So now he chases me out, now he don't need me no more!

FABIG. That's her who's doing it. He's a good man.

HAUFFE. So why does he have to hang a woman like that around his neck? Now he can see for himself how he makes out. And he could hardly wait; his first wife wasn't hardly cold and he had to rush marrying this one.

SIEBENHAAR. Well, nobody knew her too well, then.

FABIG. Oh, I knew her all right. Jesus, I'll say I did! If he'd asked me, I'd have told him all about her! If he wanted to send Gustel to her grave after her mother he couldn't have done no better. Wasn't nothing would have done it quicker than take Hanne for her stepmother.

HAUFFE. No, no. I won't say nothing. Many a man's shook his head about it. But it'll come home to roost one of these days. At first, people just wondered what was going on, but by now they expect the worst from him.

SIEBENHAAR. That's all just gossip and a lot of tongue-wagging.

(WALTHER *enters, wearing high boots, a hunting jacket, and a cap; he carries a whip in his hand. Sitting down at one of the tables he makes a sign to* FRANZISKA *who brings him a glass of beer.*)

HAUFFE. That's what you say and who knows, maybe it's true. But if the dead could speak, old Frau Henschel could tell you a story or two. She couldn't live and she didn't want to live. And what's more, she wasn't supposed to live.

SIEBENHAAR. Hauffe, you'd better watch out. If Henschel gets wind of talk like that . . .

HAUFFE. No need for me to watch out. I'll tell that to anybody, right in his face. Old Frau Henschel was supposed to die. If they gave her poison, that I can't say. After all, I wasn't there. But something smelled fishy. The woman was as healthy as can be and she could have lived another thirty years. (SIEBENHAAR *finishes his drink and gets ready to leave.*)

WALTHER. I can testify to that . . . that she was healthy. I should know my own sister after all. She was in the way, and so—she had to go.

(SIEBENHAAR *quietly leaves.*)

WERMELSKIRCH. Gentlemen, would you care for a pinch of snuff? (*In a low voice, confidentially.*) Gentlemen, I really believe you're going a little too far. Just take a look at the man. Last night, late in the evening, he was sitting here—all by himself. He was sighing, sighing so deeply—and nobody else around—I really felt sorry for him.

HAUFFE. That's his bad conscience biting him.

WALTHER. Oh, don't bother me with Henschel! I've had

him up to here! It's been finished between the two of us for a long time.

WERMELSKIRCH. No, no, Herr Siebenhaar is right; you really have to feel sorry for the man.

WALTHER. You can think what you like about him as far as I'm concerned. But what I think of Henschel . . . nobody can tell me a thing.

(HENSCHEL *and* HILDEBRANT, *the smith, enter from the right.* HENSCHEL *has* BERTHA *on his arm. There is a brief, uneasy pause.*)

WERMELSKIRCH. Come on in, Herr Henschel!

HENSCHEL. Good-morning, everybody.

FRANZISKA. Well, Bertha, how are you?

HENSCHEL. Say thank you! Now—can't you talk? Everything's all right; you've got to take things as they come. Good-morning, brother-in-law. (*He extends a limp hand to* WALTHER *who takes it with a similar lack of enthusiasm.*) How are things? How goes it?

WALTHER. Can't complain, I guess. Wouldn't mind if things were better. It seems you're a real nursemaid these days.

HENSCHEL. That's true. That's just about how it is.

WALTHER. Hardly see you anymore without the girl. Can't you leave her home with her mother?

HENSCHEL. She's always cleaning and scrubbing; so the girl's in her way. (*He sits down on the bench near the bar, not far from his brother-in-law.* THE GIRL *sits on his lap.* HILDEBRANT *sits down across the table*). What do you think, Master Hildebrant? What are we going to have? I'd say we've earned a stein of beer. Two steins of beer and two jiggers of corn!

HILDEBRANT. That beast really kicked me!

HENSCHEL. Still nothing but a foal, and as strong as that! And we put on all four irons, one after the other.—Good-morning, Hauffe.

HAUFFE. Morning!

HENSCHEL. —He's a little grumpy. We'd better leave him alone.

FABIG. Herr Henschel, you ought to buy something from me. A needlebox for the wife perhaps, or a pretty comb perhaps to put in her hair! (*Everybody laughs.*) George, the waiter, he's bought one, too.

HENSCHEL (*laughs good-naturedly with the others*). Leave me alone with your trash! (*To* WERMELSKIRCH.) Give him a stein, too! Funny little man, where does he come from?

HILDEBRANT. That's Fabig, over from Quolsdorf, I think. The worst, good-for-nothing wretch in the whole district.

HENSCHEL. Well, I got a little baggage from Quolsdorf here, too.

FABIG (*to* BERTHA). We're good old friends, huh?

BERTHA (*to* FABIG). I want some sugar candy!

FABIG. How about that now! She knows who I am all right. I'll take a look, see if I got some.

BERTHA. Outside, in your cart!

FABIG. No, here, right in my pocket! (*He gives the child some candy.*) Looks like you just can't keep out of the taverns, girl. Before, your grandfather dragged you around with him, now you got to knock around with Henschel.

HENSCHEL (*to* BERTHA). Tell him to worry about his own old trash. I'm taken care of! Go ahead and tell him.

(GEORGE *comes from the back room, animated.*)

GEORGE (*without noticing* HENSCHEL). I wouldn't have believed it—never—that fellow eats glass like it was candy, and that's the truth. Let's get on with it now, Fräulein Franziska, one round of beer; there's five of us!

FRANZISKA (*holding* BERTHA *on her arm, walks behind the bar*). Bertha won't let me; simply can't serve you just now!

GEORGE. Well what do you know, Master Henschel, and you're here too.

HENSCHEL (*without paying any attention to* GEORGE, *to* HILDEBRANT). Your health, Hildebrant! (*They clink their steins and drink.*)

FABIG (*to* GEORGE, *who tries to hide his embarrassment by lighting a cigar*). Tell me something, Herr George, are you a magician?

GEORGE. Sure I am. But why do you ask?

FABIG. Well, a little while ago there, you just disappeared like blowing out a light.

GEORGE. Yes, sure, why should I start something. I just can't get along with Siebenhaar.

FABIG (*gesturing as if he were about to slap him*). People say lightning has struck.—(*Passing* HAUFFE.) You've drawn the winner in the lottery, huh?

HAUFFE. Damn you, you worm. (*Laughter.*)

FABIG. That's right, that's just what I am.

HENSCHEL. Is that right . . . that you are down with Nentwich now?

HAUFFE. None of your business.

HENSCHEL (*laughs, calmly*). Now look at this bristly old codger! Pricks you like a hedgehog no matter where you touch him.

WALTHER. Seems you're going to be the landlord here pretty soon?

HENSCHEL (*looks at him for a moment, perplexed*). I don't know anything about that.

WALTHER. That's what I've heard; just can't remember who told me.

HENSCHEL (*drinks, calmly*). Whoever it was must have been dreaming. (*Pause.*)

HILDEBRANT. Everything's going to be upside down in this house. Who knows how it's going to turn out. But one thing I can tell you . . . you'll all wish Siebenhaar would be back.

HENSCHEL (*to* HAUFFE). You could drive over to Landshut for me. I got two new carriage-horses waiting there. You could bring them over.

HAUFFE. Spit on you, that's what I'll do!

HENSCHEL (*laughs, calmly*). Well, now you can sit there until you get blue in the face before I'll worry about you again.

HAUFFE. You'd better sweep in front of your own door!

HENSCHEL. Never mind, let's forget about it.

HAUFFE. You got enough dirt in your own house!

HENSCHEL. Hauffe, I'll tell you something. I don't like to do it, but if you want to start trouble here, I'll throw you out.

WERMELSKIRCH. Sh, sh, peace, gentlemen, peace, please!

HAUFFE. You're not the landlord here and you can't throw me out! You got no more to say around here than me. You can't tell me to shut up. Not you and not your wife either. I don't care what you two cook up, you and your wife—that don't bother me none. (HENSCHEL, *without showing any emotion, walks over to* HAUFFE, *grabs him by the chest and pushes him, protesting and struggling in vain, backwards toward the door. Just before reaching it he turns, opens the glass door with his left hand and pushes* HAUFFE *through the door. During this scene, the following dialogue is spoken.*)

HAUFFE. Let go of me, I tell you, let go! Better let go!

WERMELSKIRCH. Herr Henschel, that's not the way, I won't permit that.

HENSCHEL. I told you I'd do it. And now I'm doing it.

HAUFFE. Hey, do you want to strangle me? Let go of me, I tell you! You're not the landlord!

FRAU WERMELSKIRCH (*from behind the bar*). What's the meaning of this? But that's impossible, Ludwig! You can't let him do that!

FABIG (*when* HENSCHEL *and* HAUFFE *have almost reached the door*). Leave him alone, you can't do nothing about it. That man's like a wrestler. He can grab a table by the edge with his teeth and lift it up, and not even a glass turns over. Just let him get the idea and we'll be out on the street—all of us. (HAUFFE *is outside,* HENSCHEL *returns to his seat.*)

HENSCHEL (*sitting down while everybody is silent*). Just won't let well enough alone, the fool.

FIRST FIREMAN (*had come out of the back room and is drinking a glass of brandy at the bar*). What do I owe you? Seems it's better to get out of here. We might all be booted out before we're through.

WERMELSKIRCH. Never you mind! Have another glass of beer! That'd be the limit! After all, for the moment I'm still here!

WALTHER. If that's the way you do it, Wilhelm, once you're behind the bar, when you are the landlord instead of Wermelskirch, one thing I can tell you: you won't keep too many customers around with that kind of tricks.

HENSCHEL. Customers like that don't count anyway.

WALTHER. You can't be choosey. Hauffe's money's just as good as anybody's.

HENSCHEL. He can use what he pleases for money for all I care. But I'll tell you once again, don't start that business all over again. I'm not taking over the tavern. After all, if I did I'd be the first one to know. Well then! If I have a notion to buy a tavern some time I'll tell you about it. Then you can give me all the advice you want. And if you don't like it, don't come in! By God, just stay away!

(THE FIREMAN *leaves, slamming the door behind him.*)

WALTHER. I'd better leave, too. (*He prepares to pay.*)

WERMELSKIRCH. Herr Henschel, that's really not right. You're chasing my customers away!

HENSCHEL. Come on now! If he decides to go, is that my business? He can stick around until tomorrow morning for all I care.

WALTHER (*puts his money away again; with increasing violence*). You have no right to throw people out of here. You're not the landlord!

HENSCHEL. Anything else you want to say?

WALTHER. I could tell you a lot. Only I'd rather keep still. They're pretty nasty stories! Wermelskirch knows all about it, better than anybody.

WERMELSKIRCH. Why me? Now listen here . . .

HENSCHEL (*composed and firm*). Well, what do you know, huh? Out with it now!—The one knows one thing, the other something else, and between the two of them they don't know nothing.

WALTHER (*in a changed tone of voice*). If you only were the same you used to be! But who knows what's gotten into you. The way it used to be, you were like a rock, people coming from all over asking Henschel for advice. And when you said something, it stood up . . . you might say like the law. Like the Amen in church on Sunday . . . final. And now—nobody can even get along with you!

HENSCHEL. Just keep going.

WALTHER. Well, that's it. You must have noticed it yourself. You used to have nothing but friends and now—not a soul comes to see you and even if they wanted to come to see you, they'd stay away because of your wife. Take Hauffe; he's been working for you for twenty years and then one day —I don't know, your wife don't like him, so you grab him by the shirt and throw him out! What's wrong? All she's got to do is point a finger and you jump, instead of taking a good, strong rope and beat the nonsense out of her.

HENSCHEL. Now, that's enough! Now you shut up this minute—or I'll grab you by the shirt, too.

GEORGE. Master Henschel, now just don't you get carried away with it. Look, the man just don't know any better. (*Walks quickly into the back room.*)

WALTHER. Oh, yes, you'd do that all right! I'll believe that. If somebody comes and tells you the truth, you bat his head against the wall. But a double-dealing no-good, a windbag like this George here, he can lie to you day in, day out. Your

wife and he, they're trying to see who can do better. If yo
want them to lie to you, fine—let them lie! But as long as yo
got eyes in your head, why don't you open them just onc
and take a good look at that bastard! They're going be
hind your back in broad daylight!

HENSCHEL (*starts to go at him but restrains himself*)
What did you say, huh? Nothing. Well, that's good
(*Pause.*)

FABIG. Real April weather we're having today. One minut
the sun shines, the next there's hail.

HAUFFE'S VOICE (*from outside*). I'll get even with you
Just watch out! Never mind, we'll see each other again, a
court we'll see each other again!

WALTHER (*finishes his drink and gets up*). Bye now. And
no offense.

HENSCHEL (*puts his left hand around* WALTHER'S *wrist*)
You stay here! Understand?

WALTHER. What do you want now?

HENSCHEL. That we'll find out in a minute. I'm just tell-
you—you stay. (*To* FRANZISKA.) Run on down, tell my wife to
come here.   (FRANZISKA *leaves*.)

WERMELSKIRCH. But my dear Herr Henschel, for Heaven's
sake don't start a scandal here. I'll have the police on my
neck, I . . .

HENSCHEL (*in an outburst of terrible rage, his face blue-
red*). I'll kill you, all of you if Hanne don't come here right
this minute!

WALTHER (*in utter consternation*). Wilhelm, Wilhelm,
don't do anything silly! I didn't mean nothing. Really not!
People lie all the time, you know that.

HILDEBRANT. Willy, you're a good man. Just come to your
senses! How you look! Be reasonable now! You've been bel-
lowing so everybody in the house must have heard you.
What's the matter with you?

HENSCHEL. I don't care who hears it. But you stay, and
Hanne's coming here.

WALTHER. What do you want me to stay for? I really
don't know what for. Your business—that's no concern of
mine. I don't want to get mixed up with it and I ain't going
to get mixed up with it.

HENSCHEL. You should have thought of that before!

WALTHER. The rest of what we got to settle—we'll settle in
court. That's where we'll find out who's right. I'm sure I'll

get my money, I'm not worried . . . maybe your wife'll think
a little before she goes and perjures herself. The rest don't
concern me. I tell you, let go of me now, I haven't got time.
I got to go to Hartau—just can't wait any longer. (SIEBEN-
HAAR *comes back.*)

SIEBENHAAR. What's happened?

WERMELSKIRCH. God Almighty, I don't know! I just don't
know what Herr Henschel wants.

HENSCHEL (*keeping a tight grip on* WALTHER's *wrist*). I
want Hanne to come here. That's all.

FRAU WERMELSKIRCH (*to* SIEBENHAAR). Everybody was
quietly drinking his beer, and then Herr Henschel comes
and picks a fight, just as if he owned the place.

SIEBENHAAR (*trying to stop her*). Sh, sh, all right. (*To*
HENSCHEL.) Henschel, what's happened?

HENSCHEL. Herr Siebenhaar, I couldn't help it. I couldn't
help—that it's come to this! You can think what you like.
But I just can't help it.

SIEBENHAAR. But Henschel, you needn't apologize to me!
After all, I know you're a quiet, sensible man.

HENSCHEL. I was in service with your father . . . and even
if it looks that way . . . even if it looks ten thousand times
that way . . . I can't help what's happened. I don't know myself . . . what have I done? I've never been a rowdy. But
now that's the way it looks. Everybody is scratching me
and snapping at me, and this man here has been saying
things about my wife he'd better prove! Or else—God have
mercy on him!

SIEBENHAAR. Oh, why don't you let people talk!

HENSCHEL. Proof, proof is what I want—or God have
mercy on him!

WALTHER. I can prove it, and I'm going to prove it! There's
nobody in this room who don't know as well as I do what's
been going on. Your wife's on a slippery road. I can't help it,
I wouldn't have said nothing. But I'm not going to let you
kick me in the face. I'm no liar! I talk the truth—always.
You go and ask anybody! You ask Herr Siebenhaar here—
the honest truth. The sparrows are whistling it from all the
rooftops . . . and a lot of other things, too.

SIEBENHAAR. Better think what you are saying, Walther!

WALTHER. He's forcing me to. Why don't he leave me
alone? Why should I suffer for somebody else? You know
just as much about it as me. How did you get along with

Henschel before, when he still had his first wife? Do you think nobody knows about that? You don't even set foot into his room any more.

SIEBENHAAR. What's between the two of us is our private business. And I won't permit anybody to stick his nose into it.

WALTHER. But when first the wife dies . . . and she's quite healthy . . . and eight weeks later Gustel dies, too, then that's no private business no more, I don't think.

HENSCHEL. What?—I want Hanne!

(FRAU HENSCHEL *enters suddenly and quickly; she comes straight from her work and is still drying her hands.*)

FRAU HENSCHEL. What are you screaming about?

HENSCHEL. Good thing you're here.—This man here says . . .

FRAU HENSCHEL (*turns to go*). Oh, you stupid idiots!

HENSCHEL. You stay here!

FRAU HENSCHEL. Are you stone drunk, all of you? What's gotten into you? Do you think I'm going to give a performance for you like a monkey? (*Turns to go.*)

HENSCHEL. Hanne, I'm telling you . . . this man here says . . .

FRAU HENSCHEL. Oh, he can say what he wants for all I care.

HENSCHEL. . . . that you're deceiving me front and back . . .

FRAU HENSCHEL. What? What? What?

HENSCHEL. Is that right? Can he say that?—And that . . . my wife . . .

FRAU HENSCHEL. Me? A pack of damned lies that is! (*She holds her apron in front of her eyes and rushes out.*)

HENSCHEL. . . . that I . . . my wife . . . that the two of us . . . that our Gustel . . . Never mind! Never mind! (*He releases* WALTHER's *wrist and lets his head drop to the table, groaning.*)

WALTHER. I don't let anybody call me a liar.

CURTAIN

ACT V

(A few days later. The same room as in the first three acts.
It is night. The moon shines brightly through the window into the empty room. A candle is being lighted in
the bedroom, and after a few seconds HENSCHEL comes
out, carrying the candle in a tin candlestick. He is wearing leather pants and slippers. He walks slowly to the
table, looks back, then toward the window, undecided
what to do. He finally puts the candle on the table and
sits down by the window. His chin resting on his hand,
he looks at the moon.)

FRAU HENSCHEL (invisible in the bedroom). Husband!
Husband! What are you doing out there?—This hopping
around all the time! (Scantily dressed, she looks into the
room.) Where are you? Come on to bed! It's night and time
to sleep. Tomorrow morning you won't be able to get out of
bed again, lying there like a bag of oats, and down in the
yard everything's upside down. (Scantily dressed as she is,
she comes into the room and approaches HENSCHEL, bewildered and alarmed.) What are you doing, huh?

HENSCHEL. —Me?

FRAU HENSCHEL. What are you sitting there for and not
saying a word?

HENSCHEL. I'm looking at the clouds.

FRAU HENSCHEL. Heavens, no. I'm getting all mixed up. Just
what's up there, I'd like to know! Same trouble every night.
Nobody can get no rest that way to save his soul.—What do
you see all the time? Say something!

HENSCHEL. —They're up there.

FRAU HENSCHEL. Are you dreaming? Hey, you, Wilhelm,
wake up! Go to bed and get some sleep! Up there's nothing
but clouds—that's all there is.

HENSCHEL. If you got eyes you can see.

FRAU HENSCHEL. And if you get too confused you go
crazy!

HENSCHEL. I'm not confused.

FRAU HENSCHEL. I didn't say you are. But if you go on

267

like this you will be! (*She shivers, puts on a jacket and stirs the ashes in the stove with a poker.*)

HENSCHEL. What time is it?

FRAU HENSCHEL. Quarter to two.

HENSCHEL.—You've moved the clock around, huh?—It always used to hang by the door.

FRAU HENSCHEL. What are you going to think of next. It's hanging where it's always been.

HENSCHEL (*getting up*). I'll take a walk over to the stables.

FRAU HENSCHEL. I'm telling you, go to bed now; or I'll start making noise. You've no business in the stables in the middle of the night! At night you belong in your bed.

HENSCHEL (*quietly stops and looks at* HANNE). Where's Gustel?

FRAU HENSCHEL. What do you mean? She's in bed of course, sleeping. Always harping about that girl. She don't miss a thing. I don't do her no harm.

HENSCHEL. No, she's taken care of. She's gone to bed. She went to bed early—Gustel! And I don't mean Bertha!

FRAU HENSCHEL (*starts crying, stuffs her apron into her mouth*). I'm running away, I'm not staying around here any longer!

HENSCHEL. Go to bed, go on! I'll come in a little while. Crying won't do no good. The Lord knows who's to blame. It's not your fault. No reason for you to cry.—Our Lord and me, the two of us, we know! (*He locks the front door.*)

FRAU HENSCHEL (*vehemently unlocks it again*). What are you locking the door for? I won't let you lock me in!

HENSCHEL. Don't even know why I locked it.

FRAU HENSCHEL. Them people got you all befuddled. Some day they'll have to answer for that . . . all the stuff they put into your head. I took care of your girl just as if she was mine. That's not what she died from. But I can't wake up the dead! If one's got to die he just dies; nobody can't stop it . . . he just got to go. And you know as well as I do, Gustel wasn't a strong one. So why do you always ask me and look at me as if I'd done God knows what!

HENSCHEL (*suspiciously*). —Could be, too! That's quite possible.

FRAU HENSCHEL (*beside herself*). Somebody should have told me that at the time, and I'd rather have gone begging. Oh no! Jesus, I should have known that! Just listen to him!

I wanted to go, and who held me back, huh? Who insisted I stick around, stay in the house? Who? I've always taken care of myself. I wasn't afraid, I can work. But you wouldn't let me, remember? That's what I got for it now. Now I can suffer for it.

HENSCHEL. Yes, maybe that's true . . . that you got to suffer for it. What's got to happen—happens. What's anybody going to do about it? (*He locks the door again.*)

FRAU HENSCHEL. Leave that door open, Wilhelm, I'm telling you! I'll shout for help if you don't.

HENSCHEL. Sh, quiet now! Did you hear that? Something walking out in the hall. Hear that? Now it's going to the basin. Hear it splashing with the water? She's standing there washing herself.

FRAU HENSCHEL. Wilhelm! You—you're dreaming! The basin's in here!

HENSCHEL. That's just it! I know! They can't fool me. Who knows—who knows—(*quickly*)—that's all I got to say. —Come on now, come, we'll go to bed. Time will tell. (*While he is walking toward the bedroom door,* FRAU HENSCHEL *quietly unlocks the door and quickly glides out.*)

HENSCHEL (*takes a whip down from the frame of the bedroom door*). There's that old stick from Trieste! Wonder where that old thing's coming from? Haven't seen it for more than a year. I bought that when mother was still alive. (*He listens.*) What do you say?—That's right!—Of course!—Oh nothing!—So what! I wouldn't do that! All right!—I know what I got to do!—I won't make no fuss!—Never you mind!

(SIEBENHAAR *comes in through the door which had been left ajar; he gestures to* WERMELSKIRCH *and* FRAU HENSCHEL, *who are behind him, to stay outside. He is completely dressed, only instead of a collar he wears a silk scarf around his neck.* WERMELSKIRCH *wears a dressing-gown.*)

SIEBENHAAR. Good evening, Herr Henschel! What? Are you still up? Aren't you feeling well? Is something wrong?

HENSCHEL (*perplexed, looks at him for a moment; simply*). I just can't sleep. Can't sleep at all. I'd take something if I knew what. I don't know why. God knows what this is all about.

SIEBENHAAR. I'll tell you something, old friend. You go on to bed now, and tomorrow morning early I'll send the doctor. It's really time you did something about it.

HENSCHEL. No, I don't think a doctor can help much.

SIEBENHAAR. Don't say that, we'll see. Dr. Richter is a good man. My wife couldn't sleep for weeks, and she had such a headache she thought her head was bursting. Then, on Wednesday, she took a powder, and now she sleeps all night like a log.

HENSCHEL. Well, it's possible of course! I wouldn't mind if I could sleep again.—Is your lady really sick?

SIEBENHAAR. Oh, none of us are too well. Once next Monday's passed things'll look up again.

HENSCHEL. You're transferring the house on Monday?

SIEBENHAAR. Yes, I hope we'll be ready by Monday. Until then, there's so much to do, writing and inventories and God knows what, I hardly get out of my clothes. Listen, Henschel, go to bed now. Everybody's got his troubles. Life isn't a game—everyone of us has got to see how he can make things come out even. And if there are a lot of things going through your head, just don't take it to heart.

HENSCHEL. Thanks a lot, Herr Siebenhaar, and no offense I hope. And good luck to you and your lady!

SIEBENHAAR. But we're going to see each other tomorrow, Henschel. And don't thank me; we've helped each other many a time while we've been living in the same house. We're even, I think, so there's no cause for many words. We've been friends and I hope we'll remain friends.

HENSCHEL (*walks a few paces in silence; when he comes close to the window he looks out.*) All sorts of things are happening. Times are never the same. Little Karl never comes to see us no more—but you can't say nothing about that; maybe you were right. He wouldn't have learned nothing good here. Before of course, that was different.

SIEBENHAAR. Henschel, now I'm really lost. What do you mean?

HENSCHEL. You've never set foot in this room either . . . must be nine months at least.

SIEBENHAAR. I just had too much on my mind, that's all.

HENSCHEL. Before, that was just the time you came to see me. No, no; I know you're right. Everybody's right. I'm really not very proud of myself now.

SIEBENHAAR. Henschel, get some rest now.

HENSCHEL. No, we might as well talk about it for a while. You see, it's all my fault; I know it's my fault, and that's that. But it started even before I did this . . . with the wife . . . I mean before I married Hanne; even before then it started . . . slowly . . . real slowly it started going down-hill. First, I break the whalebone whip. Then, I remember exactly, I run over my dog. Was the best Pomeranian I ever had. Then, I lose three horses one after the other . . . that beautiful stallion I paid three hundred talers for. Then, finally, my wife dies. I felt it in my bones all right then—he had it in for me. But when the wife was dead, well, there was a moment I thought, that's it, that's all, he can't take away much more now. But, you see, he could—after all. I won't even talk about Gustel. When you lose your wife you lose your child, that's normal. No, it's not that. But somebody set a trap for me—and I walked right into it.

SIEBENHAAR. Who do you think set that trap for you?

HENSCHEL. Maybe the Devil, maybe somebody else. But choke I will, that's for sure. (*Pause.*)

SIEBENHAAR. That's a rather unhappy thought . . .

HENSCHEL. No, no, I won't deny it. I know I've turned bad —but I couldn't help it. Just kind of slithered into it. Maybe I'm guilty. Who knows? Should have watched out a little better! It's just that the Devil is smarter than me. I just walked straight ahead and right into it.

SIEBENHAAR. Henschel, you're your own worst enemy. You're battling only your own imagination, nothing that really exists. The Devil didn't do anything to you, and you didn't walk into any trap. And nobody's strangling you. That's all nonsense! Nothing but dangerous fantasies.

HENSCHEL. We'll see. Wait and see.

SIEBENHAAR. Just tell me one single thing, one really concrete thing. You'll see, there's nothing. You aren't bad and you aren't guilty, as you put it.

HENSCHEL. That I know better!

SIEBENHAAR. Well, what guilt is there?

HENSCHEL. Here, on this spot, stood the bed . . . and she was in it . . . and I promised her. I gave her my promise—and I broke it.

SIEBENHAAR. What promise is that?

HENSCHEL. You know very well! I broke it—and I was lost. That was the end. I'd lost the game. And you see, now she can't find no peace.

SIEBENHAAR. You're talking about your first wife?

HENSCHEL. Yes, yes, that's who I'm talking about! —She can't find peace in her grave. She comes and goes and never finds peace. When I'm currying the horses, there she is.—I take a strainer down from the grain bin, and I see her sitting back by the door.—I want to go to bed, in the bedroom—there she's lying in it looking at me.—She's moved the clock, she knocks on the wall, she scratches on the window. She puts her finger on my chest so I think I'm choking, so I'm gasping for air. Oh no, I know all about it. You got to live through things like that—or you don't know nothing about it. You just can't describe that kind of thing. I've been through something, believe me!

SIEBENHAAR. Henschel, for the last time: pull yourself together, get back on your feet. Go and see a doctor. Say to yourself, I'm a sick man, really sick—but chase these ghosts out of your mind. They're just figments of the imagination, mere fantasies.

HENSCHEL. That's about what you said that time. Just about the same words.

SIEBENHAAR. Could be. And I stand by what I said. What you did then . . . this marriage . . . you had a right to do it. There's no sin or guilt in it. (WERMELSKIRCH comes closer.)

WERMELSKIRCH. Henschel, why don't you come along with me. We'll light the gas lamp and play cards. We'll have a beer, or whatever you want, and we'll smoke a pipe. And then let the ghosts come! In two hours it'll be broad daylight, then we'll have some coffee and go for a ride. Hang it, you'll see you'll feel your old self again!

HENSCHEL. Maybe. We can always try.

WERMELSKIRCH. All right then, come on!

HENSCHEL. I'm never coming to your place again.

WERMELSKIRCH. Oh, poppycock; that silly business the other day! That was just a misunderstanding all around. Everybody understands now. And Hauffe—I don't even let him into the house any more. That man is really drunk all the time. Something is said in the heat of excitement—forget about it. In one ear, out the other. That's the way to look at it and that's how I look at it.

HENSCHEL. That'd sure be the best way. You're right. But —into the tavern—no, I just can't do it. Maybe I'll go traveling —I think. She can't follow me all over, can she? All right, sleep well! I'm sleepy now.

SIEBENHAAR. How about it, Henschel, come on up with me! I still got the light on, the office is heated, and we can play a game, all three of us. I won't get much sleep tonight anyway.

HENSCHEL. Yes, that's an idea. I haven't played cards for a long time.

FRAU HENSCHEL. That's right, go on up with them. You won't be able to sleep nohow.

HENSCHEL. I'm not going! You understand?

FRAU HENSCHEL. Well, if you don't go I will. Who knows what ideas you're going to get tonight. Maybe you'll start playing with the knife again. Yes, that's what he did last night. It's just not safe with him no more.

HENSCHEL. I wouldn't dream of it, going up there! He's the one who told me to do what I've done, and then he was the first to despise me.

SIEBENHAAR. Henschel, I've never despised you. You're a man of honor, always have been and always will be; don't get silly ideas now. Sometimes fate pounces on a man, and then he's got to bear it, even if it isn't easy. You have become a sick man, but you still are a good man; I'll put my hand in the fire for that.

HENSCHEL. I hope that's true, Herr Siebenhaar.—Well, let's talk about something else. It's not your fault, that's what I keep saying. I can't damn my brother-in-law either. He probably knows where he got it from. She's just making the rounds telling everybody about it. Now she's here, the next minute some place else—she's everywhere. Must have been to see her brother, too.

WERMELSKIRCH. Who's going around talking to people? Nobody's even thinking about it any more. This whole business the other day—everybody's forgotten all about it.

HENSCHEL. But, turn around any which way, it sticks to me. She knows how to go about it, she does. She's just everywhere, she makes them believe it. And even if they kept quiet about it and didn't say a word, even if they weren't after me like a pack of wolves—it wouldn't matter one bit—it still sticks to me.

SIEBENHAAR. Henschel, we're not leaving you before you put all this out of your mind. You really must calm yourself.

HENSCHEL. I'm quite calm—I'm reasonable.

SIEBENHAAR. Well then, let's be quite frank about it. You can see how your wife regrets it. The waiter is gone, he's far off by now and you'll never see him again. Anybody can stumble, no matter who it is. Just shake hands now, the two of you. Bury what has to be buried and make your peace.

HENSCHEL. No need for me to make peace. (*To* HANNE.) For all that, I'll shake your hand, that I can do. If you did something wrong, let the Lord be the judge. I'm not going to damn you.—If only . . . I mean about Gustel . . . if I could only be sure!

FRAU HENSCHEL. You can kill me on the spot if you want. I'll drop dead this minute if I had anything to do with Gustel's dying!

HENSCHEL. That's just it, that's what I've been saying: I'm it, it must be my fault!—Well, we can talk some more tomorrow. Before we're through talking a lot of water will flow into the sea.

WERMELSKIRCH. Make yourself a cozy fire and some hot coffee. After the rain the sun shines. It's the same thing in a marriage. But after a thunderstorm everything grows all the better. The main thing: hush, baby, hush. (*He holds his arms as if cradling a baby.*)—That's the way to do it. That's what you ought to get yourselves. (*Pats* HENSCHEL's *shoulders jovially.*) The old man likes that little stuff after all. Get together and buy yourself a little toy like that. Confound it all, Henschel! What in hell! A big bruiser like you—nothing easier than that. Good-night everybody!

SIEBENHAAR. Everything's going to be all right; keep your chin up!

WERMELSKIRCH. Cold blood and warm clothes—that's all you need.

(SIEBENHAAR *and* WERMELSKIRCH *leave.* HENSCHEL *walks slowly to the door and is about to lock it again.*)

FRAU HENSCHEL. Leave that door open!

HENSCHEL. Sure, what do I care.—What are you doing?

FRAU HENSCHEL (*crouches in front of the oven door; she starts up*). Can't you see? Making a fire.

HENSCHEL (*slumps down at the table*). Might as well light the lamp, too. (*He opens the drawer.*)

FRAU HENSCHEL. Looking for something?

HENSCHEL. No, nothing.

FRAU HENSCHEL. Then close it again. (*She goes to the table and closes the drawer.*) Do you want Bertha to wake from the racket? (*Pause.*)

HENSCHEL. Monday he's leaving. Then we'll be alone.

FRAU HENSCHEL. Who's leaving on Monday?

HENSCHEL. Well, Siebenhaar. I wonder how it's going to work out with the new one.

FRAU HENSCHEL. He's rich at least; he's not going to come around to borrow money.

HENSCHEL. Hanne, one of us'll have to go. One of us two.
Yes, that's the way it is. You can stare at me, but that's
the way it is.

FRAU HENSCHEL. So you want me to go? You're going to
chase me out?

HENSCHEL. We'll have to see who's the one who has to
go. Maybe it's me, maybe it's you.—If I was the one . . .
I know, that wouldn't worry you. You can take care of the
cartage business as good as any man. Like I'm saying: It
don't matter about me.

FRAU HENSCHEL. If one of us has got to go, all right, I'll
go. I'll take off and not a soul's going to see me again!
The horses and the wagons, that's all your stuff. You can't
leave all that . . . your father left it to you. So I'll go, and
that's the end of it.

HENSCHEL. Don't be so sure. One thing after another.

FRAU HENSCHEL. Oh, for goodness' sake, let's not fiddle
around. What's finished is finished.

HENSCHEL (*gets up laboriously and walks toward the bedroom*). And Bertha? What's going to become of the girl?

FRAU HENSCHEL. She'll have to go back to father, over to
Quolsdorf.

HENSCHEL (*from the bedroom door*). Never mind. Tomorrow is another day. Everything's going to be all right,
like Siebenhaar says. (*From inside the bedroom.*) Everything'll look different tomorrow. (*Pause.*)

HENSCHEL (*invisible in the bedroom*). Bertha's just swim-
ming in sweat again.

FRAU HENSCHEL. Let her sweat a little, that won't do her
no harm. The drops are running down my neck, too. What a
life—(*She opens a window.*)—better be dead.

HENSCHEL. What did you say? Can't understand a word.

FRAU HENSCHEL. Oh, go to sleep and leave me alone.

HENSCHEL. Aren't you coming?

FRAU HENSCHEL. It's getting daylight. (*She winds the
clock.*)

HENSCHEL. Who's winding the clock?

FRAU HENSCHEL. You shut up now. If Bertha wakes up
we'll be in a fine fix again. She'd go and holler for half an
hour. (*She sits down at the table, her head in both hands.*)
Best thing to do would be to run away.—(SIEBENHAAR
looks into the room.)

SIEBENHAAR. Just coming back to see if your husband's
quiet now.

FRAU HENSCHEL. Yes, yes, he went to bed. (*She calls.*) Wilhelm, Wilhelm!

SIEBENHAAR. Sh, Frau Henschel. Thank the Lord! Hurry up now and get some sleep, too.   (*Leaves.*)

FRAU HENSCHEL. What's there left to do? I'll just go and try. (*When she reaches the bedroom door she stops, transfixed, and listens.*) Wilhelm, Wilhelm, why don't you answer! (*Louder and increasingly anxious.*) Wilhelm, are you trying to scare me? Do you think I don't know you're still awake? (*In increasing terror.*) Wilhelm, I'm telling you . . . (BERTHA *has awakened and starts crying.*) Bertha, you be quiet now! Girl, I can tell you, be quiet or I don't know what I'll do. (*Almost shouting.*) Wilhelm, Wilhelm! (SIEBENHAAR *looks through the door again.*)

SIEBENHAAR. Frau Henschel, what on earth is the matter?

FRAU HENSCHEL. I keep calling him and he don't say a word.

SIEBENHAAR. Are you crazy? What are you doing?

FRAU HENSCHEL. It's so quiet!—Something's happened!

SIEBENHAAR. What?—(*He takes the candle and steps into the doorway.*) Henschel, are you asleep? (*He steps into the bedroom.—Pause.*)

FRAU HENSCHEL (*does not dare to go in*). What's the matter?—What's going on?—What's the matter? (WERMELSKIRCH *looks into the room.*)

WERMELSKIRCH. Who's in there?

FRAU HENSCHEL. Herr Siebenhaar.—It's so quiet, nobody answers.—

SIEBENHAAR (*deadly pale, rushes out of the bedroom, carrying* BERTHA *on his arm*). Frau Henschel, take the child and go upstairs to my wife!

FRAU HENSCHEL (*the girl on her arm*). For Heaven's sake, what's happened?

SIEBENHAAR. You'll find out soon enough.

FRAU HENSCHEL (*with a voice that rises from a stifled to a loud screaming*). God, he's done something to himself! (*Rushes out with the child.*)

WERMELSKIRCH. A doctor?

SIEBENHAAR. No, it's too late! He won't be able to help any more.

CURTAIN

PREFACE TO *Rose Bernd*

Rose Bernd, one of the last of Hauptmann's naturalistic dramas, first presented at the *Deutsches Theater* on October 31, 1903, is not easy to recommend to the American stage, although New York saw a professional production in the season of 1922–23 with Ethel Barrymore in the title part. Superficially the play belongs to a genre of pre-modern melodramas in which a poor working girl is seduced by a rich villain. Considered more closely, it is seen to follow the principles of naturalism according to which the heroine's fate is determined by instinct and environment—by the promptings of the sexual instinct in a vigorous peasant girl and a man married to an invalid wife, and by the moral pressure of an environment in which unwed motherhood must be concealed at all costs. The very ordinariness of the situation could only be considered an advantage to those who, whether writing fiction or drama, were resolved to look at the common aspects of life, and who prided themselves on discovering a maximum of significance in things familiar and typical. Just as the Moscow Art Theatre adopted a sea gull—Chekhov's "sea gull"—for its symbol, so the naturalistic school to which Hauptmann belonged could have adopted Frost's oven-bird about which the poet wrote

> The question that it asks in all but words
> Is what to make of a diminished thing?

Hauptmann made *much* of his diminished persons and especially of his suffering heroine, Rose Bernd. By combining compassionate objectivity with his depressing subject he made the play rise above the mediocrity of the characters and the environment. And by adding mesmeric atmosphere to the more or less automatic conduct of Rose Bernd as the pawn of instinct, Hauptmann made a compelling "poetry of naturalism" out of the girl's misfortune. It is not surprising therefore that *Rose Bernd* made a strong impression in its time. It combined "shock value" and "art" for its admirers, much as some of D.H. Lawrence's novels did at a later period.

In the spring of 1903, Hauptmann was a juror at the trial of a peasant girl accused of perjury and infanticide, and the playwright cast a vote for acquittal, along with the majority of the jurors. *Rose Bernd*, revolving around the same situation, was produced about six months later at the *Deutsches Theater*. But Hauptmann went far beyond the court trial in developing an entangling web of feelings and associations. Rose had been the playmate of squire Flamm's son, who was of her own age and died young. She was taken into Flamm's house out of sentiment after her mother died; and Flamm's love for the girl is mingled with memories of his lost son, while her attachment to Flamm reflects a fondness for her lost playmate. Thus there is much sympathy and understanding between Rose and Frau Flamm, the invalid wife of the squire. Many elements make up the seemingly simple fabric of a play that is conventional in rough outline but rather complex in texture.

In an important sense *Rose Bernd* can be linked with *Drayman Henschel* as a naturalistic tragedy. Both plays are carefully placed in a milieu, but the environment does not overshadow the protagonists, determine the action, or produce the catastrophe. The source of the drama is in the characters. At the same time, however, they do not produce the action either through their own will, as characters do in "high tragedy." As one Hauptmann scholar, H.F. Garten, says, "the protagonists of both these plays are passive—an essential characteristic of most of Hauptmann's heroes and heroines; their tragedy springs not from action but from suffering." The characters somehow stumble into the destructive flood of their destiny. They cannot excite or enthrall us nor qualify the plays in which they appear as high tragedies. But they can move us with their suffering and desperation, and they evoke compassion not only for themselves but for all lowly, and incompletely articulate humanity. The last words on Rose Bernd, spoken by August Keil, are an apt summary of the essence of the work: "What she must have suffered!"

ROSE BERND

A Play in Five Acts

CHARACTERS

BERND
ROSE BERND, his daughter
MARTHEL, her younger sister
CHRISTOPH FLAMM
FRAU FLAMM
ARTHUR STRECKMANN
AUGUST KEIL

THE SERVANT GIRL,
   in Flamm's service
A POLICEMAN

HAHN
HEINZEL
GOLISCH
KLEINERT
FRAU GOLISCH
THE HEAD MAID
THE MAID

} Farm Workers on Flamm's Estate

ACT I

(*A level, fertile field. It is a clear, warm, sunny Sunday morning in May. A path runs diagonally from the left background to the right front. The fields on the right are on a little higher ground than the path. In the front of the stage is a small potato patch on which the green tops of the potatoes have started to show. A shallow ditch, overgrown with wild flowers, is between the path and the field. On top of the bank rising about six feet above the path there is, on the left, an old cherry tree; on the right there are hazel and hawthorn bushes. Approximately parallel with the path, but at a considerable distance in the background, one sees a row of willows and alders which obviously mark the course of a brook. Clumps of old trees are scattered over the landscape and give it an almost park-like character. In the left background, the roofs and the church steeple of a village are visible between the tree tops and bushes. A crucifix stands next to the path in the right foreground.*

ROSE BERND *is a beautiful strong peasant girl of twenty-two. Her cheeks are flushed with excitement as she comes from behind the bushes at the left. She glances timidly in all directions, then sits down, leaning against the bank. She is barefoot and has rolled up her skirt; her arms and neck are bare. She starts quickly braiding one of her blond plaits which has come open. A moment later* CHRISTOPH FLAMM *emerges cautiously from the other side of the clump of bushes. He is the owner of an estate and Justice of the Peace.* FLAMM *also seems embarrassed, but at the same time amused. He is an imposing broad-shouldered man of almost forty dressed like a sportsman but without any trace of foppishness. He wears hunting stockings and*

high-laced boots, and a leather flask hangs on a strap
from his shoulder. His whole appearance is that of a
solid, active, and vivacious, altogether pleasant man.
He also sits down on the bank, but at some distance
from Rose. They look at each other silently, then break
out into uncontrollable laughter.)

FLAMM (*his high spirits still rising, sings in an ever loud-*
er voice and with mounting gusto, accompanying the song
with the gestures of a conductor).

> In forests and on fields
> That's where I find my pleasure!
> I am a hunting man!
> I am a hunting man!

ROSE (*at first frightened by his loud singing, grows more*
and more amused as the concert progresses and several
times breaks out into embarrassed laughter). Oh, no, really,
Herr Flamm!

FLAMM (*encouragingly*). Go on, sing with me, Rosie!

ROSE. But I can't sing, Herr Flamm!

FLAMM. And that, my dear Rosie, is a lie! I've heard you
singing in the yard often enough. For instance:

> A hunter from the Rhine
> A hunter from the Rhine
> is riding through the forest green.

ROSE. But I don't even know that song, Herr Flamm!

FLAMM. You know you're not supposed to call me "Herr
Flamm"! —Well? Or this one:

> Maiden, move close to me,
> Close to my favorite side.

ROSE (*anxiously*). But the people will be coming from
church any minute now, Herr Flamm.

FLAMM. All right, let them come! (*He gets up and takes*
his gun out of the hollow trunk of the cherry tree on the
left.) But I can always sling the gun around my neck. (*He*
does so.) There. And now my hat—and the pipe! (*He straight-*
ens his hat, which is decorated with cock's feathers, takes
the short-stemmed pipe from his pocket and puts it in his

mouth.) Now they can come. I'm ready. —Look at all those cherries! (*He picks a handful up from the ground and shows them to* ROSE. *—Ardently.*) Rosie, I wish you were my wife!

ROSE. Oh heavens, Herr Flamm!

FLAMM. So help me, Rosie!

ROSE (*timidly discouraging him*). Oh no, Herr Flamm!

FLAMM. Rosie, give me your honest, loyal little paw. (*He takes her hand and sits down.*) Good God, Rosie! —Look, I'm a damn queer fellow. I really like the old woman very much, you understand . . .

ROSIE (*hides her face behind her upraised arm*). I wish the earth would open up and swallow me!

FLAMM. I'm really very, very fond of her, I tell you . . . but . . . (*He loses his patience.*) . . . this is none of her business.

ROSE (*laughing against her will*). Oh no, Herr Flamm, you're a fine one!

FLAMM (*with genuine admiration*). Girl, you're beautiful! How beautiful you are! Look here, my wife . . . that's a funny business with the old woman and me . . . It's pretty difficult to explain. You know that Henriette is sick. For nine whole years she's been lying in bed . . . or once in a while she crawls out and into her wheel chair. Well, for God's sake, what good is that to me? (*He seizes her head and kisses her passionately.*)

ROSE (*frightened*). They're coming from church!

FLAMM. Nobody's coming. Why are you so nervous about the people in church today?

ROSE. Because August's there, too.

FLAMM. Hypocrites are always in church! Where else would they be? Rosie, it isn't even half-past ten; and when church lets out the bells start ringing first. Don't worry about it. And don't worry about my wife either.

ROSE. Oh, Christoph, sometimes she looks at me so I wish I'd sink into the ground.

FLAMM. That's because you don't really know my wife. She's a clever woman. She could see through half-a-dozen boards without a single hole in them. But for all that . . . she's as kind as a lamb. Even if she knew about us, she wouldn't kill us.

ROSE. Oh no! For heaven's sake, Herr Flamm!

FLAMM. Never mind, Rosie! You want a pinch, huh? . . . (*He takes a pinch of snuff.*) I'll tell you again and again:

I don't care one damn bit! (*Angrily.*) What's a fellow like me supposed to do, after all! —Well, what's the matter now? Rosie, you know how serious I am about this. Don't get mad if I rave a little once in a while!

ROSE. Christoph, you're so good to me! (*Passionately, with tears in her eyes, she kisses* FLAMM's *hand.*) But . . .

FLAMM (*startled*). Good? No wonder! Confound it, Rosie! To be good to you—that's not hard. If I were free I'd marry you right this minute. I'm all tangled up, you see. Not to mention the things that happened in the past. By now I could be Chief Forester. . . . And still, when the old man died I rushed home, quick as a bunny; I didn't hesitate one minute to give up my career. I just wasn't made for all this high-falutin' business. Even here everything is much too civilized for me. A log cabin—a gun—bear steak—that's what I like. And anybody who comes near gets a load of buckshot in his rear end!

ROSE. But you know that's impossible, Herr Flamm! —And . . . it just can't go on like this.

FLAMM (*to himself*). God damn it to hell! Is that sanctimonious milksop in such a hurry? Isn't there going to be enough left for him? —He's getting too much as it is. Oh no, my girl, I'll show him all right!

ROSE. I've really put him off long enough now. He's been waiting for more than two years, and now he's insisting. He just won't wait any more. And it really can't go on like this.

FLAMM (*furious*). That's all a lot of nonsense, you understand? First you had to slave for your father all these years. You didn't even know what it meant to be alive. And now you want to take this . . . this bookbinder in tow. It's incredible. It's not fair to exploit anybody like this—to wear a person down to the bone! If you want to let them do that to you, you've got plenty of time!

ROSE. No, Christoph, no . . . you can say that, Herr Flamm, but if you were in my shoes you'd think different. —I know how wobbly father is. And now they've given us notice to leave the house, on top of everything. They want to give it to the new man they're getting for the cows. And then—well, it's just one of his fondest hopes that things get finally straightened out.

FLAMM. Why doesn't your father marry August Keil, if he loves him so much! It seems he's simply infatuated with him! It's almost an obsession.

Rose. You're really unjust, Herr Flamm.

Flamm. You'd better say . . . well, what? . . . How shall I describe it? . . . I simply can't stand the sight of that prayerbook fanatic. To me, he's just obnoxious! God may forgive me; —and you, too—you most of all, Rosie! Why shouldn't I be frank with you? He may have his good points. It seems he's saved a few pennies. But is that a reason to crawl right into that sticky mess?

Rose. No, Christoph, don't talk like that! God help me, I shouldn't even listen to you. August's had his fill of worries, too. With his illness and his bad luck . . . he can make you feel real sorry for him.

Flamm. Oh, who can understand you women! A smart and determined girl like you, and then, all of a sudden, you come to a point where I'm absolutely dumfounded. . . . If you could see how stupid you are! Just as stupid, God knows, as a goose in a thunderstorm. "Feel real sorry for him" —what does that mean? You might as well get married to a jailbird, out of pity—or out of stupidity. Give your father a piece of your mind for once. What's he missing, your August? Tell me! He's been raised in an orphanage and yet he's made his way. If you don't want him, they'll find him another girl. They're very good at that sort of thing, those brethren.

Rose (*determined*). I don't want to! Yet, it's got to come some day, Herr Flamm! I'm not sorry for what's happened, although I've suffered often enough—quietly. I mean, all by myself—all this time. That's nothing. It's too late to change anything about it anyway. But—it's got to end; it can't go on like this—it can't, it can't!

Flamm. "It can't go on" —what do you mean exactly?

Rose. Because—because that's the way it is. I can't drag it out any longer, and father wouldn't let me, either. And he's quite right, too. Oh God, Maria and Jesus Christ! It won't be easy, I know. But to have it off my chest . . . I don't know . . . (*She clutches her breast.*) . . . I think they call it heart cramps. Sometimes my heart just aches . . . and it's got to stop!

Flamm. Well, it doesn't seem there's anything I can do about it. It's getting late. I'd better go on home. (*He gets up and shoulders his gun.*) Good-by! —Good-by, Rosie!

(Rose *stares in front of her, without replying.*)

FLAMM. What's wrong, Rosie? See you soon!

(ROSE *shakes her head.*)

FLAMM. No? . . . I haven't hurt you, have I?

ROSE. But never again—like this—Herr Flamm.

FLAMM (*in a sudden outburst of passion*). Rosie, even if this is my downfall . . . (*He takes her into his arms and kisses her passionately.*)

ROSE (*a moment later, suddenly alarmed*). Good God! Somebody's coming, Herr Flamm!

(FLAMM *alarmed, jumps up and disappears behind the clump of bushes.*)

(ROSE *quickly gets on her feet, hastily smoothes her hair and dress and looks around uneasily. She sees nobody, and, picking up her hoe, starts working in the potato patch.*

After a few moments, ARTHUR STRECKMANN *enters in his Sunday best, without being noticed by* ROSE. *He is a threshing machine operator. A tall, handsome man with broad shoulders, he has the solemn mannerism of a fop; his long, blond beard reaches down to his chest. Everything about him shows that he is convinced of his own superiority as well as of the importance of good clothes. He is, in fact, impeccably dressed, from the small forester's hat, pushed back on his head, and his morning coat worn with an embroidered vest, down to his high boots that are polished to a brilliant luster. His bearing and his dress show that he is fully aware of his unusually good looks.*)

STRECKMANN (*as if he noticed* ROSE *only now, in an affectedly resonant tone of voice*). Good-morning, Rosie Bernd!

ROSE (*startled, turns around*). Morning, Streckmann! (*Vaguely.*) Where are you coming from? —From church?

STRECKMANN. I left a little early.

ROSE (*excited and accusing*). Why? Couldn't you stand the sermon?

STRECKMANN (*off-hand*). Oh . . . just because we're having such beautiful weather! —But I left my wife and the kid in church. A fellow's got to be by himself once in a while.

Rose. I'd rather be in church.

Streckmann. That's right, that's where women belong.

Rose. I'd think you've sinned enough so it wouldn't do no harm doing a little praying.

Streckmann. I'm on very good terms with our Lord! He's not too particular about my sins.

Rose. Hm, hm.

Streckmann. He don't pay much attention to me.

Rose. What a stuck-up brute you are!

(Streckmann *bursts into a roar of affected laughter.*)

Rose. If you was a real man you wouldn't beat your wife like you do.

Streckmann (*with shining eyes*). That's just why! All the more! That's the way to do it! A fellow's got to show you women who's wearing the pants.

Rose. Don't fool yourself!

Streckmann. Oh yes! That's how it is. What's right is right. And I always get what I want.

(Rose *forces a laugh.*)

Streckmann. I hear you're going to leave Flamm?

Rose. I'm not working for Flamm. I got other things to do, like right now.

Streckmann. But you were helping out at Flamm's yesterday, eh?

Rose. So? Sometimes I help out and sometimes I don't. Why don't you worry about your own business!

Streckmann. Your father's moved, though, eh?

Rose. And where would he have moved to?

Streckmann. To Lachmann's house, in with August.

Rose. August hasn't even bought it yet! You know a lot more than I do.

Streckmann. And it seems you're going to get married pretty soon now.

Rose. Oh, go on—gab as much as you like!

Streckmann (*after a short silence, takes a few steps toward* Rose *and plants himself in front of her, legs wide apart*). Right you are! It's always early enough for that! A beautiful girl like you's never in a hurry to get married; have some fun first! I laughed right in his face, too; nobody believed him when he said it.

Rose (*quickly*). Who said it?

Streckmann. Why, August Keil!

Rose. So August said it. That's what he gets for his damn jabbering.

Streckmann (*after a short pause*). Really, August's just too miserable a creature . . .

Rose. Don't you start that! Leave me alone! I don't want to know nothing about your squabbles! When it comes to that, one's just as good as the other.

Streckmann. Well now, not when it comes to nerve.

Rose. Oh Jesus! Your nerve—we know all about that! You only have to listen to what the women have to say! No, that's true—August's not like *that*.

Streckmann (*with a roguish smile*). Did I say he was?

Rose. And you sure couldn't, either!

Streckmann (*looking at her sharply through half-closed eyes*). It's not a good idea to start a fight with me. What I want from a woman—I get!

Rose (*jeering*). Oh yes?

Streckmann. Oh yes! Want to bet, Rosie? Maybe you've made eyes at me, too, now and then. (*He comes still closer and wants to take her into his arms.*)

Rose. Don't you get ideas, Streckmann! —Stay away from me!

Streckmann. That'd be . . .

Rose (*pushes him back*). Streckmann! I'm telling you! I don't want any part of any of you men. You get on your way now!

Streckmann. I'm not hurting you, huh? (*After a short pause, he gives an embarrassed laugh tinged with malice.*) Just wait! It'll be your turn one of these days! I'm telling you, you'll come to me, no matter how saintly you're trying to look! There's a cross! And over there's a tree. —Damn it! Maybe I've done quite a few things . . . but under a cross! . . . I don't know . . . Things usually don't bother me none but I'd be ashamed to do that. What would your father and August say? They might say, for instance, that tree's hollow . . . Or that is where a gun was hidden.

Rose (*has kept on working but been listening with increasing attention. Now she turns pale as wax; trembling and without thinking*). What did you say?

Streckmann. Oh nothing. I'm not saying a thing. But—here nobody's had any idea about it; nobody's been thinking of anything; and then a girl like that puts on such an act!

Rose (*frightened, losing control of herself, jumps up and faces him*). What did you say?

Streckmann (*steady despite her furious stare*). I said, "a girl like that!"

Rose. What does that mean, "a girl like that"?

Streckmann. That don't mean anything.

Rose (*clenching her fists, stares at him in a surge of rage, hate, and fear; finally, feeling that she is powerless, she drops her hands and, almost whimpering, blurts out*). I'll see that justice is done! (*She starts weeping, holds her right arm in front of her eyes and, with the left, uses her apron to blow her nose. Sobbing and defeated she walks back to where she had been working.*)

Streckmann (*follows her with his eyes, an expression of malice and cold determination on his face. After a while, however, he can't help smiling and, finally, he breaks out into a roar of laughter.*) That's the way it is, Rosie! Don't take it to heart! What do you think of me, Rose Bernd, eh? What's the matter? Don't you worry about it. Why shouldn't you bamboozle them? Why not? It's their fault if they're so dumb! That's the women I like best, them who can do that. Sure, a fellow like me knows all about that. You know, I've known that for a long time.

Rose (*beside herself*). Streckmann! I'll kill myself! Understand? Or you leave this minute! I'm . . . I feel like . . . something terrible's going to happen!

Streckmann (*sits on the bank, hits his knees with his hands*). My, my, my! Jesus, no! Who's going to run and gab about it all over the place? Who's going to talk bad about you? That's none of my business as far as I can see. You carry on and play your tricks as much as you like!

Rose. I'm going to hang myself from the rafter when I get home! Just like Marie Schubert.

Streckmann. With that one, it was another story. She had a lot more on her conscience. And I didn't have nothing to do with it.—That sort of thing really is no reason to hang yourself. Jesus, there wouldn't hardly be any women left!—It's always like that; don't matter where you look. That's just the way it is. Why—just laugh at it! That's all. But how your father's always looking down on everybody! He just stares you into the ground. You feel like creeping into a hole when he looks at you like that—just because you've done something maybe a little bit off. So there! Let him sweep in front of his own door now!

ROSE (*trembling, in a cold sweat*). Oh Jesus, Maria and Joseph!

STRECKMANN. Isn't that right? You really put on quite a show with all your piety, the three of you, August Keil, your father and you. I can't compete with you solemn hypocrites!

ROSE (*in a desperate, last attempt*). That's a lie! You've seen nothing!

STRECKMANN. What? Seen nothing? Damn it, I must have dreamed then. I don't know . . . if that wasn't Flamm from Diessdorf! And I didn't touch a drop all morning. That wasn't him? And he didn't hold you by your braids? And he didn't throw you under the willows over there? (*Roaring with laughter.*) He really had a hold of you!

ROSE. Streckmann! I'll crack your skull!

STRECKMANN (*still laughing*). Listen to that now! What's the matter? Why shouldn't you? I don't blame you. First come, first served. That's the way it is.

ROSE (*weeps and whimpers helplessly but keeps working away*). How dare a man talk like that!

STRECKMANN (*furious, brutal*). Me dare? You're daring quite a lot yourself! I wouldn't mind daring something, though. What Flamm can have I can get any day!

ROSE (*completely thrown off balance, weeps and shouts at the same time*). I've been a decent girl all my life! Nobody can say anything against that. I've taken care of three little brothers and sisters. I've been getting up at three in the morning, and I never allowed myself even one drop of milk! Everybody knows that! Any child can tell you that!

STRECKMANN. There's no reason to set up such a howl. —They're coming out of the church now, the bell's ringing. And you might be a little more sociable with a fellow. You're simply bursting with conceit! Maybe . . . yes, it looks like it all right. But I won't talk about it and you can go right ahead working your head off and pinching pennies. But otherwise—you sure are no better than anybody else!

ROSE (*looking anxiously into the distance*). Isn't that August coming there?

STRECKMANN (*following her glances toward the village. Contemptuously.*) Where? —Oh yes, that's the two of them. They're just coming around the pastor's garden. —What do you want? You think I ought to run, eh? I ain't afraid of that prayerbook hero!

ROSE (*terror-stricken*). Streckmann, I've saved twelve talers . . .

STRECKMANN. Rosie, I bet you've saved a hell of a lot more'n that!

ROSE. All right! I'll give you every last penny I got! I'll throw every bit in front of your feet! I'll bring it to you, down to the last penny, Streckmann, but for God's sake have a heart . . . (*Imploringly she tries to grab his hands; he pulls them away.*)

SRECKMANN. I don't want money.

ROSE. Streckmann! For the love of Christ, don't . . .

STRECKMANN. I'm just wondering if you won't come to your senses.

ROSE. If one soul in the village hears about it . . .

STRECKMANN. That's up to you, Rosie. Nobody's got to know a thing about it. Just watch out, and nobody's going to hear a single word. (*In a changed tone, passionately.*) Well? It's just that I'm crazy about you . . .

ROSE. There's not many you aren't crazy about.

STRECKMANN. Maybe so. I can't help it. Wherever I go with the threshing machine, on all the farms and estates, everybody's always talking. I know how I am. Even before that Flamm fellow turned up—I won't even talk about August! —I've had my eye on you. And how that's bothered me nobody's got any idea. (*With inflexible obstinacy.*) And the devil may come and get me feet first, I don't care, what's got to happen is going to happen. Rosie, this is no joke. I got something on my mind now!

ROSE. What's that?

STRECKMANN. You'll find out soon enough.

(MARTHEL, *Rose's younger sister, comes skipping down the path. She is still a child and wears neat Sunday clothes.*)

MARTHEL (*calls*). Is that you, Rose? What are you doing here?

ROSE. I have to finish hoeing the patch. Why didn't you finish the job on Saturday?

MARTHEL. For heaven's sake, Rosie, if father sees you!

STRECKMANN. If it's likely to bring in a few pennies he won't kill her. We know old man Bernd all right!

MARTHEL. Who's that, Rosie?

ROSE. Never mind.

(BERND *and* AUGUST KEIL *are coming down the field path. Both men, the old, white-haired* BERND *as well as his younger companion, who is about thirty-five years old, are dressed in their black Sunday suits and carry their hymn books.* BERND *has a white beard; his voice is soft, like the voices of people who have had a serious lung ailment. He has the appearance of a dignified coachman who has been pensioned off.* AUGUST KEIL *is a book-binder; he has a pale face, a thin, dark mustache and a pointed beard; his hair is getting sparse. He is thin, has a narrow chest, and his entire appearance indicates a man used to working in his room. Occasionally he twitches nervously.*)

BERND. Isn't that Rosie?

AUGUST. Yes sir, Father Bernd.

BERND. You simply can't get her away from it! If she gets a notion she has to work she goes and works, and too bad if it's a Sunday. —(*He has meanwhile come close to her.*) Isn't there time for that during the week?

AUGUST. You're doing too much, Rose! You really don't have to do that.

BERND. If our good pastor would see that it'd hurt him in his soul. He wouldn't believe his eyes.

AUGUST. He's been asking about you again.

STRECKMANN (*suggestively*). And I hear he wants her for his housekeeper!

BERND (*notices* STRECKMANN *only now*). Why, there's Streckmann!

STRECKMANN. In all his glory! That girl's working away and she don't care if the bees and horse-flies buzz around her. She'd keep going even if she'd broken all her ribs. She don't have time to sleep in church.

BERND. We haven't been sleeping there either—not likely! But I wouldn't be surprised if some people had been sleeping out here, in the open air—them who refuse to be awakened. The Bridegroom is near . . .

STRECKMANN. That hits the nail on the head! But meanwhile the bride's going to pot!

AUGUST. You're feeling right jolly today.

STRECKMANN. That's right! I could hug a rock I'm feeling so good—or even the handle of the collection bag. I feel so damn chipper I could laugh till my sides split.

BERND (*to* ROSE). Put your things together, Rose, we have

to go home now. —But not like that! I'm not going home with you like that! Put that hoe over there in the cherry tree. That'd just be the thing to give offense.

AUGUST. I know some who even carry a gun on Sunday.

STRECKMANN. And some devils even a bottle of schnapps! (*He brings out his liquor bottle.*)

AUGUST. Everybody's got to account for what he does.

STRECKMANN. Right! And to pay for it, too. Come on, steel your heart and have a drink with me! (*He offers the bottle to* AUGUST *who does not pay any attention to him.*)

BERND. You know that August never touches liquor! —Where do you have your threshing machine now?

STRECKMANN. But you, Father Bernd, you'll have to do me the honor! After all, you've been a distiller. —The machine's down on the estate.

BERND (*hesitates but finally takes the bottle*). Just because it's you, Streckmann; I wouldn't take it from anybody else. —When I was still managing the estate, why, you just had to do everything that came along. But I never liked doing it—distilling liquor. And I never touched a drop, then.

STRECKMANN (*addressing* AUGUST *who is picking up a shovel that had been lying on the ground and putting it into the hollow tree*). Just take a look at that cherry tree! Bang, bang, bang! Just aim and pull the trigger.

BERND. There's people who really go hunting on a Sunday.

STRECKMANN. Like Flamm.

BERND. Right. We met him. That's really bad. I feel sorry for people like that. (STRECKMANN *is throwing June bugs at* ROSE.)

ROSE (*trembling*). Streckmann!

BERND. What's the matter?

AUGUST. What's going on?

STRECKMANN. Nothing. We got a bone to pick, the two of us!

AUGUST. Go pick your bones with whom you like. And you can eat them all by yourself for all I care.

STRECKMANN (*mean and hostile*). August, watch yourself!

BERND. Now, now. For God's sake don't start a fight.

STRECKMANN. That toad always has to puff himself up.

AUGUST. Toads are what I see sitting in ditches.

STRECKMANN. August, let's try and get along. The old man's right, let's be friends. It's really not Christian the way you always bristle! Come on now and have a drink! We'll take a drink together! You're not handsome—I got to admit that though it makes me green with envy—but you know pretty well how to read and write and you've feathered your nest pretty well! So here's to a merry wedding, and soon! (*Since* AUGUST *does not move to take the bottle,* BERND *quickly grasps it and drinks.*) I'll consider that an honor, Father Bernd.

BERND. To a merry wedding—for that I'll make an exception.

STRECKMANN. That's the spirit! That's the way. —It's no longer like it used to be when I was hitching up horses over on the estate and you were the boss. Now I'm respectable. If a fellow has a little brains he's bound to get someplace.

BERND. Well, that's how God wills it. (*To* AUGUST.) Come on, drink to a merry wedding.

AUGUST (*takes the bottle*). May God grant it. There's no need to drink to it.

STRECKMANN (*slapping his thighs*). And may he grant a lot of little Augusts! So grandfather will have some fun. And the first one's going to become Justice of the Peace! —Let Rosie have a drink, too, now.

BERND. What are you crying for, Rosie, what's the matter?

MARTHEL. It's dripping down from her eyes all the time.

AUGUST (*to* ROSE). There, take a mouthful so he's content.

(ROSE *makes a great effort to overcome her disgust and takes the bottle.*)

STRECKMANN. There now! Go to it! Take a swig!

(ROSE *trembling, drinks and returns the bottle to* AUGUST *without attempting to hide her loathing.*)

BERND (*low to* STRECKMANN, *with paternal pride*). That's some girl! He'd better hold on to her.

CURTAIN

ACT II

The living room in FLAMM's *house. The large, low-ceilinged room is on the ground floor. A door at the right opens into the hallway. A second door, in the back, connects the living room with a smaller room which* HERR FLAMM *calls his "hunt room"; it contains equipment for making cartridges, clothing, and guns which are hanging from hooks in the wall, stuffed birds that can be seen through the open door and, finally, a cabinet with the files of the registrar's office. The three windows in the left wall of the living room, its brown, open-beam ceiling, and its furnishings give the room a lived-in, comfortable air. In the left corner is a large, old-fashioned sofa covered with a flowered material; in front of it stands a dark-stained oak table with extension leaves. Antlers of stags and roebuck horns, hung close together, cover the wall above the sofa. Above the door to the hunt room hangs a glass case containing a family of stuffed partridges. Next to the door, on the right, is a key rack with a number of keys. Further along the wall is a well-filled bookcase with glass doors. On top of the bookcase sits a stuffed owl; on the wall, next to the case, hangs a cuckoo clock. A large stove, of white tiles dotted with blue, completely fills the right-hand corner. In front of the three windows, which have muslin curtains, are potted plants in bloom. The window near the table and the one further toward the front are open. Not far from the front window stands an old chest-of-drawers with a curved front, covered with a lace cloth. The top of the chest is crowded with glasses, all kinds of family souvenirs, knickknacks, etc. On the wall above it hang family photographs. Between the stove and the hall door stands an old grand piano, its keyboard turned toward the stove, and an embroidered piano stool. Several cases containing a butterfly collection hang on the wall above the piano. In the right front is a roll-top desk polished in a light color; in front of it stands a simple chair. Several other chairs of the same kind stand along the wall near the desk. Between the windows stands an old, brown leather arm chair. A large, English lamp with a wide brass edge hangs from the ceiling above the table. A large photograph of a good-looking, five-year-old boy in a simple wooden frame hangs on the wall above the desk. It is decorated with a wreath of fresh wild flowers. Below it, on the desk, stands a large glass bowl with forget-me-nots, which are stuck in moist sand. It is not quite eleven o'clock on a glorious morning in late spring. FRAU FLAMM is sitting in a wheel chair near the front window. She is about forty years old, matronly and pleasant looking. She wears a smooth, black alpaca dress with an old-fashioned bodice, and a white lace coif on her head. Around her neck is a little lace collar, and her fine, thin hands are almost covered by lace cuffs. She has a book and a fine batiste handkerchief in her lap. Her face has large, impressive features, her eyes are light blue and penetrating, her forehead high, and her temples wide. She wears her thin gray hair parted in the middle, an eminently correct hairdo. Now and then she brushes it lightly back with the tips of her extended fingers. The expression on her face indicates great kindness; it is serious without being hard. A good deal of whimsy flickers around her eyes, nose, and mouth.)*

FRAU FLAMM (*now looking pensively into the distance, sighs, and starts reading her book; then she listens, closes the book after inserting a bookmark, turns to the door and says loudly, but in a pleasant voice*). Whoever it is, come on in!—(*There is a knock, the hall door is opened a little, and* BERND's *head becomes visible.*) Who is it? Oh, it's Father Bernd, our orphanage trustee and deacon. Come right in, Father Bernd! I don't bite.

BERND. We've come to talk to the lieutenant. (*He enters, followed by* AUGUST KEIL; *both, again, are wearing their Sunday finery.*)

FRAU FLAMM. Well, well! You look pretty ceremonial!

BERND. Good-morning, Frau Lieutenant.

FRAU FLAMM. Good-morning, Father Bernd! —My husband was in the hunt room a minute ago. (*Indicating* AUGUST.) And that is your son-in-law?

BERND. Yes, Ma'am, with God's help.

FRAU FLAMM. Take a seat! I suppose you want to make the announcement? So it's going to happen finally!

BERND. Yes, thank God, we've gotten this far, at last.

FRAU FLAMM. I'm so glad! This waiting and waiting is no good. Once it's decided you might as well do it quickly. So she's finally agreed?

BERND. Yes, Frau Flamm. And it really's taken a stone off my chest. She's dragged it out such an awful long time. Now, all on her own, she's the one who's in a hurry. She'd have the wedding rather today than tomorrow.

FRAU FLAMM. I'm really glad, Herr Keil! I'm glad, Bernd! —Christel! —I think my husband will be here in a minute. So that's straightened out at last. Well, Father Bernd, you're really lucky. I'm sure you're very happy.

BERND. I am, Frau Flamm. You're quite right. Day before yesterday we talked it over, all of us. And now God's added another blessing; August's been to see Fräulein Gnadau, and she's been so charitable, she's lent him three thousand marks. So now, with this money, he's been able to buy Lachmann's house.

FRAU FLAMM. Is that right? Really? Not possible! There you can see, Father Bernd; at the time your people let you go without any allowance at all, you were so discouraged— you had no hope at all. And it was mean, the way they behaved! And now by God's grace, everything turns out well.

BERND. That's the way it is! Man's always faint-hearted.

FRAU FLAMM. Well then! You're really well taken care of! First of all, the house is right close by the church; then there's a fine piece of land that goes with it. And Rose— that much I know! —she really knows how to run a house. Well, well! You can really be content now.

BERND. How much good a lady like that can do! After God, whom do we have to thank most? —If I'd been working for Fräulein Gnadau, and if I had slaved as much for her as I did for our Lordship, I wouldn't never had anything to complain about.

FRAU FLAMM. Well, Bernd, now you've nothing to complain about anyway!

BERND. That's true. No, in a way, everything's all right now.

FRAU FLAMM. You can never count on gratitude in this life. My father had been head forester for forty years, and later on my mother had nothing to eat all the same. —You've got a good son-in-law now, you'll live in a nice house and can even do a little work on your fields. And you needn't worry about seeing that things move forward . . . you can leave that to your children.

BERND. Yes, I sure hope so. I don't doubt it'll work out. Somebody who's worked so hard to get ahead, started by selling tracts from door to door . . .

FRAU FLAMM (*to* AUGUST). Didn't you want to become a missionary at one time?

AUGUST. Yes, ma'am. It was too bad my health wasn't good enough.

BERND. . . . has learned to write and read and a trade, and is such a good Christian and such an honest man—I think I'm safe putting my head on a pillow, even if it's to sleep forever.

FRAU FLAMM. Father Bernd, did you know that my husband is transferring his registrar's duties to somebody else? He probably won't even marry your daughter.

BERND. They're busy with the rape-seed . . .

FRAU FLAMM. I know. Rose is helping them I think. This morning she came up to talk to me. If you want to go down, they're right behind the yard. Christel! —Oh, there he is . . .

FLAMM (*outside the door*). Coming! Just a minute!

FRAU FLAMM. Registry business!

(FLAMM *appears in the door to the hunt room; he wears neither coat nor vest, and his white shirt is open in front. He is busy cleaning the double barrel of a shot gun.*)

FLAMM. Here I am. Streckmann was here just now. The best thing would be to get him to thresh right now. His machine is down on the estate, but they haven't finished by a long shot . . . Heavens, here's Father Bernd!

BERND. Yes sir, Herr Flamm. We've come so we'd . . .

FLAMM. One thing after another. Just a little patience. (*Looking through the gun barrels.*) If you have some business for the registry, Father Bernd, maybe it'd be better to wait just a little while longer. Steckel—you know, the accountant—he'll be my successor. And I'm sure he'll make much more of a ceremony out of it than I would.

FRAU FLAMM (*has listened to her husband attentively, the point of her crochet hook at her chin*). No really, Christel, what kind of nonsense is that!

AUGUST (*even paler now that* STRECKMANN'S *name has been mentioned than he was before; gets up, solemnly and excited*). Herr Lieutenant, I'm here for a wedding announcement. —With God's help, I'm willing to enter holy matrimony.

FLAMM (*removes the gun from his eye; carelessly*). Is that so! Are you in a great hurry?

FRAU FLAMM (*playfully*). Now that's really none of your business, Christel. You just let them get married if that's what they want. A fine preacher you are! If that man had his way, Father Bernd, there'd be only bachelors and spinsters in the world.

FLAMM. Marriage is nothing but a confidence game! —You're August Keil, the bookbinder, aren't you?

AUGUST. At your service!

FLAMM. And you live over in Wandriss? You just bought the Lachmann property, didn't you?

AUGUST. At your service!

FLAMM. And you're planning to start a book store?

AUGUST. Yes, books and stationery. At least, I may.

BERND. He's thinking of inspirational books mostly.

FLAMM. The land that goes with the Lachmann house— that's near the big pear tree, isn't it?

BERND AND AUGUST (*together*). Yes sir.

FLAMM. Well! We're neighbors then. (*He puts the gun aside and searches in his pockets for a key-ring. Then he calls.*) Minna! Come in and wheel Frau Lieutenant's chair out! (*Although not quite at his ease, he resigns himself and sits down at the desk.*)

FRAU FLAMM. Oh, my husband's always so chivalrous! But he's right. You don't need me here. (*Addressing the neatly-dressed chambermaid who has meanwhile entered and stands behind her chair.*) Just push me into the hunt room, girl. You might smoothe your hair a little better. (FRAU FLAMM *and* THE GIRL *leave through the door to the hunt room.*)

FLAMM. I feel sorry for the Lachmanns. (*To* AUGUST.) Did you have money invested in that property? —(AUGUST *coughs, excited and embarrassed.*) Well, it really doesn't matter. Anybody who's able to get that property is certainly lucky. —So you want to . . . But the bride's missing! —How's that? Doesn't she want to?

AUGUST (*very excited and determined*). Everything's been agreed, as far as I know.

BERND. I'll go and get her, Herr Flamm.

(*He hurries out.*)

FLAMM (*visibly absent-minded, opens the roll-top of the desk and notices too late that* BERND *has left*). Nonsense, there's no hurry. (*Bewildered, he looks at the door through which* BERND *has left, then shrugs his shoulders.*) Oh, go ahead and do as you like! —I'll light a pipe in the meantime. (*He gets up, takes a tobacco pouch from the bookcase and a short pipe from a pipe rack on the wall, fills the pipe and lights it. While doing so, to* AUGUST.) Do you smoke?

AUGUST. No, sir.

FLAMM. And you don't use snuff?

AUGUST. No, sir.

FLAMM. And you don't drink? No beer, no schnapps, no wine?

AUGUST. No, sir. Nothing but the communion wine.

FLAMM. Absolutely iron principles! —That's excellent! —Come in! —Didn't somebody knock at the door? Must have been those damn dachshunds. —You play the quack now and then, just for fun, don't you? (AUGUST *shakes his head.*) I thought maybe you could heal by prayer. Seemed to me I had heard something like that.

AUGUST. That'd sure be different from quackery.

FLAMM. Oh?

AUGUST. Faith can move mountains. And if one prays and has the proper spirit . . . God's almighty, even nowadays.

FLAMM. Come in! —Wasn't there a knock again? —Come in, then! Come on in! Damn it, why the devil . . . (BERND, *himself very pale, pushes* ROSE, *pale and recalcitrant, through the door. For a moment,* ROSE *and* FLAMM *gaze fixedly into each other's eyes. Then* FLAMM *continues.*) All right, then! Wait just a minute! (*He pretends he is looking for something and goes into the hunt room. The following exchange between* BERND, ROSE, *and* AUGUST *takes place in excited whispers.*)

BERND. So what did Streckmann tell you?

ROSE. Who? No, Father . . .

BERND. Streckmann was out there, and he just kept ranting at her.

ROSE. What should he have been ranting about?

BERND. That's what I'm asking you!

ROSE. And I just don't know what you mean.

AUGUST. You shouldn't even talk to a no-good wretch like that!

ROSE. Can I help it if he talks to me?

BERND. There you are! So he did talk to you!

ROSE. What if he did! I wasn't listening anyway.

BERND. I'll have to report that Streckmann one of these days. I'll have to take him to court. As we were passing by just now where they're working with the threshing machine . . . there! Listen! Now they're starting again . . . (*The humming and pounding of the threshing machine is heard in the distance.*) . . . he shouted something—but I just couldn't make out what he said.

AUGUST. If a girl only talks to him for a minute her reputation's ruined.

ROSE. Why don't you go look for a better girl then!

FLAMM (*comes back. He has put on a collar and a hunting jacket. His bearing is dignified.*) Good-morning everybody! What can I do for you? When's the wedding supposed to take place? What's the trouble? There isn't any . . . er . . . difference of opinion about this, is there? Well, say something, somebody! Well, it seems you aren't quite ready yet. Let me make a suggestion: why don't you all go home, and sleep on it! And then, when you've made up your minds, you come back.

AUGUST (*dictatorially*). This business is going to be finished right now!

FLAMM. Keil, I don't object, that's for sure! (*Takes a pencil, ready to make some notes.*) Well then, what date do you have in mind?

BERND. Just as soon as possible we thought.

AUGUST. In four or five weeks maybe, if that's possible.

FLAMM. In four or five weeks, eh?

AUGUST. Yes sir, Herr Flamm.

FLAMM. Give me the exact date, then. But you really shouldn't rush into this, and . . .

ROSE (*deeply troubled*). It could very well wait a while, too!

FLAMM. What do you mean, Rosie? Fräulein Rose, I mean. Well, I've known her since she was a child. But now that she's going to be a bride I shouldn't be so familiar. Well now! She doesn't agree with you, it seems.

AUGUST (*having flinched at ROSE's words, is still staring at her, trying to control his violent feelings. Ominously calm.*) Well then! Good-by, Father Bernd!

BERND. You stay right here, August, I tell you! (*To* ROSE.) And you! Let me tell you something! You'd better make up your mind right now! I've had a lot of patience with you, and so has August, more than enough. We've put up with all your whims. We've kept telling ourselves, let's be patient with her, some day God Almighty will bring her to her senses. But it's getting worse and worse. Three days ago you gave me your hand, and you gave August your hand—and it was all settled! You just couldn't wait yourself. And now you've changed your mind again? What do you want? Who do you think you are? Do you think you can do anything just because you're a decent girl? Because you kept your nose clean and have worked hard and nobody can say nothing against you? You aren't the only one like that. That's nothing so special. That's nothing to be stuck up about. There are plenty of girls who don't run to every dance. There are plenty who take care of little brothers and sisters and keep house for their old father. Just because you're a decent, pious girl, that don't mean all the other girls are trash. If you'd been any different I'd have thrown you out of the house a long time ago! I wouldn't have a daughter like that! And this fellow here, August, he don't have to wait for you. A man like that, all he's got to do is hold up his finger, and the women will come running—women from the best families too, mind you. Better girls than you. Good Lord, I'm losing my patience! This pride! This impudence! Either you're going to keep your promise . . .

FLAMM. Easy, easy now, Father Bernd! Don't get excited!

BERND. Herr Lieutenant, you don't know what's been going on! If a girl keeps pushing an honest man around like that, she's no daughter of mine!

AUGUST (*close to tears*). Rose, what do you have against me? Why do you behave so beastly? I've never trusted my luck, that's the truth—why should I? It's just my fate to have bad luck. I've always told you so, Father Bernd! And yet, I've worried and I've worked, and in a way I've had God's blessing because I didn't go to the dogs. Sure I'm crying. It just happens—that's the way it is! It just would have been too much happiness for me. I was brought up in an orphanage; I've never had a home, nor a sister, or a brother. So I've held on to the Saviour.—All right, I know I'm no beauty. But I've asked you and you said yes. It's what's inside that counts. God looks at the heart! You'll be sorry for this some day! (*He again turns to go, but* BERND *holds him back.*)

BERND. I'm telling you, August, you stay right here! Do you understand what I said, Rose? Every word—this man here . . . either . . . I won't stand for it! He's been my support long before he asked to marry you. When I was sick and couldn't earn a penny, and nobody cared what happened to us, he shared his bread with us. (AUGUST *is unable to control his emotion any longer, takes his hat and leaves.*) He's been like an angel!—August!

ROSE. But Father, I'm willing, I want to. Only just give me a little time!

BERND. He's given you plenty of time! Three years he's given you! Even the Herr Pastor's talked to you . . . He's had enough now. And I can't blame him. There's a limit. He's right. But you . . . you look after yourself now . . . do what you want . . . I'm not proud of you any more!

(*He leaves.*)

FLAMM. Well, well, well! Good Lord!

(*During the foregoing,* ROSE *has alternately blushed and turned deadly pale. Obviously very upset, she was several times on the verge of losing her self-control. After* BERND *has left, her face turns terribly pale and freezes into immobility.*)

FLAMM (*closes the register and at last finds the courage to look at* ROSE). Rose!—Wake up!—What's the matter?—You aren't going to take all this sulfur and brimstone seriously, eh? (ROSE *starts shivering and her large, unmoving eyes fill with tears.*) Rose!—Be reasonable!—Look here now!

ROSE. I know—what I want—and I'm going to get it.—And if not—then—that don't matter, either!

FLAMM (*paces up and down excitedly, listens at the door*). Of course, and why not? (*He seems to be interested only in the key-rack from which he takes first one key, then another. In ever growing passion he whispers.*) Rose! Darling!—Rose!—Are you listening?—We've got to talk about all of this. Meet me at the small farm!—Sh! Mother's in the hunt room. We can't talk here.

ROSE (*struggles for words, but manages to say with great determination*). No!—Never and never, Herr Flamm!

FLAMM. Are you trying to get us all into the nuthouse?

Are you crazy, girl?—Here I've been running after you for four weeks, trying to talk some sense to you, and you behave as if I were a leper.—Now you see! That's what had to happen!

ROSE (*as before*). And if it was ten times as bad! You just go ahead, all of you! Keep hitting me over the head! I don't deserve no better. Go ahead and wipe your boots on me. But . . .

FLAMM (*stands at the table and, with a quick movement, turns to face* ROSE. *He tries to control his anger and consternation. Unintentionally, his fist suddenly slams violently down on the table.*) God damn it all to hell!

ROSE. For heaven's sake . . .

(FRAU FLAMM *appears in the door of the hunt room in her wheel chair, pushed by* A SERVANT GIRL.)

FRAU FLAMM. What's going on here, Christel?

(FLAMM *has turned pale as a sheet; he pulls himself together, takes his hat and cane and leaves by the door on the right.*)

FRAU FLAMM (*a worried expression on her face, follows her husband with her eyes, shakes her head as he leaves the room and asks* ROSE). What's been happening? What's the matter with that man?

ROSE (*overcome by her violent emotions*). Oh, dear Frau Flamm, I'm so terribly unhappy! (*She falls on her knees and hides her face in* FRAU FLAMM'S *lap.*)

FRAU FLAMM. Now . . . what on earth, girl . . . what's gotten into you?—What's the matter?—You're completely changed!—I don't understand a thing. (*To* THE SERVANT GIRL *who had pushed her chair.*) I won't need you just now. Come back a little later! Meanwhile, get the kitchen in order. (THE SERVANT GIRL *leaves.*) Now then!—Where does it hurt?—What happened?—Go on, tell me everything. That'll do you good. What's that?—What did you say?— Don't you want to marry Pastepot August?—Or is there someone else?—It's all right! One's about as good as the next one, and none of them is worth much!

ROSE (*collecting herself at last, gets up*). I know what I want to do, and that's that.

FRAU FLAMM. Oh? You see, I was just thinking you

didn't know what to do. Women sometimes don't, you know, least of all at your age. So an old woman sometimes can give some good advice. But if you know, why, that's wonderful! Then you're going to find the way out all by yourself. (*Puts on her spectacles and eyes* ROSE *sharply.*) Rosie, are you sick by any chance?

ROSE (*taken aback, confused*). Sick? . . . Why . . .

FRAU FLAMM. Just sick, the way one gets sick now and then. You don't seem to be yourself.

ROSE. But I'm not sick!

FRAU FLAMM. I didn't say you were. I was just asking. That's why I asked. Now, we have to understand each other. There's really no point our running around in circles, playing hide and seek. You don't think I don't mean well, do you? (ROSE *shakes her head violently.*) Well—that'd be something! All right, then. You and my little Kurt, you played together when you were children, you grew up together . . . until God took my only child. And when your mother died, at about the same time—I remember, she was on her death bed—she talked to me; she asked me to look after you a little if I could.

ROSE (*stares in front of her*). The best thing would be to drown myself! If that's the way it is . . . May God forgive me the sin!

FRAU FLAMM. If that's the way it is? What does that mean? I don't understand. Try to be just a little clearer. First of all, I'm a woman, so I'm not going to be shocked! And then, I'm a mother, even if I have no children left. God knows what's wrong with you, girl! I've been watching you for weeks, even if you didn't notice. Come on now and tell me the truth! Push me over to the chest, will you? (ROSE *does so.*) There! There are a lot of old things in the drawers here. Little Kurt's old things . . . Your mother once said, "My Rose, she's going to be a real mother, but she's a little hot-blooded!" I don't know, maybe she was right. (*She takes a large doll out of one of the drawers.*) Look at this! No matter what happens, a mother's nothing to look down on! You and Kurt, you used to play with this doll. It was mostly you, though; you took care of her, washed her, fed her, and changed her diapers. Once Flamm happened to come by, and you were even putting her to your breast! You brought such nice flowers this morning. You put the forget-me-nots in the bowl there, didn't you? And on Sunday you put a wreath on Kurt's grave! Yes, children and graves—that's women's business. (*She takes a child's shirt out of the drawer and holds it up by the sleeves with both hands; she talks across the raised shirt.*) Isn't that right, Rose? And I want to thank you for what you did. Your father, why he's always busy with the missions, and his Bible lessons and all that sort of thing. He thinks all men are sinners, and he wants to make angels out of all of them. Maybe he's right; I don't know anything about these things. But one thing I've learned, and that is what it means to be a mother on this earth, and how many pains she has to suffer.

(ROSE *sinks to her knees, crushed and groaning; as a sign of confession, she gratefully covers* FRAU FLAMM's *hands with kisses.*)

FRAU FLAMM (*calmly continues to talk, although a sudden light in her eyes betrays the fact that she now understands the situation and acknowledges* ROSE's *silent confession*). You see, girl, that much I've learned. I have learned it, and the world has forgotten it. I don't know much about anything else. I know about as much as everybody else, but what everybody else knows I wouldn't call really knowing anything. (*She puts the baby shirt carefully on her lap.*) You go on home now and don't worry. I want to think about all this for a while. It's all right, I won't ask any more questions now. You are something special now . . . So we have to be twice as careful. I don't want to know anything. Just trust me. Fathers don't matter anyway; I don't care if it's a judge or a tramp. We're the ones who have to bring the children into the world anyway. Nobody's going to change that. We have to think about three things now: about your father, about August—and about a lot of other things. But I have time to think about all that. I'll give it a lot of thought. At least I'm still good for something!

ROSE (*gets up and stands rigidly before* FRAU FLAMM). Oh no, Frau Lieutenant, you mustn't do that!—It just isn't possible! You mustn't worry about me. I don't deserve that from you and from nobody, I know that. I just have to eat that soup all by myself. I mustn't let somebody else do it for me. It's . . . I just can't explain it any better. You're an angel, Frau Lieutenant, so good you are! Good God, you're much too good to me. But it's just not possible! I can't accept it. Good-by, Frau Lieutenant . . .

FRAU FLAMM. Now wait a minute. I'm not going to let you go like this! God knows what you're going to do.

ROSE. No, don't worry about that, Frau Flamm. I'm not ready yet to do something foolish. If it has to be, I can always work for the child. The sky's high and the world's wide! If it was just me, and I didn't have to think of Father and wasn't so sorry for August . . . and a child just ought to have a father!

FRAU FLAMM. All right. Be a brave girl! You've always had a lot of spirit. That's just fine if you keep your head. —But if I understand you right, there's still something that I can't get through my head. Why don't you want to get married?

ROSE (*turns pale; balky and timidly*). What can I tell you?—I just don't know. I wouldn't object to it, only . . . Streckmann . . .

FRAU FLAMM. Out with it now . . . all right? Or if you want to, go home now; that's all right; you can come back tomorrow. But you listen to me: be glad! A girl has to be glad about having a child!

ROSE. I will, God knows!—And I'll get through . . . all this; but nobody can help me doing it.

(*She leaves quickly.*)

FRAU FLAMM (*follows her with her eyes, sighs, takes the little shirt from her lap and holds it up*). Now, my girl, what you have—it's a joy! There's no greater happiness for a woman! Hold on to it!

CURTAIN

ACT III

(*Fertile fields. In the right foreground, an old pear tree stands on a slightly lower, grassy triangle between the fields. Clear water bubbles from a spring into a simple basin of field stones just below the tree. In the middle distance are pastures; in the background is a large pond with water plants and reeds, surrounded by alders,*

*hazel, willow, and beech shrubs. Beyond are meadows
and, in a semi-circle, a group of very old oaks, elms,
beeches, and birches. Between bushes and trees one
sees the steeples and rooftops of distant villages; behind
the bushes to the left are the thatched roofs of the out-
lying farm buildings belonging to an estate. It is a hot
afternoon in early August. A threshing machine hums
in the distance.* BERND *and* AUGUST KEIL *are coming
from the right, both visibly tired from their work and
exhausted by the heat. They are wearing only their
shirts, pants, boots, and caps. On their shoulders they
carry each a hoe, in their hands a scythe. A cow's horn,
in which they carry their whetstones, hangs on their
belts.)*

BERND. Really pretty hot today!—About time for a little
rest!—But then, it's nice to work on your own land.

AUGUST. Only I'm just not used to cutting grass.

BERND. You kept up very well, though.

AUGUST. Oh no. And how long am I going to stand it?
I've got aches and pains in all my limbs already.

BERND. You can be satisfied with yourself, son. One's got
to get used to this work. And you're not doing this but once
in a while. Believe me, you could work along with any
farmer.

AUGUST. For one day maybe. But the second day I'd be
finished. I'm just not well enough. It's just miserable the
way I am. I've been over to the District Physician again,
too. Same as always. He just shrugged his shoulders.

BERND. There's nothing wrong with you—and you're in
God's hands. You might put a couple of rusty nails in water,
though, and drink the water two, three times a week. That
cleans the blood and makes the heart strong. If only the
weather would keep!

AUGUST. What a heat! A little while ago I thought I
heard thunder, too.

BERND (*kneels by the edge of the well and drinks, his
mouth touching the surface of the water*). There's nothing
like water! It's the best drink there is.

AUGUST. What time is it?

BERND. Must be around four. I wonder where Rose is with
the supper. (*He gets up and looks at the blade of his scythe
which he had left leaning against the tree.* AUGUST *does*

the same.) Do you have to sharpen yours? Mine will last a while longer.

AUGUST. I'll try mine like it is, too.

BERND (*drops down into the grass below the pear tree*). Come and sit down beside me. And if you got your Testament along we could strengthen our souls a bit.

AUGUST (*sits down, too, tired and relieved*). I only say, praised and thanked be the Lord!

BERND. You see, August, I was telling you all along, just leave her be. She'll find the way, that girl. So now she's seen reason. I'd been racking my brains for a long time, even before your time. Sometimes she sure was stubborn! —But—leave her alone, I thought. God knows, sometimes it was like she was butting her head against a wall . . . And nobody else could see that wall, so she'd have to grope all the more by herself trying to find a way around it.

AUGUST. That other time, what had gotten into her . . . I'll thank God on my knees now . . . but then I just couldn't understand it. And the way she suddenly . . . I still don't know what had happened, even today . . . what made her behave that way.

BERND. And how nice she was this time, when we went down to the Registrar's, compared with the last time!

AUGUST. I can't say I mind that it's not Flamm any more.

BERND. This time she didn't move a muscle and in four, five minutes the whole thing was over. Well, that's the way it goes, that's how women are!

AUGUST. I keep wondering if it had something to do with Streckmann? He shouted at you I don't know what, and then he'd been jabbering at her before . . .

BERND. Maybe, and maybe not. I just don't know. Sometimes you just can't get nothing out of that girl. It sure isn't nice that way. But I'm all the more content she's getting a husband now who can change her so she'll stop being so pigheaded. You two were meant for each other. She's a good girl, but she needs somebody to guide her, and you have a good and gentle hand.

AUGUST. When I see that Streckmann I think I see the Devil . . .

BERND. I wonder if she thought that fellow was up to no good . . . He's been a wild one all right from the time he was a boy! His mother used to complain many a time. It's possible. He's capable of anything.

AUGUST. When I see that man, I don't recognize myself.

Hot and cold it runs down my back . . . and I feel like accusing God Almighty . . . wishing he'd made me strong like Samson! I get nasty ideas—may God forgive me. (*The whistle of the threshing machine sounds.*) There he is again!

BERND. Don't you pay no attention to him.

AUGUST. Sure . . . once this is all over I'll lock myself in my four walls and we'll live a peaceful life.

BERND. A pleasant, peaceful life . . . yes . . . with God's help.

AUGUST. I don't want to hear nothing any more about the world. The whole world and all the people in it—it just disgusts me so, I could . . . why, Father, I don't know how to say it . . . When I feel bitter like that and I got everything up to here, I just laugh! I'm happy to die! I'm happy as a baby just thinking I'll die.

(*A number of farmhands, among them an old woman and two young girls are hurrying over across the fields. All of them work on* FLAMM's *estate. They are* HAHN, HEINZEL, GOLISCH, FRAU GOLISCH, OLD KLEINERT, *the* HEAD MAID *and the* SECOND MAID. *The men are dressed only in shirts and trousers, the women have rolled up their skirts and wear kerchiefs around their shoulders and their heads. They are all thirsty.*)

HAHN (*thirty years old, tanned and brisk*). So I'm the first one at the spring again! As much as you run, you can't catch up with me nohow! (*He kneels down and bends over the spring.*) I'd love to jump right into it!

MAID. Don't you dare! We're thirsty, too!—(*To the* HEAD MAID.) You got a cup along?

HEAD MAID. You just wait a while! First comes the Head Maid!

HEINZEL (*pulling both women back by their shoulders, pushes between them to the spring*). First the men, the women come after.

KLEINERT. There's room for everybody. Hey there, Father Bernd! Good-evening!

BERND. Yes, only we're still waiting for our supper.

GOLISCH. I'm wet like a rag all over. My tongue feels like a piece of wood in my mouth.

FRAU GOLISCH. Water!

KLEINERT. There's enough for all of us.

*(Everybody drinks greedily, some directly from the surface
of the spring, some from their cupped hands, their
hats, or from bottles or pots. The only sound is the
noise of their avid drinking and their sighs of relief.)*

HEINZEL *(gets up)*. Water's good, but beer would be
still better.

HAHN. I wouldn't mind a drop of schnapps, neither.

GOLISCH. August, why don't you pay for a quart!

FRAU GOLISCH. He'd better invite us for the wedding.

GOLISCH. We're all coming to the wedding, sure. It's
going to be soon now, I hear, right?

HEINZEL. I'm not going there. Won't be nothing but water
to drink, and that I can get right here! And just for sipping
some coffee . . .

HAHN.   . . . and for praying and singing, don't forget!
Who knows, maybe he'll get the Pastor from Jenkau over
and he'll have us recite The Ten Commandments.

HEINZEL. Or even the prayers! That wouldn't be so good;
I've forgotten all about that stuff.

KLEINERT. Leave August alone now! I can tell you, if I
had a girl, I wouldn't ask for a better son-in-law. He knows
what he's doing and he takes care of his business.

*(The laborers sit down on the ground in a semi-circle and
start eating their supper. They drink coffee from tin
containers and eat bread, cutting bite-size pieces from
large wedges with their pocket knives.)*

FRAU GOLISCH. There's Rosie Bernd coming around the
barn.

GOLISCH. Just look how that girl can run!

KLEINERT. She'll lift a bag of flour by herself and lug it
up to the loft. Only this morning I saw her . . . She had
a great big wardrobe on the wheelbarrow and was pushing
it over to the new house. That girl's strong as a bull. She'll
take care of her house all right.

HAHN. If I was as well off as August, Jesus, I wouldn't
mind . . . I'd even try that holy stuff, too.

GOLISCH. You got to know how it works, then it's not too
bad.

HAHN. If you think how he used to run around with his
bag in the beginning selling them tracts in the villages;
and then how he started writing letters for people . . .

And today he's got the best piece of land in Wandriss and is marrying the prettiest girl for miles around!

(ROSE BERND *comes, bringing in a basket the supper for* BERND *and* AUGUST.)

ROSE. Good-evening!

EVERYBODY. Good-evening! Good-evening!

GOLISCH. You're letting your lover starve, Rosie!

ROSE (*unpacks the food; cheerfully*). Oh, don't worry. Nobody starves to death that quick.

HEINZEL. You got to feed him well, Rosie, or he won't get fat.

GOLISCH. Yes sir, he'll just stay too damn meager for you if you don't.

BERND. Where have you been all this time, eh? We've been waiting for half an hour.

AUGUST (*in an undertone, annoyed*). Now we've got that whole crowd here again! We could have finished by now!

FRAU GOLISCH. Let him growl, girl, don't mind him.

ROSE. Who's growling, Golisch? Who'd be growling around here? August wouldn't growl for anything.

FRAU GOLISCH. And if he does, just let him; that's all I'm telling you.

HEINZEL. If he hasn't started growling yet—he will.

ROSE. I'm not worried!

GOLISCH. You two seem really crazy about each other all of a sudden.

ROSE. But we've been promised for ages, huh, August? (*She kisses him.* THE LABORERS *laugh.*) What are you laughing about? That's how it is!

GOLISCH. No . . . that's really something . . . Here I was always thinking I'd climb in her window some night . . .

KLEINERT. Hmph, you'd be lugging your bones home in your handkerchief!

HEAD MAID (*suggestively*). Oh dear, oh dear! No, no, I'd try anyways! Who'd know about it!

BERND (*darkly and quietly*). That's enough, woman!

KLEINERT. See? He's telling you where to get off. Better watch out. Old Bernd just don't see the joke sometimes.

ROSE. She hasn't said anything. Leave her alone!

KLEINERT (*lights his pipe*). Yes, here he's sitting looking peaceful as a lamb, but if he gets going, you just wouldn't believe it. I remember when he was still foreman on the

estate . . . Jesus, the women had nothing to laugh about!
He'd take care of ten like you; nothing doing about running around with fellows?

HEAD MAID. Who's running around with fellows?

KLEINERT. You ought to ask Streckmann!

HEAD MAID (*blushing*). Oh, why don't you go and ask
God Almighty himself! (*Laughter.*)

(STRECKMANN *appears; he is dusty as he has just come from
the threshing machine; he has had some brandy and is
slightly drunk.*)

STRECKMANN. Who's talking about Streckmann? Here he
is! This is him! Anybody want to start something? Good-
morning . . . good-evening, I mean . . . everybody!

FRAU GOLISCH. Speak of the devil . . .

STRECKMANN. And when I look at you it seems I'm seeing
the devil's own grandmother! (*He takes off his cap and
wipes the sweat off his forehead.*) Lord, oh Lord! I've had
enough. That grind takes the skin off your bones and breaks
your bones into splinters! Hello, August! Hello, Rosie! Hello,
Father Bernd! Jesus Christ, can't nobody talk?

HEINZEL. Leave them alone! They're too well off.

STRECKMANN. To His own, God gives while they're asleep.
A fellow like me's got to slave and can't make no headway
anyways. (*He sits down, squeezing between* HEINZEL *and*
KLEINERT. *He hands his bottle of schnapps to* HEINZEL.)
Pass it around!

FRAU GOLISCH. Go on, you've the best life of any of us,
Streckmann! What in heaven's name do you have to complain about? Here you get double and triple pay, and all
you got to do is stand next to your machine a little.

STRECKMANN. Brains! That's what it takes, you copycats!
I've got it up here! But you dumb clucks wouldn't know
anything about that. How can an old hag understand anything like that!—But for the rest . . . I sure got troubles . . .

GOLISCH. Jesus, Streckmann got troubles?

STRECKMANN. More than enough! I'm in a stew, I can
tell you . . . I've got a feeling in my belly or maybe it's
around the heart . . . I'm feeling as sick as a dog! Maybe
doing something real crazy would help.—(*To* THE MAID.)
Want me to come over, girl, and lay with you?

MAID. I'll bang a whetstone across your skull!

GOLISCH. He's got his old troubles again. It gets black
in front of his eyes, he can't see nothing—and the next

minute, plunk, he's in bed with a girl! (*Loud laughter.*)

STRECKMANN. Just go on laughing, you idiots! Laugh your fool heads off! Me, I don't feel like laughing. (*Boastfully.*) I risk losing my right arm in that machine! I risk having that piston run right through me! Go ahead, girl, go ahead and kill me!

HAHN. Why don't you set fire to a barn for a change!

STRECKMANN (*disdainfully*). Bah! I got fire enough— inside! Look at August, he's a happy man . . .

AUGUST. Never mind if I'm happy or not—that don't concern nobody.

STRECKMANN. What did I do now? Can't you be a little sociable?

AUGUST. I'll pick the people I want to be sociable with!

STRECKMANN (*stares at him for a long time darkly, full of hatred; finally, he controls his rage and grabs the bottle which is now on its way back to him.*) Give me that! A fellow has to drown his sorrows! (*To* ROSE.) What are you looking at me for? We've made our deal! (*He gets up.*) I'm going! I don't want to bother you.

ROSE. You can go or you can stay; it's all the same to me.

FRAU GOLISCH (*calling* STRECKMANN *back*). Streckmann, how did you make out the other day—three weeks ago, you know, by the threshing machine,—when we were getting the rape-seed ready? THE LABORERS *burst out laughing.*)

STRECKMANN. That's finished. I don't know nothing about it.

FRAU GOLISCH. I remember how you swore up and down you'd . . .

KLEINERT. That's enough! Stop that nonsense!

FRAU GOLISCH. I just wish he'd stop shooting his mouth off the way he does.

STRECKMANN (*returns*). What I said that time, I'm going to do it, or I'll be damned!—And that's that. That's all I got to say. (*He leaves.*)

FRAU GOLISCH. That's the easy way out now—not talking!

STRECKMANN (*returns again, starts to say something but changes his mind*). Nothing. I'm not going to swallow that bait. But if you really want to know all about it, go ahead and ask August—or Father Bernd.

BERND. What's that? What are we supposed to know?

FRAU GOLISCH. That time you went to the Registrar's . . . when you passed by and Streckmann called something after you . . .

KLEINERT. It's about time you shut up!

FRAU GOLISCH. Why? It's just a joke.—Did you really get together that time? Or didn't Rosie want to play?

BERND. May God forgive you your sins, all of you!—I'd like to know one thing, though . . . Can't you leave us alone, for God's sake? Or did we step on somebody's toes?

GOLISCH. Well, we're not doing no harm to anybody, either.

ROSE. If I wanted to that time or if I didn't, don't you get gray hair about that! Now I do and that's all that counts.

KLEINERT. That's the girl, Rosie! You tell them!

AUGUST (*has been reading The New Testament, apparently oblivious of the conversation; now he closes the book and gets up.*) Come on, Father, let's get back to work.

HAHN. That'll sure wear you out quicker than pasting prayer books and stirring the glue!

HEINZEL. But just wait till after the wedding! That'll really wear him out. A girl like Rosie, she'll sure be asking for something! (*Laughter.*)

STRECKMANN (*joins the laughter*). Oh Jesus! I'd almost said something! (*He steps back among the others.*) I'll tell you a riddle, all right? Quiet waters run deep!—It's a bad business; a man shouldn't taste blood! The thirst only gets worse and worse.

FRAU GOLISCH. What are you talking about? Where did you taste blood?

BERND. He's talking about tasting schnapps, more than likely.

STRECKMANN. I'm off!—Good-by!—I'm a good boy!—Good-by, Father Bernd! Good-by, August! Good-by, Rosie! (*To* AUGUST.) What's wrong, August? Stop moping! Everything's all right, I'm telling you! You won't see me again. But you know, you really ought to thank me. You've always been full of spite. And here I am, letting you go ahead! As soon as I said it was all right, things went smooth as pie!

(*He leaves.*)

ROSE (*vehemently and firmly*). Let him talk, August, don't pay no attention!

KLEINERT. Flamm's coming! (*He looks at his watch.*) More than half an hour already! (*The whistle of the threshing machine is heard.*)

HAHN (*while everybody is getting ready to go*). To the attack, Prussians! Misery's blowing the whistle!

(THE LABORERS *take their scythes; they and the women leave quickly. Only* ROSE, BERND, *and* AUGUST *remain.*)

BERND. It's like Sodom and Gomorrah around here! What's that Streckmann fellow been gabbing about? Do you understand anything about it, Rosie?

ROSE. No, I don't. And I've got something better to think about, too. (*She playfully punches* AUGUST.) Huh, August? We've no time for nonsense like that. We'll have to hustle these next six weeks! (*She puts the remainder of the supper back into the basket.*)

AUGUST. Come over to my house for a while, later on.

ROSE. I'll have to do the laundry, iron, make buttonholes, and I don't know what else! We haven't got much time.

BERND. We'll come over for a bite after seven.

(*He leaves.*)

AUGUST (*ready to leave, solemnly*). Do you like me, Rosie?

ROSE. I like you!   (AUGUST *leaves.*)

(ROSE *is now alone. The threshing machine hums in the distance and a thunderstorm rumbles beyond the horizon.* ROSE *puts the bread and butter, the cans, and cups back into the basket, straightens up and puts the basket on her arm. Ready to go, she seems to see something in the distance which attracts her attention. She stops, but suddenly determined, she picks up her kerchief which had dropped and hurries off. Before she is out of sight, however,* FLAMM *appears, his gun on his shoulder, and calls after her.*)

FLAMM. Rose! Halt, damn it! (ROSE *stops but does not look at him.*) I want you to give me a drink of water—I ought to be worth that much!

ROSE. There's the water.

FLAMM. I can see that, I'm not blind. But I don't like to drink like a calf! Don't you have a cup in your basket? (ROSE *opens the basket.*) That's better! And even a cup from Bunzlau! That's the kind of cup I like best anyway. (*She gives him the cup without looking at him.*) Now, please! A little more polite, all right? You'll just have to trouble yourself one more time! (ROSE *steps over to the spring, rinses the cup, fills it, and puts it down next to the spring. Then she goes back to where she left the basket, picks it up and waits, turning her back to* FLAMM.) No, Rose, that isn't the way to do it!—You can treat a tramp this way maybe; I'm not too familiar with tramps. But for the moment I'm still Flamm.—Now then, do I get a drink of water or don't I?—One—two—and—three—and that's it! Do it a little nicely and no nonsense about it! (ROSE *steps over to the spring again, takes the cup and offers it to him, her face still averted.*) No! A little higher! No, it still won't work!

ROSE. You'll have to hold it yourself.

FLAMM. How can anybody drink like this?

ROSE (*laughing against her will, turns her head*). No, really . . .

FLAMM. That's better!—That's fine! (*Apparently without any other thought in mind but to steady the cup, he puts his hands on hers. Putting his mouth to the cup, he lets himself down lower and lower until he has to use one knee to support himself.*) There! Many thanks, Rose. Now you may let go of me.

ROSE (*trying gently to disengage herself*). No, no! Let go of me, Herr Flamm!

FLAMM. Is that so? That's what you think. So you think I ought to let go of you? When I finally caught you? Oh no, my girl, it isn't as easy as that!—I can't!—Don't ask me to. Don't even try! You aren't going to get away from me! First of all, look at me properly! I'm still the same. Look into my eyes! I know, I know everything—everything! I've been talking to Steckel, so I know that you've made up your mind. Thank God, I won't have to hitch you up myself! There's somebody else now to spring the trap! I even know when the funeral—good heavens, what am I saying!—the wedding, I meant to say, is going to be. And then I've also had a serious talk with myself. Rose, this is a very hard nut to crack for me! I only hope we won't break all our teeth trying!

ROSE. I mustn't stand around with you like this, Herr Flamm.

FLAMM. Oh yes, you must! I don't care one bit, even if everybody disapproves. I just don't give a hoot whether they approve or not! If it's really God's will, why, I expect a proper good-by; I won't be put out in the cold just like that. Rose, did I do anything wrong?

Rose (*shaking her head violently*). No, Herr Flamm.
You don't have to apologize for nothing.

Flamm. No? Honest not? (Rose *shakes her head vehemently*.) Well, I'm glad about that at least. I'd always
hoped it would be like this. This way, we can think back
and remember everything as one whole piece.—Oh, Rose,
this has been a wonderful time!

Rose. And you've got to get back to your wife . . .

Flamm. If things like this only didn't flit by so fast! A
wonderful time! What's left of it now?

Rose. You have to be good to your wife, Herr Flamm!
Your wife is an angel—she saved me!

Flamm. Come, let's step over under the pear tree for a
moment. There!—Now what do you mean? I've always been
good to my old woman. We get along beautifully. Tell me,
Rose, tell me exactly what you mean. You said . . . how did
you say it? She saved you? Was that it? From what did
she save you, Rose? Of course, I'd like to know! What was
going on that time anyway? Mother always hints at all sorts
of things, but I can't make head or tail of it.

Rose. Christoph—Herr Flamm! I can't sit down here!—
What's the use? This won't get us nowhere. It's all finished—
all right, so it's over with. I know, God's going to forgive
me my sin. He wouldn't take it out on an innocent baby.
He's too merciful, he wouldn't do that!

Flamm (*remarking on the humming of the threshing
machine that is getting louder and louder*). This damned
buzzing all the time!—What was that? Rose, sit down for
a moment! I won't do anything—I won't touch you, I swear.
I want you to get all this off your chest. Do trust me just a
little!

Rose. Well . . . it's just . . . I don't know! After I'm
married you can ask your wife some time; maybe she'll
tell you what's the matter with me now. I haven't told
August yet, either.—I know he's a good man. So I'm not
worried on his account. Because he's good-hearted and a
real Christian. So—good-by now, Christoph! Good-by—good
luck!—I've got a whole lifetime ahead of me, so I'll have
lots of time to be faithful, to slave and to suffer, so as to
pay my debts and work off what I owe.

Flamm (*holding on to* Rose's *hand*). Stay one more
minute, Rose! All right, so everything's settled. But I'm not
coming to your wedding, by God! Even if I'd come to your
wedding though, I know you're right. I've loved you so much,

Rosie, loved you truly, I can't tell you how much!—I've loved you since . . . since I can remember. Even when you were still a little girl I liked you a lot. You were always so honest . . . in a million little things . . . always frank . . . when I asked you something you always had a simple answer. You never stalled or lied even when a mirror had just gone into a thousand pieces.—I've known quite a lot of women, in Tharandt and then in Eberswalde, when I was at the Forestry Academy, and later in the Army. I've always been happy with them. And yet only now I understand what happiness really means—happiness with you.

ROSE. Oh, Christel! I've loved you very much, too!

FLAMM. You've been making eyes at me ever since you were a tot! You had that gleam in your eyes sometimes when you looked at me! Are you going to think of it sometimes? Think of Flamm, the crazy old sinner?

ROSE. I sure will! And I've got a token . . .

FLAMM. Oh yes, the little ring with the stone. Are you going to come and see us once in a while?

ROSE. No, that wouldn't work. That would be like cutting my heart. It would be double the torment and double the misery. No, it has to be—it's finished! I'm going to bury myself in my house; I'm going to work and slave for two— and I just mustn't look back! There's nothing but misery and suffering in this world . . . all we can do is wait for heaven.

FLAMM. Is this going to be our last good-by, Rose?

ROSE. Father and August will be wondering already.

FLAMM. And if the fish in the water stand on their tails wondering and the birds stand on their heads, I'm not going to throw away one single second I can have with you. So it's all finished—all gone?—You aren't even going to visit my wife?

ROSE (*shakes her head*). No, I couldn't look her in the face no more. Maybe some time, later—in ten years maybe! Maybe I'll get over it some time. Good-by, Christoph! Good-by, Herr Flamm!

FLAMM. All right. Girl, I can tell you, if it weren't for my wife . . . even now . . . I wouldn't fuss around much . . . I wouldn't wait a minute to get you.

ROSE. Yes, if there wasn't always the word "if." If there was no August and no father, who knows what I'd do! Fly out into the wide world, that's what I'd like best.

FLAMM. I'd come along, Rose! Well!—so here we are!

Now just give me your hand once more . . . (*He presses her hand and their eyes meet in a last, burning good-by.*) What has to be must be—and nothing can be done about it.—And this is where we part! (*He turns resolutely and leaves with firm steps and without turning back.*)

ROSE (*follows him with her eyes, pulls herself together and says with determination*). What has to be must be! And that's that! (*She puts the cup back into the basket and is ready to take off in the opposite direction, when STRECK-MANN appears.*)

STRECKMANN (*his face pale and twisted, his manner shy and crawling*). Rose!—Rose Bernd!—Don't you hear? Wasn't that that no-good Flamm again? If I ever get my hands on him . . . I'll break every bone in his body!—What's wrong? What did he want from you again? One thing I'll tell you, this won't work . . . I won't have it! One's as good as the other! So I just won't let you give me my walking papers!

ROSE. What did you say? And just who are you?

STRECKMANN. Who I am? Damn it, you ought to know that all right!

ROSE. Who are you? Did I meet you before?

STRECKMANN. Did you . . . me . . . if you met me, girl? You find someone else who'll play the monkey for you!

ROSE. What do you want? Who are you? What do you want from me?

STRECKMANN. The hell I want! Nothing! You understand? Nothing. For Christ's sake, don't scream like that!

ROSE. I'll scream so the whole world will hear me if you don't leave me alone!

STRECKMANN. Remember the cherry tree! Remember the crucifix . . .

ROSE. Who are you? You liar! What do you want from me? Either you get on your way . . . or I'll scream for help!

STRECKMANN. You've lost your mind, girl!

ROSE. So that's one thing less to lug around with me! Who are you? Liar! You've seen nothing! I'm going to scream! I'll scream until I lose my breath if you don't take off!

STRECKMANN (*scared*). All right, Rosie, I'm going. Just stop shouting—I'm on my way.

ROSE. Go then—now—understand?

STRECKMANN. All right, all right! What do I care! (*With a clownish gesture he protects himself from an imaginary cloudburst and starts off.*)

Rose (*in an outburst of hatred*). There he goes, that no-good bastard! When you look at his back you see the best part of him! He gives me the creeps! Disgusting—that's what he is . . . spit'n polish on the outside and eaten by maggots inside! It makes you puke!

Streckmann (*turns back, pale, threateningly*). Is that so? What do you know! You really mean that? That don't sound very appetizing! But then . . . why were you all hot and bothered running after it?

Rose. Me? Running after you?

Streckmann. You haven't already forgotten, have you?

Rose. You low-down dog!

Streckmann. That's just what I am!

Rose. You rat! What do you want from me? Who are you, anyway? Eh? What did I do to you? You've been chasing after me, you've hunted me, you've snapped at me—oh, you bastard! You're worse than a bloodhound!

Streckmann. You're the one who was running after me!

Rose. What?

Streckmann. Weren't you the one who came to my house? You were the one who's been bothering me!

Rose. And you . . .

Streckmann. Well?

Rose. And you? What did you do?

Streckmann. I just never refuse a tasty dish!

Rose. Streckmann, some day you're going to die! You understand? Think of the hour when you'll have to die! When you'll be standing before your judge! I came running to you scared out of my wits . . . I was begging you . . . to step out of the way so August and I could . . . I went down on my knees . . . and you dare to say I was running after you! That was a crime that was! And I was your victim! That wasn't just a dirty trick, that was a crime, a double and a triple crime! And God will surely punish you for it!

Streckmann. Well, what do you know! I'll just have to wait and see!

Rose. So you want to wait and see? Is that what you're saying? You are disgusting—I spit on you!

Streckmann. Just remember the cherry trees! Remember the crucifix!

Rose. You swore you weren't going to talk about it—ever! A holy oath you swore; you put your hand on the cross and you swore on the cross that you wouldn't! And now you start chasing me all over! What do you want from me?

STRECKMANN. I'm just as good a man as Flamm. So either you forget about him . . .

ROSE. And if I jumped right into his bed that wouldn't be none of your business, you dirty dog!

STRECKMANN. We'll see about that! Just you wait!

ROSE. What? You raped me—you tricked me—you've broken me! Like a vulture you shot down on me! I remember all right! I wanted to get out of the house, and you tore my skirt and my jacket, and you bolted the door! I was bleeding and I wanted to get away! A crime that was, I tell you! And I'll report it . . .

(BERND *enters,* AUGUST *close behind him.* KLEINERT, GOLISCH *and the other* LABORERS *follow.*)

BERND (*stepping directly in front of* STRECKMANN). What's going on here? What did you do to the girl?

AUGUST (*pulls* BERND *back and comes forward*). Let me do this, Father!—He's asking you what you did to Rosie?

STRECKMANN. Nothing.

BERND (*pushing forward again*). What did you do to the girl?

STRECKMANN. Nothing.

AUGUST (*pushes between them*). You're going to tell us what you did to her!

STRECKMANN. I'm telling you, nothing! Not a damn thing.

AUGUST. Either you're telling us what you did—or . . .

STRECKMANN. Or? Well, what "or," eh?—Take your hands off me . . . take that hand off my throat!

KLEINERT (*trying to separate them*). Stop that!

STRECKMANN. Take your hands off my throat!

BERND. You're going to pay for this! Either . . .

AUGUST. What did you do to the girl?

STRECKMANN (*suddenly gripped by fear, retreats to the pear tree and shouts*). Help!

AUGUST. What did you do to the girl? Answer! Answer! I want to know! (*He pulls away from the others and steps in front of* STRECKMANN.)

STRECKMANN (*raises his arm and punches* AUGUST *in the face*). There's my answer! That's what I did!

KLEINERT. Streckmann . . .

FRAU GOLISCH. Catch him! August's falling!

HEAD MAID (*catches* AUGUST *as he drops to the ground*). August!

BERND (*pays no attention to* AUGUST; *shouts at* STRECK-MANN). You're going to answer for this! You'll get your come-uppance this time!

STRECKMANN. Bah, what a mess! And all because of that bitch whose got something with everybody . . . (*He leaves.*)

BERND. What did he say?

KLEINERT (*holds up* AUGUST, *who is almost unconscious, assisted by* GOLISCH, *the* HEAD MAID, HAHN, *and* FRAU GOLISCH). The eye's gone!

FRAU GOLISCH. Father Bernd! August don't look very good!

KLEINERT. This fellow didn't have much fun courting!

BERND. What's happened? What is it? Jesus Christ in Heaven! (*Steps close to* AUGUST.) August?

AUGUST. That left eye's hurting something awful.

BERND. Rose, get some water!

FRAU GOLISCH. Oh, heavens, what a misery!

BERND. Get some water, Rose, don't you hear?

GOLISCH. That'll cost him a year in prison all right!

ROSE (*as if she were coming out of a trance*). He says . . . he says . . . what does he mean?—And I hope I . . . I got a doll for Christmas, didn't I?

MAID (*to* ROSE). Are you dreaming?

ROSE. Nobody should say that to nobody! No, it won't work! I just can't do it! Maybe . . . after all . . . a girl ought to have a mother . . .

CURTAIN

ACT IV

(*The same room in* FLAMM's *house as in Act II. It is a Saturday afternoon in the beginning of September.* FLAMM *is sitting at the roll-top desk, busy with bills.* STRECKMANN *is standing near the door to the hall-way.*)

FLAMM. So I owe you two hundred and six marks and thirty pfennigs.

STRECKMANN. That's right, Herr Flamm.

FLAMM. By the way, what was wrong with your machine? One morning you weren't working at all, I believe.

STRECKMANN. I had to go to court. There wasn't nothing wrong with the machine.

FLAMM. Was that because of that . . . business with Keil?

STRECKMANN. Sure was. And then Bernd's suing me, too; I'm supposed to have insulted his daughter.

FLAMM (*takes money from a special drawer in the desk and counts it up on the big table*). That's two hundred . . . two hundred and six . . . and fifty. Now you owe me twenty pfennigs.

STRECKMANN (*takes the money and puts twenty pfennigs on the table*). And . . . I just thought I'd tell you, about the middle of December I'll be free again.

FLAMM. All right. For two days, let's say the beginning of December. By then I'll want to empty the big barn.

STRECKMANN. All right, Herr Flamm. Beginning of December then.—Good-by!

FLAMM. Good-by, Streckmann!—Tell me, what's going to happen with that business of yours?

STRECKMANN (*stops, shrugs his shoulders*). Oh, nothing much is likely to happen, Herr Flamm.

FLAMM. Oh? No?

STRECKMANN. I'll just have to take what's coming.

FLAMM. How a mere nothing can sometimes snowball! —How did you two get at each other to start with?

STRECKMANN. I can't remember a thing. I was . . . I must have been plumb crazy that time . . . but I just can't remember what happened.

FLAMM. That bookbinder fellow is usually quite peaceful, it seems.

STRECKMANN. He always tries to start something with *me*, though! But for the rest . . . everything is like wiped out in my head. I just remember that they came at me like two wild wolves. I thought they really wanted to kill me!—If I hadn't thought that, my hand wouldn't have slipped neither.

FLAMM. And nothing could be done to save his eye?

STRECKMANN. No. I really feel sorry for him. But . . . well, there's nothing I can do. It wasn't my fault.

FLAMM. Things like that are bad enough at best, but when they get to court, it's even worse. The one I feel sorry for most of all is the girl.

STRECKMANN. I'm just shaking all over, that's how I've taken that business to heart. I don't even know what sleeping is like no more, Herr Lieutenant. And I don't really have nothing against August! I just . . . simply don't remember!

FLAMM. You really ought to go and see Bernd. If you insulted his daughter and you weren't really yourself at that moment, why, you can simply apologize.

STRECKMANN. That's none of my business! That's his lookout. But if he knew where this is getting him he'd drop his suit right quick. He sure don't do the girl no good with it. Well, that's how it is! Good-by, Herr Lieutenant!

FLAMM. Good-by!   (STRECKMANN *leaves*.)

FLAMM (*excitedly to himself*). If I could only get my hands at this bastard's throat!

(FRAU FLAMM *is being pushed in from the hunt room by the* MAID.)

FRAU FLAMM. What are you mumbling about, Flamm? (*She signals the girl to leave the room.*) Did you have any trouble?

FLAMM. Yes, thank you! Quite enough!

FRAU FLAMM. Wasn't that Streckmann?

FLAMM. Yes, handsome Streckmann! Indeed, handsome Streckmann in person.

FRAU FLAMM. How's that story coming along, Christoph? Did you talk to Streckmann about Keil?

FLAMM (*busily writing*). Oh, never mind. I'm busy with the accounts.

FRAU FLAMM. Am I bothering you, Christel?

FLAMM. No, you don't bother me if you keep a little quiet.

FRAU FLAMM. Well, if I can do nothing else, that I can do, rest assured. (*Silence*.)

FLAMM (*bursting out*). Good Lord and all His saints! Sometimes I really feel like running into the hunt room, getting a gun and just shooting a miserable creature like that! It would be a pleasure to have that on my conscience!

FRAU FLAMM. Heavens, Christel, you really scare me!

FLAMM. I can't help it. I get scared myself.—That man is so bad, Mother, I can tell you, so incredibly rotten . . . at least when he wants to be . . . that a fellow like myself, who really can stand quite a lot, feels as if his stomach was turning. Of course, people like us . . . we'll never learn.

You can have learned everything all the universities in the world can teach you, you can have a stomach that can digest pebbles and ropes—but when it comes to understanding something like this . . . to such downright infamy . . . we never get beyond kindergarten!

FRAU FLAMM. What's brought all this on?

FLAMM (*resuming his entries*). I'm just talking . . . in general.

FRAU FLAMM. And here I thought it had something to do with Streckmann! You know, Christel, I can't stop thinking of this story. And whenever you feel like . . . a little more than just now . . . I'd really like to talk to you about it.

FLAMM. To me? What do I have to do with Streckmann?

FRAU FLAMM. Maybe not just Streckmann, not exactly him. But about old Bernd and Rose. Look, as far as the girl's concerned, this is really pretty serious. And if I could move around I'd have been down to see her long ago. She doesn't come here any more, after all.

FLAMM. You go to see Rose? What would you want to do that for?

FRAU FLAMM. Now listen to me, Christel. Look, she isn't just anybody! I just have to see how things are going.

FLAMM. All right, Mother. Go if you have to! But I don't think you'll get very far with that girl.

FRAU FLAMM. Get very far? How do you mean, Christel?

FLAMM. It never pays to get mixed up in other people's business. All you get for it is aggravation and ingratitude.

FRAU FLAMM. That's nothing! One just has to be able to cope with a little aggravation, and ingratitude is all you ever harvest! As far as Rose Bernd is concerned, I don't know . . . I've always had the feeling . . . that she's my daughter . . . at least half. Look, Christel, as long as I can remember . . . even at the time Father was still Chief Forester, her mother was already working in our house doing the laundry. Later . . . although I was more dead than alive myself . . . I can still see her at the cemetery, when we buried Kurtel. Apart from you and myself, nobody was as desolate as she.

FLAMM. Maybe. But what do you want to do? I really can't figure that out.

FRAU FLAMM. Well, first I'll have to ask you something.

FLAMM. Oh? Why?

FRAU FLAMM. For no reason at all. You know I never interfere with your business. But now . . . I really would

ike to know something. What's been the matter with you
ately?

FLAMM. With me? I thought you were talking about
Rose Bernd!

FRAU FLAMM. Well, I'm talking about you now.

FLAMM. You had better forget about that, Mother! That's
my business and you'd better not worry about it.

FRAU FLAMM. That's easily said! But if you have to sit
like I have to, and if you see that somebody's always restless, that he doesn't sleep at night, and you hear him sigh
all the time, and then . . . if he happens to be your husband . . . why, of course one wonders!

FLAMM. Now really, Mother, you must be crazy. That's
absolutely ridiculous! Sighing! I'd really have to be a little
off! What next? I'm not a lovesick schoolgirl after all!

FRAU FLAMM. No, Christel, I won't let you get away
with that.

FLAMM. What do you want, Mother? Are you trying hard
to be a bore? Is that it? Are you trying to bore me to
death? Drive me out of the house? Is that it? If that's what
you want you couldn't do any better.

FRAU FLAMM. You're still hiding something!

FLAMM (shrugging his shoulders). Is that what you
think? Well, so I'm hiding something! But just suppose that
I am . . . you know me well enough . . . in that respect
you really know me . . . even if everybody started standing on his head, you wouldn't get that much out of me!
(He snaps his fingers.) Everybody's got his troubles! Yesterday I had to fire the helper in the brewery; the day
before I had to throw one of the workers in the still out
on his ear. And finally, apart from all that, a life like we
have here is really boring enough to drive a fellow clear
out of his mind!

FRAU FLAMM. Why don't you find some friends? Drive
into town!

FLAMM. That's it! Sit in the "Horse" inn and play cards
with horses or walk on stilts holding hands with the Commissioner! God forbid! I've had enough of that nonsense!
I wouldn't take one single step for that kind of pleasure!
If it weren't for the bit of hunting one can do . . . if one
couldn't grab that gun now and then . . . I should have
gone to sea!

FRAU FLAMM. You see? That's it! That's what I've been
saying! You're simply completely changed! Until two, three

months ago you were gay, went out shooting birds, mounted
them, collected plants and eggs, and you were singing all
day long. It was a pleasure just watching you. And now . .
you're a different man!

FLAMM. If at least little Kurt was still alive!

FRAU FLAMM. What would you say . . . if we adopted
a child?

FLAMM. Now all of a sudden? No, Mother, now I wouldn'
want to do that any more. Before, you could never make
up your mind. Now it's too late for me.

FRAU FLAMM. It's easy to say, take a child into the
house! Of course, it seems like treason at first! It seemed
like betraying Kurt even to think of such a thing! That's
how I felt . . . What shall I say? It was like disowning
the boy completely, like casting him out, out of the house,
out of his room and his bed—and finally out of our hearts
But the main thing is, where do you find a child that you
think might give you some happiness? Well, let's forget
about it. Let's get back to Rose now. I just wonder if you
know what's the matter with her, Flamm.

FLAMM. Well now . . . of course!—Why not!—Streckmann has insinuated things about her . . . her conduct
and Old Bernd wouldn't stand for it. It's silly of course to
go to court. The woman's always the one who pays the
bill in a case like that.

FRAU FLAMM. I've written a couple of letters to Rose
and asked her to come to see me. Really, Flamm, a girl
in her situation just can't possibly know what to do and
where to turn.

FLAMM. How's that?

FRAU FLAMM. Because Streckmann is right!

FLAMM (perplexed, stupidly). What, Mother? You'll have
to be a little more explicit.

FRAU FLAMM. Now, Christel, don't fly off the handle
again! I haven't said anything to you about it before because I know how you are in things like that. Remember
the little servant girl you threw out of the house before
anybody had even time to take a breath? And the bag-
maker you beat up? The girl made a confession to me quite
a while ago . . . must be more than eight weeks ago . . .
and she simply isn't any more just Rose Bernd . . . but
there's now another one who has to be considered . . .
you know what I mean . . . the one who's on the way . . .
do you get what I mean, Flamm? Do you understand?

FLAMM (*gloomily*). No, not quite, Mother—frankly. Because I have . . . because it is . . . because today . . . these days . . . sometimes the blood rushes to my head. That's like . . . it's awful . . . like fainting! But . . . no, no . . . I'll just have to get some fresh air. It's nothing, Mother, don't worry.

FRAU FLAMM (*puts on her glasses*). What are you doing with your cartridge pouch?

FLAMM. Nothing. What am I doing with these cartridges? (*He flings the pouch away which he had instinctively picked up.*) I don't know about anything! Nobody tells me anything! One really feels like a complete idiot sometimes—like a stranger in your own house.

FRAU FLAMM (*suspiciously*). Tell me, Christel, just what do you mean?

FLAMM. Nothing, Mother! Nothing at all! Absolutely nothing! I feel already much better, my head's much clearer. But sometimes I have a feeling, like a panic, I don't know, as if suddenly there was no ground under my feet and I'd fall and break my neck.

FRAU FLAMM. Strange things you're telling me. (*Someone knocks at the door.*) Who's there?—Come in!

AUGUST (*still outside*). It's only me, Frau Flamm!

(FLAMM *hurries out into the hunt room.*)

FRAU FLAMM. Oh, it's you, Herr Keil. Do come in!

(AUGUST KEIL *comes in, still paler and still more emaciated than he had been before. He wears dark glasses and his left eye is covered with a black patch.*)

AUGUST. I've come to apologize, Frau Flamm! Good-morning, Frau Flamm!

FRAU FLAMM. Good-morning to you, Herr Keil!

AUGUST. Rose had to go to court, Frau Lieutenant, or she would have come herself. Maybe she'll come tonight, though.

FRAU FLAMM. I'm very glad to see you. How do you feel? Sit down!

AUGUST. The ways of God are miraculous! And if He punishes you you mustn't complain. To the contrary, you ought to be glad. You see, Frau Flamm, that's almost the way I feel now. I don't complain. The worse it gets the better it is—the greater grows your stake in eternity.

FRAU FLAMM (*breathing heavily*). I wish you were right, Herr Keil.—Tell me, did Rose get my letters?

AUGUST. Yes, and she let me read them. And I told her again and again, it wasn't right and she ought to go and see you.

FRAU FLAMM. I have to tell you, Herr Keil, I'm surprised that she hasn't found her way here—with everything that's happened lately. After all, she knows that I care.

AUGUST. It's just that she's been awfully shy lately, Frau Flamm. If I may say so, Frau Lieutenant, don't be mad at her. First she's really had her hands full taking care of me—and she's sure earned God's blessing for what she's done! And then, after the way that fellow insulted her she simply don't dare leave the house.

FRAU FLAMM. Of course I'm not angry at her, Herr Keil! —How does she feel otherwise? What's she doing?

AUGUST. Oh my God . . . no . . . that is . . . how shall I say . . . When she was supposed to leave for court today —it sure was something! Frau Flamm, it was almost enough . . . to get scared the way she carried on. First she didn't want to go at all, then she said she wanted me along, finally she off and leaves like greased lightning and shouts to me I shouldn't come after her.—Sometimes she's crying all day long!—So of course, one gets ideas.

FRAU FLAMM. What kind of ideas?

AUGUST. Oh, all kinds.—First of all that I had this bad luck. She's talked about that many a time. It really seems to hurt her soul. And then about Father Bernd, that he's taken it to heart so.

FRAU FLAMM. Look, Herr Keil, we're all alone here. So we can speak quite frankly, can't we? Didn't you ever think . . . I mean what Streckmann said . . . didn't you ever think, you or Father Bernd, that there might be something to it?

AUGUST. I've never given that a thought.

FRAU FLAMM. You're quite right. I don't blame you. Sometimes it's really best to put your head in the sand like an ostrich. But a father shouldn't do that!

AUGUST. Well, Frau Flamm, as far as Old Bernd's concerned, any idea . . . I mean that something might be wrong . . . any idea like that's far, far from his mind. He believes like a rock . . . he's so sure he'd let them cut off both his hands and he wouldn't change. And Herr Flamm's been to talk to him, too, trying to get him to drop that law suit . . .

FRAU FLAMM (*agitated*). Who's been to talk to him?

AUGUST. Why, Herr Flamm.

FRAU FLAMM. My husband?

AUGUST. That's right! He was talking to him for a long while. You see, for all I care . . . even though it's cost me one of my eyes . . . I'm not so anxious that Streckmann gets punished! Justice is mine, says the Lord! But father, he's just dead-set on this thing; he says, you can ask him to do anything, but don't ask him to do that.

FRAU FLAMM. So my husband's been to see Old Bernd?

AUGUST. Yes, when he got the summons.

FRAU FLAMM. The summons? What did he get a summons for?

AUGUST. Why, from the examining magistrate.

FRAU FLAMM (*more and more excited*). Old Bernd?

AUGUST. No, Herr Flamm.

FRAU FLAMM. Well—did my husband have to testify, too? What does he have to do with this business?

AUGUST. Yes, sure, he's had to testify, too.

FRAU FLAMM (*shaken*). I see! That's news to me! I didn't know a thing about it! I didn't even know that Christel had been to see Old Bernd! I wonder where my eau de cologne has gotten to! Well, August, maybe you'd better go now. I feel . . . I don't know! I can't give you any special advice anyway. I feel as if something had struck me. You go on home and wait and see. And if you really love the girl . . . just look at me! I could tell you something about it! If somebody's made like that—if he's a man the women run after or if it's a woman that the men chase after like crazy—all you can do is suffer! Suffer and be patient! I've been living like this for twelve years! (*She holds her hand in front of her eyes.*) I've had to close my eyes—or I would have gone blind!

AUGUST. I just can't believe that, Frau Flamm!

FRAU FLAMM. Believe it or don't. Life never cares what we want to believe. I'm like you—and I can't understand it either. We have to see how we can cope and be content with what we have. I've promised something to Rose. Sometimes it's easy to make a promise and very difficult to keep it. Well, I'll do all I can. Good-by now!—Of course . . . I can't expect you . . . let's hope that heaven will be merciful!

(*Deeply moved,* AUGUST *shakes* FRAU FLAMM's *extended hand and leaves without another word.*)

(FRAU FLAMM *leans her head far back, looks absently at the sky and sighs deeply several times.—*FLAMM *enters. He is very pale. Glancing sidelong at* FRAU FLAMM, *he starts to whistle softly, opens the bookcase and seems to be eagerly looking for something.*)

FRAU FLAMM. Yes, you just whistle, Flamm!—But—that . . . I really wouldn't have thought you'd do that!

(FLAMM *turns around and, without a word, lifts his hands up slightly and his shoulders very high, then lets his arms droop. Not in the least embarrassed, he looks at the floor thoughtfully rather than in shame.*)

FRAU FLAMM. You men take things so easy! What's going to happen now?

FLAMM (*with the same gesture as before, but not quite as pronounced*). I don't have any idea. I'll try to be as calm as possible and tell you how it happened. Perhaps you'll be a little more lenient in your judgment then. If not . . . why, then I'm simply very sorry.

FRAU FLAMM. Oh no, nobody can be lenient about a piece of tomfoolery like that!

FLAMM. Tomfoolery? This was no tomfoolery! But what would you rather have it be, Mother, tomfoolery or something more serious?

FRAU FLAMM. To go and destroy the whole future for a girl when we have . . . when we are responsible for her! We took her into our house! They had complete confidence in us! Oh no! It's enough to just sink into the ground! As if we had secretly planned it this way!

FLAMM. Have you finished, Mother?

FRAU FLAMM. Not by a long ways!

FLAMM. Well, in that case I'll wait a while.

FRAU FLAMM. Do you remember, Christel, what I told you when you came out with it and asked me to marry you?

FLAMM. Well? What did you tell me?

FRAU FLAMM. That I'm too old for you. A woman can be sixteen years younger but she shouldn't be even three or four years older. It would have been better if you'd believed me.

FLAMM. Oh, that's really pretty useless . . . to start talking about old stories like that! Don't we have anything more important to talk about just now? I really think we have, Mother. What's really the matter with Rose . . . I didn't have any idea of that until today. Otherwise, of course, I would have acted differently. Now we'll just have to see if things can get straightened out. And this is just why I asked you not to be so stiff-necked about it, why I wanted to try to get you to understand the whole thing. As long as . . . until I heard that this twitching character was going to marry Rose, everything was as respectable as you please. But when that was certain . . . that he would marry her . . . why, that was the end. Maybe I was getting a little mixed up. I had seen the girl grow up . . . there was something of my love for Kurt mixed up in it . . . First I just wanted to keep her out of that misery and in the end, suddenly . . . as these things happen . . . Plato already knew about that and wrote about it—about the two horses—in *Phaidros* he wrote about it . . . the bad horse simply pulled me along . . . and all the dikes burst.

(Protracted silence.)

FRAU FLAMM. You've told me a very pretty story there —and you even managed to sprinkle some learned stuff over it—and I suppose that proves that you're right . . . as you men always are! The poor woman can look out for herself! Maybe you did it just to make her happy . . . and even sacrificed yourself! No! There's simply no excuse for things like that.

FLAMM. All right, Mother, let's leave it alone for now. But remember, when Kurt died I didn't want to see the girl in the house any more. And who asked her to stay and kept her here?

FRAU FLAMM. I didn't want it to be all dead around us! I didn't need her for my own sake!

FLAMM. And I didn't say anything against it—for your sake!

FRAU FLAMM. Any tear a woman sheds for a man is just a waste! But please, save your pretty speeches, Flamm!

(THE SERVANT GIRL brings the coffee.)

SERVANT GIRL. Rose Bernd's outside in the kitchen.

FRAU FLAMM. Come here, girl! Give me a push! There, give me a hand!—(*To* FLAMM.) You can help push me out of the way—somewhere. I'm sure you'll find a little room for me in some corner. I won't be in your way. And then you can call the girl in.

FLAMM (*sternly to* THE SERVANT GIRL). Tell the girl to wait a minute. (SERVANT GIRL *exits.*) Mother, you'll have to talk to her! I can't do it! My hands are tied.

FRAU FLAMM. What am I going to tell her, Flamm?

FLAMM. You know that better than I, Mother! You know that yourself . . . you said so yourself . . . for God's sake let's not be petty now! We can't let her go like this.

FRAU FLAMM. I'm not going to clean her shoes, Flamm!

FLAMM. Nobody asked you to. Nobody's been talking about that. But you asked her to come yourself. You can't suddenly turn yourself inside out and forget all the pity and compassion you felt for her. What was it you told me a little while ago? The girl's been destroyed! And if that girl really should come to grief . . . you don't think that I'm such low-down scum that I'd go on with my life! It's either—or, don't forget that!

FRAU FLAMM. Well, Christel . . . you really aren't worth it . . . neither you nor any of you! But when you get down to it: what can a woman do?—Our hearts are bleeding . . . but it's our own fault! Why do we always pretend, over and over again, even when we are old enough and should have seen enough to know better. Still, we don't see the forest for the trees. And about that, Christel, don't make any mistake about it . . . all right, all right. I'll talk to her. Not for your sake but because it's the right thing to do. But don't get any ideas that I'll be able to put together what you've smashed to pieces. You're like children, you men . . .

(THE SERVANT GIRL *enters.*)

SERVANT GIRL. She says she's not going to wait no more!

FRAU FLAMM. Send her in!   (SERVANT GIRL *leaves.*)

FLAMM. Be reasonable now, Mother! On my word of honor . . .

FRAU FLAMM. You needn't give it—so you needn't break it!

(FLAMM *leaves.* FRAU FLAMM *sighs and starts crocheting.* ROSE BERND *enters.*)

Rose (*decked out in all her Sunday finery. Her face is drawn and her eyes glitter abnormally*). Good-afternoon, ma'am!

Frau Flamm. Sit down! Good afternoon!—Rose, I've asked you to come and talk to me because . . . You remember of course what we talked about the last time you were here? Now, a lot of things have changed since then. In many ways at least they have. Well now, I thought I'd better talk to you . . . now more than ever. You told me then I couldn't help you, that you wanted to see this thing through all by yourself. Today I've come to understand quite a few things; your peculiar behavior that other time, for instance, and that you didn't want to accept any help from me. But how you're going to manage this all by yourself, that I still don't see. Come, have a cup of coffee with me. (Rose *sits down on the edge of a chair near the coffee table*.) August was here just now. If I were in your shoes, girl, I would have told him the truth a long time ago. (*She looks at* Rose *steadily*.) Now I can't advise you to do that any longer, though. Isn't that right?

Rose. But why not, ma'am?

Frau Flamm. It's true, the older we get the less we understand other people. Everybody came into this world exactly the same way, but nobody wants to talk about it. They just can't be vulgar enough when they talk about how they come to be alive, all of them, starting with the emperor and the archbishop down to the last stable boy! And then, when the stork flies over the roof, everybody gets so terribly befuddled that they take off in all directions at once! A guest like that is never welcome.

Rose. Oh, that I could have straightened out long ago, ma'am, if only that scoundrel, that criminal . . . oh, what a liar that Streckmann is . . .

Frau Flamm. Now listen, girl, I don't understand. How can you say that man's lying? You can almost tell just by looking at you.

Rose. He's lying! He's lying! That's all I know.

Frau Flamm. What's he saying that isn't true?

Rose. Everything! Just everything!

Frau Flamm. Rose, I don't think you know what you're saying! Do you know whom you're talking to? Think a minute!—First of all, you confessed everything to me, and besides I know more than that, I know even what you didn't tell me.

Rose (*shivers and trembles; stubbornly*). You can kill me, I don't know what you mean.

Frau Flamm. Is that so?—Sh!—Is that the way you dance now? Now that I wouldn't have thought of you! That's really a surprise! I only hope you talked a little more sense when you were testifying in court!

Rose. I said the same thing in court.

Frau Flamm. Rose, pull yourself together! What you're saying is just plain nonsense! You can't lie like that when you stand in front of the judge! Listen to me now; there, drink some coffee . . . there's nothing to be afraid of. Nobody's after you and I'm not going to eat you whole, either! —You certainly haven't behaved very nice toward me; nobody can say that! And if you had told me the truth right away, it would perhaps have been a little easier to find a way out. Now it's really a bit difficult! But—no matter, we're not going to quit. We'll keep trying to find the answer. Maybe we'll hit on something—even now. Well then . . . the main thing is . . . this much I can tell you . . . that's one thing you can count on . . . you're never going to starve! —Even if your father should turn away from you and August just walks out and leaves you. There'll always be enough for you and your child.

Rose. I really don't know—what you mean!

Frau Flamm. Well, my girl, then I'll just have to talk plainly! If you don't know that or if you've forgotten, then it's just your bad conscience! Then there must be something else! And if there's still another secret you haven't told me, it can't be anything else. It's got to have something to do with Streckmann! Then he must be the man who got you into trouble!

Rose (*violently*). Oh no! How can you think that, ma'am! You're saying that . . . oh no, for God's sake, I didn't deserve that from you!—If my little Kurt only . . . my dear child . . . (*She stands in front of the picture of the boy, hysterically wringing her hands.*)

Frau Flamm. Oh no, Rose, please not that! Maybe you did deserve better from me. But we're not arguing about that just now. You're so completely changed . . . it's unbelievable how you have changed.

Rose. Why didn't my mother come and get me! She told me she'd come for me when she died.

Frau Flamm. Come to your senses now, girl! You're alive! What is the trouble?

ROSE. I don't have nothing to do with Streckmann! That man's lying . . . it's nothing but monstrous lies!

FRAU FLAMM. What did he lie about? And did he swear to it?

ROSE. What do I care if he swears or he don't!

FRAU FLAMM. Did you have to swear, too?

ROSE. I don't know . . . I'm not a bad girl! Or if I am . . . I'm even a criminal! . . . That August had to lose his eye . . . I didn't . . . that wasn't my fault! . . . It's haunting me day and night . . . what that man had to suffer—that pain! . . . Or else he'd have a right to spit on me. So I've been holding up my arms . . . trying to grab something . . . to save it from the fire . . . but they're breaking every bone in my body.

(FLAMM *enters in a state of great excitement.*)

FLAMM. Who is breaking your bones? Why don't you look at Mother! Just the opposite is true, we're trying to save you!

ROSE. It's too late! You can't do nothing now!

FLAMM. What does that mean?

ROSE. Oh, nothing! I can't wait no more. Good-by! I got to go my own way.

FLAMM. Stay here! Don't move! I've heard everything from behind the door and now I want to know the truth.

ROSE. But I'm telling the truth!

FLAMM. The truth about Streckmann!

ROSE. There wasn't nothing between us. He's lying!

FLAMM. Does he say there's been something between you?

ROSE. All I'm saying is that he's lying!

FLAMM. Did he lie under oath?

(ROSE *is silent.*)

FLAMM (*looks at* ROSE *steadily. After quite a while*). Well, Mother, don't hold all this against me and forgive me as much as you can. Now I'm dead sure that this business just doesn't concern me one bit any more. I laugh about it! I sneeze at it!

FRAU FLAMM (*to* ROSE). Did you really deny everything?

(ROSE *does not answer.*)

FLAMM. I told the truth, of course. And I don't think

Streckmann would lie at a time like that. You get into jail for perjury—so people aren't likely to lie!

FRAU FLAMM. And you didn't tell the truth, girl? Maybe you even lied under oath? Don't you have any idea what that means—what you did there? How did you get that fantastic idea? How could you even think of doing a thing like that?

ROSE (*shattered, shouts*). I was so ashamed!

FRAU FLAMM. But Rose . . .

FLAMM. It's a waste of time talking about it. Why would you go and lie to the judge?

ROSE. I was so ashamed! I was so ashamed!

FLAMM. And what about me? And Mother here? And August? Why did you have to lie to all of us? And finally even to Streckmann maybe? And to anybody else—with whom you may have had something? Oh yes, you have an honest face all right! But you were right to be ashamed of yourself!

ROSE. He's been after me, chasing me and hunting me, like a dog!

FLAMM (*laughs*). Why sure, you women always try to make us look like dogs. One day this one, the next day someone else—it's cruel enough! Go ahead, do what you like, you two! If I do as much about this business as move my little finger, I'll find myself a piece of rope and hit myself about my big donkey ears until I'm blind!

(ROSE *stares at* FLAMM *in horror.*)

FRAU FLAMM. Just remember what I said before, Rose, there'll always be enough for the two of you.

ROSE (*without moving, whispers mechanically*). I was so ashamed!—I was so ashamed!

FRAU FLAMM. Do you hear, Rose? (ROSE *rushes out.*) Rose! —Gone!—It's enough to ask the angels in heaven . . .

FLAMM (*thoroughly disturbed, tries to control his sobs*). May God forgive me, Mother . . . I can't help it.

CURTAIN

ACT V

(The living room in BERND's cottage. The room is fairly large, has gray walls and a whitewashed open-beam, wooden ceiling. A door in the rear leads into the kitchen, another door to the left opens into the entrance hall. There are two small windows in the right-hand wall. A yellow chest-of-drawers stands between the windows. An unlit kerosene lamp stands on the chest; on the wall above it hangs a mirror. In the left-hand corner is a big, tiled country stove; in the right-hand corner, a sofa covered with oilcloth, a table with a tablecloth, a lamp hanging above it. On the wall above the sofa hangs a Bible illustration with the inscription, "Suffer little children to come unto me"; below it are photographs of BERND as a soldier and several pictures showing him with his wife. In the left foreground is a glass-front cupboard well filled with painted cups, glasses, etc. A crucifix stands on the table, and a Bible lies on the chest-of-drawers. A picture, entitled "Jesus with the Crown of Thorns," hangs above the hall door. Several patchwork rugs cover the floor. In front of the windows are muslin curtains. Four or five yellow wooden chairs are placed around the room in orderly fashion. Everything looks clean but chilly. On top of the cupboard lie several Bibles and hymn books. On one side of the hall door hangs a collection box.—It is about seven o'clock in the evening of the same day on which the action of Act IV took place. Both doors are open. It is dusk, almost dark.

(Voices are heard outside the house. Then there are several knocks at the window. Finally, a voice is heard, talking through the window.)

THE VOICE. Bernd! Anybody home? Let's go around to the back door!

(Silence. Soon one hears the back door being opened, then

339

voices and steps in the entrance hall. KLEINERT *and* ROSE BERND *appear in the hall door;* ROSE, *obviously exhausted, is leaning on* KLEINERT.)

ROSE (*speaking with difficulty, in a low voice*). Nobody's home. It's all dark.

KLEINERT. I can't leave you alone like that!

ROSE. Why not, Kleinert! There's nothing wrong with me.

KLEINERT. Bah! Nonsense! Nothing wrong with you! If there wasn't I wouldn't have picked you up like you was.

ROSE. No—I just got a bit dizzy. Really! I'm all right now! I really don't need you no more.

KLEINERT. No, no, girl. I can't do that.

ROSE. Sure, Father Kleinert, really! Thanks a lot! It's all right; there's nothing wrong with me! I feel fine again. This just happens once in a while but it don't mean anything.

KLEINERT. Huh! You were half-dead when I found you back of them willows! Twisting and turning like a worm!

ROSE. Go on home, Kleinert . . . I'll light the lamp in a minute! And I got to make fire . . . go on home . . . they'll be home for supper in a minute! . . . Oh, Kleinert, no, I feel so tired, Kleinert, so awful tired, you just can't imagine!

KLEINERT. And so you want to make fire! That's nothing for you. You ought to be in bed!

ROSE. Go on home, Kleinert, go on! If Father . . . or August . . . they mustn't know about this! Do me the favor —don't do that to me!

KLEINERT. As if I wanted to hurt you!

ROSE. No, no—I know. You've always been good to me! (*She rises from the chair to the right of the door on which she had collapsed when she entered the room. She pulls a candle out from behind the stove and lights it.*) And then . . . I feel fine now. Nothing wrong with me. Don't you worry about me!

KLEINERT. That's what you say!

ROSE. Because that's the way it is. (MARTHEL *comes in from the fields, her arms and feet bare.*)

ROSE. And there's Marthel now!

MARTHEL. Is that you, Rose? Where have you been all day?

ROSE. I was dreaming I was in court.

KLEINERT. No, no, she really was in court! You look after your sister a bit, Marthel, at least until Father comes home. She don't feel right.

Rose. Martha, hurry up! Get the fire going so we can put he potatoes on. Where's Father?

Marthel. Working on August's land.

Rose. And August?

Marthel. I don't know where he is. He hasn't been out n the field today.

Rose. Do you have new potatoes?

Marthel. The whole apron full! (*She shakes the potatoes ut of her apron on the kitchen floor, just behind the door.*)

Rose. Get me a bowl and a pot so I can start peeling ight away. I can't get up and get it myself.

Kleinert. Do you want me to take a message somewhere?

Rose. To whom? . . . The gravedigger maybe?—No, no, Uncle Kleinert, not for my sake! I'm going to have a very pecial spot.

Kleinert. Well, good-night then!

Rose. Good-night!

Marthel (*lively*). Come and see us again, Uncle Kleinert!

(Kleinert, *his pipe in his mouth as always and shaking his head, leaves.*)

Marthel (*lights the fire*). Don't you feel well, Rosie?

Rose. Oh no, I'm all right!—(*In a low voice to the crucifix, wringing her hands*). Jesus, Maria, have mercy on me!

Marthel. Rose?

Rose. Yes? What is it?

Marthel. What's wrong with you, Rose?

Rose. Oh, nothing! Bring me that pot and the potatoes!

Marthel (*has got the fire going and brings an earthenware bowl filled with potatoes and a knife*). Oh no, Rosie! I'm scared the way you look!

Rose. How do I look, huh? Tell me, how? Have I got omething on my hands? Or did my eyes get burned? Everyhing looks so spooky! (*With a weird laugh.*) Oh, Jesus! Now I don't see your face! Now I see only one hand! Now see two eyes! And now just dots! Martha, I think I'm going blind!

Marthel. Rosie, what's happened to you?

Rose. May God protect you from what's happened to me! . . You'd wish to die young! Because that's what they say, f someone dies young, they say, he rests in peace. He don't ave to live and breathe. How was that with little Kurt

Flamm? I don't know! . . . I'm dizzy! . . . I've forgotten all
about it! . . . Oh, life's hard! . . . If only it'd stay the way
it's now! . . . If only I didn't wake up no more! . . . I wonder
what all this is good for . . .

MARTHEL (*frightened*). If only Father would come
home . . .

ROSE. Come here, Martha, listen to me! Don't tell Father
that I've been here . . . that I'm here . . . all right, Martha,
promise? . . . I've done a lot of things for you . . . huh, Martha?
And you've never forgotten it . . . even if it's all dark around
me now!

MARTHEL. Do you want a drop of coffee? There's just a
little left in the oven. I'm so frightened, Rosie . . .

ROSE. Don't be afraid! I'll go upstairs to the bedroom for
a while. Just for a little while . . . I think I'll lie down.
Otherwise—I'm fine . . . there's nothing wrong with me.

MARTHEL. And you don't want me to tell Father?

ROSE. Not a word—not a single word!

MARTHEL. And not August neither?

ROSE. Not a word! You've never known your mother, girl,
and I've brought you up, with a thousand fears. How many
nights didn't I stay up with you and worry about you when
you were sick. I wasn't even your age and was already half-
crooked from carrying you round. You hardly never left
this arm here! If you betray me now, it's finished between
us!

MARTHEL. Rosie, it's nothing bad, is it? Nothing dangerous, I mean?

ROSE. No, I don't think so! Come on, Marthel, help me up
. . . there . . . let me lean on you a little! . . . It's just that
we're too alone in this world! We're too alone and lost! If
only one didn't feel so lonely . . . so terribly lonely!

(ROSE *and* MARTHEL *leave by the hall door.*)

(*For a few seconds the room remains empty. Then* BERND
*appears in the kitchen. He puts down his basket and
potato hoe and, with a serious expression on his face,
looks inquiringly into the room. At the same time,*
MARTHEL *returns by the hall door.*)

MARTHEL. Is that you, Father?

BERND. There's no hot water! You know I got to have my
foot bath! Isn't Rose home?

MARTHEL. No, she's not home yet, Father!

BERND. What? Hasn't she come back from court yet? But that's impossible! It's almost eight! Has August been here?

MARTHEL. No, not yet.

BERND. Not him either? Well then, maybe she's at August's. Did you see that big cloud, Marthel? . . . about six o'clock, coming across the mountain?

MARTHEL. Yes, Father, it was getting all dark.

BERND. Some day it'll get a lot darker still! Go light the lamp on the table for me and get the Good Book ready. The main thing is to be prepared. Marthel, are you always thinking of your eternal life? That you'll be standing in front of the eternal judge? There's not many people who think of that. Just now on the way home, coming along the water, I heard somebody swearing at me. When have I ever been a slave driver? That's what he was screaming and shouting, you know: slave driver! All I done was my duty. But there's always evil men . . . bad people. Crooks! If you shut both eyes . . . watch them swindle people without saying a word . . . that way people like you. But I'm trusting our Lord Jesus. All of us need support! And just doing good works isn't enough! If Rose had thought of that a little more, maybe we'd have been spared a lot of hard and bitter things. (THE POLICEMAN *appears in the doorway.*) Who's coming?

POLICEMAN. I have a paper here for your daughter. I'd like to talk to her.

BERND. My oldest daughter?

POLICEMAN (*reading*). To Rose Bernd.

BERND. My daughter's not back from .court yet.—Can't I give her the letter?

POLICEMAN. No. I'll have to make some inquiries, too, personally. I'll be back tomorrow morning around eight.

(AUGUST *enters hurriedly.*)

BERND. Well, there's August now.

AUGUST. Is Rose here?

BERND. No. The sergeant's looking for her, too. I thought you'd be together.

POLICEMAN. There's some questions I'll have to ask her about something—and then I have this paper here to serve.

AUGUST. That Streckmann business goes on for ever and

ever. Not enough to lose an eye, but now all this trouble! May God forgive me, but there don't seem to be no end to it!

POLICEMAN. Good-night! Until tomorrow morning at eight.

(*He leaves.*)

AUGUST. Marthel, you go into the kitchen now for a while. Father, I got to talk to you about something. Go on, Marthel, and close the door. Marthel, didn't you see anything of Rose?

MARTHEL. No, nothing. (*She beckons to him secretively with her forefinger.*) I got to tell you something, August.

AUGUST. Close the door, girl. I don't have time now. (*He closes the kitchen door himself.*) Father, you'll have to drop that law suit.

BERND. Ask me anything, August! But I can't do that!

AUGUST. It's not Christian! You got to drop it!

BERND. I don't think that that's not Christian!—Why wouldn't it be? It's still as shameless now as it was before to give a girl a bad name. That's a crime and that must be punished!

AUGUST. How am I going to start this!—Father Bernd . . . you've been too hasty in this business . . .

BERND. My wife demands that, my wife who's in her grave! And my honor demands it! The honor of my family and of my girl! And finally, your honor, too.

AUGUST. Father Bernd, how am I going to tell you this if you're so unforgiving! You've just been talking about the honor of quite a heap of people. But we're not supposed to look for our own honor. We ought to worry about God's honor and nothing else!

BERND. In this case here, that's different. A woman's honor is God's honor, too. Or do you have something to complain about as far as Rose is concerned?

AUGUST. I've told you before, I'm not complaining about anything.

BERND. Or is there anything you can hold against her?

AUGUST. You know pretty well how I feel about these things, Father Bernd. Rather than getting off the straight and narrow . . .

BERND. Well then! I know that! I've known that all along! So justice will have to take its course.

AUGUST (*wiping the sweat off his forehead*). If we only knew where Rose is.

BERND. Who knows if she's even come back from Striegau
yet.

AUGUST. An interrogation like that, that don't take much
time. And she was planning to be back by five.

BERND. So she probably went shopping while she was out.
Wasn't there a few things she was supposed to buy? I
thought you were still short a few things.

AUGUST. But she didn't take any money along! And what
we still need for the store—some curtain material for the
window and the door—we were going to buy that together.

BERND. I thought she was with you.

AUGUST. I walked along the road for more than four miles
to meet her. But I haven't heard or seen nothing of her. I
met Streckmann, though!

BERND. That's like meeting the devil!

AUGUST. Oh—you know, Father, he's got a wife and children, too. Do you want to blame them for his sins? What
good does it do me if he sits in jail? If a fellow's sorry for
what he did . . . that's all I care about.

BERND. That miserable creature sorry? Hah!

AUGUST. Still, that's what it looks like.

BERND. Did you talk to him?

AUGUST. He wouldn't leave me alone! He walked next to
me and talked and talked and there just was no stopping
him. And not a soul in sight. That was out on the Jenker
Road. At last I felt sorry for him. I couldn't help it.

BERND. Did you answer him? What did he have to say?

AUGUST. He said you ought to drop the suit.

BERND. I'd sooner go to hell! If it was only for my sake,
why the whole thing wouldn't matter much. I can stand it,
I'd even laugh at it! I'm a man and I'm a Christian. But if
your child's mixed up in it, that's a whole lot different.
How could I ever look her in the face again if I asked her
to swallow that kind of stuff? And all the more now, after
his awful accident! Look, August, it's not possible and I
can't do it! Everybody's been after us because we live dif-
erent, not like everybody else. Everybody's been calling us
bigots and hypocrites and sneaks and what not. They'd just
ove it if we did that. And besides . . . that's the way the
girl's been raised . . . to live in the fear of God and to work
hard, so when a Christian man comes and wants to marry her
he can build a good Christian house with her. That's how
it is! That's how I'm going to give her away! And you want
me to leave her, with that poison sticking to her? In that

case, I'd rather eat potatoes and salt for the rest of my life than take one single penny from you!

AUGUST. Father Bernd, the ways of God are mysterious! He can test you every day. We mustn't be proud! But—much as I'd like to—it's impossible . . . I have to tell you about it, Father! Rose has been human, too!

BERND. What do you mean?

AUGUST. Oh, Father, don't ask no questions!

BERND (*sits down on a chair, at the side of the table, his face turned to the wall. When he hears* AUGUST's *last words he looks at him for a few seconds in amazement, his eyes unnaturally large. Then he turns to face the table and opens the Bible with trembling hands. In mounting agitation he flings the pages back and forth. Then he stops and looks again at* AUGUST. *Finally he folds his hands on top of the Bible, lets his head drop on his arms, his whole body twitching convulsively several times. After a while he straightens up.*) No, no—it can't be! I must have misunderstood you! Look here, if I heard right . . . really . . . I don't know . . . the whole room's turning . . . I'd have to be deaf and blind. No, August, I know I'm not deaf and blind. Don't let that Streckmann tell you stories! He's liable to try anything now. He's trapped . . . he's getting his due! So . . . he's trying to get out of the fix he's in by lying! And now he's even trying to turn you against the girl! No, August, no, no . . . don't you believe it! Don't you set no store by what he says! Anybody can see through this villain! He sure was after her long enough! If he don't get what he wants one way—he tries another. So now he figures he'll try it this way! Maybe he'll succeed and get you two apart. That's happened many a time, that people have been driven apart by a devil like that and his miserable cunning . . . people, mind you, whom God had made for each other! They never liked to see you get Rose. All right then, I'm not going to throw the girl at you! We've always had enough to eat and . . . But you listen to me! I'll put my right hand into the fire that . . .

AUGUST. But Herr Flamm's sworn to it!

BERND. Sworn, huh! Ten oaths—twenty oaths—he can swear as many oaths as he wants to for all I care! So he's perjured himself! So he's damned himself to misery for now and for all eternity!

AUGUST. Father Bernd . . .

BERND. You just wait a minute now . . . before you say another word about this! There . . . I'm taking the books . . . I'm taking my hat . . . and here I'm taking the collection box for the mission. And if what you say is right, I'm going across to see the Pastor right now. . . . If there's just this much truth in it . . . and I'll tell him, Herr Pastor, such and such has happened . . . I can't be a deacon no more. I can't look after the money for the mission no more . . . good-by! And after that nobody's going to lay eyes on me again! No, no, no! For the sake of God, no—it can't be! Now . . . you go on . . . and tell me what you have to say! But don't torture me for nothing.

AUGUST. I've been thinking the same thing! I'll sell the house and the land again! Maybe I can try again some place else.

BERND (*overcome with astonishment*). You . . . sell the house again . . . and the land . . . August? How did all this happen now . . . all of a sudden? It's almost . . . I almost feel like crossing myself—and I'm no Catholic! Has the world gone completely mad? Or maybe the day of judgment's coming! Or maybe my last hour's come! Answer me now, August, that's all I want! Answer . . . answer by your eternal life!

AUGUST. Whatever happens, Father Bernd, I'm not going to leave her.

BERND. That . . . do as you like! That's none of my business. I don't even want to know if a man wants to have a . . . creature like that in his house. I wouldn't! I'm not made like that. Well?

AUGUST. I don't rightly know . . . I can't say nothing but that something . . . must have happened . . . some time. If it was with Flamm—or with Streckmann . . .

BERND. So there's even two of them!

AUGUST. I just don't know.

BERND. Well . . . I'd better go to see the Pastor! Brush me off a little, August . . . there's the brush. I feel like a leper!

(*He steps into the hallway. At the same moment* MARTHEL *bursts in from the kitchen and talks to* AUGUST; *she terrified.*)

MARTHEL. I think something's wrong with R
upstairs! She's been home for a long time.

BERND (*comes back into the room, his expression changed by something that has frightened him*). It seems somebody's upstairs!

AUGUST. Marthel's just been telling me that Rose's home.

MARTHEL. I can hear her! She's coming down the stairs!

BERND. May God forgive me! I don't want to see her!

(*He sits down at the table again, plugging his ears with his thumbs, and lowers his head until it almost touches the Bible. ROSE appears in the doorway. She is dressed in a simple skirt and a blouse of printed cotton. She is holding herself on her feet only with great effort. On one side her hair hangs down loose, on the other it is plaited. Her face expresses a terrible stoicism and bitter defiance. For a moment she surveys the room, the old man bent over the Bible and AUGUST, who is slowly turning away from the door and pretends looking out of the window with great concentration. Groping for some support, ROSE summons all her energy to be able to speak.*)

ROSE. Good-evening, everybody! Evening!

AUGUST (*after some hesitation*). Good-evening!

ROSE (*bitter, icily*). If you don't want me here, why, I can go out again.

AUGUST (*soberly*). Where would you go now? Where have you been?

ROSE. If you ask a lot of questions you'll get a lot of answers! Sometimes more than you bargained for. Marthel, come over here a minute! (MARTHEL *steps over to* ROSE *who sits down near the stove and takes her hand. In a loud voice*). What's the matter with Father?

MARTHEL (*embarrassed, afraid, in an undertone*). How do I know?

ROSE. Wh... the matter with Father? Go ahead and ... too, August ... what's the matter with ... August, you've reason enough to despise ...ght. Oh, yes! I don't deny that.

...espise anybody in the whole world.

...I despise everybody ... everybody!

...now what you're talking about. I don't ... all in the dark ...

...right! Yes, I'll admit that ... it's very ...ear wild animals scream! But later on

. . . suddenly . . . later on it's going to get light. So one can feel how hot the fire is in hell. Marthel . . .

BERND (*has been listening, gets up and frees* MARTHEL's *wrist from* ROSE's *grip*). Don't you poison the child, too! Keep your hands off her! Go to the bedroom and go to bed! (MARTHEL *leaves weeping.*) Oh . . . to hear nothing! To see nothing! I wish I were dead! (*He immerses himself again in the Bible.*)

ROSE. Father! I'm alive! I'm sitting here! And that's something . . . that's really something that I'm sitting here! I thought you would understand that, Father! What a world . . . and you've drowned in it . . . and you can never do nothing to me again. Oh Jesus, in what a small little room you're living, all of you! And you've no idea what's going on outside that room! I know what's going on! I've found out . . . in convulsions I've found out!—Everything . . . I don't know . . . everything faded away from me . . . like one wall after another . . . and then I was standing outside, in the middle of the storm . . . and there was nothing left, below me or above me. Oh, against that . . . you're just little babies.

AUGUST (*fearfully*). Well, if it's true what Streckmann says, Rose, you've been perjuring yourself . . .

ROSE (*with a bitter laugh*). I don't know! Maybe all that's true—I can't remember now. The whole world's made of lies.

BERND (*sighs*). Lord . . . you're my refuge for ever and ever.

AUGUST. Is that the way you feel about perjury?

ROSE. That's nothing! Nothing, I tell you! What does that mean? . . . There! There something's lying . . . That's something! . . . Lying out there by the willows! That's something that counts! The rest . . . I don't care, I don't care. There I was . . . and looked up to the stars . . . and cried and screamed! But no father in heaven made a move.

BERND (*frightened, trembling*). Are you blaspheming the heavenly Father? If you've sunk that far I don't know you no more!

ROSE (*crawls toward him on her knees*). I've sunk that far! But you know me, Father! You've held me on y knees . . . you! And I've helped you, too, now and Something's sweeping over us now, over all of us struggled against it . . . I've fought . . .

BERND (*startled*). What are you talking a

ROSE. I don't know! I don't know! (*She remains on her knees, trembling, and stares fixedly in front of her.*)

AUGUST (*deeply moved by the sight, overwhelmed*). Get up, Rosie! I'm not going to leave you! Get up, I can't stand seeing you like that! We're sinners, all of us. And if somebody repents like you do, he'll be forgiven. Get up, Rosie! Father, you raise her up! We're not . . . at least I'm not one of . . . I'm not a Pharisee! You can see how she's taking it to heart! I don't care what happens, I'll stick with her! I don't want to judge—I never judge. Our Saviour in heaven never judged, neither. Oh yes, he bore our sickness for us but we thought God was punishing Him and torturing Him! Didn't you ever make a mistake? I've been thinking . . . and I don't claim I'm blameless! Even before she really knew me she had to say Amen! What's the world to me? I don't ask what they think and what they say.

ROSE. August, they were sticking to me like leeches! I couldn't walk across the street . . . and all the men were after me! So I hid myself, I was so afraid of them. But it was no good, it got worse and worse! And then . . . I stepped into one snare—and into another—and I could never catch my breath no more.

BERND. And you, you used to have such stern ideas! You were damning the Leichner girl and you despised the Kaiser girl. You were bragging, nobody could do anything to you! You were the one who hit the miller boy across the mouth! A girl who does that, you used to say, don't deserve no pity. She ought to go hang herself, you used to say! And you're talking about snares now!

ROSE. Now I know!

AUGUST. No matter what's going to happen, Rose, I'm staying with you. I'll sell my land and we'll go off, out into the world. I got an uncle who is over in Brazil. We'll get along. Somehow, we'll get along. Maybe we're ready for it only now.

R . . . . Jesus . . . what's the matter with me? Why . . . . Why didn't I stay with my baby?
. . . h who?
. . . I'm finished, August! First my body . . . azy . . . then I was spinning around and . . . came hope—and I was running like a . . . kitten in her mouth! And now the dogs . . . got it.
. . . derstand any of this, August?

August. No, not this . . .

Bernd. Do you know how I'm feeling? I feel as if one abyss opened up in front of me after another. Oh, what are we going to hear!

Rose. A curse! A curse you'll hear! I've seen you! I'll see you again . . . on the day of judgment! I'll tear out your gullet and jaws! You're going to answer me! You'll have to give me an answer!

August. Who're you talking about?

Rose. He knows—the one I mean! (*Exhausted and almost fainting she sinks down on a chair. Prolonged silence.*)

August (*trying to help* Rose). What—what's come over you? You were suddenly . . .

Rose. I don't know. If you'd asked sooner, maybe . now I don't know. Nobody's ever loved me enough.

August. Who knows which love is stronger, happy love or unhappy love!

Rose. I'm strong! I'm strong! I was strong . . . now I'm weak. Now I'm finished.

(The Policeman *comes.*)

Policeman (*in a quiet voice*). It seems your daughter's home now! Old Kleinert said she came home quite a while ago.

August. That's true, only we didn't know before.

Policeman. Well, then I might as well get it over with now. There's something to sign here. (*He puts several papers on the table, without noticing* Rose *in the feeble light.*)

August. Rose, there's something you're supposed to sign.

(Rose *bursts out laughing hysterically.*)

Policeman. If you're the one, there's nothing to laugh about, Fräulein. Here you are.

Rose. You may—stay—just a little while.

August. But why?

Rose (*with burning eyes, viciously*). You've strangled my child!

August. What's she saying? What in heaven's name are you saying?

Policeman (*straightens up, looks at* Rose *inquiringly, then continues as if he had not heard anything particularly remarkable*). It's probably about that Streckmann business.

ROSE (*as before, barks*). Streckmann? That's the one who strangled my child!

BERND. Be quiet, girl, you're out of your mind!

POLICEMAN. But you don't have a child.

ROSE. What? How else could I've strangled it with my own hands? I've strangled my baby with my own hands!

POLICEMAN. You must be mad! Is something wrong with you?

ROSE. I'm quite sane! I'm not a bit mad! I was quite sane when I woke up! (*Cold, wild, with cruel determination.*) I didn't want it to live! I didn't want it to live and to suffer the same tortures as me! I wanted it to stay where it belongs.

AUGUST. Rose, come to your senses! Don't torment yourself! You don't know what you're saying! You're going to make all of us suffer.

ROSE. You know nothing! You see nothing! You had your eyes open but you didn't see. He can go and look . . . behind the big willow . . . near the alders . . . back of the Pastor's field out there . . . by the pond . . . that's where he can see the little thing.

BERND. You did a terrible thing like that?

AUGUST. You did an unspeakable wrong like that?

(ROSE *faints. The men look at each other, frightened and helpless.* AUGUST *supports* ROSE *and tries to help her.*)

POLICEMAN. Best thing would be you come with me to the station. She can make a complete confession there. If this isn't just her imagination—why, it may be something in her favor, later on.

AUGUST (*serious and with deep feeling*). That's no imagination, Sergeant. This girl . . . what she must have suffered!

CURTAIN

SELECTED BIBLIOGRAPHY

BOOKS AND IMPORTANT ARTICLES

Bab, Julius, *Gerhart Hauptmann und seine besten Bühnenwerke,* Berlin, 1920.

Barnstoff, Hermann, *Die soziale, politische und wirtschaftliche Zeitkritik im Werke Gerhart Hauptmanns,* Jena, 1938.

Behl, Carl F. Wilhelm, *Chronik von Gerhart Hauptmanns Leben und Schaffen,* Munich, 1957.

Zwiesprache mit Gerhart Hauptmann, Munich, 1949.

Wege Zu Gerhart Hauptmann, Goslar, 1948.

Fechter, Paul, *Gerhart Hauptmann,* Dresden, *c.* 1922.

Fiedler, Ralph, *Die späten Dramen Gerhart Hauptmanns,* Munich, 1954.

Garten, Hugh F., *Gerhart Hauptmann,* New Haven, Yale University Press, 1954.

Gregor, Joseph, *Gerhart Hauptmann: Das Werk und unsere Zeit,* Vienna, 1951.

Guthke, Karl Ziegfried and Hans M. Wolff, *Das Leid im Werke Gerhart Hauptmanns,* Berkeley, University of California Press, 1958.

Hänisch, Konrad, *Gerhart Hauptmann und das deutsche Volk,* Berlin, 1922.

Marcuse, Ludwig (ed.), *Gerhart Hauptmann und sein Werk,* Berlin and Leipzig, 1922.

Muller, Siegfried, *Gerhart Hauptmann und Goethe,* New York, King's Crown Press, 1948.

Reichart, Walter A., "The Totality of Hauptmann's Work," *Germanic Review,* xxi (1946), pp. 143–49.

Schlenther, Paul (enlarged by A. Eloesser), *Gerhart Hauptmann: Leben und Werke,* Berlin, 1922. (First edition: Berlin, 1912.)

Sinden, Margaret, *Gerhart Hauptmann: The Prose Plays,* Toronto, University of Toronto Press, 1957.

Spiero, Heinrich, *Gerhart Hauptmann,* Bielefeld and Leipzig, 1922.

Voigt, F. A., *Hauptmann-Studien,* Breslau, 1936.

— and W. A. Reichart, *Gerhart Hauptmann und Shakespeare,* Goslar, 1948.

Wahr, F. B., "Theory and Composition of the Hauptmann Drama," *Germanic Review,* xviii (1942), pp. 163–73.

Ziegenfuss, Werner, *Gerhart Hauptmann,* Berlin, 1948.

See also the Gerhart Hauptmann *Jahrbücher,* especially for the years 1936, 1939, and 1948.

BOOKS CONTAINING ESSAYS AND USEFUL COMMENT ON HAUPTMANN AND HIS BACKGROUND

Bentley, Eric, *The Playwright as Thinker,* New York, 1946.

Bithell, Jerome, *Modern German Literature: 1880–1950,* London, 1959.

Block, Anita, *The Changing World in Plays and Theatre,* Boston, 1939.

Buck, Philo, *Directions in Contemporary Literature,* New York, 1942.

Clark, Barrett H. and George Freedley, *A History of the Modern Drama,* New York, 1947.

Dosenheimer, Elise, *Das deutsche soziale Drama von Lessing bis Sternheim,* Konstanz, 1949.

Eloesser, Arthur, *Modern German Literature,* New York, 1933.

Friedrich, Werner F., *An Outline History of German Literature,* New York, 1948.

Garten, H. F., *Modern German Drama,* Fairlawn, N.J., 1959.

Gassner, John, *Masters of the Drama,* New York, 1940, 1945, 1954.

Henze, Herbert, *Otto Brahm und das deutsche Theater,* Berlin, 1930.

Holl, G. K., *Hauptmann, His Life and Work,* Chicago, 1913.

Hülsen, H. von, *Gerhart Hauptmann: siebzig Jahre seines Lebens,* Berlin, 1932.

Klenze, Camillo von, *From Goethe to Hauptmann,* New York, 1926.

Lewissohn, Ludwig, *The Modern Drama,* New York, 1921.

Nicoll, Allardyce, *World Drama,* New York, 1950.

Stockius, Alfred, *Naturalism in Recent German Drama,* New York, 1903.

Witkowski, Georg, *German Drama of the 19th Century,* New York, 1909.

BIBLIOGRAPHICAL RECORD

Reichart, W. A., "Fifty Years of Hauptmann Study in America, 1894–1944," *Monatshefte über deutschen Unterricht*, xxxvii, 1945.

COLLECTED AND SELECTED WORKS OF HAUPTMANN IN GERMAN

Gesammelte Werke; 6 vols., Berlin, 1906. Subsequent editions: 1912 (6 vols.), 8 vols. (1921), 12 vols. (1922), Berlin.
Gesammelte Werke, "Ausgabe letzter Hand," ed. by C. F. W. Behl and F. A. Voigt, 17 vols., Berlin, 1942.
Augewählte Werke, 6 vols., Berlin, 1925.
Augewählte Dramen, 4 vols., ed. by H. Mayer, Berlin, 1956.

COLLECTIONS OF HAUPTMANN'S PLAYS IN ENGLISH

Lewissohn, Ludwig (ed.), *The Dramatic Works of Gerhart Hauptmann*, New York, 9 vols., 1912–29.

AUTOBIOGRAPHIES—IN GERMAN

Gerhart Hauptmann,
  Der grosse Traum, 1932
  Im Wirbel der Berufung, 1936
  Das Abenteuer meiner Jugend, 1937

The illustration for
Gerhart Hauptmann's *The Weavers*,
"Procession of Weavers on Strike,"
which appears on the cover of this
Bantam Classic is by Käthe Kollwitz,
the great German painter,
lithographer and etcher.

BANTAM CLASSICS

are chosen from the whole span
of living literature. They
comprise a balanced selection of
the best novels, poems, plays and
stories by writers whose works and
thoughts have made an indelible
impact on Western culture.

BANTAM CLASSICS

NOVELS

(continued on next page)

DRAMA

COLLECTIONS

BIOGRAPHY

NON-FICTION